Recreating the Past

Recreating the Past

A Guide to American and
World Historical Fiction
for Children and Young Adults

Lynda G. Adamson

Greenwood Press
Westport, Connecticut • London

Library of Congress Cataloging-in-Publication Data

Adamson, Lynda G.
    Recreating the past : a guide to American and world
historical fiction for children and young adults / Lynda G. Adamson.
        p.   cm.
    Includes index.
    ISBN 0–313–29008–3
    1. Children's literature—Bibliography. 2. Young adult
literature—Bibliography. 3. Historical fiction—Juvenile
literature—Bibliography. I. Title.
Z1037.A266 1994
[PN1009.A1]
016.80883′81089282—dc20   94–14435

British Library Cataloguing in Publication Data is available.

Library of Congress Catalog Card Number: 94–14435
ISBN: 0–313–29008–3

First published in 1994

Greenwood Press, 88 Post Road West, Westport, CT 06881
An imprint of Greenwood Publishing Group, Inc.

Printed in the United States of America

∞™

The paper used in this book complies with the
Permanent Paper Standard issued by the National
Information Standards Organization (Z39.48–1984).

10 9 8 7 6 5 4 3

To Frank, Frank III, and Gregory

"The past is not dead, it is not even past."

William Faulkner

CONTENTS

HOW TO USE THIS BIBLIOGRAPHY

Librarians, teachers of history and English, and others frequently select books for children and young adults about such topics as the Great Depression, the Underground Railroad, or Romans in Britain. Too often, they may be unaware of available books on the subject in either academic history or historical fiction. This annotated bibliography provides an easy reference to appropriate fiction which conveys historical ideas in a particularly meaningful way by adding the dimensions of character. Adults can assemble a basic list of books on a subject that will yield both a history lesson and a worthwhile reading experience. The 970 works selected are insightful, historically accurate, and for the most part, well written. At least 200 are award winners.

The brief annotations in the bibliography are generally divided into three parts--an introduction to the date and setting of the book; a description of the protagonist according to age, sex, and situation; and a final statement of theme. The bibliographic material includes the ISBN and current publication availability. Known awards that each work has won appear in italics at the end of the entry. The guide makes no pretense of insightful literary criticism.

The twenty-nine chapters in this annotated bibliography are arranged within historical time periods according to setting such as "Prehistory: Greece," "Canada: 1933 and After," "The United States: 1861-1965," and "Japan: Before 1199." In each section, the titles are arranged alphabetically according to the author's last name. Some of the chapters have very few entries because the titles included are the only ones available within the scope of the bibliography. These chapters, therefore, indicate geographical areas that historical fiction writers may want to investigate for future works. Seven very useful appendices and an index of authors, titles, and illustrators follow the bibliography.

- Appendix A lists works according to grade level of Readability (R=) established by the Fry Readability Graph with the Interest level (I=) appearing after each title.

- Appendix B lists works according to grade level of Interest (I=) based on findings of Lawrence Kohlberg's study of moral development, Carol Gilligan's studies on decision-making processes, and several studies on children's reading interests. The Readability level (R=) appears after each title.

- Appendix C is a brief list of Highlights in History. If the researcher does not know the date of a particular incident, Appendix C lists dates of important events in history which a work included in the annotated bibliography may cover. Some of the events listed, although not covered in any historical fiction work within the scope of the bibliography, are included as reference aids.

- Appendix D is a subject guide to works with members of minority groups as the protagonists or as major factors in the plot.

- Appendix E identifies famous persons or groups appearing in the works.

- Appendix F is a list of the works with sequels, the same characters, or in a series.

- Appendix G is a list of works by countries in Europe or the British Isles.

The bibliography may be used in several ways. A teacher or librarian may search for a time period, an interest level, a readability level, an author, a book title, a minority protagonist, a famous person or a group of people, a sequel or series, or a country's setting. For a book about the American Civil War for a sixth grade reader, one first finds "United States" in the Table of Contents. Then one locates the time period, "1861-1865," in the section of text labeled "United States." One searches the entries for those with suitable reading levels I=6 (or 8, 7, 5, and 4) and comparable interest levels. For books having Robert E. Lee as a personage, one checks Appendix E. For works with African American protagonists, one may refer to Appendix D. If a reader wants to know if other works have the same characters, Appendix F lists authors and the works that they have written with sequels, the same characters, or in a series.

Since the index lists both titles and authors, a researcher can readily find the pages on which a specific author or a specific title appears. The scope of the bibliography extends to historical fiction appropriate for children and young adults which is either in print or has recently gone out of print but may return to print because it is good literature. Because some well-written historical fiction works which have not won awards have been out of print longer than two years, they are excluded from the bibliography. Books that have either one or two asterisks following the bibliographic entry are currently out of print but may still be available from the publisher, the local library, or interlibrary loan. Books often come back into print from either the same or another publisher, especially those that have won awards. A researcher should check the current *Books in Print* to see if a book has been reprinted.

> * Books with one asterisk have been out of print since July 1992 according to the 1993-1994 edition of *Books in Print*.

> ** Books with two asterisks have been out of print longer.

A number of the books are appropriate for young adults but housed in the adult fiction sections of most libraries. Some of the books have juvenile protagonists, but the situations in which they find themselves are more complex than one normally finds in young adult books. Some are mysteries, such as Ellis Peters' novels set in the twelfth century with their detective Brother Cadfael solving murders around his Shrewsbury Benedictine monastery. Some of the others might be classified as "costume" novels, but all have accurate descriptions of the time in which they are set. The adult novels included here are generally recognized as good literature, some award-winning. On the whole, none of the novels will expose high school juniors or seniors to anything, except perhaps the history, that they have not yet encountered elsewhere.

ACKNOWLEDGMENTS

This manuscript is possible because of the help of others. Many publishers kindly supplied books recently published and not yet available in libraries or book stores. Nora Marlow and Shirley Lee, library assistants at Prince George's Community College in Largo, Maryland, handled many Interlibrary Loan requests. Barbara Rader, my editor, and Jane Lerner, my production editor, made excellent suggestions for improvement. I also thank my friend, Susan Sedgewick, for her efforts at proofreading. Without my husband, Frank, who counted words, graphed readability levels, edited, and then reedited the manuscript, this bibliography would not have been possible.

Lynda G. Adamson

INTRODUCTION

HISTORICAL FICTION: WHAT AND WHY

The historical novel, as a literary genre, evolved and rose to heights of popularity in the early nineteenth century with the novels of Sir Walter Scott in England. Some critics assert that Scott's novels are no more than "costume" novels, set in a different time period but with characters acting like they would at the time when the novel was written. Regardless of the assessment, the genre did not gain momentum in the world of Children's and Young Adult literature until the 1950s. Isolated novels, such as Eric Kelly's *The Trumpeter of Krakow*, Carol Ryrie Brink's *Caddie Woodlawn*, and Rachel Field's *Calico Bush*, written before World War II, still deserve recognition, but the work of novelists like Great Britain's Cynthia Harnett, Rosemary Sutcliff, and Henry Treece, or William O. Steele in the United States occurred after the war. Many of the best books were produced during the 1960s and 1970s by many writers included in this annotated bibliography.

In his nineteenth century commentary, *On the Historical Novel* (Rpt. Univ. of Nebraska Press, 1983), the Italian writer Alessandro Manzoni discussed the difficulties of creating a work of art that incorporates both fact and fiction. To him, the *form* of historical fiction uses dialogue in a concrete narrative with precise dates, places, and events. The *content* includes customs and art of the time period as well as social and economic class distinctions. Manzoni traces the development of the historical novel from the time of the classical epics circa 800 BC, *The Iliad* and *The Odyssey*.

One hundred years after Manzoni, George Lukacs, in *The Historical Novel* (Beacon Press, 1963), comments on the values of historical fiction. He believes that the main character must be an ordinary figure because only the everyday life of people--"the joys and sorrows, crises and confusions"--can portray the broad "being of an age." When the reader sees the "personal destinies of a number of human beings coincide and interweave within the determining context of an historical crisis . . . , the historical crisis is never abstract, the split of the nation into warring parties always runs through the centre of the closest human relationships" (41). Lukacs evaluates the genre itself by positing that the reader "should reexperience the social and human motives which led men to think, feel and act just as they did in historical reality." What he calls the "law of literary portrayal" is "that in order to bring out these social and human motives of behavior, the outwardly insignificant events, the smaller (from without) relationships are better suited than the great monumental dramas of world history (42).

This exact "literary portrayal" of the historical has led some academic historians to dismiss the validity of fictional accounts of fact. Jill Paton Walsh, a British author who writes in the historical fiction genre, says that historians have accused her of writing what is "known *not* to be true" when what she writes is "not *known* to be true" ("History is Fiction," *The Horn Book* [Feb. 1972]: 22). A situation may have occurred as she describes it although it has not been verified. Fiction itself may have happened or could possibly happen. A reader or writer just may not have personally witnessed the specific situation described in a work of fiction.

The historical novel is fiction set in a specific past time. An event in the novel may be documented, but no one today can know exactly how the people involved in the event felt or acted at the time of the event. Words spoken may be a matter of historical record, but inflection, tone of voice, or facial expression are unknown. The historical novelist attempts to recreate the scene, its time, and its participants so that it will live in the present.

Perhaps academic historians conveniently forget that any history book reflects the facts which its writer wants to include or exclude. Sharon Kay Penman comments in the afterword of *The Sunne in Splendor* that she once saw a definition of history--"the process by which complex truths are transformed into simplified falsehoods" (934). Although contemporary historians would be offended at this definition, every book, whether considered to be "fact" or considered to be "fiction," is a collection of words, with all their nuances and connotations, chosen by its author to communicate his or her ideas. A book anticipates a solitary reader reacting to its gestalt of words, or in Louise Rosenblatt's terms, transacting with its text as she discusses in *The Reader, the Text, the Poem: The Transactional Theory of the Literary Work* (Southern Illinois Univ. Press, 1978).

A text must "evoke" a response from a reader before it can come "alive." Then it exists in the "reality" of the reader's mind. In the case of "facts," the reader makes an *efferent* transaction, expecting to exact explicit information on a topic. In a fiction text, the reader expects a different transaction, one that Rosenblatt labels as *aesthetic*. Facts must be strong enough to make the reader think that he or she is absorbing valuable information. Obviously, a novel must be aesthetically strong enough to "hook" the reader's psyche, to form a transaction with the reader so that he or she will "live" along with the story as it unfolds through the author's words.

Children and young adults, like all readers, will transact with texts which evoke their response. *Aesthetic* historical fiction with its added dimension of character acting within a specific time can evoke stronger responses than *efferent* history texts. In *The House of Desdemona: The Laurels and Limitations of the Historical Novel* (Wayne State Univ., 1987), Lion Feuchtwanger notes that "it is truly remarkable how art enhances the human capacity for lived experience. Genuine historical writing helps the reader to live his own experiences and compels him to recognize himself anew" (144).

Historical fiction recreates a particular historical period with or without historical figures as incidental characters. It is generally written about a time period in which the author has not lived or no more recently than one generation before its composition. I have stated elsewhere that fiction having a setting within twenty years of the time it was written is not historical fiction. I am modifying that definition. Geoffrey Trease, a prolific British novelist of historical fiction for children, has defined historical fiction as fiction set outside the time of living memory. For

children and young adults, "outside living memory" may be as few
as five years ago. To many youngsters, the fall of the Berlin wall
had no meaning because they either had no knowledge of it or no
understanding of its significance in the twentieth century. This
bibliography, therefore, includes several books with Vietnamese
and Cambodian protagonists set more recently than 1974 so that
children may read these books and understand what it meant to be
a refugee from one of these countries.

Several books that present aspects of World War II and the
Holocaust also prove difficult to categorize as contemporary or
historical fiction. The books are set in the present time, but much
of the discussion includes grandparents telling their grandchildren
about their experiences in the concentration camps of World War
II. In several of the stories, the author uses the device of having
the child ask about the numbers tattooed on a grandparent's arm.
One book involves the grandfather vacationing with his grandson
and recognizing a man who was his best friend as a youth in
Poland. The old friend says that he has never seen the
grandparent and that age must be affecting his brain. Later, the
"friend" appears at the grandfather's funeral and explains to the
grandson that acknowledging the friendship would bring back too
many painful memories that he had spent years trying to deny.
Although the story discusses a different time period, it does not
attempt to recreate that period; these books are not included.

One might be suspicious of the unusual number of historical
novels with strong female protagonists. It may seem to many
readers that throughout history, almost all strong protagonists
have been male. But one needs to remember Scarlet, survivor of
the Civil War, or Helen, the woman who deserted her husband and
family, causing a war that raged for ten years between the Greeks
and the Trojans. And Judith, in the *Apocrypha*, pretends to allow
the Assyrian warrior, Holofernes, to seduce her, but decapitates
him instead to save her city and her people. Harriet Beecher
Stowe earned Abraham Lincoln's distinction as the woman who
started the American Civil War because she wrote *Uncle Tom's
Cabin*. Thus women have made history, but the term "feminist" did
not come into use until the late twentieth century.

Some novels set in the present jump back into the past via
diaries, letters, time travel, and even dreams. These framing
devices are historical "facts" which provide the basis for these time

shifts or other "supernatural" occurrences. Since a fiction, according to Jill Paton Walsh, is something "not known to be true," a fantasy is a fiction relying on something unable to occur in the *logical* world. Whether a work becomes labeled fiction or fantasy depends on this difference. Within these narrow confines, one must define a plot propelled by a psychological world as fantasy. If a novel, however, projects an accurate historical setting as a basis for plot progression, it belongs and is included in this guide within the past time period presented and is designated within the entry as "historical fantasy."

Creators of historical fiction must be historians as well as writers. Writers and academic historians generally have the same information available which they must shape coherently so that a reader may comprehend it. Each researches the same family *Bible*, the court record, the diary, and the letter. The historian chooses a chronological factual report while the historical fiction writer chooses to weave the facts into a narration. A reader must always remember that even the academic historian selects and reshuffles the facts to fit a unique and personal thesis. Thus, the history text has the same origin as the historical novel; the difference lies in the instrumentation. Some children and young adults find history books informative and entertaining. Too many others find them dry and unappealing. Historical fiction provides protagonists with whom to identify, family life and social mores for comparison, and quite often a mystery plot to hold interest. The disadvantage of historical fiction is that it may not completely cover an event; therefore, to be fully informed, students will need to read *efferent* history as well.

Historical fiction is valuable both aesthetically and educationally. Read prior to or simultaneously with a history text, it can provide a base for historical study of an era. Since it allows historical periods to live through people of all social and economic classes, history teachers should strongly consider supplementing their basic texts with historical fiction. Other teachers should consider assigning historical fiction because it exhibits the qualities expected in good literature and has the added advantage of factual information presented aesthetically. Parents should encourage their children to read historical fiction for all of the aforementioned reasons, in addition to the concept that it fosters comparison among the present condition and various conditions in the past which reveal that although social mores may change, human values do not. It also establishes the sense that the reader belongs in a continuum rather than being isolated in the present. Plutarch said "I am all that has been, and is, and shall be . . . ." Children and young adults reading historical fiction often discover the same about themselves.

Recreating the Past

PREHISTORY AND THE ANCIENT WORLD

EGYPT AND MESOPOTAMIA

Carter, Dorothy S. *His Majesty, Queen Hatshepsut.* Illus. Michele Chessare. Boston: Lippincott, 1987. 0-397-32178-3, 248p. R=5; I=5.

When given joint reign with her under-age half-nephew, Hatshepsut decides to declare herself sole ruler of Egypt, by saying that in a dream, her father had declared that she be Pharaoh. For twenty-two years, she survives the hostility of the strong priesthood, but after a viper poisons her daughter and guards murder her confidant, an advisor contrives to serve her poisoned wine. When one loses loved ones, money and wealth cannot replace them.

Gedge, Pauline. *Child of the Morning.* Cutchogue NY: Buccaneer, 1986 (1977). 0-89966-567-5, 300p. Paper, New York: Soho, 1993. 0-939149-85, 403p. R=8; I=10+.

Hatshepsut's father surprises her with the news that she must learn the arts of war and government because her intended husband, Thothmes, is her father's illegitimate but incompetent son. She rules Egypt for twenty years, manipulating the priests who do not want to carry out a woman's orders. Then her stepson decides to take back his throne by first murdering Hatshepsut's trusted companion Senmut. To protect Egypt while he goes away to war, Thothmes assassinates Hatshepsut by sending her poisoned wine. Living without any friends or family to give one comfort can be very lonely.

Lewis, Hilda. *The Ship That Flew.* New York: S. G. Phillips, 1958 (1937). 0-87599-067-3, 246p. R=4; I=5.

Four children find themselves transported through time in this historical fantasy on a magic ship that Peter, the oldest, sees and buys one day in a shop. When he returns to the shop, it has disappeared. The children visit Asgard and the Norse gods, William the Conqueror's as well as Robin Hood's England, the Egypt of Amenemhet the First, and other times. As they grow older, they adventure less frequently so Peter returns the ship to a man he met in Asgard and becomes a writer.

McGraw. Eloise. *The Golden Goblet.* New York: Puffin, 1986 (1961). Paper, 0-14-030335-9, 248p. R=4; I=7.

Disturbed because his older brother has taken his inheritance and will not buy him an apprenticeship, Ranofer, twelve, begins to suspect his brother's repugnant friend and discovers that the man steals gold from his employer. When Ranofer finds that his brother also steals from a queen's tomb, he reports to the palace; the guards believe him when he identifies stolen objects, and he earns an apprenticeship to a goldsmith. When a family member lacks respect for other members and acts dishonestly, one sometimes has no choice but to become an accuser. *Newbery Honor*, 1962.

McGraw, Eloise. *Mara, Daughter of the Nile.* New York: Puffin, 1985 (1953). Paper, 0-14-031929-8, 280p. R=6; I=8.

As an Egyptian slave in 1550 BC, with uncharacteristic blue eyes, seventeen-year-old Mara both reads and speaks Babylonian. She interprets for Hatshepsut's brother Thutmose's wife, a Syrian princess, while she acts as a spy both for and against Thutmose, a role which tests her loyalty to the man she loves. Since one has only one chance to live on earth, one needs to love as much as possible.

Nolan, Dennis. *Wolf Child.* New York: Macmillan, 1989. 0-02-768141-6, 40p. R=7; I=4.

Teo, at nine, is too old to help the women and not strong enough to hunt with his tribe so he makes beautiful tools of obsidian. When he finds a wolf cub that he befriends, the tribal chief makes him take the wolf into the forest after the first snow, but the wolf somehow follows the tribe and saves Teo and the chief from being killed by a mammoth. Some animals form unusually strong bonds with humans who are kind to them.

Service, Pamela F. *The Reluctant God.* New York: Atheneum, 1988. 0-689-31404-3, 211p. Paper, New York: Fawcett (Juniper), 1989. 0-449-70339-8. R=8; I=8.

In this historical fantasy, Lorna attends school in England but longs to return to Egypt and the archeological digs over which her widower father presides. In a concurrent story, Ameni trains to become a priest in 2000 BC while his twin brother prepares to become the pharaoh, Senusert III. When Lorna arrives in Egypt for her school vacation, she finds a tomb in which Ameni, alive, continues to search for eternity. Through Lorna, Ameni finds that eternity, and all gods, reside within humans.

Stolz, Mary. *Zekmet the Stone Carver: A Tale of Ancient Egypt.* Illus. Deborah Nourse Lattimore. San Diego: Harcourt Brace, 1988. 0-15-299961-2, 32p. R=4; I=3.

When Kahfre, Pharaoh of Egypt, wants a monument, he tells his vizier Ho-tep to think of an appropriate shape. Ho-tep asks the carver Zekmet, and he visualizes the regal body of lion and face of the Pharaoh, now known as the sphinx. Many humans search for immortality on earth.

Synge, Ursula. *The People and the Promise.* New York: S. G. Phillips, 1974. 0-87599-208-0, 191p. R=7; I=8.

Leah, born and married in Egypt during the 13th century BC, joins her family and Moses in the long march to Israel. Her life and that of Moses entwine as they try to accept Yahweh's plan for them. The difficulties that arise and their conflicting emotions humanize their journey.

PALESTINE AND THE NEAR EAST

Coolidge, Olivia. *People in Palestine.* Boston: Houghton Mifflin, 1965. 65-19985, 212p. R=6; I=9.**

Palestine, during the time of Jesus, from AD 1 to AD 50, has a diverse collection of inhabitants including Romans, Jews, Syrians, Arabs, Greeks, and Egyptians. Each individual has a unique view of the events of the time, and these short stories provide insights on the variations in the lives of people from different social and economic classes.

Speare, Elizabeth George. *The Bronze Bow*. Boston: Houghton Mifflin, 1961. 0-395-07113-5, 256p. Paper, Sandpiper, 1973. 0-395-13719-5. R=4; I=7.

Since they crucified his father and uncle for unpaid taxes and bound him to a vile blacksmith, Daniel, at eighteen, detests his Roman conquerors in Palestine and becomes an outlaw in the nearby mountains. Although he admires and supports another outlaw in hiding, he hears about a man who preaches nonviolence named Jesus. When his new employer leaves his forge for Daniel to work in order to follow this Jesus, Daniel becomes even more intrigued, especially when Jesus tries to heal Daniel's sister's psychological wounds. Sometimes those who are the strongest and most effective are those who use only words and love to "bend a bronze bow." *Newbery Medal*, 1962; *International Board of Books for Young People*, 1964.

Yarbro, Chelsea Quinn. *Four Horses for Tishtry*. New York: Harper, 1985. 0-06-026638-4, 218p. R=4; I=7.*

Tishtry, thirteen, has great promise as a performer in the Roman arenas with her chariot and matched horses. She works hard to become better, even with a master who cheats her, and to earn enough money to buy freedom for her Armenian family whose members are all slaves. When one tries to improve one's abilities in order to help others, one can be doubly happy with positive results.

GREECE

Coolidge, Olivia. *Marathon Looks on the Sea*. Illus. Erwin Schachner. Boston: Houghton Mifflin, 1967. 67-23307, 248p. R=6; I=8.**

Separated from his father when young, Metiochos becomes a favorite of Darius, the Persian ruler. When Metiochos meets his father again, he is an enemy, fighting for Persia at the Battle of Marathon in 490 BC. The petty pursuit of power by individuals throughout the centuries has led to the unnecessary death of millions.

Parotti, Phillip. *Fires in the Sky.* New York: Ticknor & Fields, 1990. 0-89919-930-5, 320p. R=10; I=10+.

Before battling the Greeks in the Trojan War, Troy fights the Mysian Wars. One of the Trojan leaders at Cyme is Dymas, eighteen. Dymas, however, becomes embroiled in palace intrigues involving Hecuba, queen of Troy, from which he must extricate himself to keep his reputation. Although successful, the Mysian wars greatly weaken Troy. But Dymas discovers that the Greeks have supplied a base close to Troy on Scyros and seem to be planning an attack. When greedy people desire what others have, they will fight to get it.

Purtill, Richard. *Enchantment at Delphi.* San Diego: Gulliver, 1986. 0-15-200447-5, 149p. R=7; I=9.

In this historical fantasy, Alice returns often to Delphi. She finds herself back in time when the goddess Rhea is arguing with Apollo that Delphi will always be the place to worship the goddess. In a second time shift, Alice meets Apollo and comes back to the present with a sacred cloth which she uses to bind a wound on her Greek boyfriend's head. Both Alice and her boyfriend disappear, but wherever they are, they are not together. To understand the intentions of people who have different cultural signals, one needs to know someone who can explain them.

Renault, Mary. *The Bull from the Sea.* New York: Random, 1975 (1963). Paper, 0-394-71504-7, 343p. R=7; I=10+.

When Theseus returns to Athens and forgets to raise a white sail to announce his safety to King Aigeus, he faces the tragedy of his father's death. He throws himself into cleaning up the kingdom and adding Crete to his collection of conquests by agreeing to marry Phaedra, daughter of the dead King Minos, when she comes of age. But when he meets Hippolyta, queen of the Amazons, she becomes his soul mate and bears his child Hippolytos, although they cannot marry. After Theseus marries Phaedra, encouraged by Hippolyta for political reasons, Hippolyta sacrifices herself for his life in battle, and Phaedra and his heir come to live with him in Athens. Phaedra lusts for Hippolytos, tries to seduce him, and cries "rape" when he refuses her. Theseus lives the remainder of his life in anguish because he falsely curses his son just before a tidal wave, "bull from the sea," destroys him. Rash actions almost always cause remorse.

Renault, Mary. *Fire from Heaven*. New York: Random, 1977
(1969). Paper, 0-394-72291-4, 374p. R=7; I=10+.

Alexander's life from 352 BC until he takes the throne in
336 BC after Philip's assassination seems to prove him as
rightful heir--astonishing Persian ambassadors with his political
and military acumen at age six; unnerving Demosthenes and
making him forget his speech when ten; killing his first enemy
at twelve; leading combat at Thrace when fifteen; and serving
as his father's regent, founding a city, and becoming a general
at seventeen. Alexander has a loving homosexual relationship
with his companion, Hephaiston.   On the whole, however,
Alexander seems absorbed with competition--in athletics, on the
battlefield, and in political arenas. Some people seem, through
their accomplishments, to be more mature at earlier ages than
others.

Renault, Mary. *The King Must Die*. New York: Pantheon, 1980
(1958). 0-394-43195-2. Paper, New York: Random, 1988.
0-394-75104-3, 352p. R=8; I=10+.

Theseus comes to Athens at seventeen when he has reached
the physical strength to fight for his mortal father Aigeus but
soon leaves Athens for Crete as one of the seven men sent
yearly as tribute to King Minos. In Crete, he falls in love with
Minos' daughter Ariadne, and she gives him the string to
retrace his steps out of the labyrinth after he kills another
youth nicknamed the "Minotaur" during the ritual bull dance
performed by young slaves for the decadent Cretan citizens.
Shocked when Ariadne joins other women in tearing the local
king apart by hand in the yearly ritual sacrifice to ensure the
following year's fertility, Theseus leaves her and returns to
Athens. There he breaks with tradition by uniting Eleusis,
Troizen, and Athens under masculine, as opposed to feminine,
rule. One must accept another's beliefs if one chooses that
person as a mate.

Renault, Mary. *The Last of the Wine*. New York: Random, 1975
(1956). Paper, 0-394-71653-1, 389p. R=8; I=10+.

Alexias, a young Athenian of good family, born during a
plague, becomes soldier, athlete, citizen, and pupil of Socrates
along with his schoolmate and male lover. He tries to learn
ethical and philosophical truths but sees cowardly and insolent
men who prefer power and money to human insight malign
Socrates. Some people refuse to understand that power and

control over other humans never reward like honesty and kindness.

Renault, Mary. *The Mask of Apollo*. New York: Random, 1988 (1966). Paper, 0-394-75105-1, 384p. R=8; I=10+.

When Nikeratos is nineteen, his father dies, but Niko has learned acting from him, having been in plays since he was a child and understanding the power of the talented actor over a rapt audience. He joins a small troupe and eventually gains experience and money enough to present his own productions. One day he plays Achilles for Alexander in Pella, and he becomes for Alexander the definitive Achilles, a man of moderation who refused to kill Agamemnon at the beginning of the Trojan War, and thereby, sacrificing his dear friend Patrokolus when Hector later kills him. Of great importance is the sense that one has done something to the best of one's ability and helped someone else through the attempt.

Renault, Mary. *The Persian Boy*. New York: Random, 1988 (1972). Paper, 0-394-75101-9, 432p. R=6; I=10+.

From the time Alexander the Great is twenty-six until his death, he has as his companion and lover, the Persian slave-boy Bagoas, who once belonged to the Persian king Darius. Bagoas understands Alexander's need for affection and his feelings of sympathy for his Persian subjects and stays with him throughout the fever that finally takes his life. Even kings and queens need someone who loves them for themselves rather than their political status.

EUROPE AND THE BRITISH ISLES TO 54 BC

Brennan, J. H. *Shiva: An Adventure of the Ice Age*. New York: Lippincott, 1989. 0-397-32454-5, 184p. Paper, HarperCollins, 1990. 0-06-440392-0, 208p. R=3; I=6.

Shiva is perhaps eleven and is both an orphan in her Ice Age tribe and left-handed, two misfortunes. But because she finds two things--the circle of stones and the skull of Sabre, marvels of magic, her tribe listens to her warning to treat the ogres kindly, a different species of subhumans who saved her life. When used wisely, power can benefit all involved.

Brennan, J. H. *Shiva Accused: An Adventure of the Ice Age.*
New York: HarperCollins, 1991. 0-06-020742-6, 275p. Paper,
1993. 0-06-440431-5. R=3; I=5.

A neighboring tribe discovers Shiva hiding a body she found
drowned in the river and accuses her of murdering "The Hag,"
the most sacred member of all the tribes. Shiva refuses to be
cowed by this matriarchal group, and she escapes during a
mammoth stampede just before being stoned to death. For
prehistory, all is speculation, but small statues of the Venus
figure and sophisticated cave art indicate that women may have
had high ranking in their communities.

Furlong, Monica. *Wise Child.* New York: Knopf, 1987.
0-394-99105-2, 228p. Paper, Borzoi, 1989. 0-394-82598-5. R=7;
I=7.

Wise Child, nine, becomes an orphan (although her father is
at sea, not dead) and goes to live with Jupiter, the woman
everyone accuses of witchcraft because she uses herbs to heal
people. All, however, come to her when seriously ill. Wise Child
discovers that Jupiter's only magic is her intense concentration
on detail, but the village people, incited by the priest, accuse
her of causing smallpox and arrest her for witchcraft. One must
get to know someone personally rather than believe what others
say about them.

McGowen, Tom. *The Time of the Forest.* Boston: Houghton
Mifflin, 1988. 0-395-44471-3, 110p. R=4; I=7.*

In prehistoric times, two tribal members walk away from
their tribe for five days and discover people who kill animals
for food. One of the second tribe, Wolf, sees the men and follows
them home, finding that they pen animals and plough. When a
farming girl becomes wounded in the forest, Wolf helps her.
They both become ostracized by their tribes and leave to form
their own. When a society shuns a person, that person must
make a new, and sometimes, better life elsewhere.

Pryor, Bonnie. *Seth of the Lion People.* New York: Morrow,
1988. 0-688-07327-1, 118p. R=3; I=5.

Seth, thirteen, has to face taunts of his peers because his
leg, shattered from falling rock that killed his mother, has
crippled him. Seth, however, continues his caring ways in his
prehistoric society and learns the tribe's stories from his dying

father, the Teller-of-Tales. Threatened by the tribe's leader who is only interested in hunting, Seth leaves and finds a more fertile area where the tribe can live. Goodness and concern attract more followers than bullying.

Sutcliff, Rosemary. *The Mark of the Horse Lord*. New York: Dell, 1989 (1965). Paper, 0-440-40161-5, 276p. R=7; I=8.**

Phaedrus, a former Roman slave, pretends to be Midir, king of the Dalraidian, after Midir becomes disfigured. If the people find out that Midir no longer has his looks, they will consider him unfit to be king and kill him. Carefully schooled by Midir's advisors, Phaedrus finally fools Midir's best friend into believing that he, Phaedrus, is Midir. In his disguise, Phaedrus must act like a king, and he eventually has to sacrifice his own life to save the people from their Roman enemies--a mythic and engrossing transformation. *Phoenix Award*, 1985.

Sutcliff, Rosemary. *Warrior Scarlet*. Illus. Charles Keeping. London: Oxford, 1958. 0-8098-3024-8. R=5; I=6.**

Drem, a Bronze Age boy, looks forward to wearing the scarlet cloak that will identify him as a tribal warrior after he kills a wolf. With only one arm, he fails to kill his wolf and is exiled from the tribe, but after he kills three wolves to save another outcast, tribal leaders reconsider and find him worthy of the honor. Persons with disabilities sometimes have difficulty fulfilling the requirements established by fully able people. *Carnegie Commendation*, 1958; *International Board of Books for Young People*, 1960.

Thomas, Elizabeth Marshall. *The Animal Wife*. Boston: Houghton Mifflin, 1990. 0-395-52453-0, 280p. Paper, New York: Pocket Books, 1991. 0-671-73323-0. R=4; I=10+.

During the mammoth era, Kori does not meet his father until he is a teenager. His father comes to Kori's tribe searching for a fourth wife many years after Kori's mother divorced him and left for her tribe. Kori decides to go with his father, a famous hunter. He enjoys the ways of the new tribe including the woman of a seemingly inferior group whom he captures and impregnates. After her people rescue her, Kori tries to retrieve her and his son, but her relatives kill Kori's half-brother. Kori's father's other wives leave him, and to diffuse the situation, Kori perpetrates the tribal belief that men are strong and do not need bickering women. Humans sometimes survive by studying animals, but they are sometimes less successful at understanding human habits in other groups.

Treece, Henry. *The Dream-Time*. Illus. Charles Keeping. New York: Meredith, 1968. R=5; I=7.**

In the England of prehistory, a lame boy departs from his unkind tribe and travels from place to place until he finds a home with the River People. There he uncovers his artistic talent and begins to create jewelry and make magical cave paintings before he leaves for the Red Men, and finally, for another group with two other orphans. Pictures are really abstract dreams made concrete. *Carnegie Commendation*, 1967.

Treece, Henry. *Men of the Hills*. Illus. Christine Price. New York: S. G. Phillips, 1958. 0-87599-115-7, 182p. R=6; I=7.

In prehistoric England, Lalo, son of the People of the Hill chieftain, earns his manhood by killing a wolf. Almost immediately, his tribe suffers conflicts with other tribes--the Fisher Folk, Hunter Folk, and Cattle Folk. Eventually, only he, his guardian, and his dog remain, having exhibited courage and kindness in their conflicts.

Turner, Ann. *Time of the Bison*. Illus Beth Peck. New York: Macmillan, 1987. 0-02-789300-6, 54p. R=3; I=4.**

In prehistoric times, Scar Boy, eleven, wants to find his real name. At the summer clan meeting, after he has shaped a horse from clay, he meets a painter who shows him magical cave paintings and promises to teach Scar Boy enough for him to earn the right to be called Animal Shaper. A profession sometimes chooses a person rather than vice versa.

Wolf, Joan. *Daughter of the Red Deer*. New York: NAL-Dutton, 1991. 0-525-933794, 420p. Paper, New York: Onyx, 1992. 0-451-40334-7. R=7; I=10+.

Fourteen thousand years ago, after bad water poisons women in the tribes of the Cro-Magnon Magdelenian culture of Vésère Valley in France, Mar and his peers of the patriarchian Horse Tribe capture the Mother-designate of the matriarchical Red Deer, fifteen-year-old Alin, and her friends, to be their wives. What surprises them is that a love match develops between Mar and Alin. When people treat others, even captives, kindly, a conflict may be resolved positively.

ROMAN EMPIRE TO 476 AD

Bradshaw, Gillian. *The Beacon at Alexandria.* Boston: Houghton Mifflin, 1986. 0-395-41159-9, 374p. R=6; I=10+.**

The new governor of Ephesus, a cruel man, contracts to marry Claris, fifteen, in 371. Claris's brother dresses her as a eunuch and helps her escape on a ship to Alexandria, Egypt, where she begins formal study of medicine, her real love. She succeeds at the masquerade, gaining the reputation as an excellent physician. But events eventually lead to the revelation of her sex, and a second escape pairs her with the man whom she has secretly loved for several years. Intelligent women have often had to deceive those who would keep them from pursuing their interests, no matter how altruistic.

Coolidge, Olivia. *Roman People.* Boston: Houghton Mifflin, 1959. 59-7481, 243p. R=7; I=8.**

This series of short stories introduces a soldier, a freedman, a poor Roman, two kings, a charioteer, a slave, a Roman aristocrat, a working-class Roman, and an early explorer. A broad overview of people living typical lives in Roman times makes the period come alive.

Davis, Lindsey. *Shadows in Bronze.* New York: Crown, 1991.0-517-57612-0, 343p. Paper, New York: Ballantine, 1992. 0-345-37426-6. R=7; I=10+.

The Roman "detective," Marcus Didius Falco in 70 AD works for the Emperor Vespasian. When he finds that Barnabas plans to kill him and to overthrow Vespasian, Marcus disguises himself and trails Barnabas. The chase leads Marcus to the woman he loves but does not have enough money to marry. When people do not treat others kindly, they often find themselves alone.

Davis, Lindsey. *Silver Pigs*. New York: Crown, 1989.
0-517-57363-6, 258p. Paper, New York: Ballantine, 1991.
0-345-36907-6. R=7; I=10+.

Marcus Didius Falco in Rome during 70 AD helps to uncover
a plot against the Emperor Vespasian, Nero's successor, after a
bitter civil war. A senator hires him to find the men who are
chasing his daughter because she knows where traitors have
hidden "silver pigs" (lead ingots holding silver) with which they
plan to overthrow the government. Being associated with power
does not replace the importance of human love.

Davis, Lindsey. *Venus in Copper*. New York: Crown, 1992.
0-517-58477-8, 277p. Paper, New York: Ballantine, 1993.
0-345-37390-1. R=7; I=10+.

Around 71 AD, unhappy with the salary paid him by the
Emperor Vespasian, Marcus Didius Falco decides to go back
into business for himself as a private detective in order to earn
enough money to support the woman he loves. He gets a case to
investigate the intended bride of a real estate magnate to find
if she is interested in the man himself or only his money. When
the man dies unexpectedly, the fiancée is a suspect. However,
other problems arise which both extricate and involve her.
Trying to solve a mystery requires a continuous search for
extraneous knowledge; with it, one may become aware of
different possibilities when situations require them.

Hunter, Mollie. *The Stronghold*. New York: HarperCollins, 1974.
R=7; I=10.**

Coll, eighteen, designs a unique tower to protect the
members of his Orkney Island tribe from Romans trying to
capture them for slaves. Various plots against the leader and
the leader's refusal to accept Coll's plan almost destroy them.
People who want power, but do not yet have it, will often try to
coerce their foes to destroy each other. *Carnegie Medal*, 1975.

Llywelyn, Morgan. *Druids*. New York: Morrow, 1991.
0-688-08819-8, 456p. Paper, New York: Ballantine (Ivy), 1992.
0-8041-0844-7. R=3; I=10+.

As a child fascinated by the druids, the Order of the Wise
who believed in the immortal soul, Ainvar eventually becomes
one and rises to be the spiritual leader beside Vercingetorix, the
military leader of Gaul whom Caesar defeats around 58 BC.

Although the two try to get individual tribes to fight Caesar together, Caesar's power defeats them. After watching Vercingetorix keep his dignity while the Romans spit at him and treat him like an object, Ainvar is able to escape. The act of living continues to be magic, and humans have power over the kinds of magic they create with their lives.

McCullough, Colleen. *The First Man in Rome.* New York: Morrow, 1990. 0-688-09368-X, 896p. R=7; I=10+.

Tracing the leaders of Rome from 110 BC to 106 BC with Gaius Marius, one sees the complex palace intrigue and the citizens' responses to their leaders. Both the free persons and the slaves have to be controlled so that they will accept the government's decisions.

McCullough, Colleen. *Fortune's Favorites.* New York: Morrow, 1993. 0-688-09370-1, 878p. R=7; I=10+.

Sulla returns from exile, becomes dictator, and suddenly retires while Pompey, designating himself "Magnus" ("The Great"), works his way upward. But he has as his rival, Julius Caesar, who rises to power in this third novel on first century BC Rome, following *The First Man in Rome* and *The Grass Crown*. The people and the customs in the highly structured Roman society as well as the schemes and vendettas come alive as people try to survive in their places of power.

McCullough, Colleen. *The Grass Crown.* New York: Morrow, 1991. 0-688-09369-8, 756p. Paper, New York: Avon, 1992. 0-380-71082-X. R=7; I=10+.

In a continuation of *The First Man in Rome*, the focus on Gaius Marius shifts to Lucius Cornelius Sulla during the first century BC. He has to protect his position of leadership in Rome while facing opposition and intrigue.

Sutcliff, Rosemary. *The Eagle of the Ninth.* Illus. C. Walter Hodges. New York: Oxford, 1987 (1961). 0-19-271037-0, 264p. R=9; I=9.

Marcus, a Roman soldier in Britain, becomes lame from a leg wound, resigns from his post, and buys a gladiator to be his servant. The two travel north looking for Marcus's father's lost Ninth legion, and when they see the Epidaii tribe parading the eagle insignia of the Ninth, they steal it and return home, knowing the fate of the men and Marcus's father. Sometimes one's best and most loyal friend comes from a very different background. *Carnegie Commendation*, 1954.

Sutcliff, Rosemary. *The Lantern Bearers*. Illus. Charles Keeping. New York: Walck, 1959. R=7; I=10.**

By 410, the Romans are leaving Britain, but the soldier Aquila deserts because he has always lived in Britain. Soon captured by the Saxons, however, he travels in servitude to their homeland, but upon his return to Britain, he escapes and joins the forces of Ambrosius against the Saxon Vortigern. He recognizes his nephew in battle and returns to nurse him, an enemy, before sending him back to his mother with a dolphin ring. The nephew returns the ring to Aquila, signaling his safe arrival. One's inner peace often comes from acceptance of what is truth rather than what one wants to be the truth. *Carnegie Medal*, 1959.

Sutcliff, Rosemary. *The Silver Branch*. Illus. Charles Keeping. New York: Farrar, Straus & Giroux, 1993 (1959). Paper, 0-374-46648-3. R=9; I=10.

Justin, feeling unattractive and unappreciated by his father, serves in the Roman army in Britain as a surgeon. When he suspects the legion's finance minister of betrayal, the man guesses and tries to kill him. A group of soldiers rescues Justin, and they eventually destroy the evil minister. When one tries to help others, and even live or die for them, life often gains greater meaning. *Carnegie Commendation*, 1957.

Sutcliff, Rosemary. *Sun Horse, Moon Horse*. Illus. Shirley Felts. New York: Dutton, 1978. R=7; I=7.**

Lubrin of the Iceni during the Iron Age of 100 B.C. in Britain enjoys drawing pictures of horses. After the Attribates capture his tribe, their ruler bargains with Lubrin to draw a large horse on a nearby hill. Lubrin understands that he will sacrifice himself on the horse's eye as a condition for the release of his people. Those who have loyalty to their people will pay the cost, whatever it may be, to save them.

EUROPE

476-1199

Bradshaw, Gillian. *The Bearkeeper's Daughter*. Boston: Houghton Mifflin, 1987. 0-395-43620-6, 310p. R=8; I=10+.**

After his father dies of plague around 550, John, twenty-four, goes to Constantinople to reintroduce himself to his mother whose identity he has just discovered, the Empress Theodora. She welcomes him, gets him a job, and gives him support based on his being discreet about his identity and her past. When he demonstrates a lack of ambition and when Justinian accuses him of lying, he continues to show his loyalty to her until her death. An honest person has no other human to fear.

Dickinson, Peter. *The Dancing Bear*. Boston: Little, Brown, 1972. 0-316-184268, 244p. Paper, New York: Dell, 1988. 0-440-40033-3. R=7; I=7.*

When the Kutrigur Huns invade the Emperor Justinian's Byzantium in 558, Silvester, a slave, and Holy John, the household priest, escape with the family's pet bear, but the Huns kidnap Addie, the daughter. Silvester and Holy John rescue a dying Hun and take him to the Khan's camp where they find Addie. Another warring tribe ambushes the camp, and they escape again, going to live with a Roman, also exiled from his home. High social status does not make a person humane, but caring for others does.

Haugaard, Erik. *A Slave's Tale.* Illus. Keith Eros. New York: Bradbury, 1973. 0-02-735560-8, 192p. Paper, New York: Dell, 1991. 0-440-40402-9. R=5; I=8.*

Given freedom from slavery by her master Hakon, Helga wants to do everything, including stowing away on a ship going to Frankland (France) around 997. In Frankland, only four of the men survive a vicious Norman attack and only because they have help from the priests of a new religion which interests Helga. Revenge takes enormous energy while peace relaxes and rejuvenates.

Manson, Christopher. *Two Travelers.* New York: Holt, 1990. 0-8050-1214-1, 32p. R=5; I=3.*

Isaac, servant to Charlemagne, travels to Baghdad from France in 787 and brings back a gift of peace from the calif, an elephant named Abulabaz, "Father of Wisdom." When Isaac has to leave Abulabaz with Charlemagne, the elephant pines after him. Charlemagne realizes the problem and recalls Issac to care for Abulabaz until the animal dies in 810.

Skurzynski, Gloria. *What Happened in Hamelin.* New York: Random, 1993 (1979). Paper, 0-679-83645-4, 192p. R=4; I=6.

After being denied his final payment for freeing Hamelin of its plague of rats, Gast feeds bread to the 130 children containing purple rye which keeps them from sleeping. Then on July 26, 1284, while their parents pray in church for them to sleep, Gast leads the children away from Hamelin. He plans to sell them each for a piece of silver. One must be prepared for the consequences if one decides not to fulfill one's part of a contract. *Christopher Award*, 198; *Reviewers' Choice, American Library Association Booklist*, 1979; *Horn Book Honor List*, 1979.

Sutcliff, Rosemary. *Blood Feud.* Illus. Charles Keeping. New York: Dutton, 1977. R=4; I=8.**

Thormod captures Jestin while he is herding cattle on the British coast in the tenth century, and Jestyn becomes Thormod's thrall (servant). Jestyn has to go with Thormod to his Viking home where they discover that they are more like brothers than master and servant. A blood feud in Thormod's family leads them to Miklagard (Istanbul) where Jestyn has a chance to avenge Thormod's death by killing his enemies. Jestyn finds that he cannot continue the blood feud because he has become a surgeon, helping people instead of hurting them. When people kill others to avenge wrongs which no one remembers, someone has to be sane enough to say "no more."

Treece, Henry. *The Road to Miklagard*. Illus. Christine Price. New York: S. G. Phillips, 1957. 0-87599-118-1, 254p. R=7; I=7.

After Harald enslaves the Irish giant Grummoch in 785, Turkish slavers capture him, his friend Haro, and the giant, and sell them to Abu Mazur in Spain. When Harald saves Abu Mazur from his treacherous gardener, Abu Mazur entrusts him to take his daughter to Miklagard (Istanbul). Marriba gets into trouble with young Constantine's evil mother Irene, but Harald rescues her and happily returns to the North with Grummoch while Marriba returns to Spain with Haro who loves her.

Treece, Henry. *Westward to Vinland*. Illus. William Stobbs. New York: S. G. Phillips, 1967. 0-87599-136-X, 192p. R=6; I=7.

After exile in Iceland and Greenland in 960, Red Eirik returns to Iceland where his son Leif the Lucky persuades him to sail to fertile Vinland. Leif does, and when he returns with passengers rescued from a shipwreck, they bring the plague with them, and Eirik dies from this disease. In the new land to which the rest escape, Leif's sister marries and bears Snorri, the first white American, while Leif goes to Norway and dies in 1013, comforted by his illegitimate son, born in the Hebrides.

Welch, Ronald. *Knight Crusader*. Illus. William Stobbs. New York: Oxford, 1979 (1954). R=4; I=8.**

Because Philip D'Aubigny, in 1187, has lived in Outremer (Jerusalem) all his life, he always asks visitors from Wales about his Welsh homeland. After escaping from several situations in which he has become a prisoner and helping the Christians to defeat the Infidels in Acre, Philip goes to Wales to claim his lands. There he faces new battles with those who would like to have the land for themselves. A person with integrity is always preferable to a person who uses trickery to gain power. *Carnegie Medal*, 1955.

1200-1491

Bellairs, John. *The Trolley to Yesterday.* New York: Dial, 1989. 0-8037-0582-4, 183p. Paper, New York: Bantam, 1990. 0-553-15795-7. R=6; I=6.

When thirteen-year-old Johnny's friend, the Professor, becomes distracted, Johnny discovers that the Professor has been traveling to the Constantinople of 1453 and the Egypt of 14 BC in a time machine. Johnny goes with him on one of his trips to try to help people during the Turkish invasion of Constantinople, but they fail. When they come back from the slaughter, they are relieved to be alive in the 1950's. This historical fantasy gives a sense of the battle coupled with the whimsy of time travel and the insight that changing history would perhaps be changing oneself.

Goodwin, Marie D. *Where the Towers Pierce the Sky.* New York: Four Winds, 1989. 0-02-736871-8, 185p. R=3; I=6.

In this historical fantasy, a French boy appears in Lizzie's room, and the two of them fade into 1429 in France while Joan of Arc is trying to help the people. Lizzie sees the fight from a twentieth century point of view including Joan of Arc's questionable visions and the actions of her enemies before Lizzie returns to the present. One can learn about oneself and about others when pretending to be a part of life in a different century.

Holland, Cecelia. *The Lords of Vaumartin.* Boston: Houghton Mifflin, 1988. 0-395-48828-1, 344p. R=5; I=10+.**

Everard, fourteen, inherits the castle of Vaumartin but prefers to be a scholar instead of a lord; however, a jealous uncle tricks him into combat. He survives the battle at Crécy in 1346, goes in disguise to Paris, and studies his books. After helping to save Paris from the merchant Etienne Marcel in 1357, he happily refuses to return to Vaumartin and his rightful title. People who are content with their abilities and their thoughts often need few of society's constructs.

Kelly, Eric. *The Trumpeter of Krakow.* Illus. Janina Domanska. New York: Collier, 1966 (1928). 0-02-750140-X, 224p. Paper, New York: Macmillan (Aladdin). 0-689-71571-4. R=6; I=7.

Joseph, fifteen, and his parents go to Krakow, Poland, in 1461, after an enemy burns their Ukrainian farm. With help, they establish themselves, but the desires of the alchemists to find gold almost destroys them before they have a chance to fulfill their family's promise hundreds of years before to the Polish king. Loyalty and honor almost always win, and an inherently good person can overcome evil's temptation. *Newbery Medal*, 1929.

O'Dell, Scott. *The Road to Damietta.* Boston: Houghton Mifflin, 1985. 0-395-38923-2, 256p. Paper, New York: Fawcett (Juniper), 1987. 0-449-70233-2, 240p. R=6; I=10.

Around 1225, when Ricca is thirteen, she falls in love with Francis and tries to seduce him, even after his transformation into the man known as Francis of Assisi. She accompanies him as his Arabic translator to Damietta when he tries to negotiate between the Moslems and the Crusaders, but he never changes from his chosen path. Some people who call themselves Christians in no way represent the concept of God's way of life while others almost perfect it.

Paton Walsh, Jill. *The Emperor's Winding Sheet.* Magnolia, MA: Peter Smith, 1974. 0-8446-6665-3, 288p. Paper, New York: Farrar, Straus, & Giroux (Sunburst), 1992. 0-374-42121-8. R=7; I=7.

Piers shipwrecks off the coast of Constantinople. After his rescue, he ends up in the court of Emperor Constantine XI, just before the Turks defeat him and end the Eastern Roman Empire in 1453. Piers stays with Constantine as his "lucky find" and decides to remain and help, even after given his freedom, because he admires the man. The explicit theme notes that humans "are not judged by the fate God appoints for them, they are judged by the manner in which they meet that fate."

Skurzynski, Gloria. *Manwolf.* New York: Clarion, 1981. 0-395-30079-7, 177p. R=6; I=10.*

The Polish serf Danusha becomes cook for a Knight of the Cross, who wears a leather mask and gloves, on a 1382 journey to Vienna. Her beauty leads him to renounce his vows of celibacy, and he impregnates her. Danusha marries someone else, but the child, when born, has skin which repulses those around him. Not until he is seventeen does the Knight find out about and claim him although distressed that they have the same affliction. Humans have no control over their physical appearance, and all need the unconditional love of their parents. *American Library Association Best Books for Young Adults*, 1981; *Child Study Association Books of the Year*, 1981; *Reviewers' Choice, Notable Children's Trade Book in Social Studies*, 1981.

1492-1789

Aiken, Joan. *Bridle the Wind*. New York: Delacorte, 1983. 0-385-29301-1, 224p. R=5; I=5.

At thirteen in 1815, Felix finds himself in an island monastery near the coast of France near Spain after being shipwrecked and delirious for three months. His fear of a mad abbot leads him to escape with another young "prisoner," and they travel into Spain, always pursued by brigands, one of them possessed with the spirit of the abbot who drowned trying to catch the two as they fled over the causeway. Felix discovers, with dismay, after he reaches home safely, that the boy whose company he had so much enjoyed, is actually a girl. Ingenuity, kindness, and a lot of luck in this interesting chase help the two escape their captors.

Aiken, Joan. *The Teeth of the Gale*. New York: HarperCollins, 1988. 0-06-020045-6, 307p. R=6; I=7.*

Called home from studying in Salamanca, Spain, the eighteen-year-old Felix finds that a friend in a convent has requested his help in retrieving children from their felon father. Wanting to see the friend, he agrees and finds himself part of a political intrigue of villains who think he has hidden money and heroes who admire his honesty. Although lives are lost, most survive the treacherous situation. Eventually, integrity and love overcome evil plotting.

Almedingen, E. M. *Anna*. Illus. Robert Micklewright. New York: Farrar, Straus & Giroux, 1972. R=3; I=6.**

Anna loves her country Russia and its Church. As she matures to a young woman by 1786, her intelligence and her liberal father (raised to the rank of nobility by Catherine II for the family collection of rare and valuable books) lead her to marry the man who brought the potato to Russia. Knowledge, honesty, integrity, and spiritual values undergird her relationships with everyone, including the serfs working her land.

Almedingen, E. M. *The Crimson Oak*. New York: Putnam, 1983. 0-698-20569-3, 112p. R=7; I=7.**

After 1739, Peter saves the Princess Elizabeth from a bear. But because he is only a peasant with the audacity to want to learn to write, the local police imprison him, unconcerned that he has helped the princess. Ironically, he learns to write while incarcerated, and afterwards, when the Princess becomes czarina, she gives him a job as she has promised and looks after his family. To make a commitment and fulfill it gains the respect of every honest person.

De Trevino, Elizabeth. *I, Juan de Pareja*. New York: Farrar, Straus, & Giroux, 1987 (1965). 0-374-33531-1, 192p. Paper (Sunburst), 0-374-43525-1. R=8: I=8.

During the seventeenth century, Juan is servant to Diego Velasquez in Spain while Velasquez paints members of Philip IV's court. Juan's deep religious faith and his own love of painting, which he keeps secret since Spanish law forbade servants to practice the arts, make him content with his duties. The story reveals the human need for love and friendship. *Newbery Medal*, 1966.

Carter, Peter. *Children of the Book*. London: Oxford, 1987 (1982). 272p. 0-19-271456-2. R=4; I=10.**

In 1682, three teenagers, one Muslim and two Christian, become entangled when the Turks, breaking a treaty, invade Austria. Who is in the "right" can never be clear, but war, led by one person's desire for power and ambition, like that of the

Janissary leader Vasif, causes needless death and suffering. Simultaneously, humans reveal their ability to unselfishly care for others even when in need of aid themselves. *Young Observer Teenage Fiction Prize*, 1983; *Leseratten Award* (Germany).

Hess, Donna Lynn. *In Search of Honor*. Greenville, SC: Bob Jones Univ., 1991. Paper, 0-89084-595-6, 153p. R=5; I=7.

As a young man in 1787, Jacques Chenier watches his father die outside Paris for poaching a pigeon as a present for his wife. Jacques continues the family tradition as an artisan by making sculptures in stone and wax until he is captured for helping someone take his rightful money. Both are imprisoned in the Bastille. Jacques escapes and becomes involved with Danton, Robespierre, and the French Revolution. His relationship with another man, the Bastille's oldest prisoner, helps him to understand that fame is fleeting and only peace of heart and mind makes life worth living.

Laker, Rosalind. *The Golden Tulip*. New York: Doubleday, 1991. 0-385-41560-5, 585p. Large Type, New York: Hall, 1993. 0-8161-5573-9, 896p. R=7; I=10+.

As the daughter of a temperamental but talented painter in Amsterdam during the 1660's, Francesca enjoys visiting Rembrandt but is especially happy to go to Delft to become Vermeer's apprentice. After her mother's death, her father incurs large debts. In order to pay them, he agrees to marry Francesca to an older and wealthy but unpleasant man when she loves someone else. The French invasion of Holland threatens them all but eventually solves their dilemmas when the nasty fiancée, also a traitor, dies. People controlled by excessive emotion and pride often hurt those whom they may love most.

Laker, Rosalind. *The Venetian Mask*. New York: Doubleday, 1993. 0-385-42190-7, 422p. R=6; I=10+.

In 1775, Marietta's mother, a maker of Venetian carnival masks, dies in the doorway of the house where orphans with musical talent may live and have the privilege of singing for groups of Venetian citizens. While Marietta trains there, she forms close friendships with two girls, also orphans. They all become involved in the feud between two noble families in the city. All are later separated from loved ones by either death or imprisonment before settling into a happier life. Sometimes even those who have always been willing to help others find themselves hurt by scheming people.

Newth, Mette. *The Abduction.* New York: Farrar, Straus, & Giroux, 1989. 0-374-30008-9, 248p. Paper, 1993. 0-374-40009-1. R=7; I=9.

The dual story of the Inuit Osuqo and the Dutch girl Christine gives a view of Osuqo's fear and distress at being captured along with her intended husband Poq on the foreigner's trading ship. The crew treats the two like animals, and Christine is horrified at humans being treated so cruelly. Isuqo and Poq are tried for the murder of a man on the ship where they have been kept at the insistence of an evil man. But no one knows their language so no one can defend them. Violence done to those who know neither the language nor the customs of a society makes the perpetrator no better than a child molester or abuser. *School Library Journal "Best Book,"* 1989.

Sonnleitner, A. Th. *The Cave Children.* Illus. Katarina Freinthal. Trans. Anthea Bell. New York: Phillips, 1971. 0-87599-169-6, 139. R=6; I=6.

When townspeople accuse Eva's grandmother of witchcraft because of her knowledge of herbs and healing, they escape in 1683 to the Swiss mountains with Peter, also nine. The grandmother and uncle die, leaving the children to survive in the Alpine wilderness. Their ingenuity helps them create tools and utensils to feed and clothe themselves as any primitive person must have done.

Spier, Peter. *Father, May I Come?* New York: Doubleday, 1993. 0-385-30935-X, 24p. R=7; I=3.

In 1687, Sietze sees a ship in trouble and rushes to alert his father and the crew which helps him sail the lifeboat. Three hundred years later, when another Sietze sees flares in the harbor, he runs to his father who in turn alerts his crew, and they save a pleasure boat carrying school children. Even though technology changes, the human need for help does not.

1790-1918

Avery, Gillian. *Maria's Italian Spring.* Illus. Scott Snow. New York: Simon & Schuster, 1993. 0-671-79582-1, 265p. R=6; I=6.

After Maria's uncle dies in 1877, in the sequel to *Maria Escapes*, the only living relative, a distant cousin domiciled in Italy, comes to Oxford and decides to take Maria back to Italy because she likes Greek and Latin. After visiting Venice, frustrated by having to admire all the old buildings and pictures, she pretends to be ill, but she escapes during afternoon rests with an English girl living nearby and explores the town. A foreign place can be very lonely.

Cameron, Eleanor. *The Court of the Stone Children.* New York: Dutton, 1973. 0-525-28350-1, 208p. Paper, New York: Puffin, 1990. 0-14-034289-3, 192p. R=5; I=5.

Although historical fantasy, Nina in contemporary San Francisco solves the mystery behind Dominique's father's assassination in Napoleon's France in the early nineteenth century. Nina finds a diary which Dominique translates for her, reassuring Dominique that her father never compromised his strong principles. The integration of the psychological and the logical creates a bond of timelessness between the real girl and the illusory one. *American Book Award*, 1974.

Douglas, Carole Nelson. *Good Morning, Irene.* New York: Tor, 1992 (1991). Paper, 0-8125-0949-8, 374p. R=7; I=10+.

Irene and her husband Sir Godfrey are reported to have died in the Alps after Irene escapes from the attentions of the King of Bohemia. But Sherlock Holmes discovers that they are living in Paris with Irene's spinster friend Nell while Irene tries to solve the mystery surrounding a man dredged from the Seine with a tatoo like one Irene has seen previously. One can almost never assume anything to be fact unless one sees it.

Douglas, Carole Nelson. *Irene at Large.* New York: Tor, 1993 (1992). Paper, 0-8125-1702-4, 381p. R=7; I=10+.

In 1890, Irene, her husband Godfrey, and her friend Nell rescue a man seemingly poisoned who falls at their feet in a Paris street. Quentin, an Englishman, who remembers Dr. Watson's kindness to him in India ten years previously, is in route to warn Dr. Watson that someone wants to murder him. Quentin interests Nell, but after they identify Dr. Watson's enemy and save him, Quentin disappears. Some people always hope for the best in life, always sharing their positive attitudes.

Geras, Adèle. *Voyage.* New York: Atheneum, 1983. 0-689-30955-4, 194p. R=2; I=6.*

In the early twentieth century, Mina, fourteen, and her family, take a ship to America in order to escape the pogroms against Jews in Russia. On board, she keeps her energy and helps others survive. The omniscient point of view reveals the diverse feelings of those around her on this journey. People tolerate great hardships to either gain or keep their freedom.

Hautzig, Esther. *Riches.* New York: HarperCollins, 1992. 0-06-022260-3, 44p. R=6; I=3.

In a small eastern European town sometime during the nineteenth century, an old couple decides to retire from their hard work but wants advice about what to do in their leisure time. The husband consults a respected rabbi who tells him to drive a cart around the countryside while his wife stays home to study religious writings as she wants to do. The man helps people walking along the road who have no money to pay for transportation. Giving of oneself, time and advice, may be more rewarding than giving money and quickly rushing away.

Heaven, Constance. *The Raging Fire.* New York: Putnam, 1987. 0-399-13395-X, 503p. R=4; I=10+.**

Galina sits in the classes of a non-practicing English doctor at the university in St. Petersburg during 1905. When the doctor helps a fellow revolutionary, she falls in love with him. During the transition to the Bolshevik regime, a fanatic man who loves Galina continues to track her, and as she prepares to escape from the new Soviet Union, this man becomes master of her future. Irrational people can create much pain and cause much fear in more reasonable people.

Herman, Charlotte. *The House on Walenska Street*. Illus Susan Avishai. New York: Puffin, 1991 (1990). Paper, 0-14-034405-5, 80p. R=4; I=4.

Leah writes a letter to her relatives in Minnesota from her home in Russia after her father dies. Her two little sisters and her mother think about coming to America when soldiers sweep through their house because they are Jewish and take their valuable items. Having memories of loved ones helps one to dream of a happier future. *Carl Sandburg Literary Arts Awards*, 1990.

Hesse, Karen. *Letters from Rifka*. New York: Holt, 1992. 0-8050-1964-2, 148p. Paper, New York: Puffin, 1993. 0-14-036391-2. R=5; I=5.

To tell of her journey to escape from Jewish pogroms in Berdichev, Russia, through Poland and Belgium to America from 1919-1920, Rifka, twelve, writes letters to her cousin in the margins of her beloved book of Pushkin's poetry. After surviving typhus, Rifka journeys to Antwerp for ringworm treatment and then is detained on Ellis Island because her hair has not regrown. Her facility for learning languages and her concern for fellow immigrants, a young Russian peasant and an orphaned Polish baby, show her good qualities and persuade customs officials to reunite her with her loving family.

Hooper, Maureen Brett. *The Violin Man*. Illus. Gary Undercuffler. Honesdale, PA: Boyds Mills, 1991. 1-878093-79-7, 70p. R=3; I=4.

In the 1880's, when Antonio is ten, a traveling man comes to his small Italian town looking for a Stradivarius violin, over one hundred years old. Using a clue in a diary that the "violin man" found in Milan, they ask people and finally locate it in the bottom of a trunk in the corner of an attic in a young widow's home--a prize not only for her but also for the person who will buy it. The emotional power of music can offset the cares and frustrations of daily life.

Levine, Arthur A. *All the Lights in the Night.* Illus. James E. Ransome. New York: Tambourine, 1991. 0-688-10108-9, 32p. R=5; I=4.

While the tzar's soldiers are blaming the Jews for all the troubles in Russia, Moses and his brother receive money from an older brother to travel to Palestine, leaving their mother behind. They take a small lamp with enough oil for only one night of Hanukkah, and when they have to give the lamp to a ship's captain for fare, all the stars in the sky become their lamps. Despotism unfairly separates families, and children have to face risks without the support of loving adults.

Levitin, Sonia. *A Sound to Remember.* Illus. Gabriel Lisowski. New York: Harcourt Brace, 1979. 0-15-277248-0, 32p. R=6; I=2.*

Jacov blows the shofar for Rosh Hashanah even though everyone in town except the rabbi thinks he is unqualified. When he emits only weak sounds, the villagers feel vindicated. On the last day of the holidays, they wonder whom the rabbi will choose and are surprised when he chooses Jacov again but plays on a second shofar himself, creating doubly beautiful sounds.

Matas, Carol. *Sworn Enemies.* New York: Bantam, 1993. 0-553-08326-0, 132p. R=2; I=8.

Around 1840 in Russia, Zev plots to capture Aaron, sixteen, to fulfill the Jewish quota for military service even though Aaron attends yeshiva and is exempt. Zev admires Aaron's intended bride and tries to garner her interest after Aaron's departure. But she knows Zev's identity, and he disgusts her. After others capture Zev for service, he and Aaron escape the military together although continuing to hate each other. When one tries to unfairly gain an advantage, one may foolishly weaken one's own position.

Milton, Nancy. *The Giraffe That Walked to Paris.* Illus. Roger
Roth. New York: Crown, 1992. 0-517-58133-7, 32p. R=4; I=2.

In 1826, the King of Egypt wants to send a gift to the King
of France, and he decides to send a giraffe. The giraffe travels
to Marseilles by ship, but the easiest way to get it to Paris is
by foot so the giraffe walks for forty-one days to meet King
Charles X and to move into its new home at the Paris zoo.
When one expects a gift, the wait for it often seems long.

O'Callahan, Jay. *Tulips.* Illus. Deborah Santini. Saxonville, MA:
Picture Book Studio, 1992. 0-88708-223-8, 28p. R=5; I=3.

Pierre visits his grandmother in Paris every fall and spring
at bulb planting and tulip blooming. One year, she and the
servants foil his mischievous ways with tricks of their own. The
lithesome watercolor illustrations set this story around 1900
with Pierre's knickers and the mention of a servant's
"bloomers."

Pitt, Nancy. *Beyond the High White Wall.* New York: Scribner's,
1986. 0-684-18663-2, 135p. R=3; I=6.*

After watching the murder of an innocent Jewish man by his
foreman on her family's property in the Ukraine during 1903,
Libby begins to understand the plans her family makes to leave
the home they love for America. Other incidents occur,
including the burning of their house. Although Libby regrets
leaving her friends, that her family tries to take charge of its
life pleases her. Although one has little control over life, one
should always try to participate rather than be passive.

Segal, Jerry. *The Place Where Nobody Stopped.* Illus. Dav
Pilkey. New York: Orchard/Watts, 1991. 0-531-08497-3, 154p.
R=6; I=6.

Between 1895 and 1906, the "place where nobody stopped"
was between Vitebsk and Smolensk at Yosif the baker's. The
Cossack sergeant major, however, stopped there and mistreated
Yosif, and people from all around came to hear the stories of
Yosif's tenant, a believer in logic and goodness. Some people
refuse to lower themselves to the bullying ways of others and
often are very content with their decisions.

Wheeler, Thomas Gerald. *A Fanfare for the Stalwart.* New York: S. G. Phillips, 1967. 0-87599-139-4, 191p. R=7; I=9.

At 19 in 1812, Alain Dieudonné joins the Trumpet Corps in Napoleon's French army. He reports to Moscow but soon after the French leave, his horse is killed, and he must walk through the intensely cold winter to Warsaw. He protects a governess and child on the journey and is duly rewarded for his heroic effort on his return to Paris.

Winter, Jeanette, writer/illus. *Klara's New World.* New York: Knopf, 1992. 0-679-90626-6, 41p. R=4; I=4.

When Klara is eight around 1852, her family decides, with regret, to leave Sweden and come to America where they will be able to grow crops and raise animals for food. After three months of sailing an ocean, rivers, and lakes, as well as train rides, they finally arrive in Minnesota to start a new life.

Zei, Aliki. *The Sound of Dragon's Feet.* Trans. Edward Fenton. New York: Dutton, 1979. R=3; I=5.*

Sasha, ten, daughter of a Russian physician in 1894, wonders how one hears dragon footsteps and admires the bravery of lion tamers. Her new tutor, a man having served in prison for his attempts to gain more rights for workers, tells her that courageous people are not those who have stuck their heads inside lions' mouths but those who have jeopardized their own comforts to help others. Aiding other people, whatever their needs, makes one's own life more interesting and enjoyable. *Mildred L. Batchelder Award*, 1980.

1919-1945

Aaron, Chester. *Gideon.* New York: Lippincott, 1982. 0-397-31993-2, 182p. R=7; I=9.*

By using his wits and ignoring the needs and pleas of others, Gideon survives life in both the Warsaw ghetto and Treblinka, a concentration camp, during World War II. He keeps as his guide his father's admonition that only alive can he help his people by being able to tell them what has happened. To survive the deceptions and atrocities of enemies requires enormous mental strength.

Baklanov, Grigory. *Forever Nineteen.* Trans. Antonina Bouis. New York: Lippincott, 1989. 0-397-32297-6, 168p. R=4; I=8.*

At nineteen, Volodya becomes a Russian soldier fighting the Germans in 1941. After various battles, wounds, and falling in love, he faces machine gun fire. Actors planning to re-enact World War II recover his body from the trench thirty years later. In the midst of war, one must enjoy each day and each pleasure as it occurs.

Benchley, Nathaniel. *Bright Candles: A Novel of Danish Resistance.* New York: Harper, 1974. 0-06-020461-3, 256p. R=6; I=8.*

Gens tells of his experiences from the beginning of the German occupation in Denmark in 1940 when he was sixteen and his frustration because the Danes would not fight back. He, his mother, and his father become separated during the next four years as each pursues individual efforts in the underground resistance, including being captured and imprisoned. Perhaps people become strongest when united against a common and especially evil enemy.

Bergman, Tamar. *Along the Tracks.* Trans. Michael Swirsky. Boston: Houghton Mifflin, 1991. 0-395-55328-8, 245p. R=3; I=7.

World War II starts when Yankele is seven, and his Jewish family escapes to the Urals in Russia from Lodz, Poland, before the Nazis finish building the ghetto wall around their Lodz home. After his father joins the Russian army, Yankele becomes separated from his mother when their train leaves him in a field after it stopped for a bombing raid. He spends four years wandering through Uzbekistan as one of the "abandoned" children before he finds his mother. Then they hear that his father, who had been missing in action, is alive in Poland. That some people do survive the inhumanities of war is miraculous.

Bishop, Claire Huchet. *Twenty and Ten.* Illus. William Pène du Bois. New York: Peter Smith, 1984 (1952). 0-8446-6168-6, 76p. Paper, New York: Penguin, 1978. 0-14-031076-2. R=3; I=3.

In France during World War II, Janet and her class of twenty with their teacher, a kind Catholic Sister, are evacuated into the countryside. Soon ten Jewish children arrive and hide in a nearby cave. All risk their lives by denying the Jewish children's presence when Nazis come searching for them. The comparison of the Nazi search to that of Herod and his soldiers for the baby Jesus gives added depth to this story, historical in its perspective although not technically historical fiction. *Child Study Children's Book Committee at Bank Street College Award, 1952.*

Cech, John. *My Grandmother's Journey.* Illus. Sharon McGinley-Nally. New York: Bradbury, 1991. 0-02-718135-9, 32p. R=2; I=3.

Korie's grandmother tells of seeing the gypsies twice--one gypsy rids her of headaches and the second tells her that she will one day want bread and be happy to be living. Soon Russia breaks into civil war, and her family loses almost everything. Korie's grandparents and her mother survive the initial battles, Stalin's purges, and World War II with the Nazis, to arrive in America and start their new life. When people have hope, they can survive amazing difficulties.

DePaola, Tomi. *Bonjour, Mr. Satie.* Illus. Tomi DePaola. New York: Putnam, 1991. 0-399-21782-7, 32p. R=5; I=3.**

In this historical fantasy, Monsieur Satie judges the paintings of two famous artists, Pablo [Picasso] and Henri [Matisse] whom he meets at "Gertrude's" [Stein] in Paris. Although no dates appear, the adult reader will relish the parody of Stein's writing style and of her salon where, among the guests, appear caricatures of James Joyce, Ezra Pound, Alice B. Toklas, Josephine Baker, and Ernest Hemingway. Monsieur Satie's equitable verdict when he looks at selections of the two artists' paintings will reassure readers that all decisions do not have to be either good or bad.

Dillon, Eilís. *Children of Bach.* New York: Scribner's, 1992. 0-684-19440-6, 164p. R=2; I=5.

Four children escape from Budapest, Hungary, after Nazi soldiers take away their musician parents at the beginning of World War II. The children, an aunt, and a neighbor hide in a van behind furniture being transported to an officer into Italy. They safely reach their friend's cousin who lives high in the remote Italian mountains where they can play their violins and piano without discovery. In times of war, not even talented people who have disciplined themselves are safe from people who want power over them.

Durrell, Lawrence. *White Eagles over Serbia.* New York: S. G. Phillips, 1957. 0-87599-030-4, 200p. R=6; I=9.

When the Communists and Tito take over Serbia and Croatia, the British spy Meuthen infiltrates the mountainous area where another spy has been murdered. His ability to speak Serbian and to survive in nature lead him to the White Eagles, a Royalist group which is trying to overthrow the new government. When the plot fails, the captured Meuthen escapes, ready to further reveal the brutish forces ruling the area.

Frank, Rudolf. *No Hero for the Kaiser.* Trans. Patricia Crampton. Illus. Klaus Steffens. New York: Lothrop, Lee & Shepard 1986 (1931). 0-688-06093-5, 222p. R=4; I=7.

Russian and German soldiers destroy Jan's Polish town on his fourteenth birthday in 1914. He joins the Germans and fights for two years, but on the day the Kaiser is to reward his bravery, he disappears, uninterested in German citizenship. Circumstances of war change many lives outwardly and even though people seem to acquiesce to their present situation, they may not want to relinquish their heritage. *Preis der Leseratten, Buxtehuder Bulle, Gustav Heinemann Friedenspreis, Mildred L. Batchelder, 1987; American Library Association Notable Book for Children, 1986.*

Gallaz, Christophe, and **Roberto Innocenti.** *Rose Blanche.* Illus. Roberto Innocenti. Trans. Martha Coventry. Mankato, MN: Creative Education, 1986. 0-8791-994-X, 28p. R=2; I=6.

Rose Blanche (symbolic name of Germans wanting to stop the war), in her German town during World War II, follows an army truck into which she sees the town's mayor push a little boy who does not want to go. She finds the barbed wire of a concentration camp and feeds the people with her own rations throughout the winter. One day, when she discovers the wire cut, the liberating soldiers, in the fog, think she is one of the Nazi enemies and shoots her. Not all people in a country support their government's politics or decisions, whether for good or for evil. *Mildred L. Batchelder Award, 1986; American Library Association Notable Book for Children, 1985.*

Gehrts, Barbara. *Don't Say a Word.* Trans. Elizabeth D. Crawford. New York: McElderry, 1986. 0-689-50412-8, 170p. R=7; I=7.

Anna's teenage years occur during World War II in Germany, where her father, a Luftwaffe officer, is arrested by the Gestapo for passing information to the Allies. She sees both family and Jewish friends die around her, and eventually, she and her mother must leave Berlin when Allies bomb their home. Times of war change everyone's lives. *American Library Association Notable Book for Children, 1986; International Board on Books for Young People, 1988.*

Glasco, Gordon. *Slow Through Eden.* New York: Poseidon, 1992. 0-671-62305-2, 259p. R=6; I=10+.

The two gifted physicists, Katherine and David, marry and begin their work on the atomic bomb in Berlin during World War II, but David is Jewish and must escape with their son to London where he meets a Russian spy who murders him. Katherine goes to New York and works on the secret Manhattan project while starting another life. Becoming loyal to one's husband instead of one's demanding father, when they are political enemies, can be difficult.

Gutman, Claude. *The Empty House.* Trans. Anthea Bell. London: Penguin, 1993. Paper, 0-14-036169-3, 96p. R=4; I=6.

In 1942, while David, thirteen, sleeps with his non-Jewish neighbors, his parents disappear. Others protect him by taking him to a convent and then to a home with Jewish children who have also been separated from their parents. When Nazis remove these children from the home in the early morning, David again escapes because he has spent the night in the woods with his girlfriend, a Catholic. He writes his story, not understanding why he is still free, three days after the children disappear and leave him in another empty house. So much of what happens to people seems to be purely circumstantial especially during a war.

Hackl, Erich. *Farewell Sidonia.* Trans. Edna McCown. New York: Fromm International, 1992. Paper, 0-88064-135-5, 135p. R=8; I=10+.

Found on the steps of a hospital in 1933, the infant Sidonia has a note attached to her saying that she needs parents. Foster parents take her, but Hitler's hostility pervades Austria, and Sidonia's skin coloring reveals her as a hated gypsy foreigner. She is eventually taken to her gypsy family's headquarters, placed on the last transport to Auschwitz, and dies there from grief, according to her brother many years later. When people in power have prejudice against particular groups, those groups have little chance of survival.

Haugaard, Erik. *Chase Me, Catch Nobody*. Boston: Houghton Mifflin, 1980. R=6; I=7.**

When Erik, fourteen, visits Germany during his 1937 spring vacation from his Danish school, the overt prejudice surprises him. After fellow students accuse him of taking a package of passports into the country for a stranger he met on the ferry, he escapes from the group and finds himself helping a half-Jewish girl flee to Denmark in a stolen boat. That politics in which a person is not interested can so adversely affect one's life always surprises.

Haugaard, Erik. *The Little Fishes*. Illus. Milton Johnson. Magnolia, MA: Peter Smith 1993 (1967). 0-8446-6245-3. R=3; I=6.

Guido's mother dies when he is twelve during 1943 in Italy, and he becomes one of the wandering children who survive by begging. He tries to help those he meets including a woman needing food for her newborn baby. Few families escape the destruction of war. *Jane Addams Book Award,* 1968; *Boston Globe--Horn Book Award,* 1967; *New York Herald Tribune Award,* 1967; *Danish Cultural Ministries Award.*

Hautzig, Esther. *The Endless Steppe: A Girl in Exile*. New York: HarperCollins, 1968. 0-690-26371-6, 243p. Paper, 1987. 0-06-447027-X, 245p. R=5; I=5.

When Esther is ten in 1941, Russian soldiers deport her family from Vilna, Poland, to Siberia, for being capitalists. From a life of being wealthy to a life of wondering about the next meal, she, her parents, and grandparents endure, with hope, the enormous changes in their lives. In the midst of despair, the realization that one must survive in any way possible can make the difference between who lives and who succumbs in life. *Sydney Taylor Book Awards,* 1968; *Jane Addams Book Award,* 1969.

Heuck, Sigrid. *The Hideout.* Trans. Rika Lesser. New York: Dutton, 1988. 0-525-44343-6, 183p. R=3; I=5.*

An old woman finds Rebecca, nine, in a bombed air raid shelter in 1944, but Rebecca does not remember her own name. After being registered with the Missing Persons Bureau and sent to an orphanage, Rebecca makes friends with a boy hiding in a nearby cornfield who tells her fantasy stories. After an enemy air raid, she suddenly remembers her name, allowing her to be reunited with her parents at the end of the war. Shock may be a coping mechanism that eases fear and the pain of loss of family.

Holman, Felice. *The Wild Children.* New York: Puffin, 1985 (1983). Paper, 0-14-031930-1, 152p. R=6; I=8.

After the Russian Revolution ends when Alex is twelve, and his family has been arrested, he walks over one hundred miles to Moscow. Unable to locate any others in his family, he meets shelterless *bezprizoni* ("wild children") and becomes one of them traveling illegally on trains until they make contact with someone who helps them reach Finland. Victims of war include children who lose their families and must survive on their own in any way possible. *American Library Association Best Book for Young Adults*, 1979.

Kerr, Judith, writer/illus. *When Hitler Stole Pink Rabbit.* New York: Dell, 1987 (1971). Paper (Yearling), 0-440-49017-0, 192p. R=6; I=6.

In 1933, Anna, nine, and her brother and mother rapidly leave Berlin for Switzerland after her father disappears. During the war, they resettle in France, and finally in England while Anna goes to new schools and learns different languages. Throughout her experiences, she only feels inconvenienced, but never unfortunate, because her family is able to stay together.

Laird, Christa. *Shadow of the Wall.* New York: Greenwillow, 1990. 0-688-09336-1, 144p. R=7; I=8.

Watching each member of his family either leave or die in the Warsaw ghetto of 1942, Misha, thirteen, decides that he must escape. Another orphan leads him through the slimy filth of the sewers with his false Aryan papers to freedom on the other side of the wall. Godless people destroy life, but godlike people help others keep their hope. *Janusz Korczak Award,* 1991.

Levitin, Sonia. *Journey to America.* Illus. Charles Robinson. New York: Atheneum, 1993 (1970). 0-68931829-4. Paper (Aladdin), 1987. 0-689-71130-1, 160p. R=4; I=4.

In 1938, Lisa's father realizes the danger of Hitler to Jews in Berlin so he secretly departs for America, leaving his three daughters and wife to later "vacation" in Switzerland and wait there for him to send for them. They leave everything, not allowed by the Nazis to take anything, and stay in Zurich almost a year before reuniting as a family in America where their experiences are recounted in *Silver Days* and *Annie's Promise.* People with compassion for others keep the world from annihilation by evil. *National Jewish Awards,* 1971.

Lowry, Lois. *Number the Stars.* Boston: Houghton Mifflin, 1989. 0-395-51060-0, 169p. Paper, New York: Dell, 1992. 0-440-21372-X, 137p. R=4; I=5.

Annemarie's friend Ellen has to escape from the Nazis who decide to assemble all of the Danish Jews in 1943. A false funeral for Annemarie's non-existent great aunt allows some of the Jews to gather before her uncle takes them on a fishing boat to Sweden, but not before a handkerchief covered with a drug keeps the Nazis' dogs from smelling them under the fish. Many people have given their own lives to help others whose governments have unjustly and unfairly treated them. *Newbery Medal,* 1990; *National Jewish Awards,* 1990; *Association of Jewish Libraries Award,* 1990; *Sydney Taylor Book Award,* 1989; *American Library Association Notable Book for Children,* 1990; *School Library Journal "Best Book,"* 1989.

McSwigan, Marie. *Snow Treasure*. Illus. Andre LeBlanc. New York: Dutton, 1942. Paper, New York: Scholastic, 1986. 0-590-42537-4, 156p. R=4; I=4.*

Although not historical fiction in the strict sense, the story tells of Norway's attempt to remove its gold from the Germans' grasp in 1940. Children, with Peter as the leader, ride their sleds hiding bars of gold bullion to the shore of the fiord where they bury them under snowmen. Peter's uncle retrieves the bars and loads them on his nearby camouflaged boat. When people work together, they can often achieve amazing results.

Marvin, Isabel R. *Bridge to Freedom*. Philadelphia, PA: Jewish Publication Society, 1991. 0-8276-0377-0, 136p. R=3; I=6.

A Jewish girl Rachel, sixteen, and a German soldier Kurt, fifteen, escape to Belgium across a bridge spanning the Rhine River in 1945 as American tanks rumble towards them in the dark. Captured, Kurt saves an American officer and gains his freedom. Aided by American soldiers and Belgian farmers, they arrive separately in Liège and find each other on May 8, Victory in Europe Day.

Matas, Carol. *Code Name Kris*. New York: Scribner's, 1990. 0-684-19208-X, 152p. R=6; I=7.

Jesper recalls his part in the Danish resistance as he sits inside his cell above Gestapo headquarters in Copenhagen, fingernails ripped out, waiting to be executed. In this sequel to *Lisa's War*, he has stayed in Denmark while Lisa and her brother Stefan, Jews, have escaped to Sweden. Jesper does gain his freedom and later remembers the day of liberation, May 4, by lighting candles in windows. During war, people do things which repulse and distress them in order to survive. *Canadian Lester and Orpen Dennys Award*, 1988.

Matas, Carol. *Daniel's Story*. New York: Scholastic, 1993. 0-590-46920-7, 136p. Paper, 0-590-46588-0. R=3; I=6.

At fourteen in 1941, Daniel unwillingly rides in the train taking his family from Frankfurt, Germany, where his mother's family has lived for one thousand years and his father's for six hundred, to the Jewish ghetto in Lodz, Poland. There and later in both Auschwitz and Buchenwald, he remembers the photographs snapped throughout his life before being declared a threat to society as a Jew. But he and his father survive the horror. To hate and want to destroy other humans is to succumb to the evil that thrives on the powerlessness of others.

Matas, Carol. *Lisa's War.* New York: Scribner's, 1989. 0-684-19010-9, 111p. Paper, 0-590-43517-5. R=3; I=5.

When Lisa is twelve in 1940, the Danish government surrenders, and the German planes fly over Copenhagen. Through the war, Lisa's family takes part in the Resistance until her father hears from the rabbi that the Nazis plan to round up the Jews during Rosh Hashanah; they have to escape to Sweden. Most wars are won because of the silent but effective resistance to those who abuse power. *Geoffrey Bilson Award for Historical Fiction for Young People*, 1988.

Mattingley, Christobel. *The Angel with a Mouth Organ.* Illus. Astra Lacis. New York: Holiday, 1986. 0-8234-0593-1, 30p. R=3; I=3.**

A mother tells her son and daughter about her life during World War II when her family was bombed out of its home and had to walk for many days to reach a camp for homeless people. Soldiers took away her father although he had only one arm. But after the war ended, she heard his mouth organ and knew that he had returned. During war, families learn that having each other is much more important than having material things.

Morpurgo, Michael. *Waiting for Anya.* New York: Viking, 1991. 0-670-83735-0, 172p. R=6; I=5.

On the Spanish border of France, Jo, twelve, becomes part of a plan to save Jewish children during World War II. By pretending the children are shepherds, the town gets them over the border without German patrols realizing their identity. War never makes sense, but sometimes it unites people to help the hunted flee the hunter. *School Library Journal "Best Book,"* 1991.

Oppenheim, Shulamith Levey. *The Lily Cupboard.* Illus. Ronald Himler. New York: HarperCollins, 1992. 0-06-024670-7, 32p. R=2; I=2.

In 1940, Miriam's parents take her to a Dutch farm to hide during World War II. The separation is painful, but Miriam's temporary family gives her a rabbit which she hugs while hiding from the Nazi soldiers who search the house. Such families hid many Dutch Jews at great peril to their own lives during the war.

Orgel, Doris. *The Devil in Vienna.* New York: Puffin, 1988 (1978). Paper, 0-14-032500-X. R=2; I=6.

In 1938, Inge celebrates her thirteenth birthday in Vienna, missing her best friend who has recently moved to Munich with her Nazi storm trooper father. Inge's letters do not get delivered. Not until Liselotte returns after the Austrian leader Schuschnigg bows to Hitler, does Inge realize the seriousness of her isolation as a Jew in this regime. Governments controlling friendships of children shows the possibilities of fanatical power. *Child Study Children's Book Committee Award,* 1978; *Sydney Taylor Book Award,* 1978; *Child Study Committee Award,* 1978; *Association of Jewish Libraries Award,* 1978; *Golden Kite Honor Book,* 1979.

Orlev, Uri. *The Island on Bird Street.* Trans. Hillel Halkin. Boston: Houghton Mifflin, 1984. 0-395-33887-5, 162p. R=3; I=6.

During World War II, Alex hides in the Warsaw ghetto ruins after the police take away his father. During his eleventh year, he uses his ingenuity to stay alive by finding food and supplies in empty apartments until his father returns. War's inhumanity leads people to use all their wits just to continue living. *Mildred L. Batchelder Award,* 1985; *Sydney Taylor Book Award,* 1984; *American Library Association Notable Book for Children,* 1984; *Association of Jewish Libraries Award,* 1985.

Orlev, Uri. *The Man from the Other Side.* Trans. Hillel Halkin. Boston: Houghton Mifflin, 1991. 0-395-53808-4, 186p. R=7; I=7.

When Marek is fourteen, he begins helping his stepfather take items into the ghetto in Warsaw, Poland, through the sewer system and bring out money and several babies to take to the Catholic convent. Marek himself becomes involved with hiding a man who returns to the ghetto to fight in an organized uprising against the Germans. In times of war, people make unusual, and sometimes unexpected, allegiances. *Mildred L. Batchelder*, 1992; *National Jewish Awards*, 1992; *American Library Association Notable Books for Children*, 1992; *School Library Journal "Best Book,"* 1991.

Pelgrom, Els. *The Winter When Time Was Frozen*. Trans. Maryka and Raphel Rudnik. New York: Morrow, 1980. 0-688-32247-6, 253p. R=6; I=6.**

Noortje, eleven, and her father find shelter on a Dutch farm in 1944-45 along with several other people. After the food disappears more rapidly than expected during the cold winter, the farm's owner takes Noortje to a nearby cave where she is feeding a Jewish family with a newborn baby. They take the baby inside before the Nazis discover the family. When the war ends, the baby's uncle says that the family was murdered in a concentration camp. Many Dutch citizens risked their lives to protect Jews from Hitler. *Mildred L. Batchelder Award, 1981*.

Posell, Elsa. *Homecoming*. San Diego: Harcourt Brace, 1987. 0-15-235160-4, 230p. R=6; I=6.

Olya and her Jewish family face hostility when tzar Nicholas is deposed in 1918. After their father escapes to America and their mother dies, the children get to Antwerp. There, several strangers whom they meet through the various aid societies give them money to go America. Many good people make sacrifices to help those who are in danger or less fortunate.

Reiss, Johanna. *The Journey Back*. New York: HarperCollins, 1992 (1976). 0-06-021457-0. Paper (Trophy), 1987. 0-06-447042-3, 212p. R=3; I=5

After Annie and her sister emerge from hiding at the Nazis' defeat in 1945, they return to their Dutch home with their sister and father in this sequel to *The Upstairs Room*. Annie misses the couple who hid her, but at the same time, she wants approval from her new step-mother. Although she does not like it, Annie realizes that life continues to change as people grow and go their separate ways.

Reiss, Johanna. *The Upstairs Room.* New York: Crowell, 1987 (1972). 0-690-04702-9, 196p. Paper (Trophy), 1990. 0-06-440370-X. R=2; I=5.

In 1942, Annie begins her two years of hiding from the Nazis in the upstairs room of a family in Holland. She and her sister survive deportation because of the risk this family takes to save them. What happens afterward appears in *The Journey Back.* When people selflessly help others, their own lives often change dramatically for the better. *Newbery Honor,* 1973; *National Jewish Awards,* 1973.

Richter, Hans. *Friedrich.* Magnolia, MA: Peter Smith, 1992 (1972). 0-8446-6573-8, 149p. Paper, New York: Puffin, 1987. 0-14-032205-1. R=4; I=4.

A narrator, Friedrich's friend, tells about the strange demise of Friedrich's prosperous family from 1925 in contrast to the rise of his own family. The difference between the two families is that Friedrich's is Jewish, and it suffers Hitler's punishment and ignominy until shrapnel kills Friedrich outside a bomb shelter. The question of both the narrator and any reader is why a person has to suffer for nothing other than being Jewish. *Mildred L. Batchelder Award,* 1972.

Richter, Hans. *I Was There.* Trans. Edite Kroll. New York: Puffin, 1987 (1972). Paper, 0-14-032206-X, 205p. R=3; I=7.

Three young German boys become friends in 1933 when they are eight--a Nazi official's son, Heinz; a Communist's son, Gunther; and the narrator. After the war starts, Heinz enlists but returns wounded, saying the only hero he saw was a man who jumped on a grenade to save men in his platoon. When all three later go to battle together, Heinz sacrifices himself for his friends. To accept the reality of life after being an idealist takes an adjustment of all one has previously believed.

Roth-Hano, Renee. *Touch Wood: A Girlhood in Occupied France.* New York: Four Winds, 1988. 0-02-777340-X, 297p. Paper, New York: Puffin, 1989. 0-14-034085-8. R=4; I=6.

When Renee is nine, her family leaves Alsace for Paris to escape the Nazis. Eventually she and her two sisters pretend to be Catholics and live in a Normandy convent while her parents stay in Paris, using an assumed name. War's devastation can make people wonder if they have any control over their lives. *American Library Association Notable Book for Children*, 1988.

Sender, Ruth Minsky. *The Cage*. New York: Macmillan, 1986. 0-02-781830-6, 252p. R=3; I=7.

Her mother tells Nancy about her experiences in the Lodz, Poland, ghetto beginning in 1939 through the concentration camps ending in 1945 when she barely escapes execution. Many in her family die but seven years after separation during the war, she finds some of her brothers through the Displaced Persons bureau. Surviving the horror of World War II as a Jew was a mental victory as much as a physical one.

Serraillier, Ian. *The Silver Sword*. Illus. C. Walter Hodges. New York: S. G. Phillips, 1959. 0-87599-104-1, 187p. Paper, *Escape from Warsaw*. New York: Scholastic, 1990. 0-590-43715-1. R=4; I=6.

When Ruth is thirteen, in 1940, the Nazis imprison her father near Warsaw, Poland. Through a series of occurrences, Ruth and her siblings eventually find their escaped father in Switzerland and joyfully reunite. In times of intense suffering, many people show kindness and give aid to others less fortunate. *Boy's Club of America Award*, 1960; *Carnegie Commendation*, 1956.

Sevela, Ephraim. *We Were Not Like Other People*. Trans. Antonina Bouis. New York: HarperCollins, 1989. 0-06-025508-0, 224p. R=5; I=8.

When Stalin purges the Union of Soviet Socialist Republics in 1937, a nine-year-old Jewish boy's family becomes "enemies of the people" and his army commander father is imprisoned. The boy survives hunger and loneliness during World War II, thinking he is an orphan. He finds afterwards that his whole family has miraculously survived. This powerful story about a depressing era ends on a positive note--that people sometimes survive, most often through the generosity of others, to face a future. *International Board of Books for Young People*, 1992.

Treseder, Terry Walton. *Hear O Israel: A Story of the Warsaw Ghetto.* Illus. Lloyd Bloom. New York: Atheneum, 1990. 0-689-31456-6, 41p. R=3; I=7.

Just before he turns thirteen and after his mother, brothers, and sister have died of typhus, Isaac, his older brother, and his father leave the Warsaw ghetto for the Treblinka concentration camp. Isaac keeps his faith even as he and his father walk toward the gas chamber. Keeping one's religious faith under such circumstances is a challenge.

Vos, Ida. *Hide and Seek.* Trans. Terese Edelstein and Inez Smidt. Boston: Houghton Mifflin, 1991. 0-395-56470-0, 133p. R=4; I=5.

As a Jewish girl in Holland when the Nazis arrive in 1940, Rachel at eight begins losing "privileges"--no tram riding, giving up her bicycle, not playing games, and wearing a yellow star on her clothes. Her family goes into hiding, and unlike her grandparents and uncle, they survive the war, as recounted in the sequel *Anna Is Still Here.* The importance of non-Jews during World War II in protecting Jews cannot be overstated.

Wild, Margaret. *Let the Celebrations Begin!* Illus. Julie Vivas. New York: Orchard/Watts, 1991. 0-531-08537-6, 32p. R=5; I=3.

Miriam remembers having toys, but younger children in the concentration camp have only known the camp as their home by 1945. When the interred hear that soldiers are coming, some women and Miriam stay up, after the guards are asleep, to make toys for the children to receive at a liberation party when the foreign soldiers arrive at Belsen. In the middle of despair, some humans can find hope and create something positive.

Yolen, Jane. *The Devil's Arithmetic.* New York: Viking, 1988. 0-670-81027-4, 170p. Paper, New York: Puffin, 1990. 0-14-034535-3. R=5; I=7.

In this historical fantasy of time travel, Hannah, thirteen, dreads the yearly seder with the relatives until one year she finds herself transported into a Polish village during the early 1940's as Chaka. When she sees the Nazis, she knows what will happen, but until they begin the journey to the camps, the villagers merely think she is over reacting to the Nazis' plan for their resettlement. Actually having to live as others have helps one more clearly understand what they have endured.

National Jewish Awards, 1989; *Sydney Taylor Book Award,* 1988; *Association of Jewish Libraries Award,* 1989.

Zei, Aliki. *Petro's War.* Trans. Edward Fenton. New York: Dutton, 1972. R=5; I=5.*

Petro becomes a member of the underground resistance to the Italians and the Germans after Greece declares war on Italy in 1940. He changes from a nine-year-old child interested in turtles to one who writes slogans on walls about the lack of food in Athens. Everyone in his family eventually joins the resistance by delivering messages, hiding people or distributing information. His uncle fights in the mountains, sending messages to the family via the BBC (British Broadcasting Company). By uniting against an aggressor, a group of people has a chance to defeat wanton cruelty. *Mildred L. Batchelder Award,* 1974.

Zei, Aliki. *Wildcat Under Glass.* Trans. Edward Fenton. New York: Holt, 1968. R=5; I=6.**

In Greece in 1936, Melia and her older sister Myrto realize that the adults have become more pensive and concerned about things which the girls do not understand. Then their cousin Niko comes to their island summer home and hides in a deserted windmill from Spanish Fascist spies ("Black Shirts"). Police imprison their friend's father and burn their grandfather's books. When they return to Athens and Myrto's teachers ask her to spy on her family as leader of the Youth Organization, they begin to see the seriousness of the situation. When selfish people grab power, they can whimsically destroy any challengers. *Mildred L. Batchelder Award,* 1970.

1946 and AFTER

Degens, T. *On the Third Ward.* New York: Harper, 1990.
0-06-021429-5, 243p. R=6; I=8.*

In the German (Hessian) State Hospital for Children with Tuberculosis in 1951, Wanda and her fellow patients create stories to help them endure the monotony and pain of their confinement. Their tales become their lives, but they still try to physically escape the hospital where death seems to be the only part of time that exists. When the body refuses to function normally, the mind may have to compensate.

De Trevino, Elizabeth. *Turi's Poppa.* New York: Farrar, Straus, & Giroux, 1968. R=7; I=6.**

After World War II, Turi, eight, and his father leave Budapest to walk to Cremona, Italy, where his father has a job as the director of the Violin Institute. When they arrive, his father has to prove his ability and identity by making a violin pleasing to a violinist who plays a Stradivari. Turi has faith in his father's talents, and continually encourages him to keep heading to Cremona. *Boston Globe--Horn Book Award,* 1968.

Fenton, Edward. *The Morning of the Gods.* New York: Delacorte, 1987. 0-385-29550-2, 184p. R=4; I=6.**

To combat her listlessness after her mother's death in a car accident, Carla, thirteen, goes to Greece to stay with her mother's aunt and uncle. Once there, she discovers the dichotomy between the military dictatorship threatening everyone and her uncle's mythological references which give insight into everyday life in 1974. Additionally, she begins to accept her mother's death by learning more about the customs that she knew, including the special rituals of the Greek Orthodox Easter. Sometimes, getting away from one's usual life may help one gain perspective.

Härtling, Peter. *Crutches.* Trans. Elizabeth D. Crawford. New York: Lothrop, Lee & Shepard, 1988. 0-688-07991-1, 163p. R=5; I=5.

At twelve in 1945, Thomas becomes separated from his mother at the Koln, Germany, train station. He boards the train for Vienna, Austria, to find his aunt, but her house is destroyed and she is dead. Thomas meets Crutches, a former soldier who lost a leg in Russia and who, at first, begrudgingly looks after him, and then cares enough not to want to tell Thomas when the Red Cross locates his mother. The ability of lost children after the war to adapt and survive with intermittent help from adults was a marvel. *Mildred L. Batchelder Award*, 1989; *American Library Association Notable Book for Children*, 1988.

Holm, Ann. *North to Freedom*. New York: Peter Smith, 1984 (1965). 0-8446-6156-2. Paper, New York: Harcourt Brace (Odyssey), 1990. 0-15-257553-7. R=6; I=7.

David escapes from a camp somewhere inside Russia where he has lived almost all of his twelve years and travels via Salonika through Italy in his return to Denmark and his mother. He is surprised and delighted by things he has never seen, like oranges, and sounds he has never heard, like music. Everyone has the right to life and freedom. *Gyldendal Prize for the Best Scandinavian Children's Book*, 1963; *American Library Association Notable Book*, 1965; *Junior Book Award; Lewis Carroll Shelf Award*.

Kordon, Klaus. *Brothers Like Friends*. Trans. Elizabeth D. Crawford. New York: Philomel, 1992. 0-399-22137-9, 206p. R=4; I=5.

Living in the Russian sector of Berlin, Germany, in 1950, Frank, seven, experiences major changes in his life which make him wonder about life after death. His twice-widowed mother marries a man with little compassion, and his beloved soccer player brother dies at fourteen from an unusual game injury. Having supportive neighbors and friends is especially important in times of disturbing losses. *German Youth Literature Award Runner-up.*

Roper, Robert. *In Caverns of Blue Ice*. Boston: Little Brown, 1991. 0-316-75606-7, 188p. R=4; I=7.

As a member of a mountain-climbing family in the Alps of Montier, France, during the 1950's, Louise becomes the first woman certified as a guide. Her love of the mountains leads her to the Himalayas in Nepal where she reaches a summit, barely surviving. The closeness of the family and its total respect for the challenges of the mountains accentuates its concern for the welfare of other climbers.

Rosen, Billi. *Andi's War.* New York: Puffin, 1991 (1989). Paper, 0-14-034404-7, 136p. R=4; I=5.

In Andi's small Greek village after World War II, the people take sides in a civil war. Her parents fight for democracy from the mountains above the town while Andi and her brother Paul live with their grandmother. Even the children suffer because the police knock Paul unconscious, and he eventually dies for refusing to tell about his parents. The fight for power claims lives of many people who do not even understand the battle.

Vos, Ida. *Anna Is Still Here.* Trans. Terese Edelstein and Inez Smidt. Boston: Houghton Mifflin, 1993. 0-395-65368-1, 139p. R=3; I=7.

Coming out after three years of hiding in 1945, in this sequel to *Hide and Seek*, Anna, thirteen, reacts to others with fear, including her parents whom she did not see for the entire time. Loud talking distresses her. As the year progresses, she makes friends with a Jewish woman who lost her family. Eventually, Anna identifies the woman's daughter from her photograph at an amusement park. Happy that the daughter has been safe with another family during the war, the woman reunites with her. Picking up pieces of a life fractured by war may be like using the pieces of a jigsaw puzzle which has suddenly changed its shape.

Ziefert, Harriet. *A New Coat for Anna.* Illus. Anita Lobel. New York: Knopf, 1986. 0-394-97426-3, 40p. Paper, 1988. 394-89861-3. R=4; I=2.

After World War II, clothes are scarce in Europe, and Anna needs a new coat. Anna's mother trades a gold watch, lamp, garnet necklace, and a teapot to get wool, have it spun, woven, and sewn into a coat. People who have needs often find ingenious and honest ways to obtain them. *American Library Association Notable Book for Children*, 1986.

THE BRITISH ISLES

476-1199

Anand, Valerie. *The Disputed Crown.* New York: Scribner's, 1982. 0-684-17629-7, 297p. R=5; I=10+.*

After William is crowned king of England in 1066, he tries to unite the Normans and the English while his wife Mathilde raises their many children and becomes involved in her own intrigues. His enemies continue their attempts to destroy him while others intermarry with the Normans, hoping to preserve what they have and to stabilize their lives. People often have to compromise on matters which can jeopardize their future.

Anand, Valerie. *Gildenford.* New York: Scribner's, 1977. 0 684-14890-X, 392p. R=4; I=10+.**

In 1018, Emma bears a son to Cnut, Viking king in England, who declares the son his heir even though he already has an older son, and Emma has two sons from another husband she has rejected. By 1036, Cnut's first son begins his quest to become heir and takes Brand as a servant, a young man taught by his father to be loyal to his lord. Through the intrigues, one of Emma's sons, Edward, eventually becomes England's king but without an heir. He chooses William of Normandy over Harold Godwin when Brand reveals that Harold and his brothers have falsely accused Emma of misdeeds. In order to look after Brand but at the same time acknowledge that he betrayed his lord, Edward sends him with William back to Normandy to be a caretaker for Harold's sons, the visible assurance that Edward has named William his successor. What may seem like a betrayal could be the need to reveal a discovered truth that saves someone unjustly charged.

Anand, Valerie. *King of the Wood.* New York: St. Martin's, 1989. 0-312-02939-X, 468p. R=7; I=10+. *

Ralph des Aix, born in 1068 in Normandy of an English father and a Norman mother who dies at his birth, becomes a member of William Rufus's court, the son and heir of William the Conqueror. Rufus (William II) gives Ralph land although not what he had wanted because of its association with the sinister King of the Wood, but Ralph earns his title as its master. Henry, Rufus's brother, works his way from third son to king (Henry I) at Rufus's untimely death, shot while hunting deer. In situations where inheritance depends on birth order, a younger son may be enticed to gain money through unscrupulous means.

Anand, Valerie. *The Norman Pretender.* New York: Scribner's, 1979. 0-684-16099-4, 410p. R=6; I=10+.**

In 1066, Harold Hardraada arrives on the eastern coast of England with Harold Godwin's brother Tostig to gain control of England. Soon after Harold lands, the winds finally favor William, and he sails from Normandy to England and the battle of Hastings through which William claims his throne. Wives, mothers, and children try to understand and adjust to the uncertainty surrounding the change of ruler in Britain, some realizing they must support the Norman king and others preparing for a new battle against him. People who think they are born to rule other humans go to much trouble and risk to prove their superiority.

Anand, Valerie. *The Proud Villeins.* New York: St. Martin's, 1992. 0-312-08282-7, 310p. R=4; I=10+.

After being one of the few Norman lords spared his life during the Gildenford massacre in 1036, Ivon has to face the rest of his life as a thrall in England. His grandson refuses to admit his blood ties with a Norman, thereby forfeiting his rights as a freeman and those of his own progeny. Yet they all retain the traits of their forefathers up through 1215 and the Magna Carta. Being able to forgive oneself and others takes strength, but one must always follow what one believes is right.

Anderson, Margaret. *The Druid's Gift.* New York: Knopf, 1989. 0-394-81936-X, 192p. R=6; I=8.

In this historical fantasy, Caitlin finds herself thrust into three different historical periods-- the time of the Vikings, the eighteenth century, and the twentieth century--on her island of Hirta off the coast of Scotland. Her ability to see the future helps her understand the importance of a truce between the harsh druids with their Samhain human sacrifice and the villagers who must appease their needs in turn for blessings. To change centuries of tradition takes great strength of character.

Attanasio, A. A. *Kingdom of the Grail.* New York: HarperCollins, 1992. 0-06-109979-1, 500p. R=5; I=10+.

When Ailena Valaise returns around 1150 from the Holy Land ten years after her son exiles her from the family home in Wales, she credits her youthful looks to having drunk from the Holy Grail. Her ability to recognize everyone convinces them that she is Ailena, but she eventually reveals to only a few that she is a Jewess, an impostor, come to defeat Ailena's son. Sometimes extreme measures are the only ones that have a chance of success.

Buechner, Frederick. *Godric.* New York: Atheneum, 1980. 0-689-11086-3, 178p. Paper, New York: HarperCollins, 1983. 0-06-061162-6, 192p. R=3; I-10+.

Beginning in 1065, Godric travels to Rome and Jerusalem, returns to the Isle of Farne, and becomes a hermit by the river Wear. Yet throughout all, he keeps his love for one woman. When he and the woman finally consummate their love, they realize that their relationship would hurt others. They quickly part, filled with guilt about their indiscretion. As a hermit, Godric realizes that what is important in life cannot be purchased. One's life, a series of events, continues through pains and pleasures.

Bulla, Clyde Robert. *The Sword in the Tree*. Illus. Paul Galdone. New York: HarperCollins, 1992 (1956). 0-690-79909-8, 128p. R=2; I=4.

When Shan is eleven, his uncle Lionel, gone for many years, returns to Weldon Castle and "accidently" kills Shan's father so that the family wealth will become his. Shan and his mother escape, helped by herdsmen. Shan goes to King Arthur at Camelot, and Sir Gareth returns with him to challenge Lionel. Shan wins back the castle and discovers that his father has been imprisoned in the dungeon instead of murdered. Shan's courage reunites his family.

De Angeli, Marguerite. *Black Fox of Lorne*. New York: Doubleday, 1956. R=5; I=7.**

Thirteen-year-old twins, Jan and Brus, accompany their father to Scotland in 950 where he shipwrecks and is murdered. Each of the twins watches for the other, and they eventually find their mother in Edin's Boro, safely arrived on a Danish ship thought lost at sea. Exposed to Christianity, all three begin to think that peace is better than revenge, and they change their attitudes to this more positive philosophy. *Newbery Honor*, 1957.

Hendry, Frances. *Quest for a Maid*. New York: Farrar, Straus & Giroux, 1992 (1990). Paper (Sunburst), 0-374-46155-4, 273p. R=5; I=7.

When King Alexander III dies in thirteenth century Scotland, Meg, nine, thinks that her sister has killed him with witchcraft. Her sister wants a position in the house of a woman who hopes to claim the throne for her son, but the rightful heir is Alexander's eight-year-old granddaughter who lives in Norway. Meg has her own job in the household of Sir Patrick Spens and sails with him to retrieve Margaret, the Maid of Norway, after she has supposedly perished in a storm off the Orkney islands. One has to know the truth before one can make an honest assessment of a situation. *American Library Association Notable Books for Children*, 1991.

Hodges, C. Walter. *The Namesake.* New York: Coward McCann, 1964. R=3; I=6.**

Alfred Timberleg, ten, dreams that he should take a horse harness to his namesake, Alfred, who becomes king in 871 and has to defend his people against the Danes. The Danes capture Alfred Timberleg, thinking that he is King Alfred's son. While in their custody, he hears about and writes Alfred the King about the Danes' dishonesty and planned attack. A child's devotion to an adult often reveals the adult's compassionate character. *Carnegie Commendation*, 1964.

Llywelyn, Morgan. *Brian Boru: Emperor of the Irish.* Chester Springs, PA: O'Brien Press/Dufour Editions, 1990. Paper, 0-86278-230-9, 160p. R=5; I=6.

When tenth century Vikings raid the Munster, Ireland, homestead of Brian's family, killing mother, brothers, and servants, Brian vows to rid the country of these plunderers. During his education at Clonmacnois, Brian studies battle plans of Alexander and Julius Caesar as well as how to construct masonry, make music, and conquer mathematics. At sixteen, he leaves and learns to appropriately use either weapons or generosity in his quest to unite Ireland. His honesty and his concern for his people earn respect; thousands follow him and help him to achieve his seemingly impossible goal. *Irish Children's Book Trust Book of the Year.*

McGraw, Eloise. *The Striped Ships.* New York: Macmillan, 1991. 0-689-50532-9, 229p. R=5; I=6.

In 1066, when Juliana is eleven, the striped Norman ships glide up to shore, and men jump off and kill many Saxons and burn their homes. She eventually finds her younger brother and goes with him to Canterbury. There, Juliana works while her brother begins his lessons in the monastery. After a year, their mother hears where they are and comes to get them. But she has wed a Norman friend of her Norman uncle, and Juliana decides to remain in Canterbury embroidering the tapestry, later known as the Bayeux Tapestry, which tells both sides of the story "the conquerors and the conquered."

Peters, Ellis. *The Confession of Brother Haluin.* New York: Mysterious Press, 1988. 0-89296-349-2, 164p. Paper, Warner (Mysterious), 1989. 0-445-40855-3. R=7; I=10+.

When the heavy snows of 1142 threaten to demolish the Shrewsbury abbey roof, Brother Haluin falls and hurts himself badly. Thinking of death, he confesses to Brother Cadfael and the Abbot, revealing an unexpected past of serious problems. Haluin recovers and goes on a journey with Brother Cadfael to expiate his past, and they come upon a murder.

Peters, Ellis. *Dead Man's Ransom.* New York: Fawcett, 1986 (1984). Paper (Crest), 0-449-20819-2, 190p. R=7; I=10+.

In 1141, King Stephen and Empress Maud battle anew for the throne of England. When the battle of Lincoln results in a prisoner exchange and a prisoner dies mysteriously, Brother Cadfael has to find why. He deduces that the man died from unnatural causes, and he must prove his case for murder.

Peters, Ellis. *The Devil's Novice.* New York: Morrow, 1984. 0-688-03247-8, 192p. R=7; I=10+.**

Two people arrive at the Benedictine Abbey in 1140, one a novice and the other a political envoy who soon disappears and is found murdered. The novice seems to be involved because he miscalculates actions and befuddles the other novices and the monks. But Brother Cadfael finds the connection and absolves the novice with his discovery.

Peters, Ellis. *An Excellent Mystery.* New York: Morrow, 1986 (1985). 0-688-06250-4, 190p. Paper, New York: Fawcett (Crest), 1987. 0-449-21224-6. R=7; I=10+.

When King Stephen and Empress Maud involve Henry of Blois, Bishop of Winchester, in their struggle for the crown, flames engulf Winchester, its nunnery, churches, and priory. Persons seek refuge at Shrewsbury, and one reveals the disappearance of a girl. In his role as herbal specialist, Brother Cadfael becomes concerned about the wounds received in the Crusades by one of the men, Humulis, and has to tell Humulis's friend Fidelis as well as find the girl's murderer.

Peters, Ellis. *The Heretic's Apprentice*. New York: Mysterious Press, 1990. 0-89296-381-6, 186p. Paper, Warner (Mysterious). 0-446-40000-9. R=7; I=10+.

In 1143, Elave brings his master to Shrewsbury to be buried on the Abbey grounds. Another visitor, a prelate, hears Elave proclaim that everyone will find salvation and charges him with heresy. The ensuing trial leads to murder which Brother Cadfael must solve.

Peters, Ellis. *The Hermit of Eyton Forest*. New York: Mysterious Press, 1988. 0-89296-290-9, 224p. Paper, Warner (Mysterious). 0-445-40347-0. R=7; I=10+.

King Stephen demands that Empress Maud in Oxford surrender her claim to his throne in 1142. Within the abbey at Shrewsbury, political problems also occur when a monk befriended by the mother of one of the pupils seems to cause difficulties. The pupil disappears, and someone finds a corpse in Eyton Forest, two events which bring Brother Cadfael out of the monastery to find the boy and the murderer.

Peters, Ellis. *The Holy Thief*. New York: Mysterious Press, 1993. 0-89296-524-X, 246p. Paper (Warner), 1994. 0-446-40363-6. R=7; I=10+.

In 1144, after an archer kills Geoffrey de Mandeville, Earl of Essex, Brother Haluin begins to solicit funds for the reconstruction of the Benedictine Abbey at Ramsay, which has been ruined by the Earl. When he brings Brother Tutilo with him to Shrewsbury and a troubadour with a girl singer arrives, someone steals the bones of St. Winifred and commits a murder which Brother Cadfael must solve.

Peters, Ellis. *The Leper of St. Giles*. New York: Morrow, 1981. 0-688-01097-0, 223p. R=7; I=10+.**

In 1139, Brother Cadfael becomes involved with the murder of the prospective bridegroom of a princess who loves another man. Inside the Leper House of Saint Giles is a very unlikely place to find the murderer, but there Brother Cadfael finds a lost relative for the princess. Disease does not impair human kindness.

Peters, Ellis. *Monk's Hood*. New York: Warner, 1992 (1981). Paper (Mysterious), 0-446-40300-8, 224p. R=7; I=10+.

One of the medicines that Brother Cadfael prepares is monk's hood, a soothing liniment that is poisonous if ingested. When a guest in the abbey becomes suddenly ill, Brother Cadfael recognizes poisoning and fears his own monk's oil is the source. Careful investigation reveals that the guest's stepson is not the guilty one although he has reason enough to hate the stepfather.

Peters, Ellis. *A Morbid Taste for Bones*. New York: Warner, 1994 (1985). Paper (Mysterious), 0-446-40015-7, 208p. R=7; I=10+.

Brother Cadfael accompanies Prior Robert to a small town in Wales to retrieve the bones of Saint Winifred and take them to Shrewsbury, in England, to bring honor to the Benedictine monastery in the twelfth century. A murder occurs, and the community creates a ruse which satisfies them, but Prior Robert is incensed to find that Gwytherin parish enjoys even more renown after the bones are removed. Jealousy can consume anyone, even those who have supposedly dedicated their lives to God.

Peters, Ellis. *The Pilgrim of Hate*. New York: Fawcett, 1986 (1984). Paper, 0-449-21223-8, 190p. R=7; I=10+.

In an 1141 celebration to honor the bones of Saint Winifred four years after they arrived in Shrewsbury, many pilgrims come to the St. Peter and St. Paul Abbey. Two of the pilgrims who arrive seem to have a connection to the murder in Winchester of a knight who is a supporter of the Empress Maud. Brother Cadfael solves the mystery and identifies one of the young men who remains loyal to his master, husband of the Empress Maud, after she loses her challenge to the throne.

Peters, Ellis. *The Potter's Field*. New York: Mysterious Press, 1990. 0-89296-419-7, 230p. Paper (Warner), 0-446-40058-0. R=7; I=10+.

A gift to the local clergy of a field in 1142 is transferred to the Shrewsbury Abbey of St. Peter and St. Paul in 1143. When plowing the ground, the Benedictine monks discover the body of a young woman, dead for at least a year. They believe the woman is the deceased wife of the man who gave the field away to join a monastery, but the arrival of a novice fleeing civil war in East Anglia helps Brother Cadfael to decide.

Peters, Ellis. *The Raven in the Foregate*. New York: Fawcett, 1987 (1986). Paper (Crest), 0-449-21225-4, 201p. R=7; I=10+.

When the Abbot of Shrewsbury assigns Ailnoth to the parish of the Holy Cross in 1141, his zeal disturbs the parishioners used to the kindly Father Adam, his predecessor, and Christmas morning, someone finds him drowned in the mill pond. Brother Cadfael investigates the background of the priest which soon involves one of Empress Maud's followers, illegally in the Shrewsbury territory of the king. But Brother Cadfael and his friend, Hugh, the Sheriff of Shrewsbury, find their answer.

Peters, Ellis. *The Rose Rent*. New York: Fawcett, 1988 (1986). Paper (Crest), 0-449-21495-8, 190p. R=7; I=10+.

Brother Cadfael's colleague, Brother Eluric, is murdered when he goes to pay the yearly rent of one rose to the widow who lets her cottage and garden to the Shrewsbury Abbey in 1142. In trying to solve the murder and to find the vanished woman, Brother Cadfael tries to decide who would benefit from the rental reverting to its owner and realizes that several suitors would be delighted. But along with his solution, the widow sees happiness in a new tenant.

Peters, Ellis. *St. Peter's Fair*. New York: Fawcett, 1987 (1981). Paper, 0-449-21354-4. Paper, New York: Warner (Mysterious). 0-446-40301-6, 220p. R=7; I=10+.

The annual Saint Peter's Fair in Shrewsbury occurs on July 30. At the fair in 1139, someone stabs and kills a wealthy merchant whose niece then risks her own life to fulfill her uncle's last wish. Brother Cadfael rescues her as well as identifies the murderer of her uncle.

Peters, Ellis. *The Sanctuary Sparrow*. New York: Fawcett, 1984 (1983). Paper (Crest), 0-449-20613-0, 222p. R=7; I=10+.

Liliwin, a boy acrobat and juggler accused of robbery and murder, flees from a mob into the Benedictine Abbey of St. Peter and St. Paul in 1140. The church has rights to protect him for forty days before releasing him to the law, and during that time, Brother Cadfael investigates the charges. What he finds exonerates the boy and reminds him of God's love.

Peters, Ellis. *The Summer of the Danes*. New York: Mysterious Press, 1991. 0-89296-448-0, 251p. Paper, Warner (Mysterious), 1992. 0-446-40018-1. R=7; I=10+.

A peaceful hiatus between King Stephen and his adversary in 1144 makes life less exciting so Brother Cadfael welcomes a chance to leave the abbey for Wales with Brother Mark. There, the Danish mercenaries fighting for Cadwaladr capture Brother Cadfael and a woman. While he waits for freedom from either a truce or a full war, he tries to solve the murder of one of the prisoners of Owain, Cadwaladr's brother and foe.

Peters, Ellis. *The Virgin in the Ice*. New York: Fawcett, 1984. Paper, 0-449-21121-5, 220p. R=7; I=10+.

Two orphans and their chaperon become lost in the winter cold of King Stephen's territory in 1139, but their nearest kinsman cannot come onto the king's land to look for them because he supports Empress Maud in the raging civil war. Brother Cadfael, summoned for his herb medicines to the priory of Bromfield, becomes involved. His investigation of murder leads back to the priory, and additionally, he finds unexpectedly that he has a son and he meets him.

Skurzynski, Gloria. *The Minstrel in the Tower*. Illus. Julek Heller. New York: Random House, 1988. 0-394-99598-8, 64p. Paper, 0-394-89598-3. R=5; I=3.

Alice, eight, and Roger, eleven, leave their feverish mother in 1195 to find an uncle about whom they have just heard. After being kidnapped by scoundrels, Alice escapes, finds her uncle, hears that her father died in the Crusades at Acre, and goes with him to rescue her brother and mother. What constitutes being brave in one person may be different for another. "A Stepping Stone Book."

Stolz, Mary. *Pangur Ban.* New York: HarperCollins, 1988. 0-06-025862-4, 182p. R=7; I=7.

When he is fifteen in 814, Cormac's father finally agrees with Cormac that he will never make a good farmer. He sends Cormac to the St. Benedictine Abbey. Cormac loves the abbey and its mission. Fifteen years later, while Cormac is carefully illuminating a manuscript about St. Patrick, the Vikings are spotted sailing near the Irish coast. He hides the work in the ground and keeps it from their rampages. Not for 350 years, long after the destruction of the abbey, does another monk discover it and see its value. Serving God in whatever capacity is demanding, but when one loves the job, it is joy, not labor.

Sutcliff, Rosemary. *The Shield Ring.* Illus. C. Walter Hodges. New York: Walck, 1962 (1956). R=7; I=7.**

Bjorn fears that he will be unable to keep Saxon secrets if caught and tortured by the Normans in the tenth century. As a harper, however, he is the only one who can easily infiltrate Norman camps to spy. He is caught and tortured, but he survives and escapes without compromising the safety of his people. The symbols of the past often play important roles in helping one understand the present. *Carnegie Commendation,* 1956.

Sutcliff, Rosemary. *The Shining Company.* New York: Farrar, Straus, & Giroux, 1990. 0-374-36807-4, 304p. Paper, 0-374-46616-5. R=5; I=7.

Around 600, near Edinburgh, Prosper becomes a shield barer for one of the king's three hundred men. When the men meet the Saxons in battle near York, only Prosper and one other survive. Afterward, a merchant intrigues them with stories about Constantinople, and they decide to leave Scotland for this wondrous city. The glory of war rapidly fades after the first death, but people must often fight to keep their freedom from those who would gladly take it. *American Library Association Notable Books for Children,* 1991.

Treece, Henry. *Viking's Dawn.* Illus. Christine Price. S. G. Phillips, 1956. 0-87599-117-3, 253p. R=6: I=7.

In 780, the Viking leader Harald sails with the *Nameless,* captained by a berserker (a man who loves battle). They wreck off the coast of Ireland and are captured, but four escape through a tunnel. Harald alone survives the ordeal and returns home on a Danish ship. But as a "sea traveler," he wants to return to sea and immediately prepares to sail again.

Westall, Robert. *The Wind Eye.* New York: Greenwillow, 1977. 0-688-84114-7, 213p. Paper, New York: Penguin, 1983. 0-14-03-1374-5, 159p. R=5; I=7.**

In this historical fantasy, the setting shifts from the present to the seventh-century world of the monk Cuthbertus, when Beth's father sails the *Wind Eye* into the North Sea toward Lindisfarne. Beth and her family discover that Cuthbert's reputation and personality profoundly and positively affect each of them, helping them to better understand themselves and their relationships with others. Persons caught in problems of their own creation can sometimes overcome them when given a chance to view them from another perspective.

1200-1491

Bosse, Malcolm J. *Captives of Time.* New York: Delacorte, 1987. 0-385-29583-9, 255p. Paper, New York: Dell, 1989. 0-440-20311-2, 268p. R=5; I=10.

In the fourteenth century, Anne, sixteen, and her mute brother Niklas, twelve, watch wanton soldiers spear their mother, after raping her, and discover their father dead inside the family paper mill. They leave home to find their uncle. He is trying to make a clock, and Anne's knowledge, intelligence, and artistic ability to draw the plans help him until the duke destroys the work, jealous that a bishop and a town will have the clock before he does. Anne and Niklas escape. Eventually, the forging of bells and the solution to the clock's works help Anne both spiritually and emotionally. Careless regard for life and jealousy of other's possessions have countered intelligence and love throughout human history.

Carrick, Donald, writer/illus. *Harald and the Giant Knight.* New York: Clarion, 1982. 0-89919-060-X, 32p. R=6; I=4.

Harald's family has to delay planting and fears the loss of all its animals and fruit trees when the baron's knights decide to use their land for a camp from which to practice their jousting. Harald's admiration for them quickly dies when he sees the destruction, and he suggests that his father, also a weaver, create a giant knight to scare them after they go to bed in their drunken state. Thoughtless people have to be conquered with ingenuity.

Carrick, Donald, writer/illus. *Harald and the Great Stag.* New York: Clarion, 1988. 0-89919-514-8. Paper, 1990. 0-395-52596-9, 32p. R=4; I=3.

In English medieval times, Harald feels sorrow for the great stag that the Baron so avidly hunts. He decides to confuse the hunting dogs by spreading the stag's scent in circles rather than having it lead in a solitary path to the stag. His plan succeeds, showing his concern for all forest animals.

De Angeli, Marguerite, writer/illus. *The Door in the Wall: A Story of Medieval London*. New York: Doubleday, 1989 (1949). 0-385-07283-X, 111p. Paper, New York: Dell (Yearling), 1990. 0-440-40283-2. R=6; I=6.

In 1325, Robin falls suddenly ill after his father goes to fight and his mother to serve her queen. Helped to recovery and taken home by Brother Luke who teaches him many things, Robin is able to use his swimming ability to go for aid when Welsh troops storm the castle. Brother Luke tells Robin that all walls have doors which each person must discover how to open. One must learn how to use life's opportunities rather than be overcome by life's adversities. *Newbery Medal*, 1950.

Gray, Elizabeth J. *Adam of the Road*. Illus. Robert Lawson. New York: Viking, 1942. 0-670-10435-3, 320p. Paper, New York: Puffin, 1987. 0-14-032464-X. R=6; I=6.

The motherless Adam patiently waits for his minstrel father Roger to return from France, and they walk from place to place, entertaining others until they become separated at a large fair in Winchester, England. After Adam falls off a wall, knocked unconscious, he recovers slowly and then searches for Roger in London but does not find him until the next spring when they both return to St. Alban's. The most important thing in life is being with a family or a parent who returns one's love. *Newbery Medal*, 1943.

Harnett, Cynthia, writer/illus. *The Cargo of the Madalena*. Minneapolis, MI: Lerner, 1984 (1959). 0-8225-0890-7, 236p. R=6; I=7.

When William Caxton brings the printing press to England around 1482, scribes who are losing their jobs try to stop Caxton's paper supply. Bendy discovers his brother's part in the plot but helps Caxton by giving him his partial manuscript of Malory's King Arthur tales for printing. Bendy's father confronts Matthew and tells him that by paying people not to deliver the paper, he has unknowingly supported Henry Tudor's red rose plan to dethrone Edward IV. Human decency prevails in this intriguing story. Illustrations complement the text. *Carnegie Commendation*, 1959.

Harnett, Cynthia, writer/illus. *The Sign of the Green Falcon.* Minneapolis, MI: Lerner, 1984 (1953). 0-8225-0888-5, 288p. R=6; I=6.

In 1415, recently apprenticed to Dick Whittington, the Mayor of London, Dickon becomes unwittingly involved in a Lollard plot against Henry V. Along with his brother Adam, they absolve themselves through Dickon's honesty and Adam's unselfish concern for others at Agincourt. Fifteenth century London comes alive in Harnett's illustrations.

Harnett, Cynthia. *The Writing on the Hearth.* Illus. Gareth Floyd. Minneapolis, MI: Lerner, 1984, (1971). 0-8225-0889-3, 300p. R=7; I=8.

The orphans Stephen and Lys survive in 1439 under the protection of the Earl of Suffolk because of their late father's bravery. Stephen's ability to read unsettles his friendship with the old healer Meg when he overhears her conversations with her visitors who subsequently accuse her of witchcraft. After facing the London plague, Henry VI's accusations, and William Caxton, Stephen realizes how he has misjudged her. His subsequent actions make his dream to attend Oxford become a reality. Other characters help Stephen remember that good goes deeper than evil and that one must look beneath appearances before coming to conclusions.

Konigsburg, E. L. *A Proud Taste for Scarlet and Miniver.* New York: Atheneum, 1973. 0-689-30111-1, 202p. Paper, New York: Dell (Yearling), 1985. 0-440-47201-6. R=6; I=6.

As wife to two kings and mother of two, Eleanor of Aquitaine waits in this historical fantasy for the arrival of her husband Henry II in heaven. She reminisces about her life in England and France during the twelfth century with three others who lived during the times. The importance of people in power ruling with fairness and justice cannot be overestimated.

McCaughrean, Geraldine. *A Little Lower Than the Angels.* Oxford, England: Oxford, 1987. 0-19-271561-5, 133p. R=2; I=5.

After he escapes from the stonemason to whom he is a bound apprentice, Gabriel joins itinerants presenting mystery and miracle plays throughout England in the fourteenth century. Unaware that the troupe's leader pays townspeople to act as if they have become healed, he believes that he is the cause of the miraculous changes. He eventually understands the illusion but sees that the words of the plays, known only to his two friends, a father and a daughter, must be written for future actors. He learns that humans in distress must have something to relieve their mental misery, even if only momentary. *Whitbread Book of the Year*, 1987.

Penman, Sharon Kay. *Falls the Shadow.* New York: Ballantine, 1989 (1988). Paper, 0-345-36033-8, 580p. R=5; I=10+.

In 1231, when Simon de Montfort, twenty-two, brazenly asks the Earl of Chester to restore his Earldom of Leicester, unrightful taken from de Montfort's father, Chester agrees. Until his death in 1266 at the Battle of Evesham, de Montfort creates intense upheaval among his enemies and great loyalty among his friends. In this second part of a trilogy beginning with *Here Be Dragons* and concluding with *The Reckoning*, one sees that when people believe in particular causes, they tend to sacrifice not only themselves but also others.

Penman, Sharon Kay. *Here Be Dragons.* New York: Ballantine, 1993. Paper, 0-345-38284-6, 704p. R=5; I=10+.

In this first book of a trilogy followed by *Falls the Shadow* and *The Reckoning*, members of the Plantagenet House are at war among themselves in 1183. King Henry and his son John oppose his other three sons, Henry, Richard, and Geoffrey. By 1234, Wales is united under Llewelyn, surviving the constant assaults of the Norman, now English, soldiers. When life is filled with too many political negotiations, one cannot help hurting a loved one in some unforeseen way.

Penman, Sharon Kay. *The Reckoning.* New York: Holt, 1991. 0-8050-1014-9, 593p. Paper, New York: Ballantine, 1992. 0-345-37888-1. R=5; I=10+.

In the final novel of a trilogy beginning with *Here Be Dragons* and followed by *Falls the Shadow*, Llewelyn tries to save the united Wales from both his brother Davydd and from the English king. His attempts eventually come to nothing as Edward finally kills him and executes Davydd in 1283, separates the surviving mothers and children, and makes his first born Prince of Wales. The strongest seem to win more often than those who seem to be in the right.

Penman, Sharon Kay. *The Sunne in Splendor.* New York: Ballantine, 1990 (1982). Paper, 0-345-36313-2, 936p. R=5; I=10+.

Although Richard seems to have admired his older brother Edward and loved his wife Anne, he has simultaneously been accused of murdering his two nephews, never seen after 1483, and of being deformed, also an unsubstantiated claim. Whatever the truth, the supposition must be based on Tudor historians, most likely interested in furthering their own cause after the bitter wars of the Roses between the Houses of Lancaster and York. This story of medieval England covers the royal families from 1459 to 1483, their concerns and deceits, while they accept and discard each other as power dictates. One can only hope, although never be certain, that others will know the truth.

Phillips, Ann. *The Peace Child.* New York: Oxford, 1988. 0-19-271560-7, 150p. R=6; I=6.

After her brother dies when Alys is ten in 1380, she finds that she was born into a family other than the one with which she lives. The families traded babies as peace offerings to settle a blood feud. Her concerns for both families and luck help them survive the 1382 pest (plague) in England. Keeping peace between families who have long been enemies requires creative negotiating but can work if both groups try.

Picard, Barbara. *One Is One.* Illus. Victor Ambrus. New York: Holt, 1966. R=7; I=8.**

In 1318, Stephen's miserable life with his father and his father's family ends when he goes to Richley monastery to study. He loves helping with the manuscripts but without encouragement, he leaves to become a knight. But after his squire dies of smallpox, Stephen returns to the monastery to gladly create beautiful drawings for God. After a loving parent dies, a child may have a lonely life searching for a way to love and be loved. *Carnegie Commendation*, 1965.

Picard, Barbara. *Ransom for a Knight.* Illus. C. Walter Hodges. New York: Walck, 1967. R=7; I=7.**

In 1315, after the Battle of Bannockburn, Alys and a serf travel from Sussex to Scotland to ransom her father and brother, both captured. Their adventures through London, the gypsies' theft and return of the jewels for the ransom, the Corpus Christi morality play in York, Alys near starvation during the winter journey, fill the story, but they finally arrive in Glengorman and make the rescue. People determined to succeed at almost impossible tasks are often triumphant. *Carnegie Commendation*, 1966.

Riley, Judith Merkle. *In Pursuit of the Green Lion.* New York: Delacorte, 1990. 0-385-30089-1, 440p. Paper, New York: Dell, 1992. 0-440-21103-4. R=5; I=10+.

After Margaret becomes a widow in 1356, Brother Gregory's father kidnaps her and makes her marry Brother Gregory, become Gilbert de Vilers, in the novel following *A Vision of Light.* Her strong opinions annoy Gilbert's family, but he refuses to beat her to satisfy his father. When Gilbert goes to France during the Hundred Years' War, Margaret goes to find him, bargains for his life with loaded dice, and returns with him to London. People sometimes find unacknowledged emotions when faced with new situations.

Riley, Judith Merkle. *A Vision of Light.* New York: Delacorte, 1989. 0-440-50109-1, 442p. R=6; I=10+.

Margaret of Ashbury decides in 1355 to write a book, heretical for a woman, but Brother Gregory, a friar needing food, finally agrees to be her chronicler. Throughout her life, she has survived the plague, invented forceps, and had a strong positive influence on the people with whom she has interacted. When the wealthy Margaret becomes a widow, Gregory's practical and pushy father demands that the two marry. Since they like each other, they agree. When one has valuable insights about life, one needs to share them whether one is a woman or a man and regardless of the century.

Treece, Henry. *Ride to Danger.* Illus. Christine Price. New York: S. G. Phillips, 1959. 0-87599-113-0, 253p. R=6; I=7.

In 1346, during the reign of Edward III (father of the Black Prince, Edward I), the Welsh fight the English because of unjust laws. The Welshman David gains Edward I's protection by fighting for him at Crécy where he learns about a new weapon, the bombard. In Wales, David uses the bombard to free his captured sister, but it kills innocent people, an unexpected development. Since the bomb also kills the enemy, David and his sister realize that humans sometimes pay very highly for freedom and fairness.

Wheeler, Thomas Gerald. *All Men Tall.* New York: S. G. Phillips, 1969. 87599-157-2, 256p. R=8; I=8.

Thomeline, at fifteen in 1323, becomes Hugh Staines' foundry apprentice in England. Encouraged to work with special powder, they and several others begin work on an object eventually called a cannon which helps defeat the French at Crécy in 1346. Hugh's experience and common sense guide Thomeline to extol the virtue and value of intelligence and skill rather than the empty pomp of untrained nobility.

Willard, Barbara. *The Lark and the Laurel.* New York: Dell, 1989 (1970). Paper, 0 440-20156-X, 207p. R=5; I=8.

When Cecily's father escapes to France in 1485 after the Yorkist king Richard loses to the Lancasters and Henry VII becomes king, Cecily, sixteen, goes to live with an aunt whom her father mistreated by marrying her off to an immoral crippled bastard. With her, Cecily learns to read, write, and run a rabbit farm, and she also meets Lewis Mallory, recently disinherited, with whom she falls in love. When her father returns, Cecily finds that she has been married to Lewis since she was five. An adult concerned about another's future will try to help that person's life have a meaning upon which to build.

1492-1648

Dhondy, Farrukh. *Black Swan*. Boston: Houghton Mifflin, 1993. 0-395-66076-9, 217p. R=3; I=7.

Rose, eighteen, copies the diaries of an astronomer/astrologer who lived in 1592, during the time of Shakespeare, for an old man who employs her mother. The diary posits that Christopher Marlow and his love, a former black slave, wrote Shakespeare's plays and sonnets. Woven with this theory are the racial overtones faced by blacks, either Caribbean or Muslim, in Britain. Sometimes people who have unwisely borrowed must repay their debts in ways more costly than money.

Garrett, George. *Death of the Fox*. San Diego, CA: Harcourt Brace, 1991 (1971). Paper, 0-15-625233-3, 744p. R=8; I=10+.

Sir Walter Ralegh plans his last two days of life before he is executed by James I, a king that he hates. He thinks of all the things he has done and considers his memories to be foolish but that he could have done worse. If one were to know that one's life were soon ending, one might perceive that all one's actions have been false and wasted. The important thing to do is to live in the moment and enjoy it.

Garrett, George. *The Succession*. San Diego, CA: Harcourt Brace, 1991. 0-15-686303-0. R=6; I=10+.

As William Cecil's spy rides from Scotland to London to report the birth of James to Elizabeth I, he disguises himself in several different ways so that no one will realize what he is doing. With each costume, he changes his social position, and thereby reveals that in England, Elizabeth I must keep many different types of subjects loyal to her. Elizabeth I refuses to name James her heir until just before her death, if then, to keep all her subjects off balance, waiting for the unexpected until she is actually dead in 1603. Regardless of one's station in life, mortality and change are consequences of time.

Harnett, Cynthia, writer/illus. *Stars of Fortune*. Minneapolis, MI: Lerner, 1984 (1956). 0-8225-0892-3, 288p. R=5; I=6.

A forefather of George Washington, Francis, saves Elizabeth (later Elizabeth I) from treason in 1554. By not fleeing from England with her would-be "liberators," she preserves her right to the throne. A subplot reveals how priests survived through Henry VIII's annihilation of Catholics and their property. Sometimes one must make decisions not according to what one wants but according to what one must do.

Harnett, Cynthia, writer/illus. *The Merchant's Mark*. Minneapolis, MI: Lerner, 1984 (1951). 0-8225-0891-5, 192p. R=6; I=6.

In the international wool market of 1493, a traitor jeopardizes the Fetterlock family's well-earned mark of quality for their Cotswold wool. By investigation, Nicholas and his betrothed Cecily, eleven, identify the culprit. Concern for family underscored with intelligence and reason can help everyone. *Carnegie Medal*, 1952.

Hunter, Mollie. *The Spanish Letters*. Illus. Elizabeth Grant. North Pomfret, VT: Trafalgar Square, 1990 (1964). Paper, 0-86241-057-6, 173p. R=7; I=8.

Jamie, fifteen and a caddie (guide) in Edinburgh in 1589, helps discover a plot for the Spanish to capture Scotland and England. His loyalty to his country and to his employer earns him respect. If one works hard and remains steadfast, others will appreciate the efforts.

Hunter, Mollie. *The 13th Member*. New York: Peter Smith, 1988 (1964). 0 8446-0002-X. R=7; I=8.

As a bond servant in Scotland during 1590, Adam, sixteen, helps another servant, Gilly, gain freedom from a witches' coven of thirteen members. After a trusted scholar helps them uncover a plot to murder James VI, they go to England to begin new lives based on Adam's intelligence and Gilly's healing ability. In any society, people with no status often have to identify honest people and ask for help in gaining their rights.

Hunter, Mollie. *You Never Knew Her As I Did!* New York: HarperCollins, 1981. 0-06-022678-1, 216p. R=7; I=8.*

As he reads of Mary Queen of Scots' execution, Will recalls twenty years earlier, in 1567, during his seventeenth year, when she was exiled to the island castle of Lochleven where Will was a page and the unrecognized illegitimate son of the castle lord. He helped her flee and fell in love with her, never to marry afterwards. People in political roles are often victims of situations perpetrated by those who crave power.

Llywelyn, Morgan. *The Last Prince of Ireland.* New York: Morrow, 1992. 0-688-10794-X, 368p. R=6; I=10+.

Upon the discovery that soldiers have murdered his son, Donal Cam O'Sullivan determines to defend Ireland, his home. With his clan, he flees the countryside in the cold and wet of 1602 after the battle of Kinsale, where they once lived, to the inland stronghold of Brian O'Rourke. People may seem defeated, but their loyalty can rekindle at any time.

O'Dell, Scott. *The Hawk That Dare Not Hunt by Day.* Greenville, SC: Bob Jones University Press, 1986 (1975). Paper, 0-89084-368-6, 182p. R=5; I=9.

In 1524, Tom sells William Tyndale an illegal Martin Luther manuscript of the Bible and decides to help Tyndale print his translation by taking him to Antwerp. Another man tails them, befriends Tyndale, and then betrays him. After Tyndale is hung, the traitor loses everything, an example of how the path of greed, when chosen instead of goodness, can destroy.

Pope, Elizabeth Marie. *The Perilous Gard.* Illus. Richard Cuffari. Boston: Houghton Mifflin, 1974. 0-395-18512-2, 272p. Paper, New York: Puffin, 1992. 0-14-034911-1. R=6; I=6.

After Queen Mary orders Kate to go to Elvenwood Hall in 1558, Kate finds that people think she is one of the fairy folk living in the woods. After she proves she is not, she realizes that the fairy folk are planning their sacrifice a of child which they do every seven years, and she devises a way to rescue the man who offers himself in exchange for the child. Superstitions can lead people to irrational conclusions. *Newbery Honor*, 1975.

Stolz, Mary. *Bartholomew Fair*. New York: Greenwillow, 1990. 0-688-09522-4, 152p. Paper, New York: Morrow (Beech Tree), 1992. 0-688-11501-2. R=5; I=8.

On an August morning in 1597, six people wake in London and prepare to attend the last day of the Bartholomew Fair. Of them, one is Elizabeth I. The others range from servants to noblemen. But all of them have a look at mortality in some way--either to start life anew or to realize that they have almost finished the task. Sometimes the things meant only for entertainment make one reflect about life's mysteries

Trease, Geoffrey. *A Flight of Angels*. Minneapolis, MN: Lerner, 1989. 0-8225-0731-5, 117p. R=7; I=6.

Although neither historical fiction nor historical fantasy, the story of four school children finding alabaster statues of great artistic merit hidden since 1550 in Nottingham, England, gives insight into the turmoil of the era when the statues were walled inside a cave. The children's discovery saves jobs as well. Research can lead to satisfying and interesting discoveries.

Willard, Barbara. *A Cold Wind Blowing*. New York: Dell, 1989 (1973). Paper, 0-440-20408-9, 175p. R=4; I=10.

In 1538, Henry VIII's destruction of convents and priories leaves the nuns unprotected and unreleased from vows of chastity. Piers, eighteen, son of Medley and the deceased Catherine Mallory from *The Sprig of Broom*, protects a young girl, as requested by his priest uncle before his death, and falls in love with her. They marry, and a former schoolmate accuses her of being a nun. Although she never took final vows, she dies of guilt after the birth of their child. People asserting power over others for their own pleasures are despicable.

Willard, Barbara. *The Eldest Son*. New York: Dell, 1989 (1977). Paper (Laurel Leaf), 0-440-20412-7, 175p. R=6; I=10.

Harry, eighteen in 1534, and brother of Piers from *A Cold Wind Blowing*, wants to be an iron master, but first he has to learn to train horses which he expects to inherit. After the plague kills all the horses and his daughter, Harry and his wife leave for her deceased uncle's land where Harry becomes an iron master, severing his ties with the old family homesteads. Because of family expectations, following the vocation which attracts one the most may be difficult.

Willard, Barbara. *A Flight of Swans*. New York: Dell, 1989 (1980). Paper (Laurel Leaf), 0-440-20458-5, 175p. R=4; I=10.

By 1588, while Ursula, daughter of Lilias in *The Iron Lily*, unhappily married to Robin, looks after sons of a recently widowed London relative, one of them disappears, eager to see the Spanish armada. Although attracted to each other and faithful for the rest of their lives, Ursula and the widower realize that they must refrain from love because of the complex family heritage surrounding the homestead of Mantlemass, which rightfully belongs to Harry, who has moved away. A parent cannot control the independent actions of a child, but the actions of both can impact a family's life for generations.

Willard, Barbara. *Harrow and Harvest*. New York: Dell, 1989 (1975). Paper (Laurel Leaf), 0-440-20480-1, 174p. R=5; I=9.

After Parliamentarians kill Harry Medley in the English Civil War during the 1630's, Edmund, his son of fifteen, rushes to Mantlemass as previously directed. Because Cecelia, granddaughter of Ursula in *A Flight of Swans*, has read Ursula's journal, she knows that Edmund is the true heir to Mantlemass. But her aunt, distressed by the knowledge, betrays Edmund to a Royalist who, in turn, shoots him. The others go to the New World, but Cecelia stays to see her friend. After also finding out that the family has descended from Richard, the last Plantagenet, she burns all evidence in order to start life anew. Jealousies about inheritances cause family members to do despicable things. *Guardian Award*, 1974.

Willard, Barbara. *The Iron Lily*. New York: Dell, 1989 (1974). Paper (Laurel Leaf), 0-440-20434-8, 175p. R=6; I=10.

In 1570, Lilias, fifteen, runs away after her mother dies of the plague, and her aunt says that her mother's deceased husband was not Lilias's father. Although she has a crooked shoulder, she works wonders with her herbs. Her employer finds her a husband, and she bears a daughter also with a crooked shoulder. The husband, an iron master, dies, and the man who buys the home, a Medley, with his own shoulder crooked feels a kinship with the daughter, and indeed, the family symbols lead to the discovery that Piers Medley is Lilias's father, but the great age difference between he and her mother kept them from marrying. When one knows one's forefathers, the background for strengths and weaknesses in character becomes clearer.

Willard, Barbara. *The Sprig of Broom*. New York: Dell, 1989 (1971). Paper (Laurel Leaf), 0-440-20347-3, 184p. R=7; I=10.

Lewis and Cecily Mallory, from *The Lark and the Laurel*, have a son, Roger who in 1506 is friendly with Medley Plashet. After villagers stone Medley's mother, suspected of witchcraft because of her ability to heal with herbs, Medley moves to Roger's home and falls in love with Roger's sister. Roger, the second son, wills his inheritance to Medley before entering the priesthood. Medley also discovers that his grandfather is King Richard Plantagenet. If one understands the origin of a family symbol such as the Plantagenet sprig of broom, one might begin to understand some family members' unexplained actions.

1649-1789

Burton, Hester. *Beyond the Weir Bridge.* New York: Crowell, 1970. R=6; I=7.*

Three childhood friends, two male and one female, grow apart between 1651 and 1667 in England. Richard squanders his Oxford opportunity and goes to London to work for a physician. Thomas, remaining at home, marries Richenda and becomes Quaker with her. Richard hates their change but allows Thomas to help him with the sick during the London plague. After Thomas dies and the Great Fire decimates the city, Richenda, with her son, accepts Richard's love. The characters, one by one, come to realize that a person's value can only be measured by the number of other persons helped when in need. *Boston Globe-Horn Book Award*, 1971.

Burton, Hester. *Time of Trial.* Illus. Victor Ambrus. Cleveland: World, 1964. R=7; I=9.**

Margaret, in 1803, watches a mob burn her home and her father's bookstore after he is imprisoned for writing so-called seditious tracts against using money for the war in France that could be used to repair dilapidated housing for the poor. She and the housekeeper go to the Essex coast where her fiancée's wealthy parents accuse her of social climbing and ignore her. Margaret, however, supports her father and his commitment to helping others, even while he serves his sentence. Some people concerned with others will not allow an unjust government decision to deter them. *Carnegie Medal*, 1964.

Calvert, Patricia. *Hadder MacColl.* New York: Scribner's, 1985. 0-684-18447-8, 160p. Paper, New York: Puffin, 1986. 0-14-032158-6, 144p. R=7; I=7.

In 1745, young and impetuous Hadder MacColl, who loves the Highlands of Scotland, looks forward to her brother's return from school in Edinburgh. When he returns, he brings his friend, but he has to stay home instead of return to school and fight for the Jacobites at Culloden where he dies. Hadder decides she will fulfill his dream of going to the New World by taking the journey herself. Since misplaced ideals destroy families, one must very carefully choose which ideal deserves risking one's life.

Carter, Peter. *The Gates of Paradise.* Illus. Fermin Rocker. London: Oxford, 1974. R=4; I=8.**

In 1796, William and Sophie Blake help Ben find an apprentice position. Ben is surprised that William has conversations with his dead brother and that William treats every living being equally, regardless of social status, because he believes no one can judge another. William's concern for the individual's rights causes the government to accuse him of sedition. One must let others be individuals and not unduly impose one's own beliefs on them. *Guardian Award Citation,* 1974.

Forman, James D. *Prince Charlie's Year.* New York: Scribner's, 1991. 0-684-19242-X, 136p. R=4; I=8.

When preparing for a 1780 battle against the English in North Carolina, Colin MacDonald remembers his last battle against the English when, at fourteen in 1745 at Culloden, Scotland, he swore never to fight them again. After fighting for Prince Charlie and being defeated, Colin became a British prisoner; was transported to America; and was bound out for seven years. When his love Peggy joins him, he knows he can survive. Sometimes persons must break their promises if doing so means the survival of human freedom.

Garfield, Leon. *Devil-in-the-Fog.* Magnolia, MA: Peter Smith, 1991 (1966). Paper, New York: Dell (Yearling), 1988. 0-440-40095-3. R=4; I=6.

When George Treet is fourteen, his father tells him he is a Dexter. After he moves to Sir John Dexter's and finds confusion, including the information that Mr. Treet is a villain, he discovers that he is not a Dexter but a Treet, sold to the Dexters to act as heir. His acting abilities annoy Sir John, but Lady Dexter appreciates and supports him. *Guardian Award for Children's Fiction,* 1967.

Garfield, Leon. *The Empty Sleeve.* New York: Delacorte, 1988. 0-385-29817-X.   Paper,   New   York: Dell   (Yearling). 0-440-40102-X, 207p. R=5; I=6.

In eighteenth century London, Peter and Paul, born twins, have opposite personalities. Peter becomes apprenticed to a locksmith at fourteen, but before he leaves home, an old man brings two perfectly carved sailing ships encased in bottles which Paul shifts so that he gets Peter's. As Peter becomes entangled in deceits, his ship which Paul has, begins to decay, the visible result of his transgressions, and the old man cannot repair it. *School Library Journal "Best Book,"* 1988.

Garfield,   Leon.   *Footsteps.*   New   York: Delacourt,   1980. 0-385-28294-X, 192p. Paper, New York: Dell (Yearling), 1988. 0-440-40102-X. R=4; I=6.

Before William's father dies in the late eighteenth century, he tells William that he once cheated Alfred Diamond, his business partner, and gives William a gold watch to guard. William eventually finds Diamond after discovering his address inside the watch. He becomes aware that his real enemy is Alfred's son John. By finding and saving John as well as confessing to Alfred, William stops the footsteps of his father's ghost from walking each night. *Whitbread Book of the Year*, 1980.

Garfield, Leon. *The Night of the Comet.* New York: Delacorte, 1979. 0-385-28753-4. Paper, New York: Dell (Yearling), 1988. 0-440-40070-8. R=4; I=6.

Pairs of lovers prepare to party in honor of Pigott's comet on April 6, in the mid-eighteenth century. An Irishman searches and finds his love in town while Bostock, thirteen, tries to attract the attention of his friend's sister who ignores him. Other lovers appear and all get into brief trouble before the evening concludes.

Garfield, Leon. *Smith.* New York: Peter Smith, 1991 (1967). 0-8446-6455-3. Paper, New York: Dell, 1987. 0-440-48044-2. R=6; I=7.

Smith pickpockets a man just before someone else murders him and is distressed to find a document in the deceased man's wallet which he cannot read. Smith decides to live with a blind man because his daughter will teach him to read. After he learns, he reads the document, refuses to give it to a man who puts him in prison and lets him out again. He eventually claims the reward money with his blind benefactor. *Phoenix Award*, 1987.

Garfield, Leon. *The Strange Affair of Adelaide Harris.* New York: Dell, 1988 (1971). Paper (Yearling), 0-440-40057-0. R=8; I=8.

Harris hears about Laius exposing Oedipus on the mountainside and decides to leave his seven-week-old sister in the woods. Someone finds her and takes her to the neighboring parish church. Since Harris cannot find the child, he replaces her with another baby which his parents detect. The ensuing search leads to a girl finding their daughter in the poor house while the girl is walking in the woods with a boy, not acceptable in the mid-eighteenth century. The girl's father challenges the boy to a duel. All ends well when the girl's teacher, in love with her, takes her to the New World.

Garfield, Leon. *Young Nick and Jubilee.* New York: Delacorte, 1989. 0-385-29777-7, 137p. R=3; I-3.

Two Irish orphans, Nick, ten, and Jubilee, nine, survive in London by living in parks and stealing food. When they want to attend a charity school, they adopt an accomplished thief to be their dad and apply for them at the school. Since the headmaster makes surprise visits to the homes, they have to live with the man who becomes a very good father. Many times people live up to expectations when they never realized they would or could.

Harnett, Cynthia, writer/illus. *The Great House.* Minneapolis, MI: Lerner, 1984 (1949). 0-8225-0893-1, 180p. R=5; I=6.

In 1690, Barbara and Geoffrey's architect father receives a commission for a house from Sir Humphrey outside London, and they accompany him. Geoffrey, who idolizes Sir Christopher Wren, realizes that the house should be repositioned to overlook the river. The adults recognize the merit of his idea, and as reward, Sir Humphrey sends Geoffrey to Oxford. Illustrations embellish the text.

Haugaard, Erik. *A Boy's Will.* Boston: Houghton Mifflin, 1990 (1983). Paper, 0-395-54962-0. R=6; I=6.

In 1779, Patrick overhears a British navy captain tell of his plans to capture John Paul Jones off the southern Irish coast. Patrick's concern leads him to Skellig Michael, an island famous for its relationship to St. Patrick, from where the young Patrick sails to meet Jones and warn him. Rising to prevent unpleasant occurrences may lead to a better situation for oneself.

Hendry, Frances. *Quest for a Kelpie.* New York: Holiday, 1988 (1986). 0-8234-0680-6, 153p. R=5; I=7.*

As a great great grandmother, Jeannie remembers from the time beginning in 1743 when she was ten until she turned fourteen after the British commander Cumberland's vicious attack on the Scots during the Scottish rebellion. Jeannie helps her people and the gypsies by eventually riding a kelpie, a huge horse, through the forest which her friend then uses to escape Cumberland's wrath. Trying to survive in time of war can lead one to react in unexpected ways, depending on what is appropriate for the moment. *Quest for a Kelpie Competition,* 1987.

Hersom, Kathleen. *The Half Child.* New York: Simon & Schuster, 1991. 0-671-74225-6, 176p. Paper (Half Moon), 1993. 0-671-86696-6. R=7; I=7.

Lucy's flashback to 1650 tells of Sarah, her four-year-old seemingly slow-witted sister, who disappeared on the moors near Durham, England. Lucy's love for Sarah propels her to continue searching for her. Lucy meets the man who found Sarah and placed her in a foster home and decides to marry him. The difficult lives of people, with the English Civil War as backdrop, are apparent, but their care for each other outweighs their plight.

Hodge, Jane Aiken. *Windover.* New York: St. Martin's, 1992. 0-312-07884-6, 266p. R=5; I=10+.

In 1789, Kathryn falls in love with the tutor of her two half-brothers, but her step-father becomes so enraged when the tutor asks to marry her that he banishes him. The stepfather has an unnatural interest in Kathryn which he pursues, and she marries to avoid him. When her husband commits suicide, she has to flee to London. There she meets the tutor, not dead as she had thought, and their lives begin to settle. Selfish human beings can make life miserable for those under their control.

Hunter, Mollie. *The Lothian Run*. North Pomfret, VT: Trafalgar Square, 1990 (1970). 0-86241-069-X, 221p. R=7; I=8.

In 1736, Sandy, sixteen, discovers a gang of smugglers in Scotland who start taking documents to Jacobites in France who are planning to overthrow the Hanoverians. Sandy's employer, a lawyer, is pleased with Sandy's investigation and is able to capture several people because of it. Hard work and wits help solve problems.

Laker, Rosalind. *Circle of Pearls*. New York: Doubleday, 1990. 0-385-26305-8, 519p. Large Type, New York: Hall, 1991. 0-8161-5098-2, 830p. R=6; I=10+.

Julia's father fights for the Royalists against the Parliamentarians around 1650. His being gone while she is young disturbs her life. As she grows up, she falls in love with the man whose Parliamentarian father is responsible for her own father's death, but she marries him anyway instead of Christopher Wren, her brother's close friend. Julia survives both the plague and the Great Fire of London in 1666 and lives to be old enough to mourn Wren at his death. Neighbors in a country torn by civil war often try to destroy each other's rights and sometimes succeed, but fortunately, war ends, and they can make amends.

Laker, Rosalind. *The Silver Touch*. New York: Doubleday, 1987. 0-385-23745-6, 356p. R=7; I=10+.*

In 1721, orphaned Heather, twelve, begins living and working in her uncle's London tavern. When she is eighteen, John, on delivery duty for his silversmith boss, sees her furtively drawing the cat, and his interest begins a relationship between the two and their silvermaking. As their family grows, it endures hardship and happiness which eventually lead to it having a reputation of quality and beauty in its silver designs. Having an appreciation of aesthetic beauty can sometimes ease one's feeling of loneliness.

Langenus, Ron. *Mission West.* Trans. Niesje C. Horsman-Delmonte. Illus. Willem van Velzen. Chester Springs, PA: Wolfhound/Dufour, 1990. Paper, 0-86327-239-8, 144p. R=4; I=9.

In 1649, when Cromwell's men come close to destroying Ireland, Rory, seventeen, walks west across Ireland to take a religious parchment, contents unknown, to a monastery. Because his priest foster father had been so kind before being brutally murdered by the British, Rory undergoes great difficulty but stubbornly continues his journey to fulfill his promise at the priest's death. Integrity, not tyranny, gains respect and keeps it. *Belgian Book Prize.*

McGraw, Eloise. *Master Cornhill.* New York: Puffin, 1987 (1973). Paper, 0-14-032255-8, 218p. R=7; I=7.

In 1666, Michael, eleven, returns to London after having been evacuated during the plague and finds all of his adoptive family dead. While he tries to avoid press gangs, he begins working for a mapmaker. But after the Great Fire intervenes, he realizes that his fear of putting pen to paper keeps him from being the artist that he thinks he wants to be. One has to look forward, not backward, and be pleased with life as one attempts to live it. *William Allen White Award nomination.*

Malterre, Elona. *The Last Wolf of Ireland.* New York: Clarion, 1990. 0-395-54381-9, 127p. R=6; I=6.

Devin discovers wolf pups in 1786 near his home in Barne's Gap, Ireland. He saves the pups in secret because each wolf killed earns money for the killer. He learns that the wolf is loyal to those who befriend it. When the last wolf pup is fully grown and becomes mortally wounded, it returns to the one that loved and cared for it, Devin. Some animals seem to sense the kindness of humans more than other humans.

Paton Walsh, Jill. *A Parcel of Patterns.* New York: Farrar, Straus, & Giroux, 1992 (1983). Paper, 0-374-45743-3, 139p. R=6; I=10.

For a year beginning in 1665, Mall, sixteen, watches people die in her small village when the plague arrives from London in a damp package of dress patterns. Trying to save her fiancée as she nurses family and friends, she has someone tell him she has died, a plan that backfires when he comes to the town to help those left, gets sick, and dies instead. Humans may never understand why a plague can destroy so many without any apparent reason.

Sutcliff, Rosemary. *Bonnie Dundee.* Magnolia, MA: Peter Smith, 1984. 0-8446-6363-8. R=9; I=9.

An orphan stable boy, son of an artist, recalls the Highland march of 1689 which Colonel John Graham of Claverhouse bravely led for King James against William of Orange. He remembers the kindness of the man and the importance of the mysterious gypsy "tinklers" who helped save his own life. Humans (and animals) follow those with whom they share values.

Wulffson, Don L. *The Upside-Down Ship.* Niles, IL: Whitman, 1986. 0-8075-8346-4, 136p. R=4; I=6.*

In the 1760's, Bruce, a young dreamer, returns to Aberdeen, Scotland, after being the only survivor from a wrecked whaling ship off the icebergs of Greenland. In a flashback, he tells how he kept alive off the resurfaced ship's stores while having as his companion a polar bear cub whose mother he had killed. His brother, irritated that their mother died thinking Bruce dead, denies him a home after Bruce's arduous journey. But Bruce meets and marries, sorry for the pain of his experience but missing its intensity. One often longs for difficult situations to end, but finds that memories of surviving them can make life more satisfying.

1790-1848

Cole, Sheila. *The Dragon in the Cliff: A Novel Based on the Life of Mary Anning.* Illus. T. C. Farrow. New York: Lothrop, Lee & Shepard, 1991. 0-688-10196-8, 211p. R=6; I=6.

Although the inhabitants of Lyme Regis in England disapproved, Mary Anning, when seven, began combing the beach for curiosities with her father which he then cleaned and sold to tourists. In 1810, her father dies, and she continues working to support her family. In 1812, she discovers the "crocodile," a fossil measuring seventeen feet, whose origin of fish or fowl geologists argue. Her discoveries continue, and a woman also interested in fossils gives her books to read. But Mary Anning is never mentioned in any of the scientific papers since women, and certainly women from low economic classes, were not considered to be scientists. However, if the curiosities had not thrilled her, and she had allowed herself to be controlled by her neighbors' opinions, the study of fossils would have been greatly delayed in England.

Conlon-McKenna, Marita. *Under the Hawthorn Tree: Children of the Famine.* Illus. Donald Teskey. New York: Holiday House, 1990. 0-8234-0838-8, 153p. Paper, New York: Puffin, 1992. 0-14-036031-X, 160p. R=7; I=7.

Using their mother's story of her childhood and her family, three children walk through Ireland to find aunts they have never met during the potato famine in the late 1840's. They finally reach their destination after having seen many people in the same condition, sick and starving. This strong story shows the desperation of parents who cannot feed their children and the strength of children who try to help themselves. *International Reading Association Award*, 1991.

Flanagan, Thomas. *The Year of the French.* New York: Holt, 1989. Paper, 0-8050-1020-3, 528p. R=9; I=10+.

Five narrators--a Protestant clergyman, a solicitor, a wife, a schoolmaster, and a soldier tell the story surrounding the events of August and September 1798 when the French come to help the Irish rebel against the English at Vinegar Hill and fail miserably. Another character, the poet Owen McCarthy, becomes involved in the rebellion because he is *fey* (has a "second sight") and because he has a mythic sense of being Irish. People who have themselves in mind rather than the common good sometimes destroy everything they might have achieved.

Heaven, Constance. *The Wind from the Sea.* New York: St. Martin's, 1993. 0-312-008921-X, 502p. R=6; I=10+.

In 1793, Isabelle and her brother Guy escape from France to England to live with their mother's brother. Guy becomes involved with raids to France while Isabelle decides to marry Robert who, like Guy, also has a secretive job. When the war ends, Robert and she look forward to representing England to the Russian government in St. Petersburg. Marrying for love instead of money is always more emotionally fulfilling.

Mooney, Bel. *The Stove Haunting.* Boston: Houghton Mifflin, 1988. 0-395-46764-0, 126p. R=5; I=5.*

When Daniel, eleven, and his parents move from London to the West country, he looks inside an old stove in the rectory where they live and finds himself caught in the year 1835. As an orphan in the same house, he watches honest men condemned to Australia for sedition when all they were doing was talking about ways to make better lives for their families. Through his journey to another time, Daniel realizes the power of money to corrupt persons with the best of intentions.

Overton, Jenny. *The Ship from Simnel Street.* New York: Greenwillow, 1986. 0-688-06182-6, 144p. R=7; I=7.

When Polly meets a soldier, she decides to marry him against her mother's wishes. She follows him to Spain and comes home to have her baby. Everything in her life connects to the kinds of cakes created in the bakery which has belonged to her family for over one hundred years--hot cross buns, cradle cake for babies, simmel cake for mother's day, macaroons, and many more. Although many children complain, most parents only want what they consider the best for their children.

Paton Walsh, Jill. *A Chance Child*. New York: Farrar, Straus &
Giroux, 1991 (1978). Paper, Sunburst, 0-374-41174-3, 192p.
Paper, New York: Avon (Flare), 1991. 0-380-48561-3, 144p. R=5;
I=8.

In this historical fantasy, Creep lives in the 1820's in a boat
near a foundry, maligned along with other children who must
endure sordid conditions and hard labor. Christopher and his
sister Pauline talk to Creep, but only after he floats away on
one of England's canals do the two realize that Creep does not
live in the twentieth century. They see the name "Creep" on a
bridge over 150 years old, and they find information about him
in the Parliamentary papers, but they never see him again.
Sometimes one must have a feeling of being in a particular
place and time to understand the terrible conditions that people
living then had to endure.

Paton Walsh, Jill. *Grace*. New York: Farrar, Straus, & Giroux,
1992. 0-374-32758-0, 256p. R=6; I=9.

In 1838, in a raging storm, Grace and her father see a
shipwreck from their lighthouse and decide to risk the waves to
retrieve people they see hanging on a rock which will soon to
be covered by another tide. Because of the money and gifts
Grace receives from strangers for her heroism, she imagines
that she made the rescue out of greed rather than concern. That
fear weakens her so that consumption invades her body and
kills her. Although often unrelated, emotional distress can
weaken the body's defenses against disease.

Roberts, Ann V. *Louisa Elliott*. New York: Avon, 1990 (1989).
Paper, 0-380-70991-0, 800p. R=6; I=10+.

In the late nineteenth century, Louisa returns to York,
England, at her mother's death and falls in love with a married
man by whom she has children. She eventually realizes that
although she has compromised her honor, she actually loves her
cousin with whom she reunites and eventually marries after her
father dies. Liaisons among parents and others can lead to
unexpected family relationships which may remain unrevealed
for many years.

Williams, Jeanne. *The Island Harp.* New York: St. Martin's Press, 1991. 0-312-06570-1, 338p. R=5; I=10+.

After the landowner's agents burn her family's homes, and her grandfather dies from the resulting burns in 1844, Mairi MacLeod, seventeen, becomes the *de facto* head of her Scottish clan and inherits the role of harper. Unlikely help from a member of the gentry, Iain, who leases part of the estate, surprises her, especially when she falls in love with him. Not until the birth of a son, Mairi's song landowners deceiving the Celtic clans, and Iain's surprise return after news of his death in Afghanistan, will Mairi consent to marry him. In order to live honestly with oneself, one must do what one believes is right.

1849-1918

Anderson, Margaret. *The Journey of the Shadow Bairns.* Illus. Patricia H. Lincoln. New York: Knopf, 1980. 0-394-94511-5, 177p. R=4; I=6.*

Elspeth, thirteen, and her brother leave Glasgow, Scotland, in 1903 with boat tickets for Canada to see their aunt and uncle after their father is killed on his job, and their mother dies from illness. Once there, after difficulties, they decide to settle with people they met on the journey, never seeing their own relatives. Learning to think before acting takes much control, but it is often a good decision.

Avery, Gillian. *A Likely Lad.* New York: 1994 (1971). 0-671-79867-7. R=4; I=6.

In 1895, Willy, bored at six, runs away from his London home but soon returns. At twelve, he runs away again, but this time, he is upset because his father wants him to quit school, which he loves, and begin working "up the ladder" at his father's company. A parallel plot involves the rivalry of Willy's family with that of his mother's sister's family over the possible inheritance of their aunt's money. When the dog eats all the money, Willy's father is pleased and gladly permits Willy to stay in school. Some people never overcome the idea that money is more important than education.

Avery, Gillian. *Maria Escapes.* Illus. Scott Snow. New York: Simon & Schuster, 1992 (London: Collins, 1957). 0-671-77074-8, 258p. R=6; I=6.

An orphan, Maria finds refuge with her uncle in Oxford, England, after running away from boarding school in 1875. He allows her to stay, impressed with her knowledge of Latin and Greek and lets her study with the young boys next door. Her interest in a boy she hears about who lived nearby during the seventeenth century leads her to do research at the Bodelian Library. Her "absent-minded" uncle is kind and tolerant.

Bawden, Nina. *The Peppermint Pig.* New York: HarperCollins, 1975. 0-397-31618-6, 192p. Paper, New York: Dell, 1988. 0-440-40122-4, 160p. R=6; I=4.

In 1901, Poll's father goes to America, leaving the family in Norfolk, England, to await his summons for them to join him. Poll enjoys watching the runt pig they raise but anguishes when it becomes their food. The family sacrifices and faces its difficulties by caring for each other. *Guardian Award for Children's Fiction*, 1976; *Yorkshire Post Award*, 1976.

Clements, Bruce. *The Treasure of Plunderell Manor.* New York: Farrar, Straus, & Giroux, 1987. 0-374-37746-4, 180p. Paper, 1991. 0-374-47962-3. R=2; I=5.

Laurel, alone in the world, begins work at Plunderell Manor in 1853 in England as the maid to its mistress Alice, who is kept enclosed in a tower room by her uncle and aunt. Laurel solves the riddle which reveals where Alice's deceased parents hid the family treasure and then she saves Alice's life by helping her escape from her evil guardians. Being honest can gain greater rewards than stealing or cheating.

Cookson, Catherine. *The Harrogate Secret.* New York: Summit, 1988. 0-671-65941-3, 352p. R=4; I=10+.*

From the time near the end of the nineteenth century when Freddie is ten until Belle, his love, is available to marry him, he is involved with situations at The Towers, home of the wealthy in his small coal-mining and shipbuilding English town. His blind sister uses her gifts of hearing and smelling to help him warn people in times of danger, and he uses his own gifts to rise from poverty to possibility. One must always do what one thinks is right for oneself and for others.

Cookson, Catherine. *The Moth.* New York: Summit, 1986. 0-671-44076-4, 294p. Large Type, New York: Charnwood/Ulverscroft, 1987. 0-7089-8386-3, 480p. R=7; I=10+.

In his twenties in 1913 after his father dies, Robert goes to work building furniture for his uncle's business. He meets Agnes from the upper class. When they fall in love, her brothers threaten to disown her, but Robert's unexpected inheritance at his uncle's death frees them to marry. People judged according to class denies them as individuals.

Cookson, Catherine. *The Parson's Daughter.* New York: Summit, 1987. 0-671-63293-0, 390p. R=8; I=10+.*

When her dog rushes under the fence separating the land on the estate next to her family's parsonage, Mary Ann, twelve, unexpectedly meets a boy, David, sitting near the river. She discovers from her mother that he is illegitimate, but he becomes her friend. She matures and marries one man who dies, and then another, before her daughter runs away. After the death of her second husband, David, become wealthy with his inheritance, returns to marry her and take her back to Australia with him. Sometimes life's duty and responsibility must come before happiness.

Cookson, Catherine. *The Rag Nymph.* New York: Simon & Schuster, 1993. 0-671-86477-7, 351p. R=6; I=10+.

When Millie is seven in 1854, she is thrust upon "Raggie Aggie," a woman who sells rags in a sleazy part of town. Knowing that Millie must be protected, Aggie changes her own way of life to ensure Millie grows up in safety. When someone needs a person, that person will often sacrifice in order to help.

Cookson, Catherine. *The Wingless Bird.* New York: Summit, 1991. 0-671-66620-7, 383p. Large Type, New York: Thorndike. 1-56054-211-X, 601p. R=5; I=10+.

In 1913, Agnes, twenty-two, feels that she must get away from her mother's unhappiness and her father's selfishness of making her work in his stores. She meets and marries a wealthy, upper-middle class man, Charles, as both their fathers try to stop them. Charles's subsequent bout with tuberculosis and his ensuing death helps unite Agnes with Charles's war-wounded brother and a happier life. The road to real contentment may seem convoluted, but it may be the best route.

Garfield, Leon. *The December Rose.* New York: Puffin, 1988 (1987). 0-14-032070-9, 208p. R=8; I=8.

Barnacle, a London chimney sweep in the late nineteenth century, changes his fortunes by selling a locket that he took from one of the houses in which he worked. The locket and his experiences also help reveal happenings concerning *The December Rose*, a boat. Just because one has been less fortunate financially does not mean that one does not want to help others have a better life. *School Library Journal "Best Book,"* 1987.

Green, Roger J. *The Throttlepenny Murder*. New York: Oxford, 1989. 0-19-271601-8, 197p. R=7; I=7.

During 1885 in England, Jessie Smith's despicable boss meets his death in a graveyard which five people observe, their presences unknown to each other. Blamed for the murder, Jessie, thirteen, is sentenced to hang. She gains a reprieve, but someone else unjustly suffers. The lower social and economic classes often bear biased accusations because they cannot protect themselves against those with more money.

Gunn, Neil. *Young Art and Old Hector*. New York: Walker, 1991. 0-8027-1177-4, 255p. R=3; I=10+.

At eight, Young Art runs to Old Hector, a neighbor, when his family frustrates him in the late nineteenth century Scottish highlands. Old Hector shares with him concepts of wisdom that he does not quite understand, but he feels protected and honored to be with him. Trying to have a good life when others own the water in which the salmon swim and laws thwart simple pleasures is difficult, but love of family and friends offsets its heartaches.

Harrison, Ray. *Patently Murder: A Sergeant Bragg and Constable Morton Mystery*. New York: St Martin's Press, 1991. 0-312-07058-6, 255p. R=4; I=10+.

In 1890, Catherine Marsden becomes involved in a London mystery when she tries to give money to a young girl sitting in a doorway and realizes that the girl is dead. As a newspaper reporter in her early twenties, Catherine and her police friends identify the child as a prostitute and solve the murder by a connection between her and another man recently murdered. For someone with no morals, extermination of anyone who threatens prosperity seems to be an easy choice.

Heaven, Constance. *The Craven Legacy.* New York: Putnam, 1986. 0-399-13235-X, 328p. R=5; I=10+.**

In the 1880's, Della's father is arrested for a murder he did not commit, and Della moves from London to the Yorkshire Dales, where her father's family lives, to teach. There she finds her family's secrets and falls into unrequited love with the married mill owner whose wife regularly leaves him to spend weeks in London. Circumstances reveal her father innocent and alive instead of drowned at sea, the wife dead, and the possibility of a happy future. When unscrupulous people want someone else to be found guilty of their crime, proving that person's innocence can be difficult.

Holt, Victoria. *The Captive.* New York: Doubleday, 1989. 0-385-26332-5, 357p. Paper, New York: Fawcett (Crest), 1990. 0-449-21817-1. R=6; I=10+.

At eighteen, Rosetta (named for the Rosetta stone), her parents, Lucas, and John sail to Africa, but off the Cape in the late eighteenth century, the ship wrecks. Although Rosetta, Lucas, and John escape, pirates capture them and sell Rosetta to a Turkish pasha. She is freed, and in England, she tries, in turn, to free John of a false charge of murder against him. As people mature and experience different situations, they change, and many times, the friendships they have made also change.

Holt, Victoria. *The Road to Paradise Island.* New York: Fawcett, 1993 (1985). Paper, 0-449-45253-0, 368p. R=4; I=10+.

Around 1890, Annalice, eighteen, discovers the diary of her namesake dated nearly one hundred years earlier. Becoming obsessed with understanding the aspects of her namesake's life, Annalice's brother Philip goes to Australia to search for the island noted on the map accompanying the diary. Annalice goes to find him and discovers unexpected complications. Greed causes some people to make irrational choices.

Holt, Victoria. *Secret for a Nightingale.* New York: Fawcett, 1987 (1986). Paper (Crest), 0-449-21296-3, 371p. R=3; I=10+.

Surprised during her childhood by the response of an injured man in India when she helps him, Susanna realizes that she has an ability to heal. Her gift continues through an unfortunate marriage, the distressing death of a child, and her work during the Crimean war before she realizes that she loves a physician whom she previously mistrusted. Unless one knows all the details of a situation, one can easily arrive at false conclusions.

Holt, Victoria. *The Silk Vendetta.* New York: Fawcett, 1988 (1987). Paper (Crest), 0-449-21548-2, 425p. R=4; I=10+.

Lenore and her grand'mère live in the country home of a wealthy British silk merchant where grand'mère sews and weaves silk on the looms in the late nineteenth century. Because Lenore refuses to respond to the amorous advances of one of the sons, he trails her until after her husband (his brother) and his sister are murdered. He then accuses her of the deeds until a French count detects the deception. People sometimes try to take advantage of those whom they see as belonging to a lower social class.

Holt, Victoria. *Snare of Serpents.* New York: Doubleday, 1990. 0-385-41385-8, 373p. Paper, New York: Fawcett (Crest), 1991. 0-449-21928-3. R=4; I=10+.

When Davinia is sixteen in Edinburgh around the time of the second Boer War in 1899, her mother dies, her father blames the governess of theft and fires her, and then hires a new governess. Soon he dies mysteriously, and Davinia, charged with his murder but found "not proven," has to leave the country for Africa. Her marriage and return to Scotland help her find the truth behind the accusation. Some people can hide their misdeeds for life; others must reveal them so that they may die in peace.

Howker, Janni. *Isaac Campion.* New York: Greenwillow, 1987. 0-688-06658-5, 83p. Paper, New York: Dell (Yearling). 0-440-40280-8. R=4; I=8.

Isaac is twelve in 1901 when his brother, eighteen, takes a friend's bet that he can jump an iron fence, and instead, impales himself on one of its sharp spikes. Isaac's father, an English horse dealer, continues his feuds with others in the town. When Isaac's uncle asks him to go to America with him, Isaac knows that he must. Sometimes people have to separate from their parents to escape old prejudices and begin new lives.

Hunter, Mollie. *A Pistol in Greenyards*. Illus. Elizabeth Grant. North Pomfret, VT: Trafalgar Square, 1990 (1968). 0-86241-175-0, 192p. R=6; I=8.

In 1854, Connal, fifteen, threatens a sheriff trying to evict his family from their highland Scottish home because the wealthy Lowlanders want better grazing land for their sheep. Those in the glen fiercely support each other, but even their strong loyalty cannot protect them against their attackers. Groups without money lack the power of those which have it.

Leonard, Hugh. *Parnell and the Englishwoman*. New York: Atheneum, 1991. 0-689-12127-X, 265p. R=6; I=10+.

Kitty O'Shea tries to help her husband's political career in Ireland by appealing to Charles Stewart Parnell in 1880. Parnell and Kitty begin an affair which produces three children, accepted by Kitty's husband as his own. When news of the affair becomes public, even after O'Shea dies and Kitty and Parnell marry, Parnell loses the people's support and dies from either heart break or exhaustion. When two people decide to either live apart or together, only they can know how they treat each other in privacy.

Levin, Betty. *Put on My Crown*. New York: Lodestar, 1985. 0-525-67163-3, 184p. R=2; I=7.*

Vinnie at fourteen and the two children for whom she is nursemaid become shipwrecked on the way to Canada in 1855. They reach an island off Scotland where the local parents have lost many of their children to disease. The islanders try to keep the children traveling with Vinnie, but eventually a tourist boat arrives and retrieves them. Although people may be kind and helpful, they may also be motivated by desires contrary to those of the people they seem to be helping.

Mellecker, Judith. *The Fox and the Kingfisher*. Illus. Robert Andrew Parker. New York: Knopf, 1990. 0-679-90539-1, 40p. R=6; I=3.

In this historical fantasy, a boy and girl, upset at their father's announcement that he will remarry after their mother's death in 1902, turn into a fox and a bird with the help of the stable boy's magic key. They discover that being animals is lonelier than being someone's child so they decide to return home. When one has one's wish fulfilled, one sometimes finds that the wish is not what one wants.

Newman, Robert. *The Case of the Baker Street Irregular.* New York: Aladdin, 1984 (1978). Paper, 0-689-70766-5, 200p. R=3; I=6.

Andrew, fourteen, goes from Cornwall to London with his male tutor after his aunt dies in the 1890's. The man disappears, and through unexpected events, Andrew meets Mr. Sherlock Holmes, finds the man, and reunites with his mother. Andrew realizes that his mother has suffered during her long separation from him and that trying to forget the past will be worth the effort.

Newman, Robert. *The Case of the Etruscan Treasure.* New York: Atheneum, 1983. 0-689-30992-9, 173p. R=4; I=5.

When his mother stars in a New York play during the 1890's, Andrew and his friend come to America with her and their Scotland Yard friend, Inspector Wyatt, joins them later. They become involved with a crime boss who wants the inspector to help him find files removed from a building destroyed by fire. The man responsible for the arson thinks he is a victim and wants to be recognized for his accomplishments, although they include murder and arson.

Newman, Robert. *The Case of the Frightened Friend.* New York: Atheneum, 1984. 0-689-31018-8, 168p. R=3; I=4.**

Andrew's friend from school fears for his life when he returns for the holiday to his late nineteenth century London home and stepmother. Andrew tells his Scotland yard friend, Inspector Wyatt, and the investigation leads to finding a spy in high government places. Andrew tries to understand why someone would betray his country for mere personal gain.

Newman, Robert. *The Case of the Indian Curse.* New York: Atheneum, 1986. 0-689-31177-X, 168p. R=4; I=5.**

Andrew and Sara become concerned when Beasley, Inspector Wyatt's friend, becomes ill. Wyatt has recently become Andrew's stepfather. After Andrew and Sara are kidnapped at Beasley's shop, they discover that a group called Thugs from India are trying to kill the person who threatens to reveal their identification. They drug Beasley so that when an Indian, supposedly his friend but actually the Thug leader, hypnotizes him, he will reveal the man's name if he knows it. When the Indian finally confronts the infiltrator, he tries to break his neck. Some people will resort to any method to get their way.

Newman, Robert. *The Case of the Somerville Secret.* New York: Atheneum, 1983. 0-689-30825-6, 184p. R=3; I=5.*

Andrew and Sara help their Scotland Yard friend, Inspector Wyatt, solve the murder of a former military man in London's 1890's. The process leads to a mentally retarded child, sixteen, who looks like a monster with six toes, but who turns out to be less a monster than the people who try to destroy him for personal gain. When people start deceiving others, stopping the lies becomes almost impossible.

Newman, Robert. *The Case of the Threatened King.* New York: Atheneum, 1982. 0-689-30887-6, 212p. R=4; I=4.*

When Andrew's friend Sara is kidnapped just before the Serbian ambassador to England's daughter is kidnapped, Inspector Wyatt of Scotland Yard suspects an attempt on the visiting King of Serbia's life. This late nineteenth century setting forms a backdrop for a fast-paced mystery.

Newman, Robert. *The Case of the Vanishing Corpse.* New York: Aladdin, 1985 (1980). Paper, 0-689-71037-2, 221p. R=3; I=5.

Andrew and his actress mother dine in London one evening during his summer vacation from school and meet briefly with George Bernard Shaw. Then Andrew meets the local constable, Peter Wyatt, during one of his walks with Sara. After they proceed to find who stole Andrew's mother's diamonds and murdered a man on their street, Peter is promoted to Scotland Yard. When people are lonely, they may choose friends who seem inappropriate but who like them in return.

Newman, Robert. *The Case of the Watching Boy.* New York: Atheneum, 1987. 0-689-31317-9, 171p. R=5; I=5.

In the 1890's, Andrew becomes friends with Markham at school, and they both unwittingly kidnap a child for a woman who says the boy is hers. What they discover in London is that the boy is the son of the rightful heir to the Rumanian throne, and those who would usurp the throne are trying to use the boy as a ploy for his father, disguised as English, to abdicate. In solving the situation, Andrew realizes that history occurs in discussions made by a few people in private rooms rather than in public and that the people who may be more prepared to govern are much happier doing something else.

Perry, Anne. *Belgrave Square.* New York: Fawcett, 1993 (1992). Paper (Crest), 0-449-22227-6, 361p. R=7; I=10+.

In London, around 1890, someone murders Weems, a moneylender who has a side business in blackmail. The police eventually identify the murderer, and after they do, they find an unexpected complication. Even when people have been absolved from guilt by others, if they are guilty, they cannot escape from themselves.

Perry, Anne. *The Face of a Stranger.* New York: Ivy, 1991 (1990). 0-8041-0858-7, 328p. R=8; I=10+.

People tell William Monk that he is a police detective in the 1890's, but he has amnesia since a recent accident on a London street and does not remember if he is or not. He still has to work on cases, and his current assignment involves the murder of an aristocrat who was a Crimean war hero. He eventually solves the crime but not before thinking he might have been provoked to do it himself. Not being able to remember one's past can create a whole new experience of living.

Peyton, K. M. *The Maplin Bird*. Illus. Victor Ambrus. Cleveland: World, 1965. R=5; I=9.**

By the time Toby is sixteen in the late 1860's, only a sailboat remains of his inheritance from his father. He has to sail away on it when his uncle tries to take it for his own children. After Toby and his sister Emily get work, a wealthy boy pays Toby to help him retrieve a yacht wrecked while he was smuggling. But police arrest the boy, and Toby's leg is broken in the struggle to escape. The boy's sister nurses Toby to health, and Toby and Emily survive their struggles. Goodness and selflessness impress thoughtful people, and they are often willing to help such people overcome their ordeals. *Carnegie Commendation*, 1964.

Pullman, Philip. *The Ruby in the Smoke*. New York: Knopf, 1987. 0-394-98826-4, 230p. Paper, 1988, 0-394-89589-4. R=4; I=8.

In London during 1872, sixteen-year-old Sally faces the death of her father in a shipwreck off the coast of China. She becomes involved in a situation where people deceive her and others die or are murdered before she finds her true identity and how carefully her father prepared for her future. Material wealth never substitutes for love. *Children's Book of the Year* (Great Britain), 1987; *International Reading Association Book Award*, 1988; *School Library Journal "Best Book,"* 1987.

Pullman, Philip. *Shadow in the North*. New York: Knopf, 1988. 0-394-99453-1, 320p. Paper, Borzoi, 0-394-82599-3, 336p. R=4; I=8.

When a woman arrives in Sally's office and says that she lost all her money on an investment that Sally suggested in a shipping line when one of the ships disappeared in mid-ocean, Sally determines to find out what happened. Her investigation reveals that a wooden match magnate who has begun making explosives and a steam gun has dubious connections to the shipping line. After the magnate causes the death of her friend and unborn child's father Fred, Sally accepts his proposal of marriage based on him repaying the investment that the woman lost. He does, but Sally destroys both him and his factory. People who have power often seek their own benefits rather than trying to find what is best for others. *International Reading Association Children's Book Award*, 1988.

Pullman, Philip. *Spring-Heeled Jack: A Story of Bravery and Evil.* Illus David Mostyn. New York: Knopf, 1991. 0-679-91057-3, 112p. Paper, 0-679-81057-9. R=7; I=5.

When the three orphans escape from their nineteenth century London orphanage, Spring-Heeled Jack, a magazine cartoon character in this historical fantasy, helps to save them. The two stories, one in cartoons and one in text, occur simultaneously as the children are reunited with their long lost father aboard a ship pulling out from port for America. *School Library Journal "Best Book,"* 1991.

Pullman, Philip. *The Tiger in the Well.* New York: Knopf, 1990. 0-679-90214-7, 407p. Paper (Borzoi), 1992. 0-679-82671-8. R=4; I=8.

Sally only wants to look after her young illegitimate daughter when she gets a court summons in 1881 accusing her of desertion and demanding custody of her child from a man whom she does not know. In trying to prove her innocence, Sally finds out about a plot to extradite a man unjustly accused of various crimes merely because he is Jewish. She falls in love with him, but not before discovering that the force behind her troubles is none other than Ay Ling, the man she thought she had murdered in *The Ruby in the Smoke.* When people unite to work with each other, much more can be accomplished than when working alone.

Roberts, Ann V. *Morning's Gate.* New York: Morrow, 1992. 0-688-11074-6, 639p. Paper, New York: Avon, 1993. 0-380-70992-9. R=6; I=10+.

Zoe comes to York, England, to find about her deceased grandmother, Letitia, because Zoe feels that she herself is more like her grandmother than either of her parents. In her research, she meets a man, a distant cousin, who has diaries and photographs of her grandmother's brothers, one who fought in World War I in France. The two fall in love, and simultaneously, discover the reasons for her grandmother's individuality and strength. Investigating the past leads to sometimes painful and sometimes pleasurable revelations, but very often to the satisfaction that comes with understanding.

Sutcliff, Rosemary. *Flame-Colored Taffeta.* New York: Farrar, Straus & Giroux, 1986. 0-374-32344-5, 120p. Paper, Sunburst, 1989. 0-374-42341-5, 144p. R=7; I=7.

Damaris, twelve, and Peter, thirteen, help a wounded stranger in the mid-eighteenth century on the southern coast of England. Since the area harbors smugglers, the young man may be a spy. One must help others, regardless of their affinities.

Uris, Leon. *Trinity.* New York: Doubleday, 1976. 0-385-03458-X, 384p. Paper, New York: Bantam, 1983. 0-553-25846-X. R=8; I=10+.

When Seamus is eleven in the Ireland of 1885, his friend Conor's grandfather Kilty dies. Kilty had endured the potato famine and the continuing unrest between the Irish Catholics and the ruling British Protestants. After witnessing the destruction of Catholic homes and businesses in the same year of Kilty's death, Seamus and Conor become part of the battle to win Ireland's freedom from England with Conor rising to leadership in the Irish Republican Army and Seamus becoming a reporter, able to record the history of the process. People who sacrifice other people for monetary gain must also be willing to face their wrath when the wronged join forces to retaliate.

1919-1945

Anderson, Margaret. *Searching for Shona.* New York: Knopf, 1979. 0-394-93724-4, 159p. Paper, 1989. 0-394-82587-X, 160p. R=4; I=4.*

In 1939, Marjorie's wealthy uncle decides to evacuate her, an orphan, from Edinburgh, Scotland, to her Canadian relatives. At the train station, she sees a girl from the orphanage, with whom she had played in the park, being evacuated to central Scotland. They decide to change places. Six years later, after Marjorie has discovered Shona's parents, the two meet. But the real Shona refuses to associate with her past, and Marjorie happily continues in her newly found comfort as Shona. Feeling needed and wanted by others far outweighs the benefits of material wealth bestowed out of duty, not love.

Bawden, Nina. *Carrie's War.* Illus. Colleen Browning. New York: HarperCollins, 1973. 0-397-31450-7, 159p. Paper, New York: Dell, 1989. 0-440-40142-9. R=4; I=6.

Evacuated from London in 1939, Carrie, an eleven-year-old girl, and her younger brother stay in a small Welsh town. They and another evacuee befriend a young boy unable to speak clearly, and are, in turn, protected by the woman caring for him. Carrie sees their house afire from the train as she returns to her family, but with no way to contact them, thinks that her rash behavior caused the fire. Carrie's son finds out thirty years later that she did not. But her mistaken guilt about the fire and unfounded fears have controlled her life, just as many incidents of childhood can wrongfully affect adult choices. *Carnegie Medal Commendation*, 1973.

Bawden, Nina. *Henry.* Illus. Joyce Powzyk. New York: Lothrop, Lee & Shepard, 1988. 0-688-07894-X, 119p. Paper, New York: Dell, 1990. 0-440-40309-X. R=5; I=5.

The female narrator (presumably the author) tells of her family (without a father) that evacuated to a farm in Wales during World War II and of Henry, the baby squirrel that lived with them. She and the two boys are almost jealous of the attention their mother gives to Henry, but they have the farm animals, the owners, and their school to keep them occupied during the long separation. Finding something on which to focus apart from one's problems may give life extra meaning. *Parenting's Reading-Magic Awards*, 1988; *American Library Association Notable Book for Children*, 1988.

Baylis-White, Mary. *Sheltering Rebecca*. New York: Lodestar, 1991. 0-525-67349-0, 99p. Paper, New York: Puffin, 1993. 0-14-036448-X, 112p. R=5; I=6.

When Clarissa goes to visit her grandparents, she asks for information about their lives for her school project. Her grandmother tells about her life in England beginning in 1937, before marrying and moving to Australia. She met Rebecca, a German refugee who could speak little English, and they became friends. Rebecca introduced Clarissa's grandmother to her brother after he was freed from a German concentration camp at the end of World War II, and she married him. Thus Rebecca's brother is Clarissa's own grandfather. One must treat all relationships with care because each one may affect one's later life in an unexpected way.

Cooper, Susan. *Dawn of Fear*. Illus. Margery Gill. San Diego: Harcourt Brace, 1988 (1970). 0-15-266201-4, 157p. Paper, New York: Macmillan (Aladdin), 1989. 0-689-71327-4, 224p. R=6; I=6.

During World War II, Derek and his family outside London have to go to their shelter almost every night for an air raid. One night, a bomb makes a direct hit on his friend's house, and the next day, Derek faces a different life. The vacuum caused by a friend's death can force a person to readjust relationships with those still living.

Gardam, Jane. *A Long Way from Verona*. New York: Macmillan, 1988 (1971). 0-02-73581-3, 192p. R=5; I=6.**

When Jessica is nine, an author speaks at her school. From that time, Jessica knows that she wants to be a writer. When thirteen, her poem wins a *London Times* contest, and all the painful experiences of the school year fade away. Growing up is never easy, but being intelligent and thoughtful as well as enduring the World War II air raids makes the process even more difficult. *Phoenix Award*, 1991.

Hunter. Mollie. *Hold On to Love.* New York: Harper, 1984.
0-06-022688-9, 288p. R=7; I=10.*

In the sequel to *A Sound of Chariots*, Bridie, fifteen, works
and attends night school in Edinburgh in 1939. She meets a
young man who also loves ideas and words, but she is afraid to
commit her interest until after he leaves for World War II.
Trying to find one's true identity at the end of adolescence is
never an easy process.

Hunter, Mollie. *A Sound of Chariots.* New York: Harper, 1972.
0-06-022669-2, 241p. Paper (Trophy), 1988. 0-06-440235-5. R=8;
I=8.

Bridie, in adolescence, is faced with men returning wounded
to rural Scotland from World War II, including her father. She
becomes almost overwhelmed by the concept of time and the
fear of death. But she loves words, and her ability to tell
riveting stories intrigues her classmates. Even in sorrow, the
human spirit can soar when it takes comfort in the ordinary
things of life like colors, words, community, and love. *Child
Study Children's Book Committee at Bank Street College Award,
1972; Phoenix Award, 1992.*

Hunter, Mollie. *The Third Eye.* New York: Harper. 1979 (1973).
0-06-022677-3. R=6; I=9.*

Jinty, at thirteen, has been called *fey* (having a second
sight), when she takes a weekend job in 1935 at an earl's house
near Edinburgh. She realizes that the earl is planning to escape
a family curse of the oldest son who dies before inheriting the
title by taking his own life. But she knows that revealing his
plan will ruin his social position. Learning the "secrets" of
adulthood experience cause one to rapidly leave the innocence
of childhood behind.

Kemp, Gene. *The Well.* Illus. by Chantal Fouracre. New York: Faber, 1984. 0-571-13284-7, 90p. R=3; I=5.**

In 1935, Annie's older brother Tom tells her that a dragon lives in the well that no one but he can see. After she starts wearing glasses, her older sister runs away to London, she gets her own kitten, and she realizes that Tom's world of enchantment does not exist. She knows that the good things in her own world, like her kitten and playing cricket with Tom and his friends, are enough. When one's family seems to be happy, one's own life may seem better balanced.

McCutcheon, Elsie. *Summer of the Zeppelin.* New York: Farrar, Straus, & Giroux, 1985. 0-374-37294-2, 168p. R=5; I=5.**

In the summer of 1918, a German zeppelin bombs a small village in England near Elvira's home. Elvira, twelve, and her friend also meet a German prisoner working nearby who speaks English, and she tries to help him return to Germany to find his sister since his parents are dead. She knows her father, away for three years as a British soldier, would want her to be kind. People have similar needs regardless of nationality or race.

Magorian, Michelle. *Good Night, Mr. Tom.* New York: HarperCollins, 1982. 0-06-024079-2, 318p. Paper (Trophy), 1986. 0-06-440174-X. R=4; I=6.

In 1939, after evacuating from London, Willie, eight, lives with Mr. Tom, a crotchety old man who is still mourning the loss of his wife and child forty years after their deaths. The discovery that Willie's mentally unbalanced mother has abused him, and that Willie needs him, changes Mr. Tom. This poignant novel shows that the human desire for bonding, in the midst of loneliness, can develop between seemingly incompatible people. *Guardian Award for Children's Fiction,* 1982; *International Reading Association Children's Book Award,* 1982; *American Library Association Notable Book for Children,* 1982.

Magorian, Michelle. *Not a Swan.* New York: HarperCollins, 1992. 0-06-024215-9, 407p. R=4; I=8.

In 1944, Rose, at seventeen, and her two older sisters stay in a small English coastal village while their mother performs abroad for the troops. By the end of the summer, Rose has matured enough to love others, regardless of their class or circumstance. A magazine accepts her first short story for publication. The lingering Victorian mores clashing with the unconventional times of war reveal both the best and worst in persons in all facets of their lives.

Morpurgo, Michael. *Why the Whales Came.* New York: Scholastic, 1990. 0-590-42911-6, 141p. Paper (Apple), 1992. 0-590-42912-4. R=5; I=5.

The Birdman lives on the Isles of Scilly, and Gracie's parents forbid her, at ten, to have contact with him because he is supposedly mad. But in 1914, circumstances lead her to him, and what she discovers is a deaf man who carves beautiful birds and knows why others think a nearby island is cursed. When a whale beaches nearby, he begs the townspeople to help send it back to sea, and Gracie's mother, changed by the Birdman's gifts of food while Gracie's father serves in the navy, galvanizes the people to action. Half-true stories have lives of their own and can hurt people unjustly.

Paton Walsh, Jill. *The Dolphin Crossing.* New York: Dell, 1990. Paper, 0-440-40310-3. R=5; I=7.*

During World War II, John, seventeen, meets an evacuee from London, and they sail John's boat, the *Dolphin*, across the English Channel to transport soldiers from Dunkirk, France, during the German invasion. While John lies unconscious for three days after being shot, his friend takes the boat alone and does not return. That humans must die defending against an aggressor remains a distressing reality.

Paton Walsh, Jill. *Fireweed.* New York: Farrar, Straus, & Giroux, 1970. 0-374-32310-0, 144p. Paper, 1988. 0-374-42316-4. R=3; I=6.

Refusing to stay evacuated in Wales, Bill, fifteen, returns to London only to find his aunt's house off-limits after being bombed. He meets Julie whose parents think she is dead because the ship on which she was supposed to have sailed for Canada sank. They do odd jobs and sleep in bomb shelters. Later, they set up house in a bombed-out area and look after a young orphaned boy. Difficult circumstances can bring forth small acts of heroism.

Peyton, K. M. *The Edge of the Cloud.* Magnolia, MA: Peter Smith, 1992 (1969). 0-8446-6566-5. Paper, New York: Puffin, 1989. 0-14-030905-5, 192p. R=6; I=10.

In the second of the Flambards trilogy, Christina and Will decide they will marry as soon as Will becomes twenty-one. Will begins stunt flying with a friend, but the friend is killed. When Will's father unexpectedly dies, Will enlists in the air force for World War I, and he and Christina decide to marry early. Life's surprising turns are similar to the unexpected wind currents that buffet a plane in midair. *Carnegie Medal*, 1970; *Guardian Award for Children's Fiction*, 1970.

Peyton, K. M. *Flambards.* Magnolia, MA: Peter Smith, 1992 (1967). 0-8446-6533-9. Paper, New York: Puffin, 1989. 0-14-034153-6, 224p. R=5; I=9.

An orphan, Christina, twelve, in 1908, goes to live with an uncle and his two sons, one a horse lover, the other a horse hater. As she watches the careless Mark ruin things and people, including impregnating a servant, and the careful Will, who defies his father by flying airplanes, she realizes that she loves Will and refuses Mark's marriage proposal. Someone who is steadfast and honest may seem less attractive than one who is rowdy and reckless, but generally the former will be more protective of another's needs. *Carnegie Commendation*, 1967; *Guardian Award for Children's Fiction*, 1970.

Peyton, K. M. *Flambards in Summer.* Magnolia, MA: Peter Smith, 1992 (1969). 0-8446-6567-3, 208p. R=6; I=9.

By 1916 in the third book of the Flambards trilogy, Christina is already a widow at twenty-one and benefactor of Will's fortune. She returns to Flambards, finds that she is pregnant, offers to adopt Mark's son, and decides that she and Dick, the former stable boy who taught her to ride horses, can have a happy marriage while rebuilding the house and rejuvenating its lands. When one's life has been torn apart, one has to carefully restructure it so that life has a new meaning. *Guardian Award for Children's Fiction*, 1970.

Peyton, K. M. *Thunder in the Sky.* Illus. Victor Ambrus. London: Oxford, 1966. Cleveland: World, 1967. R=6; I=8.**

Sam, sixteen, and his brother Gil work on the barges in 1914 after their other brother enlists for Britain in World War I.

They each get new skippers, and when Sam suspects his skipper of spying, he finds instead that Gil is guilty. After Gil dies saving the other barges from a Zeppelin bomb fire, Sam decides to go to war using Gil's recent enlistment papers. During war, one may wrongly suspect people of the enemy's nationality of being spies. *Carnegie Commendation*, 1966.

Prince, Alison. *How's Business*. New York: Four Winds, 1988. 0-02-775202-X, 176p. R=3; I=4.**

How, a boy in London in 1944, hates sleeping in the bomb shelter, but he enjoys wandering around the city trading or selling small items. His evacuation north to the Fens does not stop his activity, but he has difficulty adjusting to the area because his aunt forbids him from seeing the one friend he makes, a naturalized citizen from Germany. But he refuses to be cowardly, and by being brave almost to the point of foolishness, he helps others.

Raymond, Patrick. *Daniel and Esther*. New York: McElderry, 1990. 0-689-50504-3, 165p. R=5; I=8.

Daniel meets Esther in 1936 at their progressive British school and eventually they seek each other's company as Daniel begins to study and compose orchestral music. When World War II is declared, Daniel's father calls him to America. The Jewish Esther has to return to Austria where her parents, Jews, have become stranded without their passports. In the face of war and the pain of separation, one can only hope that important relationships will one day be renewed.

Rees, David. *The Exeter Blitz*. New York: Elsevier Nelson, 1980. Paper, New York: Granada, 1980. 0-583-30405-2, 126p. R=6; I=8.**

One family of five, each person in a separate area of town, survives the German bombing of Exeter during a 1942 "Baedeker" raid. With home destroyed and friends dead, they reorder their lives and reconstruct Exeter. Revealed through omniscient point of view, the children find love and honor and courage within themselves and others, especially as they forge new and unexpected relationships. *Carnegie Medal*, 1979.

Rundle, Ann. *Moonbranches.* New York: Macmillan, 1986. 0-02-777190-3, 163p. R=4; I=7.*

In 1914, Frances' father, a schoolmaster, joins the army. She goes to stay with her aunt, a housekeeper on a country estate in England. In this historical fantasy, Frances finds that looking into the opal on a ring she finds unites her with the family's son, drowned at seven. His evil twin brother, only two years older than Frances, pursues her during her visit. Frances also "sees" a woman, an artist like her but now dead, who bore a child out of wedlock and seems to have been one of Frances' own grandmothers. Having to outsmart someone who seems to have only diabolic intentions takes much ingenuity.

Shaw, Margret. *A Wider Tomorrow.* New York: Holiday House, 1990. 0-8234-0837-X, 130p. R=6; I=10.*

When Bobby is sixteen, her grandmother decides to tell Bobby about her own life from 1912 until 1917. Bobby discovers that her grandmother, thought never to have married, actually was married during the war when serving as an ambulance driver in France. She was married to a British lord, but his death from influenza soon after their marriage kept her from telling and possibly making his mother doubly unhappy. Bobby's grandmother became interested in the rights of women and children and got herself elected to Parliament as a suffragette. Bobby decides after hearing her story that she will go to university rather than to America with her boyfriend. One must always be the most one can be without compromising to the whims or will of others.

Turnbull, Ann. *Speedwell.* Cambridge, MA: Candlewick, 1992. 1-56402-112-2, 119p. R=4; I=4.

During 1930 in England, Mary's father loses his job. Mary tries to train the homing pigeons while he looks for work away from home. Her mother does not understand her interests which are unlike other eleven-year-old girls. With each family member contributing what little he or she can, people can survive difficult times.

Westall, Robert. *Blitzcat.* New York: Scholastic, 1989. 0-590-42770-9, 230p. Paper, 1990. 0-590-42771-7. R=4; I=4.

During World War II, Lord Gort, a cat in England, uses her *psi trailing* to search for her master. Her travels take her by the south coast near Dunkirk, into Dover, Coventry, and other places where her uncanny senses help her alert the inhabitants to an impending German bombing raid. Westall reveals the cat's movements through the people she meets and thereby keeps the story from seeming like an animal fantasy. *Smarties Book Prize*, 1989.

Westall, Robert. *Fathom Five.* Magnolia, MA: Peter Smith, 1993 (1980). 0-8446-6664-5. Paper, New York: Knopf (Borzoi), 1990. 0-679-80131-6, 256p. R=3; I=8.

Chas, sixteen in 1943 (the protagonist in *The Machine Gunners*), and a friend discover a floating olive oil can containing a message which names a ship soon to arrive in the harbor. Their sleuthing eventually uncovers a German soldier pretending to hate Germans as he plans to alert a submerged German submarine when to torpedo the ship. Many heroic deeds accomplished during a war remain unheralded in order to keep a war zone secure.

Westall, Robert. *The Kingdom by the Sea.* New York: Farrar, Straus, & Giroux, 1990. 0-374-34205-9, 176p. Paper, 1993. 0-374-44060-3. R=3; I=6.

When Harry escapes a bomb in 1942, his family does not reach the shelter, and their house is destroyed. Assuming himself without family or home, Harry leaves and finds people who help him along the English coastline until one man makes him come home to say goodbye, where he finds his family relocated--damaged, irritable, and accusing. War changes people sometimes so that they cannot reestablish former relationships. *Guardian Award for Children's Fiction*, 1991.

Westall, Robert. *The Machine-Gunners*. New York: Greenwillow,
  1976. 0-688-84055-8, 186p. Paper, New York: Random, 1990.
  0-679-80130-8, 192p. R=3 I=7.

  Chas, fourteen, cuts the machine gun off a downed German
fighter plane near his home in England in 1941 and asks a
wealthy but lonely boy to hide it in his unused bomb shelter.
The police suspect that the Irish Republican Army may have
stolen the gun, but when Chas and his friends become excited
and shoot at, but miss, people they think are Germans, Chas
loses his war souvenir. (He redeems himself in *Fathom Five*.)
Young people may act rashly and jeopardize not only their
safety, but also that of others around them. *Carnegie Medal*,
1976.

1946 and AFTER

Geras, Adèle. *The Tower Room*. San Diego: Harcourt Brace, 1992. 0-15-289627-9, 150p. R=5; I=9.

Just after Megan enters boarding school, her parents die, and in 1962, as a senior at eighteen, she falls in love with a new laboratory instructor and runs away with him to London. Megan realizes that love without the worries of looking for lodgings and jobs has more lustre. When people are lonely, they may be tempted to disappoint those who trust them in order to satisfy their own desires.

Hendry, Diana. *Double Vision*. Cambridge, MA: Candlewick, 1993. 1-56402-125-4, 271p. R=7; I=9.

At fifteen in England during the early 1950's, Eliza wants to be either carefree like her friend Jo or regal like her older sister but not like herself. She falls in love with Jake, an intellectual too old for her. After he leaves for Ecuador, Jo gets pregnant and married, and Eliza's sister marries. Although Jake sends her a gift, she understands that the old order has changed, and she can proceed with her life. When others seem confident with their choices, one may feel frustrated not to have the same assurance.

Hill, Susan. *The Glass Angels*. Illus. Valerie Littlewood. Cambridge, MA: Candlewick, 1992. 1-56402-111-4, 93p. R=5; I=5.

Tilly and her widowed seamstress mother try to survive after World War II in England. Her mother becomes ill, and water leaks through the roof which ruins the wedding dress waiting to be sewn after Christmas. Tilly goes for help to the family for whom her mother is making the dress. People will generally be happy to help someone truly in need, if only given a chance.

Magorian, Michelle. *Back Home*. New York: Harper, 1984. 0-06-08449-3, 352p. Paper (Trophy), 1992. 0-06-440411-0. R=4; I=7.

In 1945, Rusty returns to England from America where she has been living as an evacuee during World War II. Rusty has difficulty adjusting to the paucity of goods, and her insufferable boarding school, and the family resents her father who thinks that as a veteran, he can dictate his desires without challenge. War causes schisms in societies and families, many of which may never be repaired; those that are rejoined may have to establish new boundaries.

Morpurgo, Michael. *Mr. Nobody's Eyes*. New York: Viking, 1990. 0-670-83022-4, 138p. R=6; I=5.*

In 1947, Harry's widowed mother meets a man, marries him, and has a baby. At ten, Harry feels ignored and lonely, but a chimpanzee which escaped from the circus keeps him company while he runs away to Bournemouth from London. Although accused by his stepfather of things for which he is not guilty, Harry appreciates his concern when his stepfather rescues him; he knows that his stepfather actually cares.

Rowlands, Avril. *Milk and Honey*. New York: Oxford, 1990. 0-19-271627-1, 143p. R=9; I=6.

In 1958, Nelson's family sails from Jamaica to England. In London, they face rudeness because they are "coloured," but Nelson, twelve, makes friends with a woman who treats him like an adult and requests his help weeding her garden. Civilized behavior and honor know no racial boundaries.

Westall, Robert. *Echoes of War*. New York: Farrar, Straus, Giroux, 1991. 0-374-31964-2, 90p. R=4; I=7.

In a collection of five stories, various young people become exposed to aspects of war--the wounded hero remembering Dresden's fires, the dead woman on shore after a bombing, a shell-shocked grandfather. They all indicate that one will never know all of the aspects of war and how they can affect participants emotionally, mentally, physically, and spiritually.

THE AMERICAN COLONIES

BEFORE 1600

Baker, Betty. *Walk the World's Rim*. New York: HarperCollins, 1965. 0-06-020381-1, 192p. R=4; I=7.

Esteban, a black slave, convinces a young Indian to go to Mexico with him and six hundred other men in 1527 to look for the legendary wealth of the seven cities of Cibola. Once there, the Indian waits in a monastery for Esteban's visit, but Esteban does not come. Not until Cortez asks the Indian to feed his horse does the Indian see Esteban and realize that slaves cannot move freely. After they leave with Coronado's expedition, the Cibulans shoot Esteban in the back. Just because one is a slave does not mean that one is not kind and caring.

Bird, E. J. *The Rainmakers*. Minneapolis, MN: Carolrhoda, 1993. 0-87614-748-1, 120p. R=6; I=4.

Around 1250 AD, in the Mesa Verde area of Colorado, Cricket, eleven, finds an orphaned bear cub. While Cricket plays his flute like Kokopelli, the Anasazi god of mischief, the bear dances, and the much needed rain starts. Crickett and the bear become famous, and their rain dancing eventually helps them find Cricket's lost sister, thought kidnapped into slavery by an enemy tribe. When one selflessly tries to help others, one may unexpectedly help oneself.

Gear, Michael, and Kathleen O'Neal Gear. *People of the Sea.* New York: Tom Doherty, 1993. 0-312-93122-0, 425p. R=5; I=10+.

Twelve thousand years ago on the Pacific coast (now California), the healer Suncatcher tries to understand what has happened to the mammoth on which his people have depended for food and clothing. Instead of finding out, he has to cope with a rival from another tribe for his sacred position as healer and to retrieve his inner strength after falling in love with a woman hunted by her demented husband. A willingness for new ways that will bring more positive results can be very difficult for a people to achieve.

Hooks, William H. *The Legend of the White Doe.* Illus. Dennis Nolan. New York: Macmillan, 1988. 0-02-744350-7, 48p. R=4; I=4.

Virginia Dare was the first child born in the colonies in North Carolina during 1587, but she and the other colonists disappeared, never to be heard from except for the word "Croatoan" written on a tree outside their fort. A legend arose that she became a beautiful young woman, but when someone shot her, she transformed into a white doe which roamed the coastal woods. When things happen for which no answers exist, magical stories may attempt to find solutions.

James, J. Alison. *Sing for a Gentle Rain.* New York: Atheneum, 1990. 0-689-31561-9, 211p. R=5; I=10.

In this historical fantasy, when James is sixteen, he has a recurring dream about an Indian girl whom he does not recognize. Simultaneously, he discovers a book about the Anasazi in his amateur archaeologist grandfather's library. He sees a beautiful Anasazi pot in a museum, goes to the place where it was found, and has an unusual experience uniting the past of 1300 AD with his present as he tries to understand the Native American identity of the father he never knew. People trying to research their families may sometimes experience unexpected reactions to the information they find.

Kittleman, Laurence R. *Canyons Beyond the Sky.* New York: Atheneum, 1985. 0-689-31138-9, 212p. R=6; I=6.*

Evan, twelve, goes to spend the summer out west at an archeological dig under his father's direction and has an experience which takes him into life 5000 years ago. He thinks he has had a dream, but he later relocates the place where he had his experience and excites his father by showing him the ruins of a complete village, a site for which his father has been searching. Sometimes parents do not realize that their children have grown enough to become interested in new ideas and places and that they should be treated as individuals.

Haugaard, Erik. *Leif the Unlucky.* Boston: Houghton Mifflin, 1982. 0-395-32156-5. R=7; I=8.**

In 1406, at a Viking outpost in Greenland, Leif, fifteen, has to protect himself against another who challenges his hereditary leadership. The ensuing duels bring tragedy, but Leif survives and keeps his position. Trying to keep groups of people together when internal stresses exist remains difficult, and often, thankless.

O'Dell, Scott. *The King's Fifth.* Illus. Samuel Bryant. Boston: Houghton Mifflin, 1966. 0-395-06963-7. R=4; I=7.

Esteban, in 1541, when seventeen, waits in a California prison to be tried for hoarding the king's fifth of gold. Through flashbacks, one finds that Esteban was cartographer of Captain Mendoza's expedition and that he threw his gold into a desert sinkhole because desire for gold was causing the men to destroy each other. One may have more freedom inside a cell if, outside, one is enslaved by money. *Newbery Honor,* 1967.

Shuler, Linda Lay. *She Who Remembers.* New York: NAL-Dutton, 1988. Paper (Signet), 0-451-16053-3, 478p. R=5; I=10+.

Because of her blue eyes, Kwani's Anasazi tribe banishes her. A Toltec magician rescues her and takes her to the Place of the Eagle Clan where she finds that she is the one chosen to carry on knowledge of the ancient secrets to the women of the tribe. She learns them from the old wise woman, "She Who Remembers." At the birth of her child, Kwani realizes that she must return to her people rather than go with the Toltec magician to his. One of the big mysteries in life is how one should make the best decisions for a promising future.

Shuler, Linda Lay. *Voice of the Eagle.* New York: Morrow, 1992. 0-688-09519-4, 600p. Paper, New York: NAL-Dutton, 1993. 0-451-17681-2. R=5; I=10+.

In the sequel to *She Who Remembers*, set around 1272, Kwani, her baby, and Tolonqua return to Cicuye. After a long life and Tolonqua's death, Kwani has a vision telling her to return to the House of the Sun (Mesa Verde) where she became "She Who Remembers." She has to leave her pregnant daughter, also journeying, but in the opposite direction. At the House of the Sun, Kwani dies, but her granddaughter, blue-eyed like Kwani, enters another city with her parents almost simultaneously. The sense that time is cyclical rather than linear allows one to mentally fuse the past and the present with the future.

Spinka, Penina Keen. *White Hare's Horses.* New York: Atheneum, 1991. 0-689-31654-2, 154p. Paper: New York: Fawcett (Juniper), 1992. 0-449-70407-6. R=4; I=7.

The Aztecs and their powerful horses come to White Hare's Chumash home on the California coast in 1522, when she is thirteen. Instead of staying friendly, the Aztecs decide to take human sacrifices from the Chumash people, but White Hare thwarts them by stealing their horses and freeing the hostages. Sometimes even the meekest of people will show bravery when their friends and family are threatened.

1600-1699

Bulla, Clyde Robert. *A Lion to Guard Us.* Illus. Michele Chessare. New York: HarperCollins, 1981. 0-690-04097-0. Paper (Trophy), 1989. 0-06-440333-5, 118. R=2; I=3.

Amanda, Meg, and Jemmy sail toward America from England in 1609 after their mother dies. Their ship wrecks in Bermuda, but they eventually reach Jamestown and their father. They bravely face an unknown future as long as they have the lion door knocker from their old home as a symbol of their father's protection.

Bulla, Clyde Robert. *Pocahontas and the Strangers.* Illus. Peter Burchard. New York: Crowell, 1971. 0-690-62903-6, 180p. Paper, New York: Scholastic, 1987. 0-590-43481-0. R=3; I=6.

When her tribe plans to sacrifice Captain John Smith, Pocahontas claims him as her possession, and thereby, saves him. She then becomes the liaison between her people and the white settlers around 1612. While the settlers keep her hostage for more food and stolen guns, she meets and marries John Rolfe. They travel to England with their child, and during their long stay, Pocahontas dies. Her willingness to reconcile probably kept the English settlers and the Native Americans from going to war sooner.

Bulla, Clyde Robert. *Squanto, Friend of the Pilgrims.* New York: Crowell, 1954. 0-690-76642-4, 106p. Paper, New York: Scholastic, 1990. 0-590-44055-1, 112p. R=2; I=4.

In the early 1600's, Squanto goes to London and becomes accustomed to the white man's ways although he wants to return to America. He gets the chance to sail with Captain John Smith in 1614, but once on American land, another captain immediately captures him and takes him to Spain to be sold into slavery. His English helps free him, and he goes back to London and finally to America in 1619 to find that a disease has killed his entire tribe. His experiences, although painful, make him invaluable as a communicator for both the Native Americans and the pilgrims from the Mayflower.

Clapp, Patricia. *Constance: A Story of Early Plymouth.* New York: Peter Smith, 1992 (1968). 0-8446-6647-5. Paper New York: Puffin, 1986. 0-14-032030-X. Paper, New York: Morrow (Beech Tree), 1991. 0-688-10976-4, 256p. R=4; I=10.

In 1620, Constance, fifteen, arrives on the Mayflower and describes in her journal the disease, disorganization, and deceit surrounding the first year at Plymouth. She also meets Native Americans and falls in love with one of the young men who came on the Mayflower with her. Constance's account of the first settlers learning to live with each other's talents and idiosyncrasies breathes life into dreary Plymouth. *American Book Award Finalist,* 1969.

Clapp, Patricia. *Witches' Children.* Paper, New York: Peter Smith, 1992 (1982). 0-8446-6572-X. Paper, New York: Puffin, 1987. 0-14-0324070, 160p. R=6; I=8.

Mary Warren, bound in 1692 to a Salem, Massachusetts, couple, begins socializing with ten young girls and Tituba, a slave who reads tarot cards and palms. After Mary and the others start accusing people of being witches, Mary becomes concerned with the capricious allegations. When she refuses to continue meeting with the group, the girls name her as a witch. She feels strong remorse for aiding evil and making false accusations in the name of God. *American Library Association Best Books for Young Adults,* 1982; *Jefferson Cup,* 1983.

Dalgiesh, Alice. *The Thanksgiving Story.* Illus. Helen Sewell. New York: Scribner's, 1988 (1954). 0-684-18999-2, 32p. Paper, New York: Macmillan (Aladdin), 1984. 0-689-71053-4. R=5; I=3.

After sailing from Holland to England on the *Speedwell,* the Hopkins children sail from England to America on the *Mayflower,* arriving in the Massachusetts winter. During their first year, they and the Plymouth settlers meet the English speaking Samoset and Squanto. They also meet Massasoit who teaches them how to plant food, leading to the first Thanksgiving feast. People who choose to change their lives by sailing to a new, unsettled land must be very courageous and industrious.

Dillon, Eilís. *The Seekers*. New York: Scribner's, 1986. 0-684-18595-4, 136p. R=4; I=9.

Edward leaves England and his family for New England in 1632 when his fiancée's father decides he will go and take his daughter. After a difficult sailing, they try to adjust to the religious zeal and hard work expected of them, and to survive the illnesses, but eventually Edward and Rebecca prefer England. For people who choose to leave their homes, adapting to the accompanying hardships may be easier than for those who must leave because of another's choice.

Fleischman, Paul. *Saturnalia*. New York: HarperCollins, 1990. 0-06-021913-0, 128p. Paper (Trophy), 1992. 0-06-447089-X. R=6; I=8.

A group of characters--masters and servants--live their lives in Boston during December, 1681. William, an Indian apprentice to the printer Mr. Currie, enrages Baggot the tithingman because he knows all the answers to his tricky questions. During this test of wills and wits, William realizes that he must use his intelligence to preserve the history of his people rather than succumb to the wishes of his white authorities. People who try to fulfil their ideals often have to overcome roadblocks of stupidity and control. *American Library Association Notable Books for Children*, 1991; *School Library Journal "Best Book,"* 1990.

Haugaard, Erik. *Cromwell's Boy*. Boston: Houghton Mifflin, 1990 (1978). Paper, 0-395-54975-2. R=6; I=8.

When he recalls his service under Cromwell, Oliver remembers a night time ride to escape being caught as a spy. In 1086, he is in Boston and again rides into the night to encourage friends to curtail King James' power in the colonies. Despots in any country often cause citizens to rise against them.

Holmes, Mary Z. *Two Chimneys*. Illus. Rick Whipple. Austin, TX: Raintree/Steck-Vaughn, 1992. 0-8114-3506-7, 48p. Paper, 0-8114-6431-8. R=4; I=4.

An English family of five comes to Jamestown, Virginia, in 1628 with twelve indentured servants. The summer heat kills some of the servants and family members, but Katherine Eastwood survives and loves her new home. Many men who brought their families to Virginia only wanted to give them a good life unavailable to them as families with no inheritance. "History's Children" series.

Levin, Betty. *Mercy's Mill*. New York: Greenwillow, 1992. 0-688-11122-X, 241p. R=4; I=5.

In this historical fantasy, Sarah, thirteen, moves with her mother, stepfather, and siblings, including her five-year-old foster sister, to the country. While her parents are busily rebuilding the old dam and mill, Sarah meets a boy who speaks correct English but does not understand some of the simple things she mentions. She eventually finds that he is a runaway slave who has come into a different time period in his attempt to find a girl who knew him both in Colonial times and when a runaway slave. He thinks that the girl needs help. A subplot involves abused children, including the boy, the foster sister, and Sarah's stepfather. The past can never change, but one can always try to make the present and the future better.

Lobel, Arnold, writer/illus. *On the Day Peter Stuyvesant Sailed into Town*. New York: HarperCollins, 1987 (1971). Paper (Trophy), 0-06-443144-4, 48p. R=4; I=2.

When Peter Stuyvesant arrives from Holland to govern New Amsterdam in 1647, the city is dirty and disorganized. After several years, the city improves, and the people all celebrate, never comprehending the city's future--to become New York City. People working together can accomplish much good. *Christopher Award*, 1972.

Luhrmann, Winifred Bruce. *Only Brave Tomorrows.* Boston: Houghton Mifflin, 1989. 0-395-47983-5, 190p. R=3; I=9.

In 1675, Faith's father, whom she has hardly seen, takes her from her Sussex, England, home and moves her to Massachusetts. An Indian massacre kills several people in their Springfield community, including her father. Faith marries, but for a while, her husband does not realize that she loves him and not another man who made the Atlantic voyage with Faith. Accepting the benefits and blessings of what one has rather than wishing for something more takes understanding of oneself.

Petry, Ann. *Tituba of Salem Village.* New York: Crowell, 1988. 0-690-04766-5. Paper, New York: Harper (Trophy), 1991. 0-06-440403-X, 254p. R=6; I=6.

After having been sold by her mistress to a minister, Tituba and her husband depart Barbados. In Salem, five girls misinterpret Tituba's skills with herbs and tarot cards to the town's citizens, and the people convict her for being a witch. People acting in a crowd sometimes lose their individual integrity and condemn others unjustly without fear of retribution.

Smith, Claude Clayton. *The Stratford Devil.* New York: Walker, 1984. 0 8027-6544-0, 191p. R=5; I=9.**

At twelve, Ruth, who hates the Puritan's Sunday meetings in 1650, has felt lonely since the death of her father. As she matures and the townspeople continue to question her behavior, she discovers the identity of her real father. She marries for protection from the people, finds herself widowed on the same day, and is convicted for witchcraft soon after. People are sometimes victims of situations and events that are outside their control.

Speare, Elizabeth George. *The Witch of Blackbird Pond.*
Boston: Houghton Mifflin, 1958. 0-395-07114-3. Paper, New
York: Dell (Laurel Leaf), 1978. 0-440-99577-9, 256p. R=6; I=6.

In 1687, the orphaned Kit travels from Barbados to New
England, unannounced, to live with her only relative, her
mother's sister. She cannot adjust to the uncompromising and
bleak lifestyle. A Quaker woman, whom the community thinks
is a witch, helps her endure the agony, including Kit's being
accused of witchcraft when she is actually teaching a child to
read. Uninformed people can be vile, hostile, and malicious.
Newbery Medal, 1959; *International Board of Books for Young
People*, 1060.

Waters, Kate. *Sarah Morton's Day: A Day in the Life of a
Pilgrim Girl.* Photographs by Russ Kendall. New York:
Scholastic, 1989. 0-590-42634-6, 32p. Paper (Blue Ribbon), 1991.
0-590-44871-4. R=3; I=3.

At Plimoth Plantation in Massachusetts around 1627, Sarah
spends her day milking, mucking the garden, pounding spices,
polishing brass, studying, playing knickers (marbles), and
talking to her friend. Since her father died soon after their
journey and her mother remarried, Sarah seeks her new father's
approval by trying to do her best. The photographs of the
restored Plimoth Plantation enhance the ideas and events in
the text.

Wisler, G. Clifton. *This New Land.* New York: Walker, 1987.
0-8027-6727-3, 125p. R=6; I=5.

Escaping from England and King James I's religious
tyranny, Richard and his family leave the Netherlands in 1620
for the New World. At twelve, Richard feels the loss of the old
and the fear of the new as his mother dies aboard their ship.
His group under Miles Standish first meets the Native
Americans Samoset and Squanto, who thankfully, both speak
English. They say that their leader, Massasoit, is very willing
to trade with the colonists. To have freedom to practice one's
religion, one may sometimes have to make sacrifices as harsh
as leaving one's home. "Walker's American History" series.

1700-1774

Anderson, Joan. *Spanish Pioneers of the Southwest.* Photos by George Ancona. New York: Dutton, 1989. 0-525-67264-8, 64p. R=7; I=4.

In the eighteenth century, a young boy in the area now called New Mexico is pleased to be asked to guard the pueblo. His warning of someone in the distance causes the guards to close the gates, but all are relieved to find that the newcomer is a friend. When young people have to take adult responsibility, it can lead them to act more maturely.

Anderson, Joan. *A Williamsburg Household.* Photos by George Ancona. New York: Clarion, 1988. 0-89919-516-4. Paper, 1990. 0-395-54791-1, 48p. R=7; I=2.

In 1770, Rippon and his family are slaves to Williamsburg families. They make contact with each other when they run errands around town. The life is very difficult, but some come to understand that just being alive, in itself, must not be underestimated.

Byrd, Max. *Jefferson: A Novel.* New York: Bantam, 1993. 0-553-09470-X, 424p. R=7; I=10+.

A look at Thomas Jefferson through the eyes of his young secretary in Paris beginning in 1784 shows a man difficult to categorize. The secretary watches the enigmatic Jefferson in his diplomatic dealings with the French, his political parryings with his fellow Americans, and his disparate relationships with women. Jefferson's behavior tends to belie the rumors that Jefferson bore children by one of his slaves because he only chooses married women as his friends. No one can ever know everything about another human being.

Dalgliesh. Alice. *The Courage of Sarah Noble.* Illus. Leonard Weisgard. New York: Scribner's, 1987 (1954). 0-684-18830-9, 64p. Paper, New York: Macmillan (Aladdin), 1991. 0-689-71540-4, 64p. R=3; I=3.

In 1707, Sarah, eight, goes with her father to build a new house in Massachusetts. She stays with a Native American family while her father returns to their former home to get her mother. When they return, Sarah's mother refuses to believe anyone else can care for her child better than she. *Newbery Honor*, 1955.

Edmonds, Walter. *The Matchlock Gun.* Illus. Paul Lantz. New York: Putnam, 1989 (1941). 0-399-21911-0, 64p. R=6; I=3.

Left with his family when his father goes to defend the settlement from Indians in 1757, Edward, at ten, has to keep Indians from burning his own home. After they throw tomahawks at his mother, Edward saves the family by shooting a gun which is twice as long as he is tall. When faced with an emergency, people can overcome their fears and inhibitions to perform actions they thought impossible. *Newbery Medal*, 1942.

Field, Rachel. *Calico Bush.* Illus. Allen Lewis. New York: Macmillan, 1987 (1931). 0-02-734610-2, 224p. Paper, New York: Dell (Yearling Classic), 1990. 0440-40368-5. R=6; I=7.

In 1740, after sailing from France to America, Marguerite, twelve, becomes bound out to a family that moves north to Maine. An older Scottish woman who knows how to heal with herbs helps her endure the loss of her Catholic religion and her French nationality as skirmishes leading to the French and Indian war begin. When Marguerite saves the family from Indians, her courage leads the family to offer her freedom, but she decides to stay where someone cares for her. *Newbery Honor*, 1932.

Grimes, Roberta. *My Thomas: A Novel of Martha Jefferson's Life.* New York: Doubleday, 1993. 0-385-42399-3, 320p. R=5; I=10+.

In 1772, Martha Skelton, a twenty-two year old widow who had been determined not to remarry, marries Thomas Jefferson, a young lawyer and legislator. She keeps a journal in which she records the pain and pleasure of their years together until she dies after childbirth in 1781, and Jefferson leaves Monticello for ten years, distraught at his loss. People in the public's eye often find that having a private life is very difficult and that others who dislike them will sometimes tell false stories about them.

Keehn, Sally. *I Am Regina.* New York: Philomel, 1991. 0-399-21797-5, 240p. Paper, New York: Dell, 1993. 0-440-40754-0. R=4; I=6.

When Regina is eleven in 1755, Allegheny Indians kill her father and brother and kidnap her and her sister. Regina spends four years living as an Indian, forgetting English and longing for any sign of human tenderness. White men finally free her, and she finds her mother and other brother. She learns that anyone, regardless of race, can be loving and kind as well as cruel and heartless.

Martinello, Marian L., and Samuel P. Nesmith. *With Domingo Leal in San Antonio 1734.* San Antonio, TX: University of Texas, 1980. Paper, 0-933164-40-8, 78p. R=6: I=4.

Domingo, at ten in 1734, becomes bored with watching the cattle and is relieved when he must take the adze to the nearby mission for repair work. After he watches the blacksmith and rides with a soldier, he spies enemy Indians watering their horses. He realizes that all people tend to have the same kind of responsibilities no matter what their jobs, and although the jobs may not seem exciting, they give security and comfort.

Michener, James. *Centennial.* New York: Random, 1974. 0-394-47970-X. Paper, New York: Fawcett, 1987. 0-449-21419-2. R=7; I=10+.

The town of Centennial, Colorado, is home for an eclectic assortment of people from its beginning in 1760 to its high point at the time of the Civil War as it becomes the center of a great cattle empire on through its demise during the 1890's. The Arapaho brave, the French trapper with two wives, and the disillusioned Mennonite with his child bride, come alive in the town as does the unscrupulous actor who uses a dead banker's money to amass his own wealth. When people no longer can find ways to thrive in an area, it dies as the people move on.

Moore, Ruth Nulton. *The Christmas Surprise.* Illus. Allan
Eitzen. Scottdale, PA: Herald Press, 1989. 0-8361-3499-0. R=6;
I=5.

In 1755, Delaware and Shawnee Indians raid Kate's family
and kill her parents while Kate hides in the root cellar. Kate's
uncle, an itinerarnt preacher, takes her to Bethlehem,
Pennsylvania to stay in the Moravian settlement. The Moravian
policy of non-violence, even when the Indians threaten to raid
on Christmas Eve, surprises Kate. But when she sees the lonely
Nathan, a young Indian boy whose parents were killed by
whites, she finally understands that all humans have the same
needs and pains.

Pope, Elizabeth. *The Sherwood Ring.* Magnolia, MA: Peter
Smith, 1992 (1958). 0-8446-6416-2, 266p. Paper, New York:
Puffin. 0-14-034911-1. R=7; I=8.

In this historical fantasy, Peggy leaves Scotland after her
father's death to live in the family's New York state home. A
girl on horseback greets her at the train, and after research
and ghostly encounters, Peggy finds out that the girl lived in
1773, and her British family was very involved in the American
Revolution. Family intrigue and plots can jeopardize others
outside the family unit. *American Library Association Notable
Book*, 1958.

Rappaport, Doreen. *The Boston Coffee Party.* Illus. Emily A.
McCully. New York: HarperCollins, 1988. 0-06-024825-4, 64p.
Paper, 1990. 0-06-444141-5. R=2; I=2.

When Sarah and her sister Emma try to buy sugar in 1775,
the only merchant who has it charges too much. Their mother's
friends discover that the same merchant is hiding coffee,
waiting for the price to rise. They meet and, acting together,
take the coffee from the greedy merchant and distribute it for
an equitable price. "An I Can Read Book."

Richter, Conrad. *The Light in the Forest.* Cutchogue NY:
Buccaneer, 1991 (1953). 1-56849-064-X, 180p. Paper, New York:
Bantam, 1990. 0-553-26878-3. R=4; I=4.

When True Son is fifteen in 1765, the whites demand that
the Cuyloga or Delaware Indians release their white captives.
Although he has lived in Cuyloga for eleven years and thinks of
himself as a Cuyloga, True Son has to face the whites whom he

has learned to hate, including his biological parents. Kindness and love have no racial or social boundaries.

Rinaldi, Ann. *A Break with Charity: A Story about the Salem Witch Trials.* San Diego, CA: Gulliver, 1992. 0-15-200353-3, 257p. R=5; I=8.

Fourteen years after 1692, Susanna recalls her part in the Salem witch trials when she had first desired to be part of the group which gathered at Reverend Parris's with Tituba. Although she knows the narrow-minded and selfish attitudes of the girls who name people as witches, including her parents, for entertainment, she does not tell anyone for a long time because of her fear. People who have little concern for others and are bored with life may harm others for their own amusement.

Rinaldi, Ann. *The Fifth of March: A Story of the Boston Massacre.* San Diego, CA: Harcourt Brace, 1993. 0-15-200343-6, 333p. Paper, 0-15-227517-7. R=4; I=7.

As indentured servant to John and Abigail Adams around 1770, Rachel knows what is happening politically in Boston. In addition to looking after the Adams' children and hearing the discussions of the Adams's visitors, she gets herself "educated" by reading from Henry Knox's bookstore, developing a friendship with a young British soldier, and having a friend Jane who alerts her to ensuing riots, one which becomes known as the "Boston massacre." Even though one may be appreciative of another's gifts, one sometimes has to return the boon in order to keep or earn one's independence.

Rockwood, Joyce. *Groundhog's Horse.* Illus. Victor Kalin. New York: Holt, 1978. 0-8050-1173-0, 115p. R=4; I=4.**

The Cherokee youth Groundhog, eleven, sneaks away from home in 1750 to find his horse which has been stolen by the Creek enemies. He rescues it as well as a young Cherokee boy kidnapped by the Creeks two years previously. Groundhog attributes his successful journey home to the instincts of his horse, refusing to accept praise for something he sees as having occurred accidentally.

Speare, Elizabeth George. *The Sign of the Beaver*. Boston: Houghton Mifflin, 1983. 0-395-33890-5, 144p. Paper, New York: Dell (Yearling), 1984. 0-440-47900-2. R=4; I=5.

After Matt and his father go to Maine to build a new home in 1768, Matt's father leaves him alone while returning to Massachusetts to retrieve the other family members. Someone visits and steals Matt's gun. Then, an Indian living nearby hears his cries and helps him when bees mercilessly sting him. They begin to trade reading lessons for lessons in trapping, fishing, and finding trails. Only by assisting others can one gain contentment. *Newbery Honor*, 1984; *Child Study Children's Book Award*, 1983; *Christopher Award*, 1984; *Scott O'Dell Award for Historical Fiction*, 1984; *American Library Association Notable Book for Children*, 1983; *School Library Journal "Best Book,"* 1983.

Steele, William O. *Wayah of the Real People*. Illus. Isa Barnett. Williamsburg, Va: Colonial Williamsburg, 1964. R=4; I=5.**

When Wayah, an eleven-year-old Cherokee, arrives in Williamsburg to attend school in 1752, he has to learn both the customs and the words of the white people. Steps shock him as does the bell and the "teeth" of a piano. Returning home after one year greatly relieves him, but his new ability to act as translator benefits his tribe. By learning how others are different, one can begin to understand why problems arise and how to negotiate solutions.

THE UNITED STATES

1775-1783

Avi. *The Fighting Ground.* Illus. Ellen Thompson. New York: HarperCollins, 1984. 0-397-32074-4, 160p. Paper, 1987. 0-06-440185-5. R=4; I=6.

When Jonathan is thirteen in 1778, he spends one day fighting the Hessians near Trenton, New Jersey. When he discovers that the people with whom he is fighting have killed Tory farmers, and he watches that same group then kill the Hessians, his concept of war changes. A close view of real war can expose the fear, shame, and hatred associated with it. *Scott O'Dell Award for Historical Fiction,* 1985; *American Library Association Notable Book for Children,* 1984.

Benchley, Nathaniel. *Sam the Minuteman.* Illus. Arnold Lobel. New York: HarperCollins, 1969. 0-06-020480-X, 64p. Paper, 1987. 0-06-444107-5. R=2; I=2.

When Paul Revere's message reaches Concord that the British are coming, and someone rings the church bells to alert the people, Sam and his father take their guns and join other "minutemen" to protect the town's supplies. The marching British shoot at the small band of men, killing eight, and wounding Sam's friend John. Their battle starts a war in 1775 that lasts for eight years. A person's carelessness can cause many people anguish for many years. "An I Can Read Book."

Berleth, Richard. *Samuel's Choice.* Illus. James Watling. Niles, IL: Albert Whitman, 1990. 0-8075-7218-7, 36p. R=4; I=4.

In 1775, Samuel, a fourteen-year-old slave in Brooklyn, decides to help the Sons of Liberty fight the British by sailing them across Gowanus Creek in his master's boat. The Maryland commander asks him to be his orderly. By helping the Americans, unlike his master, Samuel gains his freedom.

Caudill, Rebecca. *Tree of Freedom.* Illus. Dorothy Bayley. Magnolia, MA: Peter Smith (1949). 0-8446-6401-4, 284p. Paper (Puffin), 1988. 0-14-032908-0. R=7; I=7.

In 1780, when Stephanie's family moves from the Carolina colony to Kentucky, she plants an apple seed transported from France by her great-grandmother, her "tree of freedom." Her brother, after fighting Indians allied with the British, decides to study law in Williamsburg to help illiterate persons, like their father, learn their rights. One must have knowledge, or one's freedom can be threatened, even in the wilderness. *Newbery Honor*, 1950; *New York Herald Tribune Award*, 1950.

Collier, James and Christopher. *The Bloody Country.* New York: Four Winds, 1976. 0-02-722960-2, 192p. Paper, New York: Scholastic, 1985. 0-590-4126-9, 180p. R=4; I=7.

After Indians scalp his mother and brother-in-law and the government claims his father's mill, Ben cannot understand why his father refuses to return to Connecticut from the Wyomming Valley of Pennsylvania in 1782. When Ben sees the former slave Joe, freed by a technicality in Pennsylvania law, in the woods enjoying his new status, he begins to comprehend his father's need to stay and be free from working for others.

Collier, Christopher and James. *My Brother Sam Is Dead.* New York: Four Winds, 1984 (1974). 0-02-722980-7, 224p. Paper, New York: Scholastic, 1985. 0-590-42792-X, 182p. R=4; I=5.

Beginning in 1775, the British kill young Timmy's ten-year-old friend, his father dies of cholera on a British ship, and his brother is executed for cattle theft when protecting the family's stock. Timmy is never certain whether the Tories (like his father was) or the rebels are right and wonders much later in his life if the same goals could have been achieved without war. Timmy survives, but one wonders how his hope can continue in light of losing so much. *Newbery Honor*, 1975.

Collier, Christopher and James. *War Comes to Willy Freeman.* Magnolia, MA: Peter Smith, 1992. 0-8446-6596-7. New York: Delacorte, 1983. 0-385-29235-X, 192p. R=6; I=6.

When Willy, thirteen, accompanies her father to Fort Griswold, Connecticut, where he will fight in the Revolutionary War, and thereby gain freedom for his family, she sees a British soldier gore him to death. The British capture her mother, and Willy begins searching for her in New York at Sam Fraunces's Tavern. Willy has to protect herself as a black female and is very aware of the problems inherent in her identity.

DeFord, Deborah H, and Harry S. Stout. *An Enemy Among Them.* Boston: Houghton Mifflin, 1987. 0-395-44239-7, 203p. R=5; I=8.

When Margaret goes to another Pennsylvania town in 1776 to care for her wounded brother, she helps an enemy Hessian in the same hospital. The Hessian, as a prisoner of war and a trained cobbler, comes to Margaret's house to help her father instead of going to prison, and discovers a Loyalist traitor in the small town as he begins to love Margaret and become good friends with her brother. Relating to people as individuals breaks the artificial barriers created by wars.

Edwards, Sally. *George Midgett's War.* New York: Scribner's, 1985. 0-684-18315-3, 138p. R=4; I=6.**

At fourteen, George lives in Ocrakoke on the Outer Banks of the North Carolina colony in 1777, not bothered by the war. But when British soldiers murder a mute woman nearby because she hides valuable salt, he and his father take the salt and other supplies on a hazardous journey by land and sea all the way to Valley Forge, Pennsylvania. When something happens to a loved one, a person's whole concept of life can change.

Forbes, Esther. *Johnny Tremain*. Illus. Lynd Ward. Magnolia, MA: Peter Smith, 1992 (1943). 0-8446-6600-9. Paper, New York: Dell, 1987. 0-440-44250-8. R=3; I=6.

After Johnny severely burns his hand in 1774, he has to support himself by delivering newspapers rather than creating beautiful silver objects. Soon blackmailed by a Tory, he quickly learns about differences between Whigs and Tories and becomes an ardent Whig. Johnny learns that all people have value, even if they remain unskilled or illiterate. *Newbery Medal*, 1944.

Fritz, Jean. *Early Thunder*. Illus. Lynd Ward. New York: Coward McCann, 1967. 0-698-20036-5, 256p. Paper, New York: Puffin, 1987. 0-14-032259-0. R=7; I=7.

In Salem, Massachusetts, Daniel West, fourteen, can see no reason for the American colonies in 1775 to defy the British king, especially after the Tories throw stones though a judge's window who lies dying of smallpox. His attitude gradually changes, even though his physician father's does not, because some of the Whigs are people whom he admires. Deciding what one thinks is right and just is always difficult, but even more so when one realizes that what is right is against the law.

Gauch, Patricia L. *This Time, Tempe Wick?* Illus. Margot Tomes. New York: Putnam, 1992 (1974). 0-399-21880-7, 48p. R=4; I=4.

In 1781 on her Pennsylvania farm, Tempe Wick has to protect her horse from soldiers in General Washington's army. She hides the horse inside the house and staves off the men for three days. Using one's wits may help save something of value.

Hoobler, Dorothy and Thomas. *The Sign Painter's Secret: The Story of a Revolutionary Girl*. Illus. Donna Ayers. Englewood Cliffs, NJ: Silver-Burdett, 1991. 0-382-24143-6, 55p. Paper, 0-382-24345-5. R=3; I=3.

Annie becomes a spy while British soldiers use her house as headquarters in Philadelphia during 1777. She risks her life to take a message to General Washington at Valley Forge, but she and her family realize that they must endure their separation from each other and place themselves in danger for a greater good--defeating the British. "Her Story" series.

Jensen, Dorothea. *The Riddle of Penncroft Farm.* San Diego: Harcourt Brace 1989. 0-15-200574-9, 180p. Paper (Odyssey), 1991. 0-15-266908-6, 242p. R=3; I=5.

After moving to the Philadelphia area from Minnesota, Lars, eleven and lonely, finds himself being visited by a family ghost who lived during the Revolutionary War, in this historical fantasy. He learns about the time and the roles of ancestors of families still living in the area during the *first* American civil war as his "shade" calls it, and learns a lot about himself. History becomes muddled as the years pass, and only careful research can help one begin to find the truth about events and people.

Moore, Ruth Nulton. *Distant Thunder: A Sequel to the Christmas Surprise.* Illus. Allan Eitzen. Scottdale, PA: Herald, 1991. Paper, 0-8361-3557-1, 160p. R=6; I=6.

In 1777, Kate, fifteen, lives with her aunt in Bethlehem, Pennsylvania, while her parents serve as Moravian missionaries in the outlying areas. The town becomes both a hospital for wounded Continental Army soldiers including the Marquis de Lafayette and a prison for British Hessian soldiers. Kate and her cousin rescue an escaped Hessian and help nurse him back to health in the non-violent Moravian tradition. The events make 1777 a painful year, but Kate's mother becomes reunited with her long-lost brother who had been adopted by the Seneca tribe. People of all races and faiths can live together if they accept each other as human beings.

O'Dell, Scott. *Sarah Bishop.* Boston: Houghton Mifflin, 1980. 0-395-29185-2. Paper, New York: Scholastic (Point), 1991. 0-590-44651 7, 240p. R 3; I=0.

Having lost her family of three during 1776, Sarah Bishop eludes the British who think she started a fire from which she was actually trying to escape. She flees, cuts her hair, finds a cave, and learns to survive in the wild. Although one may long for companionship, if people befriend on their terms rather than meeting equally, solitude may be a more satisfying choice.

Rinaldi, Ann. *A Ride into Morning: The Story of Tempe Wick.* San Diego: Gulliver, 1991. 0-15-200573-0, 289p. R=3; I=7.

Tempe Wick, twenty-two, hates the war in 1781 and only enjoys riding her horse which soldiers decide that they can use. Mary, fourteen, meets Henry, Tempe's estranged brother, in a camp, and Henry creates a way for Tempe to keep her horse. Tempe has to decide if she will tell her mother that Henry is alive rather than dead has she has told her previously. War often forces people to make decisions based on insufficient knowledge or unstable circumstances.

Rinaldi, Ann. *Time Enough for Drums.* New York: Holiday, 1986. 0-8234-0603, 249p. Paper, Mahwah, NJ: Troll, 1989. 0-8167-1269-7. R=4; I=9.

During the Revolutionary War in Trenton, New Jersey, Jem waits for her sixteenth birthday, hating the lessons she must endure with her harsh but handsome tutor, a despised Tory. What she soon finds, however, is that he actually spies for the Americans and is in love with her. His love helps her cope with the deaths in her family and her haughty, deceitful sister, married to a British officer. Choices made during war rarely resolve a situation, but one must always make them according to one's convictions.

Steele, William O. *The Buffalo Knife.* San Diego: Harcourt Brace, 1990 (1952). Paper (Odyssey), 0-15-213212-0. R=4; I=4.

In 1782, Andy, nine, loses the knife his uncle gives him, at the beginning of his family's flatboat journey down the Tennessee River. The family survives the arduous journey including the white water rapids and the Chickamauga Indians shooting at them with flame and flint arrows supplied by the British. Feelings of guilt for being irresponsible often seem more distressing than an unrelated serious physical danger.

Steele, William O. *Flaming Arrows.* Illus. Paul Galdone. Magnolia, MA: Peter Smith, 1992 (1958). 0-8446-6506-1. Paper, San Diego: Harcourt Brace (Odyssey), 1990. 0-15-228427-3, 146p. R=5; I=5.

Chad, eleven, and fellow settlers assemble in the nearby fort when Chickamaugas make their 1784 autumn raid on Cumberland. Although the people accuse one boy's father of betraying them to the Indians, the boy risks his life for people inside the fort during the battle. A child does not necessarily have the same values as a father, especially if the father has compromised the safety of a community for his own benefit.

Steele, William O. *Winter Danger*. Illus. Paul Galdone. Magnolia, MA: Peter Smith, 1992 (1954). 0-8446-6508-8. Paper, San Diego: Harcourt Brace, 1990. 0-685-02109-2, 131p. R=5; I=5.

In the 1780's, Caje's woodsman father takes him to his aunt's home for the winter. Concerned about eating the family's meager food supply, Caje, eleven, leaves, but soon returns with a bear he discovered hibernating and shot to feed them for the rest of the winter. One may benefit oneself through concern for others.

Tripp, Valerie. *Meet Felicity: An American Girl*. Illus Dan Andreasen. Mankato, MN: Pleasant Company, 1991. 1-56247-003-5. Paper, 1-56247-004-3, 69p. R=4; I=4.

Felicity loves horses, and in 1774 in Williamsburg, Virginia, she rises very early every morning to make friends with the beautiful horse owned by a nasty man who beats and starves it. Since he will not sell the horse, she decides to help it go free by jumping it over a fence. Sometimes one must make decisions that seem to be breaking the law in order to protect something or someone from evil intentions. "The American Girls Collection."

Turner, Ann. *Katie's Trunk*. Illus. Ronald Himler. New York: Macmillan, 1992. 0-02-789512-2, 32p. R=3; I=3.

At the beginning of disagreements with the British over taxes leading to the American Revolution, Katie's family is branded as "Tory." When rebels ransack her house, she hides in her mother's wedding trunk. When her friend's father, a rebel, feels her under the clothes, he diverts the other men and tells no one about her presence. In a war, many persons on either side are neither good nor bad; they only have differing opinions.

Wibberley, Leonard. *John Treegate's Musket*. Magnolia MA: Peter Smith, 1992 (1959). 0-8446-6655-6. Paper, New York: Farrar, Straus & Giroux (Sunburst), 1986. 0-374-43788-2, 224p. R=6; I=7.

Peter Treegate becomes an apprentice in 1769 and soon has to protect himself from another apprentice whom he watches

commit a murder. Shipwrecked during his escape, Peter washes
ashore in South Carolina, where Maclaren, an exiled Scot who
fought at Culloden in 1746, rescues him. Peter's amnesia
thwarts his return to Boston until 1775 at the beginning of the
American Revolution. Help often comes from unlikely sources.
*Southern California Council on Literature for Children and
Young People's Awards: Excellence in a Series.*

Wibberley, Leonard. *Peter Treegate's War*. New York: Farrar,
Straus & Giroux, 1960. 60-9229, 156p. R=7; I=7.**

Fighting with Maclaren rather than his estranged father,
Peter, first in *John Treegate's Musket*, now sixteen, becomes
imprisoned on a British warship but escapes. His fate becomes
more connected to Maclaren's when he recognizes a picture of
Maclaren's clan's tara in the home of a British soldier whom
Peter forces to surrender. Sometimes one may feel stronger
emotional ties to a person outside one's family.

Wibberley, Leonard. *Sea Captain from Salem*. New York:
Farrar, Straus & Giroux, 1961. 61-6967, 186p. R=6; I=7.**

Peace of God Manly sails to Paris to tell Benjamin Franklin
about the surrender at Saratoga. He tries to capture British
ships in the English channel. He is captured instead, but
escapes, and his exploits help France's leaders decide to fight
for the Americans against the British in 1778. A brave person
challenges only those who might be an equal or a better, but
never a lesser, competitor.

Wibberley, Leonard. *Treegate's Raiders*. New York: Farrar,
Straus & Giroux, 1962. 62-9528, 218p. R=6; I=7.**

Peter, twenty-one, after surviving situations in *John
Treegate's Musket* and *Peter Treegate's War*, meets George
Washington, who in 1780, is distressed at Benedict Arnold's
treason and thinks the war will be won in the cities, Peter
thinks, however, that the American Revolution will be won on
the frontier. Peter leads his men into battles along the frontier
at King's Mountain, Tennessee. After being captured and
rescued, he journeys to Yorktown for the British surrender.
Sometimes people who seem to be loyal to a cause may be more
concerned about their own interests than those of their
colleagues; others will fight for their friends until death.

1784-1814

Avi. *Something's Upstairs: A Tale of Ghosts.* New York: Orchard/Watts, 1988. 0-531-08382-9, 120p. Paper, New York: Avon, 1990. 0-380-70853-1, 128p. R=3; I=4.

In this historical fantasy, Kenny's family moves from California to Providence, Rhode Island, into a house dating from 1792. When he sees the ghost of a slave rising out of a stain in the floor of his bedroom closet, he becomes involved in solving the boy's murder in 1800. Only by changing the memory can the ghost be freed from the room.

Collier, James Lincoln, and Christopher Collier. *The Clock.* Illus. Kelly Maddox. New York: Delacorte, 1992. 0-385-30037-9, 162p. R=3; I=8.**

In 1810, Annie's father decides that she, at fifteen, will go to work in the local mill instead of becoming the school teacher that she prefers, because he needs money to pay for his spendthrift ways. The mill overseer propositions her, and when she rebuffs him, he manages to murder her crippled friend by having him climb up the frozen waterwheel to free it from the ice. When people become pawns for the foibles of others, survival at any cost becomes their major goal.

Collier, Christopher and James. *Jump Ship to Freedom.* New York: Delacorte, 1981. 0-385-28484-5, 192p. Paper, New York: Dell (Yearling), 1987. 0-440-44323-7, 192p. R=5; I=6.

In 1787, Daniel retrieves money his dead father earned as a soldier that his master, Ivers, has claimed from his mother. Daniel jumps from Ivers' ship in the West Indies where Ivers plans to sell him. Soon after, Daniel returns to Philadelphia, and there he encounters General Washington and Alexander Hamilton. He learns about lying at all levels of politics, but one honest man saves his soldier's notes (money) for him so that he can buy his and his mother's freedom.

Collier, Christopher and James. *Who Is Carrie?* New York: Delacorte, 1984. 0-385-29295-3, 192p. Paper, New York: Dell, 1987. 0-440-49536-9. R=6; I=6.

Captain Ivers tries to detain Carrie in 1785, but she escapes to Sam Fraunces, who then takes her with him to be George Washington's steward. Eventually, they reconstruct the family's situation and understand that Carrie is Willy's (*War Comes to Willy Freeman*) younger sister, and therefore, free. When one lacks freedom, one is vulnerable to the whims of unscrupulous people.

Collier, Christopher and James. *The Winter Hero.* New York: Scholastic, 1978. Paper, 0-590-42604-4, 153p. R=4; I=8.

Soldiers fighting in the Revolutionary War return to New England, where increasing taxes distresses them because they have less money for necessities. Justin, fourteen, becomes involved in Shay's 1787 Rebellion against the wealthy wanting to take property for payment, and the only time he stops fleeing is to try to save his brother-in-law. Seemingly inconsequential actions make people heroes in the eyes of others, but what people know and admit about themselves is more realistic.

Fleischman, Paul. *Coming-and-Going Men.* Illus. Randy Gaul. New York: HarperCollins, 1985. 0-06-021884-3, 147p. R=6; I=7.

Four stories of 1800 centered around New Canaan, Vermont, present a shadow man who prides himself on reading character in silhouettes, a chandler who kills crows and represses his misdeed, a painter who decides to forego illusion after a July 4th experience, and a peddler of dyes and essences. They all deal with illusion and the unknown, illustrating that humans sometimes respond to situations in the ways that they do not anticipate.

Fleischman, Paul. *Path of the Pale Horse.* New York: HarperCollins, 1983. 160p. 0-06-021905-X, 147p. Paper (Trophy), 1992. 0-06-440442-0. R=4; I=8.

In 1793, Lep Nye's sister goes to Philadelphia to help a man who has been a family benefactor for twenty years. When Clara does not write, Lep goes to find her in the city which is undergoing a yellow fever epidemic and discovers various frauds. Disappointed at his failure to save friends, Lep, as many people might, pledges himself to find as many medical cures as possible.

Greeson, Janet. *An American Army of Two.* Illus. Patricia Rose Mulvihill. Minneapolis, MN: Carolrhoda, 1991. 0-87614-664-7, 48p. Paper, 0-87614-547-0. R=3; I=3.

In 1812, on the coast of Massachusetts, Rebecca and Abigail see British ships in the harbor. When they hide behind a tree playing "Yankee Doodle" on a fife and drum, they trick the British into thinking the American troops are marching, and the ships leave. Ingenuity coupled with bravery can sometimes be an effective way to mislead an enemy. "On My Own Book."

Lyons, Mary E. *Letters from a Slave Girl: The Story of Harriet Jacobs.* New York: Scribner's, 1992. 0-684-19446-5, 146p. R=7; I=7.

Harriet, a slave girl of twelve in 1825 living in North Carolina, knows how to read and teaches herself how to write by wording letters to her deceased mother. Her new master, after her old one's death, angles to seduce her without his wife's knowledge, but he never quite succeeds. Harriet has to endure other degradations as she bears children and becomes separated from members of her family before she gains her freedom. The hardships some people must face when controlled by those with no compassion are difficult to comprehend.

McPhail, David, writer/illus. *Farm Boy's Year.* New York: Atheneum, 1992. 0-689-31679-8, 32p. R=4; I=2.

A boy in Maine, in the 1800's, lives his twelfth year helping his parents and enjoying himself with his friends. He sees his father saw ice blocks from the pond to sell in summer. He makes maple syrup, forges a scythe, goes swimming in the same pond during summer, marches in the Fourth of July parade, picks apples, and shoots a goose for Thanksgiving. The pleasures of people in all ages often correlate to their feelings of accomplishment.

Manson, Ainslie. *A Dog Came, Too.* Illus. Anne Blades. New York: McElderry, 1993. 0-689-50567-1, 32p. R=4; I=2.

When Alexander Mackensie travels with friends across the land now known as America in 1793, Our Dog follows him, warning the group of wild animal dangers along the way. Although the group loses Our Dog, he searches for it along a river across country and eventually reunites with its members on their return from the Pacific Ocean. Sometimes humans seem to think that they understand and can communicate with their dogs; perhaps they can.

Morrow, Barbara, writer/illus. *Help for Mr. Peale.* New York: Macmillan, 1990. 0-02-767590-4, 32p. R=7; I=2.

When Rubens is ten in 1794, his father, the painter and naturalist Charles Wilson Peale, decides to move the family to a new house in Philadelphia, which will become a museum. He and his brothers, Rembrandt, Titian, and Raphaelle, pack all of the items except very large ones. Rubens realizes that carrying them in a parade to the new house will entertain the neighbors. Solving problems takes time; careful thought often works.

Roesch, Ethel & Paul. *Ashana.* New York: Random, 1990. 0-394-56963-3, 404p. Paper, New York: Ballantine, 1991. 0-345-37298-0. R=7; I=10+.

In the 1790's, when Russian fur traders come to Alaska, one of them takes Ashana, fifteen, as his mistress, unconcerned that she is already married. Ashana bears him two children but continues to see her husband secretly until he is killed. Ashana refuses to deny her heritage and teaches it to her children. Using guns to conquer people can gain control of people's bodies but not of their minds or of their spirits.

Sanders, Scott R. *Aurora Means Dawn.* Illus. Jill Kastner. New York: Bradbury, 1989. 0-02-778270-0, 32p. R=7; I=4.

A family with seven children leaves its home in Connecticut in 1800 to travel to cheap land in Aurora, Ohio. A terrible storm blocks the way, but with the help of people two towns away, they get their wagon freed from fallen trees and continue their journey. One must make sacrifices for a better life.

Sanders, Scott R. *Bad Man Ballad*. New York: Bradbury, 1986. 0-02-778230-1, 241p. R=5; I=7.

In 1813 in the Ohio valley, Eli, a young girl, and a lawyer search for the giant who killed a dwarf when he threatened the girl while the dwarf thought no one else was around. What Eli finds in the giant is a gentle, kind man without speech whom Eli knows needs protection. When all that people have are clues and no facts, they often make the wrong conclusions.

Shub, Elizabeth. *Cutlass in the Snow*. Illus. Rachel Isadora. New York: Greenwillow, 1986. 0-688-05928-7, 48p. R=4; I=3.

In 1797, Sam and his grandfather sail to Fire Island, rumored to be a pirate haven, off Long Island, New York, to pick Christmas holly and see the unusual land and tree formations. After staying overnight because of a snowstorm and seeing unidentified lights, they find a chest of gold coins the next day. Sometimes, although rarely, one may find something very valuable.

Wibberley, Leonard. *The Last Battle*. New York: Farrar, Straus & Giroux, 1976. 0-374-34349-7, 198p. R=3; I=7.**

Manly Treegate, in 1812, captains a ship sailing to New Orleans on the eve of a war between the British and the French. His uncle Peter escapes problems in Spain, and they reunite in New Orleans after horrible and unnecessary slaughter of the British. When one tries to serve a greater cause than oneself, one's life becomes worthwhile.

Wibberley, Leonard. *Leopard's Prey*. New York: Farrar, Straus & Giroux, 1971. 0-374-3-4378-0, 184p. R=6; I=6.**

When Peter Treegate's nephew Manly, thirteen, sails near Norfolk one day in 1807, a British ship captures him and impresses him into service. Peter's friendship with an escaped Haitian slave leads to Manly's rescue and return to Boston. If one is kind to all people, that kindness may be unexpectedly and happily reciprocated at a later time.

Wibberley, Leonard. *Red Pawns*. Magnolia, MA: Peter Smith, 1992 (1973). 0-8446-6558-4. 183p. R=5; I=7.

At eighteen in 1811, Manly Treegate listens to his uncle Peter when he warns him that Indian tribes will become "red pawns" in the battle to keep the American boundary east of the Ohio River. Manly goes to the frontier, and after getting help from a guide, he finds how to defeat the Indians. But the two sides declare war anyway. One needs to understand the differences between cultures in order to solve problems rather than become assertive and declare that one's own way is the best and only solution.

1815-1845

Anderson, Joan. *Christmas on the Prairie.* Photos by George Ancona. New York: Clarion, 1985. 0-89919-307-2, 48p. R=7; I=4.

In 1836, the Curtis children look forward to Christmas in their new home but worry about it since the school master refuses to cancel school on Christmas Eve, a heathen celebration. But they take cookies to the neighbors and Christmas morning, they find presents in their stockings and their father's wooden shoes. As long as people and freedom are present, Christmas can be observed.

Avi. *The True Confessions of Charlotte Doyle.* New York: Orchard/Watts, 1990. 0-531-08493-0, 215p. Paper, New York: Avon, 1992. 0-380-71475-2, 240p. R=3; I=6.

In 1832, Charlotte, thirteen, sails on the *Seahawk* from England to Rhode Island to join her family. On board as the only passenger, she finds herself in the midst of intrigue and a murder for which she is accused. When she reaches home after the developments on her voyage, she cannot adjust to the restrictions put on her by her family and returns to the sea. *Newbery Honor,* 1991; *Boston Globe–Horn Book Award,* 1991; *Golden Kite Award,* 1990; *Judy Lopez Memorial Award,* 1991.

Blos, Joan. *A Gathering of Days.* New York: Scribner, 1979. 0-684-16340-3, 144p. Paper, New York: Macmillan, 1990. 0-689-71419-X, 160p. R=7; I=7.

From 1830-1832, the New Englander Catherine Cabott keeps a journal of her fourteenth year during which one friend dies; another goes to Lowell, Massachusetts, to become a factory worker; her widowed father remarries; and she aids a runaway slave. Her emotional stability in coping with these changes and her growing maturity permeate the entries. She shows her belief that something worth doing is worth doing well and that a life unchanging becomes stagnant. *Newbery Medal,* 1980.

Blos, Joan. *Brothers of the Heart.* New York: Scribner's, 1985. 0-684-18452-4, 176p. Paper, New York: Macmillan (Aladdin), 1993. 0-689-71724-5. R=4; I=9.

His legs crippled, Shem is unable to handle physical tasks, but his strong clerical abilities support him in 1837-38. When he cannot walk with his employer through the deep Canadian snow, an old Indian woman, left to die by her tribe, finds and helps him. When he returns to his home, his innocent recounting of his experiences make him a hero, and those who once shunned him realize that visible disabilities in no way reflect his strength of character.

Brady, Philip. *Reluctant Hero: A Snowy Road to Salem in 1802.* New York: Walker, 1990. 0-8027-6974-8, 159p. R=2; I=7.

After his father breaks his leg, Cutting, although only thirteen, must make a two-week journey through snow with sled and oxen from New Hampshire to Salem, Massachusetts, to sell shingles and furs so that his family can have food. He saves a young girl from the unwanted advances of a nasty brute, and the man pursues him until they face each other within two days' journey from Cutting's home. Even though the consequences may be painful, people often try to help those being threatened by others. "Walker American History" series.

Carrick, Carol. *The Elephant in the Dark.* Illus. Donald Carrick. New York: Clarion, 1988. 0-89919-757-4, 135p. Paper, New York: Scholastic, 1990. 0-590-42995-7. R=4; I=4.

Although at first fearful of the strange animal, young Will learns to care for an elephant left in Cadbury, Massachusetts, in the 1800's. Orphaned after his mother dies, he becomes despondent when his employer sells the elephant, so he decides to leave. Will's employer understands his attachment to the elephant and gives him money and wishes him good luck for his journey to find it.

Carrick, Carol. *Stay Away from Simon!* Illus. Donald Carrick. New York: Clarion, 1985. 0-89919-343-9. Paper, 0-89919-849-X, 64p. R=5; I=4.

When Simon appears at school, Lucy, eleven, in the 1800's, is fearful of him because of his slow wits. Trying to escape from him during a snow storm after school, she becomes lost. When Simon finds and saves Lucy and her brother, Lucy realizes that

Simon only wants her to know that he can finally count to ten. Listening to tales of others rather than getting to know them personally can create serious errors in judgement.

DeFelice, Cynthia. *Weasel.* New York: Macmillan, 1990. 0-02-726457-2, 119p. Paper, New York: Avon (Camelot). 0-380-71358-6. R=3; I=4.

A strange man, later identified as Ezra, arrives at Nathan's cabin in 1839, shows him his dead mother's locket, and leads him to his father who is almost dying from gangrene. When Nathan, eleven, and his sister hear the story of what happened, and after Nathan escapes from the nasty man Weasel who caused his father's and Ezra's pain, he has to deal with his feelings of hatred. Killing an amoral person may get rid of the person, but the murderer loses by taking another person's life.

De Hartog, Jan. *The Peculiar People.* New York: Pantheon, 1992. 0-679-41636-6, 319p. R=8; I=10+.

By 1834, the United States calvary has begun removing Native Americans from their hunting grounds including the Mahanoy Indians, and Quakers have become abolitionists, starting stations along the Underground Railroad. During this time, the Quakers have disagreements among themselves about the appropriateness of their support for the Indians and the slaves, but two people remind them of their commitment to equality, and eventually forty of them leave their homes in Pendle Hill, Pennsylvania, to go to Kansas and build a school on the Mahanoy reservation. What makes life worth living is the pleasure of helping others in need.

Fox, Paula. *The Slave Dancer.* Illus. Eros Keith. New York: Bradbury, 1982 (1973). 0-02-735560-8, 192p. Paper, New York: Dell (Yearling), 1991. 0-440-40402-9. R=4; I=6.

Slavers capture Jessie, thirteen, in 1840 and take him on board a ship in New Orleans bound for Africa to purchase slaves from black African *cabocieros* because he can play the fife for the slaves to dance and exercise. Horrified by the situation, and powerless, he barely copes. When the ship wrecks, only Jessie and one of the slaves survive; Jessie never listens to music again. That some humans have the ability to sacrifice other humans for money, including their own race and culture, can never be understood. *Newbery Medal,* 1974.

Fritz, Jean. *Brady.* Illus. Lynd Ward. New York: Puffin, 1987 (1960). Paper, 0-14-032258-2, 223p. R=3; I=5.

After Brady accidentally finds a site for Underground Railway transfers in 1836, he rushes home to tell his parents, and they refute his claim, telling him not to spread such foolish stories. After his minister father is injured in a fire, Brady helps his uncle transport slaves to another station without telling his father. When his father hears, he writes in the family Bible that Brady has completed a man's job. People must weigh what they say about others because they may be unwittingly jeopardizing that person's safety.

Fritz, Jean. *The Cabin Faced West.* Illus. Feodor Rojankovsky. New York: Coward McCann, 1958. 0-698-20016-0, 124p. Paper, New York: Puffin, 1987. 0-14-032256-6. R=7; I=4.

Ann wants to return to Gettysburg in 1784 after her family moves to the West Country, beyond any of the colonies. At ten, she misses her friends and her school, but she meets a local boy who has had no schooling. He wants to learn how to write, and she teaches him. When George Washington stops at her house to eat dinner and talks about the wonder of the western settlements, she realizes that she is living in an exciting time.

Henry, Joanne L. *A Clearing in the Forest: A Story about a Real Settler Boy.* Illus. Charles Robinson. New York: Four Winds, 1992. 0-02-743671-3, 64p. R=7; I=5.

El, nine in Indianapolis during 1833, dislikes his school teacher so his parents send him to a boarding school in a nearby town, a change which he appreciates. But he also enjoys coming home in the summer and the experiences--some good like taking the stage to Cincinnati, and some bad, like getting caught in a tornado. People must do what they think is right in a situation regardless of the opinions of others.

Holmes, Mary Z. *See You in Heaven.* Illus. Rick Whipple. Austin, TX: Raintree/Streck-Vaughn, 1992. 0-8114-3502-4, 48p. Paper, 0-8114-6427-X. R=2; I=4.

A large slave family copes with its hard life and strives to remember its history on an Alabama plantation in 1836. Elsy, at 12, begins her "adult" work in the cotton fields just before the master sells her sister to a Texan. A strong love of family and heritage shines through the difficulties that each person faces. "History's Children" series.

Highwater, Jamake. *Legend Days*. New York: HarperCollins, 1984. 0-06-022304-9, 147p. R=7; I=7.

When Amana is ten, her parents die of the "sickness," and she has a vision of herself as a great Indian warrior. Soon she is married to her ill sister's old husband, and the two mates share a love of adventure although not the marriage bed, until buffalo trample him. The Northern Plains Indians' beliefs controlled their methods of surviving cold, heat, and disease.

Hooks, William H. *The Ballad of Belle Dorcas*. Illus. Brian Pinkney. New York: Knopf, 1990. 0-394-94645-6, 40p. R=4; I=4.

In this historical fantasy, Belle Dorcas, free issue (her father is the master and her mother a slave), wants to marry a slave, against her mother's wishes. She marries him, the master dies, and the new master prepares to sell her husband. A conjure woman gives her a potion which turns her husband into a tree during the day and back to a human at night. In times of family separation, such a trick would be a welcome foil.

Hotze, Sollace. *A Circle Unbroken*. New York: Clarion, 1988. 0-89919-733-7, 224p. Paper, 1991. 0-395-59702-1. R=4; I=9.

When Rachel, or Kata Wi to the Dakota Sioux tribe into which she was sold seven years before, is found and returned to her family in 1838, she cannot adjust to her father's refusal to hear anything about her life when she lived with the Sioux tribe. She enjoys her siblings but becomes ill and fears she too will die like her Aunt Sarah who returned home after being captured by Comanches for the same seven years. Rachel requests to return; her father finally understands that she must, but he forbids her to mention the Sioux life when she comes to visit. The Sioux perception of whole life as an unbroken circle helps Rachel understand what she must do. Life for her and her father has been broken, never to mend as either wants. *Carl Sandburg Literary Arts Awards*, 1989.

McCall, Edith S. *Message from the Mountains*. New York: Walker, 1985. 0-8027-6582-3, 122p. R=2; I=5.

Jim, fifteen, cannot find his father in the caravan which returns from Santa Fe to Franklin, Missouri, in 1826, nor any message of his whereabouts. After Jim decides not to join Kit Carson on a departing caravan because his boss breaks his leg, Jim finds a note from his father telling Jim to wait for him. When parents have only their wits and little or no education, they sometimes have to separate themselves from their children in order to earn money to support them. "Walker's American History Series for Young People."

Moeri, Louise. *Save Queen of Sheba*. New York: Dutton, 1981. 0-525-33202-2, 116p. Paper, New York: Avon (Camelot), 1990. 0-380-71154-0, 112p. R=6; I=6.

King David, twelve, and his sister, Queen of Sheba, six, survive the Sioux raid on their portion of the wagon train but afterwards cannot find their father and his wagon. Almost scalped, King David walks along the trail with Queen of Sheba, and after days of recovery and enormous effort, they become reunited with their father. Having another person for whom to care can help the caretaker.

Monjo, F. N. *The Drinking Gourd*. Illus. Fred Brenner. New York: HarperCollins, 1992 (1970). 0-06-024330-9, 64p. Paper, 1983. 0-06-444042-7. R=2; I=3.

When young Tommy misbehaves in church, his father sends him home alone. He discovers four escaped slaves in his barn who say they are following the "drinking gourd," the North Star to Canada. His father hides them in the hay wagon and takes them to the river to cross in a boat. Tommy realizes that his father is breaking the law by participating in the Underground Railway but agrees that, although the monetary reward for return of the slaves is substantial, giving humans life and freedom can have no price. "An I Can Read Book."

O'Dell, Scott. *Island of the Blue Dolphins*. Illus. Ted Lewin. Boston: Houghton Mifflin, 1990 (1960). 0-395-06962-9, 192p. Paper, New York: Dell (Yearling), 1987. 0-440-43988-4. R=6; I=6.

In the early nineteenth century, when Aleuts kill many of the men on her island and the others escape, Karana is the only human remaining after a wild dog kills her brother. She has to survive, and to do so, she has to overcome tribal taboos including one that women must not make weapons. The ingenious ways that humans cope with their circumstances cannot be overstated. *Newbery Medal*, 1961; *Southern California Council on Literature for Children and Young People Awards*, 1961; *International Board of Books for Young People*, 1962; *Friends of Children and Literature Award* (FOCAL), 1981.

Paterson, Katherine. *Lyddie.* New York: Lodestar, 1991. 0-525-67338-5, 192p. Paper, New York: Puffin, 1992. 0-14-034981-2. R=4; I=8.

In 1843, when Lyddie is thirteen, her family begins to fall apart. Her father dies, and work and worry overcome her mother. Lyddie goes to the mills in Lowell, Massachusetts, works hard, helps others who need her, and witnesses the overseer taking advantage of some of the girls by threatening to fire them if they will not comply with his sexual advances. Although she loses her job and has nowhere to go, she suddenly realizes that she has earned enough money to pay for college and that her Quaker friend back home will wait for her until she is ready to marry him. Caring for others and being cared for bring the human spirit back to life.

Raines, Kerry. *A Birthday for Blue.* Illus. Michael Hays. Niles, IL: Albert Whitman, 1989. 0-8075-0774-1, 32p. R=3; I=2.

In 1816, Blue and his family travel the Cumberland Road toward Illinois on his seventh birthday. His father plants trees for him as a birthday gift while the family shares the work on the long journey.

Rinaldi, Ann. *Wolf by the Ears.* New York: Scholastic, 1991. 0-590-43413-6, 252p. Paper, 0-590-43412-8. R=2; I=8.

Harriet Hemings, possible daughter of Thomas Jefferson, born into slavery, keeps a diary from 1819 when she is eighteen until she leaves Monticello to help her people by separating from them and passing as white. Although never acknowledged by Jefferson as his daughter, Harriet looks like him and has benefit of being educated at his expense. Often people have to do things differently to help people other than themselves.

Shura, Mary Francis. *Kate's Book.* New York: Scholastic, 1989. Paper, 0-590-42381-9, 204p. R=4; I=5.*

In 1843, Kate's father decides to move her family to Oregon. Her older brother prefers to stay and study medicine, but Kate, at eleven, finds a friend in the wagon train who helps her endure the long, difficult journey. An interesting perspective concerns women and children who wanted to stay at home but were obligated to follow their husbands and fathers to find land. Males and females sometimes have different dreams, but they need each other to help them come true.

Shura, Mary Francis. *Kate's House.* New York: Scholastic, 1990. Paper, 0-590-42380-0, 183p. R=4; I=4.

In the sequel to *Kate's Book*, Kate and her family arrive in Oregon in 1843. They have to learn to cope with the animals lurking in the night and the need to quickly build a house. Kate's friend's brother disappears while another brother dies from falling off a horse before they find out that Kate's mother will have a baby to bless their new home. The hardships of the wagon train only served as preparation for the difficulty of setting up new homes for those who went west; only by helping each other could any have survived the ordeal.

Whelan, Gloria. *Next Spring an Oriole.* Illus. Pamela Johnson. New York: Random, 1987. 0-394-99125-7, 62p. Paper, 0-394-89125-2. R=5; I=3.

Libby, ten, and her parents travel from Virginia to Michigan to settle in 1837. They help an Indian girl recover from measles by nursing her in their wagon, and her family reciprocates by bringing food to help Libby and her parents survive through the winter. To receive an unexpected reward for a good deed can be very gratifying. "A Stepping Stone Book."

Wisler, G. Clifton. *Piper's Ferry.* New York: Lodestar, 1990. 0-525-67303-2, 131p. R=4; I=5.

In 1836, Tim, fourteen, leaves his family and stepfather for Texas and relatives where he decides to stay and fight to free Texas from Mexico. Because he first feels lonely, he talks to the family's bound servant, formerly a slave, and realizes that he, Tim, has the benefit of being able to leave when he wants. War is always terrible, but one has to protect home and family from despots.

1846-1860

Ackerman, Karen. *Araminta's Paint Box.* Illus. Betsy Lewin. New York: Atheneum, 1990. 0-689-31462-0, 32p. R=8; I=3.

When Araminta's family moves from Boston to California in 1847, her paint box falls off the wagon. It undergoes a series of travels and adventures all its own until it arrives in her father's office with gold in it as payment for his treatment of a snake-bite patient.

Armstrong, Jennifer. *Steal Away.* New York: Orchard/Watts, 1992. 0-531-08583-X, 207p. R=6; I=6.

Mary, when thirteen, learns about her grandmother's experience in 1855 when, as an orphan, she escaped from her aunt and uncle's home in Virginia with the slave girl they had given her on her arrival to live with them. Mary meets the woman, a retired teacher still in Canada in 1896 who, with her grandmother, tells the story of their journey north. For people who disavowed slavery, having to be in the company of people who owned slaves but professed to be righteous Christians was painful.

Avi. *The Man Who Was Poe.* New York: Orchard/Watts, 1989. 0-531-08433-7, 208p. Paper, New York: Avon, 1989. 0-380-71192-3, 213p. R=2; I=5.

Edmund's aunt and sister disappear in Providence, Rhode Island, during 1848. The man Edmund finds to help him is a writer, a Mr. Poe, who seems to confuse the real situation with a story he is writing until Edmund, eleven, finds both his mother, gone for a year, and his sister, sailing away on a boat. In real life, the facts control the artist rather than the opposite.

Blumberg, Rhoda. *Bloomers!* Illus. Mary Morgan. New York: Bradbury, 1993. 0-02-711684-0, 32p. R=9; I=4.

Libby Miller visits Seneca Falls, New York, in 1851, wearing blousy pants, later named "bloomers," after the woman who wrote about them in a magazine called *The Lily*. Her cousin Elizabeth Cady Stanton immediately wants a pair. The men are horrified with the indecency of this apparel, but the women are delighted to have clothing in which they can more easily climb stairs and move around with greater comfort. When people want to change things, they have to ignore the disapproval of those who want things to remain the same.

Coerr, Eleanor. *Chang's Paper Pony*. Illus. Deborah Kogan Ray. New York: Harper, 1988. 0-06-021329-9, 64p. Paper (Trophy), 1993. 0-06-444163-6. R=2; I=2.

Having left China because of war, Chang and his grandfather run a hotel for gold miners near San Francisco, California, around 1850. The miners seem rude to Chang as he works and studies, but when Chang finds gold in one miner's cabin, the miner buys Chang a pony, something he has desperately wanted. "I Can Read Book." *John and Patricia Beatty Award, 1989.*

Coerr, Eleanor. *The Josefina Story Quilt*. Illus. Bruce Degen. New York: HarperCollins, 1986. 0-06-021349-3, 64p. Paper (Trophy), 1989. 0-06-444129-6. R=2; I=2.

Faith longs to take Josefina, her pet hen, on her family's wagon bound for California in 1850. When her father finally agrees, the hen saves the family valuables, including quilts, from robbers. Leaving family and familiarity can be less painful when one takes a beloved pet or toy. "An I Can Read Book."

Conlon-McKenna, Marita. *Wildflower Girl*. New York: Holiday House, 1992. 0-8234-0988-0, 173p. R=5; I=6.

In a sequel to *Under the Hawthorn Tree*, Peggy at thirteen cannot find work in Ireland and decides to go to America around 1850, although she regrets having to leave her brother and sister. After a job when her employer beats her, she secures a position as a kitchen maid in a wealthy Boston home where she works hard and begins to feel that some of the staff are her family. Beginning a new life in a new country takes courage and perseverance, and to be happy takes caring for others.

De Angeli, Marguerite. *Thee, Hannah!* New York: Doubleday, 1970 (1940). 0-385-07525-1, 96p. R=4; I=4.

In 1850, Hannah, a Quaker in Philadelphia, wants to wear pretty clothes like her friend. A runaway slave, however, tells Hannah that her Quaker bonnet identifies her as an abolitionist available to help slaves find the Underground Railway. Hannah becomes proud of her symbolic clothing.

Donahue, Marilyn Cram. *Straight Along a Crooked Road.* New York: Walker, 1985. 0-8027-6585-8, 188p. R=5; I=7.**

Luanna's father decides to leave their well-established home in Vermont in 1850 to investigate the opportunities in California. On their journey of nearly two years, including their stops for the winter, Luanna, fourteen, receives news of her best friend's death from typhoid. Her brother dies on the trail, and she falls in love. When people from different families have to live and work together, differences as well as similarities in their value systems become very obvious.

Donahue, Marilyn Cram. *The Valley in Between.* New York: Walker, 1987. 0-8027-6733-8, 227p. R=4; I=7.

At thirteen in 1857, Emmie seems to get into trouble by taking off her shoes and getting muddy, but such actions are offset by the tensions which develop in her California town. After the Mormons are called back to Utah, gold is discovered, Indians begin rampaging, and the Civil War becomes imminent. In the next few years, Emmie learns that she likes to be a part of events--from removing flood mud out of the kitchen to being appreciated by Tad, a handsome young man. People need to learn to live each day fully, not mourning for the past but by eyeing the future.

Fleischman, Paul. *The Borning Room.* New York: HarperCollins, 1991. 0-06-023785-6, 112p. Paper (Trophy), 1993. 0-06-447099-7. R=3; I=6.

Georgina tells the story of her family from the time she is nine in 1850 until nineteen, when she takes her place in the borning room for the birth of her first child. Her Ohio family of abolitionists keeps its integrity and intelligence in the face of hypocrisy. A final chapter has her reflecting on her wealth--the children and grandchildren who have entered life and left it in that one room. Allowing individuals in a family to practice their beliefs can be difficult, but it can lead to the harmony that ultimately keeps a family together. *American Library Association Notable Book for Children,* 1992; *School Library Journal "Best Book,"* 1991.

Fleischman, Sid. *Humbug Mountain.* Illus. Eric Von Schmidt. Boston: Little, Brown, 1988 (1978). Paper (Joy Street), 0-316-28613-3, 149p. R=2; I=4.

When Willy is thirteen, his family goes in search of Sunrise, the town his grandfather has founded on the Missouri River. When they find it, the river has receded, and no one lives there. Willy's father has to publish one of his newspapers with unusual stories to entice people to come. Although this story always edges fantasy, the logic never fails as each family member rises to fulfill his or her job when needed. *Boston Globe--Horn Book Award, 1979.*

Gregory, Kristiana. *The Legend of Jimmy Spoon.* San Diego: Harcourt Brace 1990. 0-15-200506-4, 164p. Paper, 1991. 0-15-243812-2. R=7; I=7.

Jimmy, twelve, bored with his life working in his Mormon father's store in 1854 in Utah, leaves with Shoshoni boys to see their mother when they promise him a horse. He does not realize that he is expected to stay with the tribe, but he has to live with them, becoming a son, until he proves his manhood and has enough respect from the tribe to make his own choice of going or staying. All people try to make life happier for those who grieve. *"Great Episodes."*

Gurasich, Marj. *Letters to Oma: A Young German Girl's Account of Her First Year in Texas, 1847.* Illus. Barbara Mathews Whitehead. Fort Worth, TX: Texas Christian, 1989. Paper, 0-87565-037-6, 161p. R=6; I=7.

When the German government threatens her professor father in 1847, Tina's family leaves for the freedom of Texas. In letters to her grandmother, Oma, during her fifteenth year, she tells of crossing the Atlantic in an over-crowded ship, killing a nine-foot panther, her first kiss, the birth of a sister, and the death of her mother. The clock Oma gave her symbolizes the love and tradition in her family. But when faced with retrieving her kidnapped sister, she quickly understands that people are much more important than possessions. *Western Heritage Awards*, 1990.

Hamilton, Virginia. *The House of Dies Drear.* Illus. Eros Keith. New York: Macmillan, 1984 (1968). 0-02-742500-2, 247p. Paper (Collier), 0-02-043520-7. R=4; I=5.

When Thomas's father takes a job teaching history at an Ohio college, his family moves into a house once owned by a wealthy abolitionist, Dies Drear, who helped 40,000 slaves at his Underground Railway station. The caretaker, Pluto, frightens the family with his secrecy, but soon Thomas and his father begin to solve the puzzle of the house with its tunnels and hidden entrances. When stories are retold often enough, they gain lives of their own, and sometimes reality is of much less magnitude than the tale. *Ohioana Book Awards*, 1969; *Edgar Allen Poe Awards*, 1969.

Holland, Cecelia. *The Bear Flag.* Boston: Houghton Mifflin, 1990. 0-395-48886-9, 422p. Paper, Windsor, NY, 1992. 1-55817-635-7. R=6; I=10+.

As the flag to proclaim California's independence rises in 1846, Cat begins to battle for its emancipation from those like Kit Carson and John Frémont who would ruin the state by gaining control over it. Cat, having become widowed during the trip to California from Boston, meets a Russian who helps her as she opposes the men and with whom she falls in love. People often have to fight for freedom in unexpected ways.

Holland, Cecelia. *Pacific Street.* Boston: Houghton Mifflin, 1992. 0-395-56144-2, 260p. R=4; I=10+.

In 1850, Mitya comes to San Francisco and meets the voluptuous blonde Daisy, the tiny black Mammy, and Gil. They work to make The Shining Light, a saloon, successful after Mitya helps build it. As the lawlessness of San Francisco rises and vigilantes sweep the city, Mammy tries to kill Gil in order to keep Daisy at the saloon, but Mitya saves him so they can all escape. People sometimes become successful by manipulating others to gain control.

Hoobler, Dorothy and Thomas. *Next Stop, Freedom: The Story of a Slave Girl.* Illus. Cheryl Hanna. Englewood Cliffs, NJ: Silver-Burdett, 1991. 0-382-24145-2, 55p. Paper, 0-382-24347-1. R=2; I=3.

Emily, ten, and her brother Isaiah, sold away from their parents, escape from their master with Harriet Tubman, "Moses," on the Underground Railway. A Quaker girl shows Emily her letters, the alphabet, because Emily was never allowed to learn to read. That some slaves were able to overcome their subjugation to the whims of other humans was a triumph. "Her Story" series.

Hoobler, Dorothy and Thomas. *Treasure in the Stream: The Story of a Gold Rush Girl.* Illus. Nancy Carpenter. Englewood Cliffs, NJ: Silver-Burdett, 1991. 0-382-24144-4, 55p. Paper, 0-382-24346-3. R=4; I=4.

Amy keeps a diary from 1848 to 1850 where she records the gold fever that hit California before it became a state. Her family rents their home from John Sutter, but when Amy finds gold, the family begins shopkeeping in San Francisco and sells the first Levi Strauss jeans. Amy's enterprising family members survive by being honest and helping both themselves and the miners. "Her Story" series.

Hopkinson, Deborah. *Sweet Clara and the Freedom Quilt.* Illus. James Ransome. New York: Knopf, 1993. 0-679-82311-5, 32p. R=3; I=3.

When Clara, eleven, hears about different places, she sews a pattern into her quilt to indicate their location, like a map. She finally sews in the boat that can take her across the Ohio River to the Underground Railway. Ingenuity can help enslaved people.

Howard, Elizabeth. *Out of Step with the Dancers.* New York: Morrow, 1978. 0-688-32141-0, 223p. R=4; I=7.**

In 1853, when Damaris is sixteen and in love with Matthew, her father decides that his family will become members of the Shaker community in New Lebanon, New York. She tries, but she can never accept being single all her life, so she returns to her hometown to live with friends. What a parent may want or decide for a family may not be best for every one of the members.

Hurmence, Brenda. *A Girl Called Boy.* New York: Clarion, 1982. 0-395-31022-9, 180p. Paper, 1990. 0-395-55698-8. R=6; I=6.**

This historical fantasy time shift involves Boy, eleven, a girl who finds herself back in 1853 where slaves think she is a runaway. When she sees the courage of the slaves, she learns to be proud of her heritage in a very short time. People need to accept their past and to build a positive future from it. *Parents' Choice Award*, 1983.

Kherdian, David. *Bridger: The Story of a Mountain Man.* New York: Greenwillow, 1987. 0-688-06510-4, 147p. R=3; I=8.

Jim Bridger, eighteen, fulfills his service as a bound-out boy and joins an expedition going up the Mississippi River into the wilderness to trap furs. He discovers his love of the mountains, and while looking for beaver, a great salt lake. When people have a chance to follow their dreams, they are often satisfied with the choice.

Kroll, Steven. *Mary McLean and the St. Patrick's Day Parade.* Illus. Michael Dooling. New York: Scholastic, 1991. 0-590-43701-1, 32p. R=7; I=3.

After Mary McLean and her family make the grueling eight-week journey to America from Ireland in 1849 during the potato famine, she finds out about the St. Patrick's Day parade in New York. In a mixture of fact and fantasy, she meets a leprechaun who promises to help her find the perfect shamrock she needs in order to ride with Mr. Finnegan in the parade.

The positive family values override the hardships of the Irish immigrants through storytelling and love.

Lampman, Evelyn Sibley. *White Captives*. New York: Atheneum, 1975. 0-689-50023-8, 181p. R=4; I=5.**

In 1851, Olive's family begins the journey from Illinois to New Mexico, but only Olive, twelve, and her little sister survive when Apaches ambush their lone wagon, killing the others in retaliation for whites who murdered members of their tribe, and taking their belongings. The two become white slaves to the Apaches. Olive's frail sister dies before their master decides to trade Olive to the whites for a horse. The belief that one must kill to gain power will always threaten peace.

Lasky, Katherine. *Beyond the Divide*. New York: Macmillan, 1983. 0-02-751670-9, 264p. Paper, New York: Dell (Laurel Leaf), 1986. 0-440-91021-8. R=7; I=10.

In 1849, Meribah and her father, shunned by the Holly Springs, Pennsylvania, Amish community, leave the rest of the family for the West. Their group of wagons includes unsavory people who refuse to respect the rights of others. Meribah learns about herbs to treat illness. After the train leaves her father and her behind, she learns about survival from Yani (Mill Creek) Indians. Faith and belief in things unseen may help one to accept or at least overcome disappointment. *Best Book for Young Adults*, 1983; *American Library Association Notable Book*, 1983; *National Council of Teachers of English Recommended Book*, 1983.

McGraw. Eloise. *Moccasin Trail*. New York: Puffin, 1986 (1952). 0-14-032170-5, 256p. R=5; I=7.

After a bear mauls him at age twelve, the Crow tribe adopts Jim, and he spends six years counting "coup" (the number of whites scalped) and wearing eagle feathers like a young brave. When he encounters his younger siblings at a nearby white settlement, they tell him they need his signature for land in Willamette Valley, Oregon, since their parents have died on the trail. Their mutual mistrust eventfully fades when each realizes that the other has abilities and talents that they all need to succeed. When a person's expectation of another is unfulfilled, learning to accept the other person is often difficult. *Newbery Honor*, 1952; *Junior Literary Guild Selection*; *Lewis Carroll Shelf Award*, 1963.

MacLachlan, Patricia. *Sarah, Plain and Tall.* New York: HarperCollins, 1985. 0-06-024102-0, 64p. Paper (Trophy), 0-06-440205-3, 1987. R=3; I=3.

Left motherless at birth, Caleb and his sister Anna welcome Sarah from Maine, the woman who answers their father's advertisement for a wife. Fearful that she will leave them after the one-month trial visit, Caleb listens for the "future" in everything she says. Although Sarah longs for the sea, she says that she will miss the family more, so she stays. *Newbery Medal*, 1986; *Scott O'Dell Award for Historical Fiction*, 1986; *Golden Kite Award*, 1986; *Christopher Award*, 1986; *Jefferson Cup Award*, 1986; *International Board of Books for Young People*, 1988; *Garden State Children's Book Awards*, 1988; *American Library Association Notable Book for Children*, 1985; *School Library Journal "Best Book,"* 1985.

MacLachlan, Patricia. *Skylark.* New York: HarperCollins, 1994. 0-06-023333-8, 80p. R=3; I=3.

Anna and Caleb are happy that Sarah, who came from Maine to the prairie to meet their father in *Sarah, Plain and Tall*, marries him and becomes their new mother. The ensuing drought renews their concerns that she might return to Maine, and she does; however, she takes them with her. When someone begins loving another, being with that person becomes more important than any other aspect of life.

Morpurgo, Michael. *Twist of Gold.* New York: Viking, 1993. 0-670-84851-4, 246p. R=5; I=7.

Around 1850, when the plague begins spreading through Ireland, a kind British soldier gives Sean, fourteen, and Annie, eleven, money to sail to America to look for their father. Leaving their dying mother, they find help from several people in their travels from Boston to California, but twice they lose and regain the O'Brien family symbol, a golden torque, before they find their father and their mother, thought dead, at the end of their journey. People need the help of others to accomplish something that would be impossible for them to achieve alone.

Morris, Neil and Ting. *Featherboy and the Buffalo.* Illus. Anna Clarke. Englewood Cliffs NJ: Silver Burdett, 1985. 0-382-06890-4, 21p. R=6; I=3.**

Featherboy, a Sioux too young to hunt, follows three crows as they fly to the cliffs, and there he spies buffalo in the distance for his hungry tribe. He rushes back to tell his people, and they celebrate their good fortune. Even the young can help when they are given the chance.

Morrow, Barbara, writer/illus. *Edward's Portrait.* New York: Macmillan, 1991. 0-02-767591-2, 32p. R=5; I=2.

Young Edward dreads having to stand still for over a minute to have a daguerreotype taken in the mid-1800's. He succeeds, however, with the help of the photographer's stories of Indians in the west. Making a connection between the present and future is sometimes difficult.

Morrow, Honoré. *On to Oregon!* New York: Morrow, 1946 (1926). 0-688-21639-0. Paper (Beech Tree), 1991. 0-688-10494-0, 239p. R=6; I=5.

John's family leaves Missouri for Oregon in 1844 when he is thirteen. On the journey, both of his parents die, and he brings the other six children one thousand miles through snow and mountains into Oregon. When one has no choice, one learns very quickly to take responsibility.

Murrow, Liza K. *West Against the Wind.* New York: Holiday, 1987. 0-8234-0668-7, 232p. Paper, Mahwah, NJ: Troll, 1988. 0-8167-1324-3. R=4; I=7.

In 1850, Abby and her family travel from Missouri to California to join her father. At fifteen, on the trail, she matures into a young woman. After they arrive, she realizes that they had their "gold" with them all along. She merely had to cleanse herself of her superficiality through the difficulties of the trip to find out who she really was.

Nixon, Joan Lowery. *Caught in the Act: The Orphan Quartet Two.* New York: Bantam, 1988. 0-553-05443-0, 151p. Paper (Starfire), 1989. 0-553-27912-2. R=4; I=5.

After Mike parts from his sisters and brothers, he lives with the Friedrichs in Missouri--a family with a secret. The father blames Mike for several incidents on the farm which are actually the work of his son Gunter, but Mike has a chance to prove without question that Gunter is the culprit before he moves to another place. Beating older children only creates children afraid of adults rather than repentant for supposed misdeeds.

Nixon, Joan Lowery. *A Deadly Promise.* New York: Bantam, 1992. 0-553-08054-7, 169p. Paper, 1993. 0-553-56177-4. R=7; I=8.

Sarah, seventeen, follows her father into the west from Chicago in *High Trail to Danger* during the nineteenth century and finds him just before someone murders him. In this sequel, her sister joins her after Sarah discovers that her father had uncovered a scheme where powerful and wealthy men had been defrauding the illiterate silver miners in town. The men involved had him killed. Sarah exposes their crimes. Doing what is right often takes courage.

Nixon, Joan Lowery. *A Family Apart: The Orphan Train Quartet One.* New York: Bantam, 1987. 0-553-05432-5, 163p. Paper (Starfire), 1988. 0-553-27478-3. R=4; I=6.

Frances, years later, tells her granddaughter of the time when she was thirteen in 1860. Frances and her five brothers and sisters leave their widowed and destitute mother in New York City for St. Joseph, Missouri, to be adopted along with other Children's Aid Society orphans. In order to protect her youngest brother by being placed with him, Frances cuts her hair and pretends to be a "Frankie". Her hard work and bravery in transporting slaves along the Underground Railway for her new family help her begin to understand her mother's sacrifice and keep her welcome in her new family even as a female. *Western Writers of America Spur Award*, 1987.

Nixon, Joan Lowery. *In the Face of Danger: The Orphan Train Quartet Three.* New York: Bantam, 1988. 0-553-05490-2, 152p. Paper (Starfire), 1989. 0-553-28196-8. R=5; I=5.

Megan, twelve, goes to Ben and Emma's house in Kansas territory, unhappy to be separated from the rest of her family and blaming herself for all their problems. She shows her bravery, however, when she saves the neighbors and Emma from a known killer by cajoling him to use his ammunition as he displays his marksmanship in hitting targets she names. Making excuses to hide behind when things go wrong rarely helps one to overcome one's fears. *Western Writers of America Spur Award,* 1988.

Nixon, Joan Lowery. *A Place to Belong: The Orphan Train Quartet Four.* New York: Bantam, 1989. 0-553-05803-7, 149p. Paper (Starfire), 1990. 0-553-28485-1. R=7; I=6.

After Danny and Peg's foster mother dies around 1860, Danny coerces his foster father Alfrid to bring his own mother west from New York City and marry her. The situation does not work as Danny would like, but everyone is happy with the arrangements that do result. One has to do what is generally best for oneself as long as it does not hurt someone else.

O'Dell, Scott. *The Dark Canoe.* Illus. Milton Johnson. Boston: Houghton Mifflin, 1968. 0-395-06960-2, 160p. R=7; I=9.

In the mid-nineteenth century, Nathan, sixteen, goes with his brother Caleb, obsessed by Ahab in Herman Melville's *Moby Dick,* to Baja, California, to search for a ship sunk when Caleb was its captain. They find that the Indians worshipped their dead blond brother and that he probably disobeyed Caleb's orders for steering the ship by heading ashore instead to search for gold. People who only seek wealth seem to destroy anything or anyone that blocks their path.

O'Dell, Scott. *Zia.* Illus. Ted Lewin. Boston: Houghton Mifflin, 1976. 0-395-24393-9, 224p. Paper, New York: Dell (Laurel Leaf), 1978. 0-440-99904-9, 144p. R=4; I=6.

In the sequel to *Island of the Blue Dolphins,* Karana's niece Zia tries to rescue her, is captured, escapes, and finally convinces a captain at the Santa Barbara mission to bring Karana from her island. Although Zia and Karana have difficulty communicating, Zia understands that Karana dislikes the mission rules and misses her home. When a person has been functioning successfully alone, having to undergo a dramatic change in lifestyle may be fatal.

Olson, Arielle. *The Lighthouse Keeper's Daughter.* Boston: Little, Brown, 1987. 0-316-65053-6, 32p. R=4; I=3.

In the 1850's, Miranda keeps the island lighthouse's fourteen lamps lit with whale oil during a blizzard while her father is stranded ashore. The fisherman reward her heroic efforts with gifts of dirt for her to plant summer flowers on the rocky terrain. *Friends of American Writers Juvenile Book Merit Award,* 1988.

Paulsen, Gary. *Nightjohn.* New York: Delacorte, 1993. 0-385-30838-8, 92p. R=3; I=7.

When Sarny is twelve in the 1850's, a new slave comes to the plantation and begins to teach her letters. When her master sees her write "bag" in the dirt, he harnesses the woman who looks after her to a cart and beats her for not pulling him fast enough and then cuts two toes off the man who confesses teaching the word to Sarny. The wounded man escapes but returns during the night to continue teaching Sarny to read. People who have to endure the cruelty of others can only be pleased when one of them outwits the cruelty.

Roop, Peter and Connie. *Keep the Lights Burning, Abbie.* Illus. Peter E. Hanson. Minneapolis, MI: Carolrhoda, 1985. 0-87614-275-7, 40p. Paper, 0-87614-454-7. R=1; I=1.

When Abbie's father goes to the mainland for food and medicine, a storm rises which keeps him from returning in one day. His young daughter Abbie, in 1853, keeps trudging up the steps in the lighthouse to keep the lights burning each night while the storm rages. When one knows that something must be done to help people survive, one can sometimes achieve things thought to be beyond one's ability.

Shaw, Janet. *Changes for Kirsten: A Winter Story.* Illus. Renee Graef. Madison, WI: Pleasant Company, 1988. 0-937295-44-2, 65p. Paper, 0-937295-45-0. R=3; I=4.

Kirsten wants to go trapping for fur with her older brother and his friend in 1854, and they finally agree because she knows so much about animals in the woods. One day she and her brother find the best trapper in the area dead, and since he has no family, they sell his furs and buy a house to replace theirs which burned. One's learning can often help one achieve unexpected things.

Smucker, Barbara. *Runaway to Freedom*. Magnolia, MA: Peter Smith, 1992 (1977). 0-8446-6585-1. Paper, New York: HarperCollins (Trophy), 1979. 0-06-440106-5, 154p. R=4; I=5.

After being sold and separated from her mother, Julilly, twelve, travels from Virginia to Mississippi with a despicable overseer who whips the slaves without provocation. A white man comes from Canada and helps her and three others escape and begin the long, arduous journey to Canada. People's values are not related to skin color.

Tate, Eleanora E. *The Secret of Gumbo Grove*. New York: Bantam, 1988 (1987). Paper (Starfire), 0-553-27226-8, 200p. R=3; I=5.

Raisin's love of history when she is eleven leads her to investigate the backgrounds of the people buried in the nearby overgrown cemetery. Although not strictly historical fiction, Raisin's research reveals much about the pride of ownership and the pain of slavery during the nineteenth century. Knowing about the past helps in understanding what people have either endured or died for and in realizing what needs to be changed to make life better.

Taylor, Theodore. *Walking Up a Rainbow*. New York: Delacorte, 1986. 0-385-29435-2, 275p. Paper, New York: Dell, 1988. 0-440-20039-3. R=6; I=8.

After her parents die in a buggy accident in 1852 when Susan is fourteen, she has to find a way to pay her father's debt or lose her home. Her attempt takes her from Iowa to California to Panama to New Orleans and back to Iowa. On her journey, she meets both entertaining and unsavory characters. A person who wants to achieve a goal may have to take many risks without knowing whether the outcome will have been worth the effort.

Tunbo, Frances G. *Stay Put, Robbie McAmis.* Illus. Charles Shaw. Fort Worth, TX: Texas Christian, 1988. 0-87565-025-2, 158p. R=3; I=4.

Separated from the rest of the wagons while crossing a river during a storm in 1848, Robbie, twelve, plants crops and builds a cabin for his grandmother and the four other children. After almost a year, the family reunites, amazed that each member is still alive and well. Humans can perform to their potential when needed. *Western Heritage Award*, 1989.

Turner, Ann. *Nettie's Trip South.* Illus. Ronald Himler. New York: Macmillan, 1987. 0-02-789240-9, 32p. R=5; I=4.

Nettie, ten, goes South with her journalist brother in the 1850's and writes her friend about what she sees. Nettie vomits at seeing slaves sold at auction because she realizes that if her skin were black, she would be treated the same awful way and have only one name. People who have compassion want to get rid of injustice toward others.

Turner, Ann. *Third Girl from the Left.* New York: Macmillan, 1986. 0-02-789510-6, 153p. R=4; I=9.**

Deciding not to be tied to a life of drudgery through marriage and children in Maine, Sarah, eighteen, becomes a mail-order bride and goes to Montana to marry a rancher in the mid-1800's. Only a month after her arrival, when her sixty-year-old husband dies, she inherits the ranch, and with the help of her Chinese cook, she decides to stay and learn how to manage it. If one has different goals in life from those with whom one lives, one may have to move elsewhere to form bonds with those who think similarly.

Winter, Jeanette, writer/illus. *Follow the Drinking Gourd.* New York: Knopf, 1992 (1988). Paper (Dragonfly), 0-679-81997-5, 48p. R=4; I=3.

Peg Leg Joe, an old sailor, wanders from plantation to plantation to teach slaves a song about following the drinking gourd to freedom during the early nineteenth century. Many slaves do as the song suggests by escaping at night and following the group of stars that look like a dipper to the Ohio River where an abolitionist waits to ferry them across and takes them to "safe" houses on their way to Canada and freedom. People helping each other achieve amazing goals.

1861-1865

Ackerman, Karen. *The Tin Heart.* Illus. Michael Hays. New York: Atheneum, 1990. 0-689-31461-2, 32p. R=5; I=3.

Mahaley and her best friend Flora each has one side of a tin heart showing their strong friendship even though they live on opposite sides of the Ohio River in the 1850's. The issue of slavery divides their fathers, but the girls refuse to let it sever their friendship. When parents feel strongly about a subject, they may try to keep their children apart.

Alphin, Elaine Marie. *The Ghost Cadet.* New York: Holt, 1991. 0-8050-1614-7, 192p. R=4; I=4.

When Benjy, twelve, and his sister Fran, sixteen, visit their father's mother for the first time in New Market, Virginia, Benjy's interest in history leads him to the nearby battlefield. In this historical fantasy, he encounters Hugh, a Virginia Military Cadet, killed in the Battle of New Market in 1864. He helps Hugh, a ghost, find his family heirloom watch lost in the battle in what Hugh calls "the War Between the States." After Benjy returns the watch to VMI as Hugh requests, he gains confidence in himself and realizes that he will no longer allow himself to be belittled by others.

Beatty, Patricia. *Charley Skedaddle.* New York: Morrow, 1987. 0-688-06687-9, 192p. Paper, Mahwah, NJ: Troll. 0-8167-1317-0. R=3; I=6.

The orphaned Charley dislikes the man his older sister plans to marry, so he leaves home and hides as a stowaway on a ship sailing from New York's harbor to the south where he becomes a Union Army drummer boy in 1864. Distraught by the destruction and remembering his brother, killed at Gettysburg, he deserts and runs away to the mountains. There he proves his bravery by helping an old woman who was once a member of the Underground Railway. The bravest people are those who act without others watching. *Scott O'Dell Award for Historical Fiction*, 1988.

Beatty, Patricia. *Jayhawker.* New York: Morrow, 1991. 0-688-09850-9, 214p. R=4; I=5.

In 1858, Lije, twelve, meets abolitionist John Brown when he comes to his family's Kansas farm and takes Lije's father on a raid into Missouri against the slave owners. After Lije's father is killed when they are trying to rescue slaves, Lije becomes a spy for the Jayhawkers (abolitionists in Kansas) in Missouri, known as bushwacker country, while the Civil War rages around him. People with power and conviction have to guard against evil in the world. *School Library Journal "Best Book,"* 1991.

Beatty, Patricia. *Turn Homeward, Hannalee.* New York: Morrow, 1984. 0-688-03871-9,208p. Paper, Mahwah, NJ: Troll, 1990. 0-8167-2260-9, 193p. R=6; I=6.

In 1864, the Yankees deport Hannalee and her brother from Georgia to Indiana. They escape from employers, and their long journey home takes them into the middle of a horrible battle. Hannalee's intelligence and determination keep the war from completely destroying the family.

Beatty, Patricia. *Wait for Me, Watch for Me, Eula Bee.* New York: Morrow, 1990 (1978). 0-688-10077-5, 221p. R=4; I=5.

In 1861, Comanches capture Lewtie and his sister Eula Bee, three, after killing five others in their family. Because he is brave, the Comanches allow Lewtie to herd the horses, and he uses a horse to escape. He eventually rescues Eula Bee, who for several months shows no recognition of him because she has adapted to her kind Comanche mother. Love and care win people much faster than forcing them to submit to hardships.

Beatty, Patricia. *Who Comes with Cannons?* New York: Morrow, 1992. 0-688-11028-2, 192p. R=4; I=4.

In 1861, Truth, twelve, goes from Indiana to stay with her North Carolina relatives, also Quakers. When her uncle hides runaway slaves, Truth is surprised but happy to find a way to support their quest for freedom through peaceable means. When one has strong beliefs about human rights, one sometimes has to find ingenious ways to enforce them.

Beatty, Patricia, and Phillip Robbins. *Eben Tyne, Powdermonkey.* New York: Morrow, 1990. 0-688-08884-8, 227p. R=6; I=6.

In 1862, Eben serves as powdermonkey on the Merrimack out of Norfolk, Virginia, when it is defeated by the North. He has an option of fighting with the North against pirates rather than being imprisoned for the duration of the war, and he does. If one does not have enough information to make a good decision, relying on the advice of a trusted person may be the only choice.

Brink, Carol Ryrie. *Caddie Woodlawn.* Illus. Trina S. Hyman. New York: Macmillan, 1973 (1935). 0-02-713670-1, 288p. Paper (Aladdin), 1990. 0-689-71370-3. R=6; I=5.

Unaffected by the American Civil War in 1864 because her father in Wisconsin paid someone to fight for him, Caddie enjoys playing with her brothers. When eleven, she realizes that her "prissy" female cousin may not be as bad as she has thought. Having no alternatives, Caddie accepts the standards appropriate for females, and her family shows loyalty for their Indian friends and patriotism toward America. *Newbery Medal,* 1936.

Clapp, Patricia. *The Tamarack Tree: A Novel of the Siege of Vicksburg.* New York: Lothrop, Lee, & Shepard, 1986. 0-688-02852-7, 224p. Paper, New York: Puffin, 1988. 0-14-032406-2, 256p. R=3; I=7.

Arriving in Vicksburg, Mississippi, from London in 1859, Rosemary does not understand the concept of owning another human being and begins helping her brother in the Underground Railway. What surprises her is that she likes people she meets who own slaves. After the Battle of Vicksburg in 1863, she returns to London, engaged to a Yankee, and her brother reunites with his Confederate fiancée. For outsiders, customs are difficult to understand, and for those used to them, difficult to change.

Climo, Shirley. *A Month of Seven Days.* New York: Crowell, 1987. 0-690-04656-1, 152p. Paper, New York: Troll. 0-8167-1476-2. R=5; I=5.

In 1864, when Zoe is thirteen, Union soldiers billet in her Georgia home, expecting her mother to cook and clean for them.

When Zoe hears that the captain is superstitious, she creates incidents and with tales to accompany them which frighten him into leaving. Zoe discovers that in war, one cannot be certain which side some people support.

Fleischman, Paul. *Bull Run.* New York: HarperCollins, 1993. 0-06-021447-3, 104p. R=5; I=5.

Ten people from both the Union and Confederate sides express their positions and thoughts about the Civil War in separate chapters. In some instances, they interact; all, however, are connected to the Battle of Bull Run in 1861. The vicious maiming of war destroys so much that one can only hope that the victory will be worth the fight.

Forman, James D. *Becca's Story.* New York: Scribner's, 1992. 0-684-19332-9, 180p. R=6; I=8.

In 1860, Becca, fifteen, has two boyfriends with whom she enjoys attending fairs and singing in their Michigan school productions. But soon, their stable world collapses when the Civil War begins. First, one joins the army, and then the second enlists and is soon declared missing, presumed dead. When war intervenes, even if the battles are far away, it changes one's life forever.

Gauch, Patricia L. *Thunder at Gettysburg.* Illus. Stephen Gammell. New York: Putnam, 1990 (1975). 0-399-22201-4, 46p. Paper, New York: Bantam, 1991. 0-553-15951-8. R=2; I=4.

While trying to escape the battle at Gettysburg, July 1-3, 1863, Tillie finds herself in the middle of it. Surrounding her are wounded soldiers whom she helps by bringing pails of water to them. Relieved after the Union wins and hearing that her family in town is safe, she realizes that she never wants to forget either the living or the dead from this awful experience.

Hansen, Joyce. *Out From This Place.* New York: Walker, 1988. 0-8027-6817-2, 135p. Paper, New York: Avon (Camelot), 1992. 0-380-71409-4. R=4; I=5.

After escaping from a Charleston, South Carolina, plantation and eventually being captured by Confederate soldiers, Easter, fourteen, returns to the Charleston area to get the boy she has raised. In this sequel to *Which Way Freedom?*, the slaves depart soon after her arrival for the coastal islands where they gain freedom and where she searches for Obi from whom she was previously separated. Easter learns very rapidly in the school created for former slaves, and after the war ends, she decides to attend school in Philadelphia and become a teacher. People are generally willing to work when it assures their freedom and gives them a future to anticipate.

Hansen, Joyce. *Which Way Freedom?* New York: Avon, 1986. Paper (Camelot), 0-380-71408-6, 128p. R=4; I=5.

Obi and Easter escape from their plantation when they hear they will be sold in 1861, but confederate soldiers find them. Obadiah again escapes to the South Carolina coastal islands where he joins Union troops and meets a "colored Yankee" who begins teaching him to read. Wounded but alive near the end the war, he looks forward to finding Easter and the little boy she stayed to save, the story told in *Out From This Place.* The inhumanity of some people reveals itself in the relationship of some whites to slaves and some slave overseers to their subordinates.

Hickman, Janet. *Zoar Blue.* New York: Macmillan, 1978. R=4; I=7.*

In 1862, tired of working at the jobs required by the German Society of Separatists in Zoar, Ohio, and missing a friend who ran away to fight in the Civil War, Barbara leaves for her uncle's house in Pennsylvania. There, she realizes that all chores everywhere are mundane. Her route back to Zoar and those she loves leads through Gettysburg just after the battle. Most people appreciate the value of what they have only after they lose it. *Ohioana Awards,* 1979; *Child Study Association Book of the Year,* 1978.

Hunt, Irene. *Across Five Aprils.* Englewood Cliffs, NJ: Silver Burdett, 1993 (1965). 0-382-24358-7, 212p. Paper, New York: Berkley, 1987. 0-425-10241-6, 190p. R=7; I=7.

For the five years beginning in 1861 when Jethro turns nine until 1865, the Civil War divides his Illinois family just as it divides the country. Rapidly pushed toward adult responsibilities, Jethro has to face the dilemma of the war symbolized through the strong respect or hatred of various people for either Abraham Lincoln or Robert E. Lee. One sees that time often dictates circumstance, and few complex situations have simple solutions. *Newbery Honor*, 1965; *Society of Midland Authors Book Awards*, 1965.

Jones, Douglas C. *The Barefoot Brigade.* New York: Tor, 1988 (1980). Paper, 0-8125-8459-7, 311p. R=7; I=10+.

In 1861, Noah steals a pig, is apprehended, and then sentenced to join the Rebel army to fight against the North. During the four long years, he meets Martin Hasford, a man wanting to be a minister but who left his family, described in *Elkhorn Tavern*, to fight for the South. After the war ends, they start walking back to Arkansas, and Rebel soldiers in Virginia shoot Noah because they think he might have had something to do with the assassination of Abraham Lincoln. Even though surrender may seem to end a war, nothing changes human emotions except the people themselves.

Jones, Douglas C. *Elkhorn Tavern.* New York: Tor, 1989 (1980). 0-8125-8457-0, 311p. R=7; I=10+.

Early in the Civil War, in 1861, after his father has joined Southern forces, Roman, fifteen, sees the jaywalkers (Northern partisans) from Missouri in his Arkansas valley. He, his mother, and sister prepare for their arrival and escape severe loss, but the Battle of Pea Ridge decimates the area. An Indian brings a Yankee with a severed arm to their home, and during his convalescence, he and Roman's sister fall in love. Enduring fighting armies is difficult but facing marauders who kill families and take their food at the same time makes survival a challenge.

Kassem, Lou. *Listen for Rachel.* New York: Avon, 1992 (1986). Paper (Flare), 0-380-71232-8, 176p. R=4; I=7.

Rachel's parents die in a fire when she is fourteen, and she goes to live with her grandparents, whom she has never met, in Appalachia. She feels comfortable in their beautiful mountain valley as she learns how to heal with herbs, falls in love, and worries during the Civil War when beloved cousins and her fiancée go to fight. Accepting others for who they are makes one's own life more content.

Keith, Harold. *Rifles for Watie.* New York: Crowell, 1991 (1957). 0-690-04907-2. Paper (Trophy), 1987. 0-06-447030-X), 334p. R=7; I=9.

Battling Watie's raiders, a Confederate group in Kansas during 1861, Jeff Busey at sixteen discovers the sordidness of war. Jeff becomes a Union spy and discovers that the man supplying guns to the Confederates for gold is his own superior officer. In war, neither side behaves with total innocence or evil; what helps humans endure war is knowing that, if they survive, they can return home to loving family and friends. *Newbery Medal*, 1958.

Lyon, George Ella. *Cecil's Story.* Illus. Peter Catalanotto. New York: Orchard/Watts, 1991. 0-531-08512-0, 32p. R=6; I=3.

When Cecil's father goes to fight in the Civil War, Cecil becomes concerned about his mother having to leave to get his father if wounded or what will happen to the family if he does not come home. He decides that he can be useful regardless of what occurs. Everyone has fears of being unable to cope with the unknown.

Meyer, Carolyn. *Where the Broken Heart Still Beats: The Story of Cynthia Ann Parker.* San Diego: Gulliver, 1992. 0-15-200639-7, 196p. Paper, 0-15-295602-6. R=5; I=8.

Lucy tells the story of her aunt, Cynthia Parker, who when recaptured from the Comanches along with her daughter in 1861, was thirty-four, and had no desire to live with whites. Cynthia almost escapes twice to be with her Comanche chief husband and two warrior sons but finally dies of grief after her daughter dies of fever. People must realize that what may be best for them personally may not be best for those they think that they are helping.

Mitchell, Margaret. *Gone with the Wind.* New York: Macmillan, 1975 (1936). 0-02-585390-2, 1037p. Paper, New York: Warner, 1993. 0-446-36538-6, 1024p. R=8; I=10+.

When the Civil War begins, Scarlett O'Hara is sixteen and in love with a neighboring plantation heir Ashley, who surprises her by marrying Melanie. Scarlett marries Melanie's brother in retaliation, and within a year, becomes a war widow with an unwanted child. Scarlett leaves for Atlanta where Sherman ravages the city and returns home to Tara to find similar destruction. To keep the plantation solvent, she marries a businessman, and after he dies, she marries Rhett Butler, a southerner become wealthy from blockade running. Scarlett's hard bargaining contrasts with her foolish and continuing love for Ashley, but she does not see his weakness or realize that she loves Rhett until after Rhett decides to leave her. When one's civilized life abruptly ends and one has to struggle to survive, one must often make decisions that conflict with one's innate beliefs.

O'Dell, Scott. *Sing Down the Moon.* Boston: Houghton Mifflin, 1970. 0-395-10919-1. Paper, New York: Dell (Yearling), 1992. 0-440-40673-0. R=4; I=7.

In 1864, Spanish slavers capture Bright Morning and her friend, taking them south to sell as menial houseworkers. They escape, only to return home in time to join their Navaho tribe on its forced walk to Fort Sumner, where United States soldiers guard them. Humans who take freedom from other humans deserve neither kindness nor respect. *Newbery Honor*, 1971.

Perez, N. A. *The Slopes of War.* Boston: Houghton Mifflin, 1990 (1984). 0-395-35642-3, 202p. Paper, 0-395-54979-5. R=6; I=8.

While Buck, eighteen, fights for the Union Army, Bekah, fifteen, stays at home in Gettysburg. The battle that occurs in the first days of July, 1863, changes their lives and their loves. One must try to keep freedom from those who would take it away.

Porter, Connie. *Meet Addy: An American Girl.* Illus. Melodye Rosales. Madison, WI: Pleasant, 1993. 1-56247-076-0, 69p. Paper, 1-56247-075-2. R=3; I=3.

Addy is surprised during the summer of 1864 to hear her parents talk about escaping slavery. Before they can flee, their master sells some of the family, but they are reunited in Philadelphia after the war. With all of the terrible things that happen to people, to know that some people have successfully reunited with their families after a war is somewhat reassuring. "The American Girls Collection."

Reeder, Carolyn. *Shades of Gray.* New York: MacMillan, 1989.
0-02-775810-9, 152p. Paper, New York: Avon (Camelot), 1991.
0-380-71232-6. R=6; I=6.

After losing his entire family during the Civil War, Will,
twelve, goes from town to live with his mother's sister on her
family's farm. Dismayed that his uncle has refused to fight,
Will needs a long time to understand his uncle's beliefs. To
keep others' opinions from ruling one's life takes much strength
and courage. *Scott O'Dell Award for Historical Fiction*, 1990;
Child Study Children's Book Award, 1989; *Jefferson Cup
Award*, 1990; *American Library Association Notable Book for
Children*, 1990.

Rinaldi, Ann. *In My Father's House.* New York: Scholastic, 1993.
0-590-44730-0, 323p. R=5; I=8.

When Oscie is seven in 1852, her widowed mother remarries,
and Oscie verbally spars with her stepfather until the
Confederate surrender at Appomattox Court House in 1865, in
the family's front room. Oscie matures into an intelligent young
woman, educated by a Northern tutor who teaches her both
knowledge and integrity. Oscie learns, with difficulty, that she
must accent the strengths in others rather than their
weaknesses.

Rinaldi, Ann. *The Last Silk Dress.* New York: Holiday, 1988.
0-8234-0690-3, 350p. Paper, New York: Bantam, 1990.
0-553-28315-4. R=2; I=7.

When Susan is fourteen in Richmond, Virginia, the Civil
War begins. She unexpectedly finds her older brother who had
left home before she knew him and learns family secrets best
kept silent. Accepting responsibility for her actions during the
war becomes a challenge, but she shows that what a young
woman may need most is to know she is loved, especially by her
family.

Shaara, Michael. *The Killer Angels.* New York: Random, 1993
(1974). 0-679-42541-1, 400p. Paper, New York: Ballantine, 1993.
0-345-34810-9, 355p. R=3; I=8.

In the third year of the American Civil War, 1863, on June
30, the Army of Northern Virginia, led by Robert E. Lee, a man
who neither owns slaves nor believes in slavery, begins to
march toward Gettysburg to meet the Army of the Potomac. On

the next three days, military leaders on both sides, projected through an omniscient point of view, make decisions about their men which lead to the defeat of Lee's army and the eventual victory of Union soldiers in the war. People who fight in wars do so for various reasons, sometimes forgetting why the war was initially begun. *Pulitizer Prize*, 1975.

Shore, Laura Jan. *The Sacred Moon Tree: The Trials and Adventures of Phoebe Sands in the Great War between the States, 1861-1865*. New York: Bradbury, 1986. 0-02-782-790-9, 209p. R=4; I=7.**

During the Civil War, Phoebe has varied experiences including a trip from Pennsylvania to Richmond by foot through the middle of battles while pretending to be a boy. After the war, her parents reunite, and her father, with one leg shot off, regains his will to live by inventing a prosthesis that is neither heavy wood nor noisy tin. When one's family is together and happy, the worst of situations seems to get better.

Shura, Mary Francis. *Gentle Annie: The True Story of a Civil War Nurse*. New York: Scholastic, 1991. 0-590-44367-4, 184p. R=5; I=7.

When Annie is ten and her widowed father moves them to Wisconsin, Annie learns to nurse first her father and then others. When the Civil War begins, she knows that she must help, and her best contribution would be to comfort the wounded. Annie, a real woman, in this pseudo-historical novel, shows that kindness and care are two of the best gifts any human can give to another.

Steele, William O. *The Perilous Road*. Magnolia MA: Peter Smith, 1992 (1958). 0-8446-6507-X. Paper, San Diego: Harcourt Brace (Odyssey), 1990. 0-15-260647-5, 154p. R=6; I=6.

Chris, eleven, becomes annoyed with federal troops who take all the family's food stored for the winter during the American Civil War and decides to support the Rebels. His brother, however, joins the Union Army in 1863, and before Chris knows, he almost jeopardizes his brother's life by reporting a federal wagon train's movement to the Rebels. Regardless of one's allegiance, war is a terrible state for everyone. *Newbery Honor*, 1959; *Jane Addams Book Award*, 1958.

Wisler, G. Clifton. *Red Cap.* New York: Lodestar, 1991. 0-525-67337-7, 160p. R=4; I=6.

Ransom decides to run away from his Frostburg, Maryland, home to join the Union Army in 1862 when he is thirteen. Captured and imprisoned in Andersonville, South Carolina, his loyalty symbolized by his red cap, the kindness of one of the enemy keeps him alive, although barely, to tell about the war. While war destroys so much, it can also illuminate the human goodness of those willing to sacrifice for others.

Wisler, G. Clifton. *Thunder on the Tennessee.* New York: Dutton, 1983. 0-525-67144-7, 154p. R=6; I=6.*

Willie's father decides to head a Texas regiment fighting for the Confederates in 1862. Willie, fifteen, joins him, enjoys the victory at Shiloh, and although grieving for his father's death, he decides he must continue fighting until the war ends. To protect home and beliefs, people have to resist those who threaten them. *Western Writers of America Spur Award*, 1984.

Yep, Laurence. *Dragon's Gate.* New York: HarperCollins, 1993. 0-06-022972-1, 275p. R=4; I=6.

In 1865, Otter comes to the Sierra Mountains from China to join his adoptive father and uncle in building the transcontinental railroad. In their pursuit of a better life, the three endure the difficult work and slave treatment by hostile foremen as well as a blinding, a loss of fingers from frostbite, and public humiliation. Being with people about whom one cares can help one cope with the unpleasant surprises that life sometimes offers. *Newbery Honor*, 1994.

1866-1889

Alexander, Lloyd. *The Philadelphia Adventure.* New York; Dutton, 1990. 0-525-44564-1, 150p. Paper, New York: Dell, 1992. 0-440-40605-6. R=9; I=9.

In Philadelphia, just before the Centennial Exposition of 1876 begins, President Grant asks Vester Holly to thwart the anticipated kidnapping of the children of Don Pedro, the leader of Brazil. Holly, with the help of intelligent friends, finds the children and reaches the Exposition Hall just in time to defuse dynamite set by the kidnapper. The characters know each other's strengths which helps to solve the mystery.

Avi. *Emily Upham's Revenge.* New York: Morrow, 1992 (1978). Paper (Beech Tree), 0-688-11899-2, 192p. R=4; I=4.

Around 1875 after her father disappears, Emily Upham, seven, leaves Boston to live with her uncle in North Brookfield. When her uncle ignores her, she and a youth she meets decide to rob her uncle's bank to get money for her return to Boston. Another robber, however, thwarts their attempt, and that robber happens to be Emily's father. Emily eventually gets the money, and in Boston, gives it to charities but says that she burned it. Helping others is the best use of ill-gotten wealth.

Avi. *Punch with Judy.* New York: Bradbury, 1993. 0-02-707755-1, 167p. R=4; I=5.

In 1870, Punch, eight, becomes a member of a traveling medicine show when its owner sees him trying to earn coins by dancing jigs for any audience who will watch. The show succeeds until hard times hit the countryside. Eventually the group realizes that the only entertainment that will sell is humor. Wanting to be loved and accepted will lead a person to do things to gain approval.

Bartone, Elisa. *Peppe the Lamplighter.* Illus. Ted Lewin. New York: Lothrop, Lee, & Shepard, 1993. 0-688-10269-7, 32p. R=7; I=2.

Since young Peppe's mother is dead and his father sick, he needs to make money to help support his eight sisters including one who lives in Italy and looks after even more people. When he gets a job as a lamplighter in New York's Little Italy before electricity, his father chastises him. But when Peppe refuses to light the lamps one night, his father realizes that the job is very important for assisting people, including the youngest sister, home safely. Even the most menial job helps in ways people do not realize until it is not done. *Caldecott Honor*, 1994.

Beatty, Patricia. *Be Ever Hopeful, Hannalee*. New York: Morrow, 1988. 0-688-07502-9, 216p. Paper, Mahwah, NJ: Troll, 1990. 0-8167-2259-5. R=4; I=6.

After the Civil War ends, in this sequel to *Turn Homeward, Hannalee*, Hannalee, thirteen, and her mother and two brothers move to Atlanta to find work. With only one arm, her brother has difficulty locating employment and becomes involved with dishonest people. He never commits a crime and is finally absolved from all suspicion. When one's family is together, the worst problems seem possible to overcome.

Beatty, Patricia. *Bonanza Girl*. New York: Morrow, 1993 (1962). 0-688-12280-9, 224p. R=6; I=6.

Ann Scott, her widowed mother, and brother Jemmy travel to Idaho territory in 1884 where another woman convinces Mrs. Scott to open a tent restaurant instead of teaching school. When a friend discovers a silver mine, they move the restaurant to the claim area and expand their efforts by collecting money in the saloons for a church. Having older female role models may inspire a young woman to try different things.

Beatty, Patricia. *The Coach That Never Came*. New York: Morrow, 1985. 0-688-05477-3, 164p. R=3; I=6.

Paul, thirteen, discovers his family's past from his grandmother when he visits Colorado for the summer. His investigation of a gaudy belt buckle shaped like a heart reveals an outlaw in the family who ambushed a stagecoach in 1873, killed the passengers, and was killed, in turn, by Ute Indians for ruining their sacred cave. Some of the past's secrets may be waiting to be found if one carefully investigates them.

Beatty, Patricia. *Nickel-Plated Beauty*. New York: Morrow, 1993 (1964). 0-688-12360-0, 272p. Paper, 0-688-12281-7, 240p. R=4; I=4.

In 1886, Hester coerces her siblings into earning enough money by digging clams, picking berries, and gathering oysters to buy their mother a stove. Additionally, Hester works at her aunt's hotel and is exposed to women's rice powder and red flannel bled for its color to be used as rouge. People working together can accomplish much more than alone.

Bedard, Michael. *Emily*. Illus. Barbara Cooney. New York: Doubleday, 1992. 0-385-30697-0, 40p. R=2; I=2.

In the 1880's, a little girl moves to Amherst, Massachusetts, on the same street as Emily Dickinson--a woman called "The Myth." Emily sends a note to the girl's mother asking her to visit and play the piano, but when the girl and her mother arrive, Emily stays upstairs to listen rather than joining them in the parlor. Why people do certain things remains a mystery.

Brenner, Barbara. *Wagon Wheels*. Illus. Don Bolognese. New York: HarperCollins, 1978. 0-06-020669-1, 64p. Paper, 1984. 0-06-444052-4. R=2; I=2.

In 1878, the Muldie family travels from Kentucky to homestead in Kansas. After his wife dies on the way, Mr. Muldie leaves Johnny, eleven, to stay with his younger brothers while he looks for hilly land. The boys cope with a prairie fire and a poisonous snake before safely rejoining their father.

Byars, Betsy C. *The Golly Sisters Go West*. Illus. Sue Truesdell. New York: HarperCollins, 1986. 0-06-020884-8, 58p. Paper, 1989. 0-06-444132-6. R=1; I=2.

May May and Rose begin their performing career as soon as they can figure out how to tell their horse to start hauling their wagon. Their confused performances, which tend to change depending on who gets to be first, delight their audiences. They enjoy traveling in the west and entertaining people along the way. "An I Can Read Book."

Byars, Betsy. *Hooray for the Golly Sisters*. Illus. Sue Truesdell. New York: HarperCollins, 1990. 0-06-020899-6, 64p. Paper, 1992. 0-06-444156-3. R=1; I=1.

Rose and May May, the Golly sisters, enjoy their road show in the 1800's. They make mistakes but improve on their act each time. They realize that if they want something, they may have to get it for themselves. "An I Can Read Book."

Carter, Peter. *Borderlands.* New York: Farrar, Straus & Giroux, 1990. 0-374-30895-0, 424p. R=6; I=8.

When his widowed mother dies in 1871, Ben, at thirteen, and his seventeen-year-old brother luckily get a job herding cattle from Texas to Abilene, Kansas. In Kansas, gamblers murder his brother, but Ben's declared vengeance toward the murderer is assuaged when he hears someone else has killed him. Ben finds an advisor who starts his business ventures although they eventually leave him penniless when a New York financier fails. Then Ben goes to kill buffalo on the Plains, a job which he finds is no more than the lucrative slaughter of both buffalo and Native Americans. The profanity fits the time, the place, and the many types of characters.

Conrad, Pam. *Prairie Songs.* Illus. Darryl Zudeck. New York: HarperCollins, 1985. 0-06-021337-X, 167p. Paper (Trophy), 1987. 0-06-440206-1. R=8; I=5.

When the doctor and his wife become Nebraska neighbors of young Louisa, all their books entice her, especially the one containing Tennyson's poem "The Eagle." But the death of a newborn child and the hard life defeat the doctor's wife, while Louisa and her family continue to adjust and accept the difficulty of surviving on the prairie. In order to adapt to change, one must be able to accept its demands. *Judy Lopez Memorial Award*, 1986; *Society of Midland Authors Book Awards*, 1986; *Western Writers of America Spur Award*, 1986; *International Reading Association Children's Book Award*, 1986; *Western Heritage Awards*, 1986.

Cooney, Barbara, writer/illus. *Hattie and the Wild Waves.* New York: Viking, 1990. 0-670-83056-9, 40p. Paper, New York: Puffin, 1993. 0-14-054193-4. R=7; I=3.

In the late nineteenth century, Hattie and her family entertain their German relatives on Sunday, and during the week, her father builds houses. Throughout her young life of going to the family summer home on the ocean, moving from Brooklyn to a huge estate on Long Island, her sister's marriage, and her brother's going to work, Hattie likes to draw pictures and paint. One has to be attune to one's inner self to decide what one wants to do as one grows up. *Lupine Award*, 1991.

Cross, Gillian. *The Great American Elephant Chase.* New York: Holiday House, 1993. 0-8234-1016-1, 193p. R=4; I=8.

Tad, fifteen, orphaned at his birth, departs his aunt's home when he hides in an elephant's railroad car cage, and the train leaves the station before he has time to get out. He travels with the elephant, Khush, and its mistress over two thousand miles to her sister's home, trying to avoid a man who wants to steal Khush. But after the journey, Khush will not leave Tad, and the two continue their travels west. Some animals have more sense of the goodness in humans than other humans do.

Emerson, Kathy Lynn. *Julia's Mending.* New York: Avon 1990 (1987). Paper (Camelot), 0-380-70734-9, 136p. R=4; I=4.

When she is twelve, Julia's parents leave New York City in 1887 to become missionaries in China. They send her to a cousin's family in Liberty Falls, New York. At first, she hates their country ways, thinking that a cousin has taken her journal which has disappeared. But after she breaks her leg and begins talking to them, she finds that the baby took her journal by mistake so she adjusts and makes friends. Outward appearances can be a deceptive indication of a person's inner character.

Fahrmann, Willi. *The Long Journey of Lukas B.* Trans. Anthea Bell. New York: Bradbury, 1985. 0-02-734330-8, 280p. R=5; I=7.*

When his grandfather decides to go to America to earn money for his unpaid home by using his carpentry skills in 1870, Luke, fourteen, goes with him to search for his father who left several years earlier to escape his debts. Although Luke's father departs town before Luke arrives, he leaves Luke sixty paintings. They are such high quality that Luke sells enough of them on board ship back to Germany that he earns enough money to buy a shop. Sometimes the decision people must make for themselves upset others, especially their parents, who want to control their lives.

Fleischman, Paul. *Graven Images.* Illus. Andrew Glass. New York: HarperCollins, 1982. 0-06-021907-6, 85p. Paper (Trophy), 1987. 0-06-440186-3. R=6; I=8.

In the late eighteenth century, three people let themselves be influenced by graven images--a binnacle boy, a copper saint weathervane, and a marble statue commissioned by a ghost. Of the three, two are associated with murder, but the third gives a boy hope for his pursuit of love. People sometimes allow themselves to be influenced by strange things that could have no impact on their lives. *Newbery Honor*, 1983; *American Library Association Notable Book for Children*, 1982; *School Library Journal "Best Book,"* 1982.

Fleischman, Sid. *The Ghost in the Noonday Sun.* Illus. Peter Sis. New York: Greenwillow, 1989 (1965). 0-688-08410-9, 144p. Paper, New York: Scholastic (Apple), 1991. 0-590-43662-7. R=3; I=4.

The day after Oliver is twelve in nineteenth century Nantucket, a ship's captain kidnaps him and sails him out to sea. Oliver and a sailor, presumably killed by the captain, eventually hoodwink the captain by hitting him on the head and making him think he is dead and seeing ghosts. When they escape their sinking ship, they take food instead of booty, are rescued, and finally return safely home.

Fleischman, Sid. *Jim Ugly.* Illus. Marcia Sewall. New York: Greenwillow, 1992. 0-688-10886-5, 130p. Paper, New York: Dell, 1993. 0-440-40803-2. R=3; I=5.

In 1894 in the West, when Jake is twelve, his father dies, and Jake tries to get his father's dog, Jim Ugly, to follow him. Instead, Jake follows the dog and finds that his father is still alive and is hiding from a bounty hunter who thinks his father has diamonds. People who stoop to dishonesty often begin to suspect everyone they see of also being criminal.

Fleischman, Sid. *The Midnight Horse.* Illus. Peter Sis. New York: Greenwillow, 1990. 0-688-09441-4, 84p. Paper, New York: Dell, 1992. 0-440-40614-5. R=3; I=4.

When Touch, an orphan, arrives in a New Hampshire town in the 1870's, he discovers that his great-uncle is the grouchy judge. He is also a miser who plans to cheat Touch out of the items his father left for him. A series of events including magic tricks finally unseat the judge, and the village survives his unsavory laws. *Edgar Allen Poe Award*, 1992; *School Library Journal "Best Book,"* 1990.

Fleischman, Sid. *Mr. Mysterious & Co.* Illus. Eric Von Schmidt. Boston: Little, Brown, 1990 (1962). Paper, 0-316-28614-1, 152p. R=3; I=4.

In 1884, the Hackett children perform with their father in a magic show as they travel across the country in a wagon. They have mishaps, but they also have fun. A loving attitude within a family makes unpleasant situations seem much less threatening.

Gipson, Fred. *Old Yeller*. New York: HarperCollins, 1990 (1956). 0-06-011545-9. Cutchogue, NY: Buccaneer, 1992. 0-89966-906-9. Paper (Trophy), 1990. 0-06-440382-3, 184p. R=5; I=5.

During Travis's fourteenth summer in the 1860's, his father leaves him in charge of the Texas family homestead while he goes to Florida. An old dog arrives, and against Travis's wishes, his brother and mother want to keep Old Yeller. Old Yeller, in turn, protects Travis and saves him from wild hogs, but Travis has to kill him because the dog contracts hydrophobia when a wild wolf bites him. Broken loyalty between humans and animals can be as painful as that between humans and other humans. *Newbery Honor, 1958.*

Gregory, Kristiana. *Jenny of the Tetons*. San Diego: Harcourt Brace, 1989. 0-15-200480-7, 120p. Paper, 1991. 0-15-200481-5. R=6; I=9.

Her family ambushed and killed when she is only fifteen in 1875, Carrie refuses to have any dealings with Indians. The woman who helps her most to recover from her grief is the Shoshoni wife of a white man who welcomes her into their home. All people are individuals and do not necessarily have the same character traits as others of their race or culture. *Golden Kite Award, 1990.*

Hancock, Sibyl. *Old Blue*. Illus. Erick Ingraham. New York: Putnam, 1980. 0-399-61141-X, 48p. R=3; I=3.**

When Davy goes on his first cattle drive with his father, the trail boss, he gets to ride up front of the cattle with the leading steer, Old Blue. After a bad snow storm, Davy suggests that a bell around Old Blue's neck will help them follow when they cannot see in the snow or in the dark. In 1878, Old Blue leads the cattle to Kansas City with his bell. Using one's imagination can help solve problems. *American Library Association Notable Book for Children, 1980.*

Harmon, Susan. *Colorado Ransom*. New York: Walker, 1991. 0-8027-4125-8, 169p. R=6; I=10+.

In 1872, Forrest Bates hires a drifter named Shannon to help him in his gold mine which is beginning to produce. Olivia, the woman Forrest has rescued from Indians and to whom he has proposed marriage, dislikes Shannon and suspects him when Forrest Bates is murdered. She writes Forrest's nephew and heir, and he comes to settle the property and the mystery. Although she falls in love with the nephew, she refuses to marry him immediately. People sometimes need to prove to themselves that they can survive for a time without help from others.

Harvey, Brett. *Cassie's Journey: Going West in the 1860's*. Illus. Deborah K. Ray. New York: Holiday House, 1988. 0-8234-0684-9, 40p. R=6; I=4.

In the 1860's, Cassie travels for eight months from Illinois to California with her family in a wagon built by her father. All the families in the wagon train suffer hardships but realize that they must continue the journey past the "elephant" (the difficult mountain crossings). Sometimes one must endure great hardship to improve one's prospects.

Harvey, Brett. *My Prairie Christmas*. Illus. Deborah Kogan Ray. New York: Holiday House, 1990. 0-8234-0827-2, 32p. R=4; I=4.

Elenore, ten, worries about how different Christmas will be since her family's move from Maine to the Dakota Territory in 1889 until her father goes out in a blizzard on Christmas Eve and does not return. The family copes with the situation by knowing that their father's safe return is more important than how they celebrate Christmas. Their best present is their father's reappearance on Christmas Day. People are more important than possessions.

Harvey, Brett. *My Prairie Year*. Illus. Deborah Kogan Ray. New York: Holiday House, 1986. 0-8234-0604-0, 40p. Paper, 1993. 0-8234-1028-5. R=7; I=4.

At nine in 1889, Elenore moves with her family from Maine to Dakota Territory and begins a new life with each day designated for a specific chore. The family copes with nature--a vicious tornado and a raging prairie fire, but they have the comfort of their neighbors on Friday visits to town and the yearly threshing events. They learn that "home" means family, not location. *American Library Association Notable Book for Children*, 1986.

Hill, Elizabeth Starr. *The Banjo Player.* New York: Viking, 1993. 0-670-84967-7, 197p. R=7; I=5.

At twelve in 1888, Jonathan leaves New York on the Orphan Train after being homeless and almost dead from the Great Blizzard, headed for New Orleans and possible adoption. He is pleased with his new family and enjoys practicing on the banjo that the hired man on the farm gives him. He soon trades places with an orphan working in a New Orleans restaurant who wants farm life, and eventually Jonathan joins a show on a riverboat, delighted to be performing with another orphan he knew from New York. If one faces a difficulty and surmounts it successfully, one has a good chance of overcoming the next obstacle.

Holland, Isabelle. *The Journey Home.* New York: Scholastic, 1990. 0-590-43110-2, 212p. Paper (Apple), 1993. 0-590-43111-0. R=2; I=5.

When their mother dies, Irish Catholics Maggie, twelve, and Annie, seven, travel by train with the Children's Aid Society to Kansas to be adopted. They find hostilities there against people who are strangers or different. They also discover that people have to be assertive and agreeable to bond with each other.

Howard, Ellen. *The Chickenhouse House.* New York: Atheneum, 1991. 0-689-31695-X, 52p. R=4; I=2.

In the late 1800's, Alena and her family move one hour from her grandparents to the chickenhouse on their new farm. They live in the tiny house for a year until they have time to build a large six-room farmhouse. Alena likes the coziness of the little house so much that she has difficulty adjusting to the new house.

Howard, Ellen. *Sister.* New York: Atheneum, 1990. 0-689-31653-4, 148p. R=5; I=6.

The birth and sudden death of a sister, in the sequel to *The Chickenhouse House*, interrupts Alena's last year in school during 1886 in the Midwest. She needs to help her mother recover from the loss. At the same time, she wants desperately to get her diploma. Her teacher helps her find a way. Life is many pieces, sometimes fitting snugly, and other times, not meshing very well. *American Library Association Notable Book for Children*, 1991.

Hurmence, Brenda. *Tancy*. Boston: Houghton Mifflin, 1984. 0-89919-228-9, 224p. R=7; I=8.**

Tancy, sixteen, has to adjust to her emancipation at the end of the American Civil War in 1865, but her ability to read secures her a job in an office registering other former slaves. She finds that her master was actually her father, and she spends time trying to find both her mother and the mother of a young child for whom she cares. When one searches for something, one must be prepared for what one finds. *Golden Kite Award*, 1985; *North Carolina Literary and Historical Association Award*, 1984; *School Library Journal "Best Book,"* 1984; *American Association of University Women Award*, 1984.

Jones, Douglas C. *Gone the Dreams and Dancing*. New York: Tor, 1987 (1984). Paper, 0-8125-8453-8, 323p. R=7; I=10+.

Liverpool Morgan tells the story of the end of the Comanches and their half-white leader Kwahadi beginning in 1875. Liver helps Kwahadi retrieve the bones of his mother through a complex process in order for Kwahadi to bury them next to his Comanche "mother" and thus end that part of his life's cycle. When a people try to impose their customs on others who neither want nor need them, disharmony often occurs and may destroy ideals within each group.

Jones, Douglas C. *Roman*. New York: Tor, 1989 (1986). 0-8125-8455-4, 389p. R=10; I=10+.

After his father returns from the Civil War in 1865, Roman (*Elkhorn Tavern*) leaves his home in Arkansas, goes to fight the Cherokees, and ends up in Leavenworth, Kansas. His success there leads people to want him to become a politician. But he decides to buy his partner's shares in their meat-packing and garbage-collecting businesses and sell the businesses in order to return to Arkansas and the woman he loves. After people have been exposed to a very different kind of life from that in which they grew up, they may decide they like the site of their earlier life better.

Jones, Douglas C. *The Search for Temperance Moon*. New York: Holt, 1991. 0-8050-1387-3, 324p. Large Type, New York: Thorndike, 1991. 1-56054-244-6. R=7; I=10+.

After the Civil War ends, someone murders Temperance Moon, an outlaw queen, in the Indian Nations. Her daughter, the madame of Fort Smith, Arkansas's best brothel, hires an ex-marshal to find the murderer even though the judge has declared the case closed. As people remember Temperance in all her wildness, they also remember her kindness to those who needed help. When people decide to judge others, they often do so without assessing the motivations behind the actions.

Karr, Kathleen. *It Ain't Always Easy.* New York: Farrar, Straus & Giroux, 1990. 0-374-33645-8, 229p. R=2; I=6.

In 1882, the orphans Jack, eleven, and Mandy, eight, meet and live in the coal bin of a bakery until its owner evicts them. They have a series of experiences which lead them to Pennsylvania, and further problems. But Jack returns to New York to get help from the woman at the Children's Aid Society. She and a man from Nebraska rescue Mandy, and the four of the them head to Nebraska to become a family. People who mistreat children seem to have a psychological need to hurt those weaker than they are.

Karr, Kathleen. *Oh, Those Harper Girls!* New York: Farrar, Straus, & Giroux, 1992. 0-374-35609-2, 182p. R=6; I=6.

Lily's father has a payment due on his Texas ranch in 1869, and after several misfortunes, he must think of a new scheme to get the money. Lily, thirteen, leads her five older sisters into cattle rustling, which fails. Then they rob a stage coach which yields them no money, but they are arrested and jailed. Eventually proclaimed innocent after their exploits attract reporters willing to pay for their story, they go on a stage tour enacting the events and earn the money for the ranch. Every group of disparate personalities needs someone to show leadership and organize its endeavors.

Lawlor, Laurie. *Addie Across the Prairie.* Illus. Gail Owens. Niles, Il: Whitman, 1986. 0-8075-0165-4, 128p. Paper, New York: Pocket Books (Minstrel), 1991. 0-671-70147-9. R=5; I=3.

While traveling across the prairie with her family to the Dakota Territory after the Civil War, Addie saves herself and her brother from a rapidly moving fire in the first in the series of books about Addie. Her bravery and quick thinking show that people can often overcome fears when they know they must act swiftly to survive.

Lawlor, Laurie. *Addie's Dakota Winter*. Illus. Toby Gowing. Niles, IL: Whitman, 1989. 0-8075-0171-9, 160p. Paper, New York: Pocket Books (Minstrel), 1993. 0-671-70148-7. R=5; I=4.

In the second book about Addie after *Addie Across the Prairie*, Addie has lived for one year in Dakota Territory. In 1884, when she goes to school, she meets Tilla, a Norwegian girl who quickly learns English. Although Tilla is not the perfect friend of Addie's imagination, Addie learns to accept Tilla for herself. People often unfairly assess others based on their own expectations rather than on the actual qualities the other possesses.

Lawlor, Laurie. *Addie's Long Summer*. Illus. Toby Gowing. Niles, IL: Whitman, 1992. 0-8075-0167-0, 173p. R=3; I=5.

During Addie's twelfth summer in 1886, in the third book about Addie after *Addie Across the Prairie* and *Addie's Dakota Winter*, her two cousins, fifteen and seventeen, come to visit the sodhouse farm. Elizabeth's affectations awe Addie until she sees her shallowness after almost losing her best friend Tilla because Elizabeth disapproves of her. When Addie discovers that the cousins have their own painful secrets, she learns compassion. People often guard themselves with unbecoming defenses so as not to have to face the truth.

Lawlor, Laurie. *George on His Own*. Morton Grove, IL: Whitman, 1993. 0-8075-2823-4, 191p. R=5; I=5.

When he is twelve in 1887, George, the brother of Addie in *Addie Across the Prairie*, *Addie's Dakota Winter*, and *Addie's Long Summer*, spends money he earns selling gopher tails to buy the trombone he has been borrowing to play in the town band. His father, distressed that George's sister has died of measles and angry that George did not buy a horse, decides to return the trombone. But George runs away and thwarts his father's plan. Asserting independence from parents becomes especially difficult when parents want a child to do something different from what the young person thinks is right.

Levin, Betty. *Brother Moose*. New York: Greenwillow, 1990. 0-688-09266-7, 214p. R=4; I=6.

In the 1870's, Louisa and Nell travel from an orphan's home in Canada to two sets of people who have offered to become their foster parents. After unexpected events and Louisa's mistreatment by her new foster family, an old Indian and his grandson take them into Maine to search for Nell's benefactor. The most important thing in life is to have someone who cares, regardless of background or financial circumstances.

MacBride, Roger Lea. *Little House on Rocky Ridge.* Illus. David Gilleece. New York: HarperCollins, 1993. 0-06-020843-0, 353p. Paper (Trophy), 0-06-440478-1. R=3; I=3.

In 1894, when Rose is seven, her parents Laura Ingalls and Alfonso Wilder decide to leave Dakota by wagon for the Missouri Ozarks where they hope to farm. When they arrive, they buy a farm which needs restoration and a barn. When neighbors come from miles around to "raise" the barn, the family no longer feels lonely and overworked, and Rose looks forward to her friendship with children living in town. Helping people often results in receiving help later. Ninth in the *Little House* series.

MacLachlan, Patricia. *Three Names.* Illus. Alexander Pertzoff. New York: HarperCollins, 1991. 0-06-024036-9, 32p. R=5; I=2.

A child's great grandfather tells of his experiences on the prairie going to school with his dog, Three Names. He loved to play fox-and-geese, hide-and-seek, and best of all, marbles. He enjoyed seeing his friends at school and each summer looked forward to September. Sometimes one needs to hear stories about one's family to appreciate what one has. *School Library Journal "Best Book,"* 1991.

McMurty, Larry. *Lonesome Dove.* New York: Simon & Schuster, 1985. 0-671-50420-7, 843p. Paper, New York: Penguin, 1993. 0-671-74471-2. R=9; I=10+.

The two partners of a business in Lonesome Dove, Texas, Gus and Call, decide to lead cattle stolen from Mexico on a cattle drive to Montana, an area where they can stake their own settlements during the 1870's. They take an assortment of people and meet other diverse characters on their journey which includes stampedes, lynchings, outlaws, storms, drought, gunfighting, and hostile Indians. Individuals need different stimuli to keep them content with their lives. *Pulitzer Prize,* 1986.

Martin, C. L. G. *Day of Darkness, Night of Light*. Illus. Victoria
M. Williams. New York: Dillon, 1989. 0-87518-357-3, 46p. R=4;
I=3.

An enormous fire sweeps toward Menominee, Michigan, in
1871, when Daniel is thirteen. The women and children seek
safety on a boat in the great lake nearby while the men, except
the cowards dressed as women, finally subdue the fire in the
swamp just outside town. Having to fight danger takes courage.

Myers, Walter Dean. *The Righteous Revenge of Artemis Bonner*.
New York: HarperCollins, 1992. 0-06-020846-5, 140p. R=4; I=5.

Artemis, fifteen, rushes to Arizona from New York in 1880
to help his aunt find his deceased uncle's treasure and to
avenge his uncle's death by killing the murderer, Catfish
Grimes. On his way, Artemis meets a young Cherokee who
accompanies him on his quest through Seattle, Anchorage, and
Tombstone. After he returns to New York, Catfish's jilted
mistress notifies him that Catfish is not dead as thought but
living on his uncle's money in Kansas. Artemis plans his trip
back to Kansas. Although improbable, the adventure is
entertaining.

O'Dell, Scott. *Streams to the River, River to the Sea: A Novel of
Sacagawea*. Boston: Houghton Mifflin, 1986. 0-395-40430-4.
Paper, New York: Fawcett (Juniper), 1988. 0-449-70244-8, 164p.
R=4; I=7.

When the Shoshone Sacagawea is thirteen, an enemy tribe
kidnaps her and makes her marry a French trader. When she
and her son accompany him on the Lewis and Clark expedition
to the Pacific, she falls in love with Clark. She realizes,
however, that she is Shoshone, not white, so she refuses Clark's
offer to go back East with him. She leaves her husband, and
returns to her tribe. Treating people with kindness costs
nothing and may gain the help that they are able to give. *Scott
O'Dell Award for Historical Fiction*, 1987.

O'Dell, Scott, and Elizabeth Hall. *Thunder Rolling in the
Mountains*. Boston: Houghton Mifflin, 1992. 0-395-59966-0,
128p. R=3; I=7.

The Blue Coats (American soldiers) fight Sound of Running
Feet's Nez Perce tribe while her father Joseph is its chief. She
eventually escapes the soldiers and walks toward Canada with

her intended husband, only to be betrayed by another tribe, the Assiniboin, before she again escapes and goes to search for Sitting Bull. Hate and greed only destroy people and places; they never build them. *Notable Children's Trade Books in the Field of Social Studies*, 1993.

Peck, Richard. *Voices after Midnight*. New York: Delacorte, 1989. 0-385-29779-3, 182p. Paper, New York: Dell, 1990. 0-440-40378-2. R=3; I=5.

Chad at fourteen, Luke at eight, and Heidi at sixteen, spend two weeks in New York City with their parents in a house where the children find themselves back in 1888 with the house's inhabitants. This historical fantasy reveals Luke's intense love of history and his understanding of how people felt in the past. What the children also find is their own individual senses of being, an unexpected result of their unusual experiences.

Roberts, Willo Davis. *Jo and the Bandit*. New York: Atheneum, 1992. 0-689-31745-X, 185p. R=6; I=5.

Jo and her brother are traveling on a stagecoach to Texas in the late 1860's, when a gang robs it. Jo's observations as an artist help her remember specific details about the men and horses. With her drawings for "wanted" posters and ideas for capture, she impresses her uncle, a judge. Her logic and intelligence finally gain his respect. The talents of young people should be appreciated and nurtured.

Robinet, Harriette Gillem. *Children of the Fire*. New York: Atheneum, 1991. 0-689-31655-0, R=5; I=5.

Hallelujah, eleven, an orphan of a slave escaped on the Underground Railway lives with kind foster parents. She helps save people in the destructive Chicago Fire of 1871 where she meets a wealthy white girl while both are lost from home. They work together and become friends during the emergency. When people treat each other like humans, they discover that all have similar emotions, regardless of color, class, or country of origin. *Friends of American Writers Juvenile Book Merit Award*, 1992.

Sandin, Joan, writer/illus. *The Long Way to a New Land.* New York: HarperCollins, 1981. 0-06-025194-8, 64p. Paper (Trophy), 1986. 0-06-444100-8. R=2; I=2.

In 1868, Carl Erik and Jonas's parents decide to leave Sweden for America because a drought is causing famine. They happily sail via England to America in anticipation of a better life. "An I Can Read Book."

Sandin, Joan, writer/illus. *The Long Way Westward.* New York: HarperCollins, 1989. 0-06-025207-3, 64p. Paper (Trophy), 1992. 0-06-444198-9. R=2; I=2.

In 1868, young Carl Erik and Jonas sail with their parents from Sweden to New York and take the train to Minnesota. They look forward to their new life without social classes and to learning English. Supportive family can help new experiences be exciting rather than frightening. "An I Can Read Book."

Santmyer, Helen H. *And Ladies of the Club.* Columbus OH: Ohio State Univ., 1982. 0-8142-0323-X, 1348p. Paper, New York: Berkley, 1988. 0-425-10243-2, 1440p. R=9; I=10+.

Sally and Anne start the Waynesboro, Ohio, Ladies Club after the Civil War in 1868. The group of women is composed of a judge's wife who supports women's suffrage and temperance, her daughter who commits the "indecency" of marrying for love, a lonely woman intellectual, a general's wife happy until her family faces scandal, and a gifted teacher who sacrifices for her students. Anne herself marries a physician who follows her father's footsteps but whose background tests Anne's courage. Sally becomes the town's wealthiest citizen, married to a German immigrant who loves both her and the American dream. They and those after them witness the events of Waynesboro and how they affect each person until the last charter member, Anne, dies of old age. One's happiness is an inward achievement of refusing to succumb to life's tragedies.

Stevens, Carla. *Lily and Miss Liberty.* Illus. Deborah Kogan Ray. New York: Scholastic, 1992. 0-590-44919-2, 80p. R=4; I=3.

Lily, excited that the French have given the statue of Miss Liberty to the United States, wants to give money for the pedestal. Her parents and grandmother help her make cardboard crowns for people to wear in honor of Miss Liberty, and her friend Rachel helps her sell them. When people work together, they can often accomplish much more than when working alone.

Stevens, Carla. *Trouble for Lucy.* Illus. Ronald Himler. New York: Clarion, 1979. 0-395-28971-8, 80p. Paper, 0-89919-523-7, 80p. R=3; I=3.

In 1843, young Lucy and her puppy leave Independence, Missouri, in a wagon train going to Fort Walla Walla, Oregon. On the trail, Lucy's mother delivers a baby girl. The family's love becomes clear against a background of concern for the mother's health.

Turner, Ann. *Dakota Dugout.* New York: Macmillan, 1985. 0-02-789700-1, 32p. Paper (Aladdin), 1989. 0-689-71296-0. R=3; I=3.

A grandmother remembers the discomforts of a sod house in Dakota in the nineteenth century and how she misses it when her family finally has money to move to a large house. Sometimes things that seem awful as they occur bring back many poignant memories. *American Library Association Notable Book for Children*, 1985.

Turner, Ann. *Grasshopper Summer.* New York: Macmillan, 1989. 0-02-789511-4, 166p. Paper, Mahwah, NJ: Troll, 1990. 0-8167-2262-5. R=2; I=4.

Sam's family leaves Kentucky for the Dakota Territory in 1874, his father looking for a new start after the Civil War. After they build a sod house and their corn starts growing, the locusts descend for at least a hundred miles around to eat everything including the green stripes on a neighbor's dress. Although only twelve, Sam helps his family to stay on the farm by secretly writing his grandfather for money that he plans to repay by trapping animals. Concern for family can make one's own life more rewarding.

Uchida, Yoshiko. *Samurai of Gold Hill.* Illus. Ati Forberg. Berkeley, CA: Creative Arts Books, 1985 (1972). Paper, 0-916870-86-3, 119p. R=4; I=6.

Koichi, at twelve, sails from Japan in 1869 to the United States where his father and partners attempt to start a tea and silk farm. Even though saboteurs destroy the farm, he hears news from Koichi sees an Indian ritual very similar to a

Buddhist one and realizes that his culture is not as unique as he had thought. Diligence may not reap visible rewards but those who work honestly and fairly can hope for satisfaction. *Commonwealth Club of California Book Awards*, 1972.

Welch, Catherine A. *Danger at the Breaker*. Minneapolis, MN: Carolrhoda, 1991. 0-87614-693-0, 48p. Paper, 1992. 0-87614-564-0. R=3; I=3.

When Andrew is eight, he stops school and begins working in the breaker house of a Pennsylvania coal mine because his family needs money. On his first day, an explosion in the mine frightens them, but his father, who is down in the mine, survives. In the 1800's, life in mining areas was difficult, dangerous, and dreary.

Whelan, Gloria. *Hannah*. Illus. Leslie Bowman. New York: Knopf, 1991. 0-679-91397-1, 64p. Paper, New York: Random, 1993. 0-679-82698-X. R=3; I=3.

When the new teacher comes to live with a poor family in their Michigan home in 1887, she decides that Hannah, nine, should go to school with the rest of the children even though she is blind. Hannah learns to count with an abacus made from acorns and knitting needles. The other students help her win a contest so that she has money to buy a Braille writing machine. When one sincerely tries to accomplish something, usually others will feel proud if they can help.

Wilder, Laura Ingalls. *By the Shores of Silver Lake*. Illus. Garth Williams. New York: HarperCollins, 1961 (1939). 0-06-026417-9, 292p. Paper, 1973. 0-06-440005-0. R=5; I=3.

After scarlet fever blinds Laura's sister Mary, the family moves to the Dakota Territory where Laura's father can find work. In 1880, more homesteaders arrive, and Laura dislikes all the people around the new town. At thirteen, she still loves the outdoors and the family as it creates its own entertainment of singing to her father's fiddling and playing checkers. Fourth in the *Little House* series. *Newbery Medal*, 1940.

Wilder, Laura Ingalls. *Farmer Boy*. Illus. Garth Williams. New York: HarperCollins, 1961 (1933). 0-06-026421-7, 372p. Paper, 1973. 0-06-440003-4. R=4; I=4.

Growing up on a farm in New York State, around 1875, Almanzo Wilder learns to sow and harvest crops, care for animals, and become self-sufficient. The cobbler, butter-buyer, and horse dealer come to the farm to trade. Almanzo's love of the animals leads his father to give him a colt to break and train when he is only ten. Some people show their abilities and have strong interests when they are very young.

Wilder, Laura Ingalls. *The First Four Years.* Illus. Garth Williams. New York: HarperCollins, 1971. 0-06-026427-6. Paper, 1972. 0-06-440031-X, 137. R=7; I=6.

Four difficult years follow Laura's marriage to Manly Wilder, but they survive illness and poor crops and have a daughter whom they name Rose. Neighbors and family helping makes life's setbacks easier to endure. Eighth in the *Little House* series.

Wilder, Laura Ingalls. *Little House in the Big Woods.* Illus. Garth Williams. New York: HarperCollins, 1961 (1932). 0-06-026431-4, 238p. Paper, 1973. 0-06-440001-8. R=2; I=2.

The year of 1872, when Laura is five, her family lives in the woods of Wisconsin. She loves the family togetherness when her father tells stories, and they prepare meat, vegetables, and fruits for the long, snowy winter. And when spring comes, they enjoy the maple syrup rising from the trees and celebrate with a dance to which all the neighbors and relatives come. First in the *Little House* series.

Wilder, Laura Ingalls. *Little House on the Prairie.* Illus. Garth Williams. New York: Harper, 1961 (1935). 0-06-026446-2, 338p. Paper, 1973. 0 06 080357-0. R=3; I=3.

When Laura is six, her family travels to Indian territory and settles in a house on the prairie which her father builds with the help of neighbors. They survive a prairie fire and a possible Indian uprising. When Laura's Pa hears that the United States government plans to move them three miles out of Indian territory to another place, he packs his family and leaves Missouri before the government interferes. Sometimes one must try to keep control of one's future rather than letting someone else dictate it. Second in the *Little House* series.

Wilder, Laura Ingalls. *Little Town on the Prairie.* Illus. Garth Williams. New York: HarperCollins, 1961 (1941). 0-06-026451-9, 308p. Paper, 1973. 0-06-440007-7. R=5; I=5.

Laura does so well in her speech at a School Exhibition that she wins a teaching certificate at fifteen. She regrets having to leave home but is pleased to know that she can make money for her blind sister Mary to attend college in Iowa. Laura undergoes the restlessness and uncertainties common to any fifteen-year-old but uses her growing maturity to overcome them. Sixth in the *Little House* series. *Newbery Honor*, 1942.

Wilder, Laura Ingalls. *The Long Winter.* Illus. Garth Williams. New York: HarperCollins, 1961 (1940). 0-06-026461-6, 334p. Paper, 1973. 0-06-440006-9. R=5; I=4.

The winter of 1880-1881 in Dakota Territory is one blizzard after another for Laura and her family. They cope, however, with very little food and using hay for fuel. Although the intense and interminable cold almost defeats her, Laura revives as soon as the Chinook wind rises overnight in April and melts the snow. Fifth in the *Little House* series. *Newbery Honor*, 1941.

Wilder, Laura Ingalls. *On the Banks of Plum Creek.* Illus. Garth Williams. New York: HarperCollins, 1961 (1937). 0-06-026471-3, 340p. Paper, 1973. 0-06-440004-2. R=5; I=3.

When Laura is seven, the family moves into a Minnesota sod house. Grasshoppers destroy the crops, and Laura's father has to leave home to find work. Laura realizes that having the family together is more important than having Christmas presents. Third in the *Little House* series. *Newbery Honor*, 1938.

Wilder, Laura Ingalls. *These Happy Golden Years.* Illus. Garth Williams. New York: HarperCollins, 1971 (1943). 0-06-026481-0, 289p. Paper, 1973. 0-06-440008-5. R=3; I=6.

When Laura, at fifteen, leaves home to teach school, Almanzo Wilder transports her back home on weekends. For the next three years, they go on buggy rides as she begins to appreciate him and eventually decides to marry him. When she is teaching away from home, Laura lives with a family that argues, making her realize how wonderfully warm and secure her own home is. Often people need to see other situations to appreciate their own good fortune. Seventh in the *Little House* series. *Newbery Honor*, 1944.

1890-1913

Angell, Judie. *One-Way to Ansonia.* New York: Bradbury, 1985.
0-02-705860-3, 183p. R=4; I=6.**

In 1893, Rose, eleven, arrives at Ellis Island from Russia
where her family and neighbors have suffered in pogroms led
by Czar Nicholas's soldiers. She and her brother and sisters
meet their father and his new wife. As they readjust to each
other, Rose stuns her family by choosing to attend a night
school in addition to working all day, but her independence
leads her out of their poverty in the New York ghetto. Few
people have the courage to follow their dreams when they must
forego old ethnic traditions no longer valid in their new
environments.

Beatty, Patricia. *Behave Yourself, Bethany Brant.* New York:
Morrow, 1986. 0-688-05923-6, 172p. R=3; I=4.

When Bethany is eleven in 1898, her mother dies in
childbirth, and her preacher father decides to become a circuit
rider and move to another town in Texas. While staying with
her relatives, Bethany feels especially guilty for spending
money on a fortune teller at the local fair. When she discovers
that someone has gambled away the money that was supposed
to build her father's new church, she succumbs even further to
sin by agreeing to draw a card from a deck in hopes of winning
the money back. She does win by drawing the high card, and
her cousin, whom she has recently learned to respect,
understands Bethany's concern for her father. Parents
sometimes make decisions which children may not like but to
which they have to adjust until they become independent.

Beatty, Patricia. *Sarah and Me and the Lady from the Sea.*
New York: Morrow, 1989. 0-688-08045-6, 182p. R=3; I=5.

Marcella's father loses his investment when a flood destroys
his Portland, Oregon, dry goods store in 1894, when she is
twelve. The family has to stay in their summer beach home in
Washington state. At first she feels superior to the peninsula
people, but soon she becomes grateful for their help. Since
Marcella's mother and siblings know nothing of cleaning and
cooking, things their servants had done before, they have to

learn, and to their surprise, they discover that they like being independent and useful. Sometimes seemingly awful circumstances reveal unexpected strengths in people.

Bethancourt, T. Ernesto. *The Tomorrow Connection.* New York: Holiday, 1984. 0-8234-0543-5, 134p. R=2; I=8.**

Ritchie and Matty, black and white jazz musicians of eighteen in 1976, time travel back to 1942, 1912, and finally 1906 when they meet Houdini. After they tell him about all of his tricks, even the ones not yet invented in 1906, he has them travel with him to San Francisco where they finally the find the key to return them to 1976. When real life seems deadening, traveling to a fantasy world can be invigorating.

Collier, James Lincoln. *My Crooked Family.* New York: Simon & Schuster, 1991. 0-671-74224-8, 181p. Paper (Half Moon), 1993. 0-671-86693-1. R=4; I=7.

In 1910, Roger, thirteen, and his little sister almost starve while their alcoholic parents drink away what little money they have. A man approaches Roger about working for him, and Roger decides that buying food is better than being caught stealing it. He becomes involved with a robbery and finds that his father has preceded him in the crime. Once someone has committed one crime, committing another may be easier.

Conrad, Pam. *My Daniel.* New York: HarperCollins, 1989. 0-06-021314-0, 137p. Paper (Trophy), 0-06-440309-2. R=4; I=5.

Ellie's grandmother from Nebraska comes to see her family in New York. During their visit to the Natural History Museum, her grandmother Julia recalls her twelfth year in the early twentieth century when her brother Daniel found dinosaur bones. Although not strictly historical fiction, Julia's poignant memories of her brother, her parents, and their farm recreates a vivid sense of time and place. The distance between generations lessens when people share their memories and emotions. *Western Writers of America Spur Award*, 1989.

Cooney, Barbara. *Island Boy.* New York: Viking, 1988. 0-670-81749-X, 32p. Paper, New York: Puffin. 0-14-050756-6. R=5; I=2.

When Matthais is little, in the nineteenth century, his father moves his entire family to an island off the coast of New

England. Matthais grows and becomes a ship's captain on the East Coast. But he returns to the island and raises a family, including his grandson Matthais whose mother is living with old Matthais when he dies. Sometimes one must leave home and see new places before one knows where one really feels "at home." *School Library Journal* "*Best Book*," 1988.

Cross, Verda. *Great-Grandma Tells of Threshing Day.* Illus. Gail Owens. Morton Grove, IL: Albert Whitman, 1992. 0-8075-3042-5, 40p. R=4; I=3.

As a child during the early 1900's in Missouri, a great-grandmother remembers her favorite time of the year, threshing day in June. The neighboring families came to help-- fathers working in the field and mothers preparing food. The narrator remembers that all enjoyed being together with everyone sharing the work. Their cooperation allowed neighbors to get their wheat threshed in one day, a major achievement.

De Angeli, Marguerite. *The Lion in the Box.* New York: Doubleday, 1975. 0-385-03317-6. Paper, New York: Dell, 1992. 0-440-40740-0, 80p. R=3; I=4.

In 1901, Lili, seven, wants a doll for Christmas which her widowed mother cannot afford. But someone who has met her mother sends them a Christmas box, saying a lion is inside. They enjoy their gifts, and Lili gets her doll. But the fellowship of the four sisters and a brother, plus the paper decorations on their tree, would have also kept them happy.

Dexter, Catherine. *Mazemaker.* New York: Morrow, 1989. 0-688-07383-2, 202p. R=4; I=5.

In a historical fantasy, Winnie disappears into a schoolyard maze and finds herself in a dilapidated maze in 1889 instead of 1989. While desperately trying to get back to 1989, she meets people who live in the town and observes their situations and superstitions. By following a cat, she is able to finally return to 1989. In 1989, she searches for William, the mazemaker who disappeared from 1889 to tell him he is welcome to return. Winnie gains perspective about herself and her town by seeing it as it once was and then reading about its history.

Dionetti, Michelle. *Coal Mine Peaches*. Illus. Anita Riggio. New York: Orchard/Watts, 1991. 0-531-08548-1, 32p. R=7; I=K.

A grandchild tells about her grandfather who came from Italy, where he worked in a coal mine and called lumps of coal "peaches," to America for work on the Brooklyn Bridge in New York City. There, he met her grandmother, also Italian. They had five children, one of whom is her father. Family stories give a sense of history, security, and accomplishment.

Doctorow, E. L. *Ragtime*. New York: Random, 1975. 0-394-46901-1, 288p. Paper, New York: Fawcett, 1987. 0-449-2148-1, 352p. R=6; I=10+.

In the postwar era of 1902 to 1917, a white upper middle class flag manufacturer, a Jewish immigrant silhouette artist, and a black jazz pianist, try to cope with their situations. Throughout the story, the three families meet each other in varied circumstances, with the white family looking after the jazz pianist's girlfriend and child, and the starving Jewish artist becoming a movie maker who marries the flagmaker's wife after the flagmaker sinks on a transatlantic ship. The jazz pianist turns revolutionary when police mistake his girlfriend's actions and shoot her. People have to struggle to overcome situations into which they have either been born or placed through unfortunate circumstances.

Edmonds, Walter. *Bert Breen's Barn*. Syracuse, NY: Syracuse Univ., 1991 (1975). Paper, 8156-0255-3, 80p. R=5; I=6.

Tom, thirteen in 1910, decides to buy the deceased Bert Breen's barn and move it to his home to shelter the cows he plans to raise. While Tom is earning the money, the Breen's widow dies, and Tom has to buy the barn from the New Yorker who purchases the land after her death. Others know money might be on the land, and they threaten Tom when they search for it, but he discovers Breen's money in the floor. This suspenseful mystery ends satisfactorily when the person who most deserves the money gets it. *National Book Award*, 1976; *Christopher Medal*, 1976.

Edwards, Pat. *Little John and Plutie*. Boston: Houghton Mifflin, 1988. 0-395-48223-2, 172p. R=4; I=5.*

In the late nineteenth century, John, nine, becomes friends with Plutie when John and his mother leave home after John's father goes to a saloon after promising not to and has his money stolen. After Plutie breaks a white man's window, the man beats him, but John's father helps Plutie by promising the man that Plutie will pay properly for his mistake. Young people often choose friends based on their character rather than the color of their skin.

Froelich, Margaret. *Reasons to Stay*. Boston: Houghton Mifflin, 1986. 0-395-41068-1, 181p. R=4; I=7.**

After Babe's mother dies in 1906, she escapes her dishonest stepfather with her two siblings and goes to her friend's grandparents' house. Soon after, she locates her own grandparents, but realizes that they will never accept her. Trying to piece together a fragmented family may not be worth the difficulty if its members do not love each other.

Goldin, Barbara Diamond. *Fire! The Beginnings of the Labor Movement*. Illus. James Watling. New York: Viking, 1992. 0-670-84475-6, 54p. R=3; I=4.

Rosie, living in Brooklyn, wants to work with her sister in the garment factory instead of going to school since in 1911, eleven-year-olds are allowed to work. But the factory burns, killing 146 people including their cousin. As a result, Rosie decides to stay in school and campaign for a garment workers' union. Jewish immigrants from Russia, accustomed to the terror of the pogroms, hesitated to assert themselves even with hazardous working conditions like locked factory doors and no fire escapes. Unless challenged, some people will take advantage of those less fortunate in any country. "Once Upon America Series."

Gregory, Kristiana. *Earthquake at Dawn*. San Diego: Harcourt Brace, 1992. 0-15-200446-7, 192p. R=6; I=6.

Daisy, fifteen, sets out with Edith Irvine, a famous photographer, on a journey around the world in 1906. Their trip is abruptly terminated in San Francisco when a devastating earthquake occurs before their scheduled departure. They survive, help others who hastily construct tents out of doors to escape further aftershock fatalities, and return to Edith's home with both photographs and mental pictures of the horror they have experienced. In times of severe stress, the safety of humans becomes the most important goal for compassionate people. "Great Episodes."

Griffin, Peni. *Switching Well.* New York: McElderry, 1993. 0-689-50581-7, 218p. R=5; I=5.

In 1891, Ada, twelve, wishes she lived in 1991, and simultaneously Amber, in 1991, wishes she lived one hundred years earlier. They switch lives through a water well. Ada is surprised by the changes in 1991. Amber is dismayed that a deaf child is almost committed to a school for the retarded and that Christians seem to have more rights and recognition than Jews. Having a chance to see what people have to endure or accept in different times may help one understand or decide to change one's own life.

Gross, Virginia T. *The Day It Rained Forever: A Story of the Johnstown Flood.* Illus. Ronald Himler. New York: Viking, 1991. 0-670-83552-8, 52p. Paper, New York: Puffin, 1993. 0-14-034567-1. R=3; I=4.

When the damn breaks in the torrents of rain above Johnstown, Pennsylvania in 1887, Christina's mother hears a baby cry outside, and she finds and saves it. The family cares for the baby, fearful that someone will claim it, but with over two thousand people dead in the flood, no parents come forth. The baby replaces the baby born dead in their family only two months before. When people make decisions, they must consider the effects of those decisions on the lives of others.

Hamilton, Virginia. *The Bells of Christmas.* Illus. Lambert Davis. San Diego: Harcourt Brace, 1989. 0-15-206450-8, 64p. R=4; I=4.

Jason, twelve, and his family, the Bells, celebrate Christmas in 1890 at their Ohio home, where they have lived for one hundred years, along the National Road stretching from east to west. Jason loves the holiday, the gifts, the family coming together, going to church, and this year, best of all, his father's new mechanical wooden leg designed and made by his uncle. The ritual and excitement of a Christmas family holiday make it an event not to be missed. *American Library Association Notable Book for Children,* 1990.

Hamm, Diane Johnston. *Bunkhouse Journal.* New York: Scribner's, 1990. 0-684-19206-3, 89p. R=3; I=8.

Sandy leaves Denver in 1911 after his drunken lawyer father humiliates him in front of others. He goes to live with a cousin on her husband's Wyoming ranch. As he writes his journal, he continues to worry about his father and feels responsible when he dies. The people he has met help him sort out his emotions, and he decides to return to Denver for at least one year of college. Because children often do not know the history of their parents' relationship, they may feel accountable for situations when they actually had no control over the origin or the outcome. *Western Heritage Awards*, 1991.

Harvey, Brett. *Immigrant Girl: Becky of Eldridge Street*. Illus. Deborah Kogan Ray. New York: Holiday House, 1987. 0-8234-0638-5, 40p. R=5; I=4.

When she is ten in 1910, Becky Moscowitz leaves Grodno, Russia, and the threat of pogroms against Jews, with her family of seven for New York. As a foreigner, she studies hard to escape the label "greenie." Her grandmother only speaks Yiddish because she wants the family to remember its heritage as it continues to follow Jewish religious customs with other immigrants around Hester Street. To survive in a new country, one needs to learn the customs, but one does not have to forget family or religious traditions.

Highwater, Jamake. *Eyes of Darkness*. New York: Lothrop, Lee & Shepard, 1985. 0-688-41993-3, 189p. R=8; I=9.

As Alexander East faces the hundreds of dead Sioux at Wounded Knee in 1890, he recalls his own life as a young Native American who loved his people but lost touch with them and his roots when his father made him begin living with whites. He remembers being eight and earning his name Yesa ("winner") by leading his tribal lacrosse team to victory. At sixteen, he danced the Bear Dance for his dying friend. And afterwards, he left the reservation for the white man's schools, becoming a successful physician. Sometimes to be true to oneself, one must oppose choices other's may have made.

Hooks, William H. *A Flight of Dazzle Angels*. New York: Macmillan, 1988. 0-02-744430-9, 169p. R=4; I=8.*

Annie Earle, fifteen, her retarded brother, sixteen, and her mother all have health problems. Annie Earle's clubfoot keeps her from dancing and enjoying people her own age. Since Annie Earle's wealthy mother seems near death in 1908 in their Southern town, her aunt tries to position herself as legal guardian over the children and the wealth, but Annie Earl and her mother avoid the interference when Annie Earl's new friend helps. A person with a disability often develops other traits strong enough to compensate.

Hoppe, Joanne. *Dream Spinner.* New York: Morrow, 1992. 0-688-08559-8, 228p. R=4; I=7.

Mary, fifteen, moves with her new stepmother and father to a different house. She reads an article on dreaming in a science magazine and begins dreaming about the people who lived in the house in 1893. She dreams the name of an old railroad station on the property about which no one else seems to know. But research reveals that the station and the people about which she dreams were real. Sometimes a different perspective on a situation, no matter how unusual, helps one understand the present more readily.

Howard, Elizabeth Fitzgerald. *Chita's Christmas Tree.* Illus. Floyd Cooper. New York: Bradbury, 1989. 0-02-744621-2, 32p. Paper, New York: Macmillan (Aladdin), 1993. 0-689-71739-3. R=3; I=2.

As the twentieth century begins, Chita and her father leave their Baltimore, Maryland, home to look for a tree in the nearby woods for Santa to bring on Christmas. As days pass, Chita helps prepare the cookies and decorations, and she worries that Santa will not know which tree to bring. Rituals make holidays special. *American Library Association Notable Book for Children*, 1990.

Howard, Ellen. *The Cellar.* Illus. Patricia Rose Mulvihill. New York: Atheneum, 1992. 0-689-31724-7, 52p. R=2; I=2.

Around 1900, everything seems to be slightly wrong to little Faith--being pecked by the hen, falling into the cellar, getting burrs in her feet, not making neat and even sampler stitches. But when she goes into the cellar alone to get apples for the family, she successfully returns. She finally realizes that her brother's teasing has plagued her day.

Howard, Ellen. *Edith Herself.* Illus. Ronald Himler. New York: Atheneum, 1987. 0-689-31314-4, 132p. R=3; I=4.

After Edith's mother dies around 1890, she has to live with her sister who has a son near her age. Her sister's husband is strict, and his mother smells, but the most upsetting part is her blackouts. Although later diagnosed as the onset of epilepsy, she is treated as if she has a terrible disease. Fearful that Edith will have a spell at school where the children will laugh, her sister tries to keep her at home, but Edith wants to go to her one-room school. Adjusting to a new home is difficult, but a misunderstood health problem can exacerbate the situation. *School Library Journal* "*Best Book,*" 1987.

Howard, Ellen. *Her Own Song.* New York: Atheneum, 1988. 0-689-31444-2, 160p. R=3; I=5.

When Mellie's adoptive father is knocked unconscious in a work accident, and she, at eleven, is left alone because her aunt is vacationing and her mother dead, she finds out about her past. The Chinese laundry man takes her to Portland hospitals to find her father and then to his home to eat. She seems to know the room although she has never been there--or at least she thinks not until she finds and reads her adoption papers. She discovers that she was sold to the Lui family and then forcibly removed by police because Chinese in 1908 were prohibited from having white children. Mellie or Mei-Le is relieved to have so many people who care about her after feeling very lonely. What seems like abandonment can sometimes be very strong love.

Irwin, Hadley. *I Be Somebody.* New York: Dutton, 1988 (1984). Paper (NAL), 0-451-15303-0, 160p. R=4; I=4.

In 1910, Rap is ten. His Aunt Spicy with whom he lives decides that they will accompany other people from their Oklahoma town to Athabasca, Canada, to homestead. On the train, she dies, but not before telling him the identity of his father. Education is one major way that a person can be "somebody" in a prejudiced world.

Jones, Douglas C. *Come Winter.* Little Rock AR: Univ. of Arkansas, 1992 (1989). 1-55728-259-5, 432p. R=10; I=10+.

In the third novel after *Elkhorn Tavern* and *Roman*, Roman returns to Arkansas from Kansas where he lives until his death in 1899. His marriage unfulfilling, he fathers a child out of wedlock, and continues his role as the town's leading banker with political power but involved in unsavory situations. Sometimes money and power seem to squeeze happiness from people's lives, even those who have tried to keep their values.

Jones, Douglas C. *Remember Santiago.* New York: Tor, 1992 (1988). 0-8125-0386-4, 354p. R=7; I=10+.

Eben Pay comes to Fort Smith, Arkansas, meets a Cherokee woman, marries her, and has a half-blood child. When she dies after childbirth, he is distraught and decides to join the army in its 1898 fight in Cuba. Being involved in a disorganized fiasco along with Theodore Roosevelt and Clara Barton helps him overcome some of his despondency, so he returns home to his son. Recovering from the loss of a loved one often takes a long time.

Jones, Douglas C. *Winding Stair.* New York: Holt, 1979. 0-03-050936-9, 277p. R=6; I=10+.**

Soon after Eben Pay, a young lawyer, arrives in Fort Smith, Arkansas, he sees the results of four murders and a rape as well as the psychological scars on the only survivor, Jennie, eighteen. Although four men are captured, convicted, and hung, Pay continues to be affected by the process and by Jennie. Without law and order, some humans will take what is not theirs and ruin other people's lives without seeming to care about the results.

Kinsey-Warnock, Natalie. *The Wild Horses of Sweetbriar.* Illus. Ted Rand. New York: Cobblehill, 1990. 0-525-65015-6, 32p. R=3; I=2.

When the narrator is eight, she and her mother live on an island off Nantucket during 1903 while her father stays at the lighthouse. She loves the sea, the geese, and the ten wild horses, but she becomes concerned for them because of the scarcity of food for them in the very cold winter. Nature has both very beautiful and very cruel aspects, and learning to accept the latter is sometimes difficult.

Kudlinski, Kathleen. *Earthquake! A Story of Old San Francisco.* Illus. Ronald Himler. New York: Viking, 1993. 0-670-84874-3, 64p. R=3; I=5.

Early in the morning on April 18, 1906, Phillip awakens to dogs barking all over San Francisco. In his father's livery stable, he calms the horses, also upset, until an earthquake throws him over, followed by after shocks. Soon the wind blows and spreads the fires caused by gas lines exploding throughout the city. He, his family, and the horses escape the devastation.

When a disaster occurs, one must look after the people and animals as quickly as possible. "Once Upon America" series.

Lasky, Katherine. *The Night Journey.* Illus. Trina. S. Hyman. New York: Puffin, 1986. Paper, 0-14-032048-2, 152p. R=6; I=6.

When Rache is thirteen, her grandmother Sachie relates the story of her family's escape from Russia and the Jewish pogroms in 1900. They hid under chicken crates, paraded as Purim players, and crossed the border with cookies hiding gold inside. Sachie went through a very stressful situation. Many humans have helped others so that they may continue their lives without fear. *National Jewish Awards,* 1982; *Sydney Taylor Book Award,* 1981; *American Library Association Notable Book for Children,* 1981; *Association of Jewish Libraries Award,* 1982.

Leighton, Maxinne Rhea. *An Ellis Island Christmas.* Illus. Dennis Nolan. New York: Viking, 1992. 0-670-83182-4, 32p. R=2; I=2.

Krysia, six, arrives with her mother and brother at Ellis Island from Poland at the turn of the twentieth century to meet her father, already in New York. After their long sea voyage, they enjoy the beautiful Christmas tree and find that Saint Mikolaj (Saint Nicholas) comes to America as well as Poland. Leaving all one has to come to a new country takes great courage.

Leonard, Laura. *Finding Papa.* New York: Atheneum, 1991. 0-689-31526-0, 185p. R=6; I=5.

Abby, thirteen, and her older brother and sister take a train to San Francisco from Estes, Kansas, to join their widowed father and his intended bride. When they arrive in 1905, he is away prospecting for gold so they all three take jobs. When he returns, he marries someone the children met on the train instead, and they all separate for new adventures. Some people need to have different stimuli in their lives and seek jobs other than working in an office.

Levinson, Nancy Smiler. *Clara and the Bookwagon.* Illus. Carolyn Croll. New York: HarperCollins, 1988. 0-06-023838-0, 64p. Paper (Trophy), 1991. 0-06-4441134-2. R=2; I=2.

Clara's father thinks that farmers have no time for reading and nearly refuses to let Clara borrow a book from the new book wagon librarian in 1905. When he discovers that the books are free, he decides to let the librarian teach her to read so that she can borrow books. "An I Can Read Book."

McCall, Edith. *Better Than a Brother.* Minneapolis, MN: Walker, 1988. 0-8027-6783-4, 133p. R=3; I=6.

As 1899 turns to 1900, Hughie, thirteen, worries about the valuable gold locket given to her by her grandmother that she has lost in the snow. One of the ice workers on the nearby lake tells her that he has found it and will give it to her in return for sexual favors. But her friend, a boy, finds out and coerces her to tell her father. Doing something one has been told not to do can lead to serious, unexpected problems.

McKenzie, Ellen Kindt. *Stargone John.* Illus. William Low. New York: Holt (Redfeather), 1990. 0-8050-1451-9, 67p. R=4; I=4.

As the nineteenth century ended, nine-year-old Lisa accompanies her first-grade brother to the one-room school house. John only talks to her and refuses to respond to the hostile new teacher. Loving help from the blind former teacher reveals John's real intelligence and alleviates Lisa's suffering for her brother's "stargone" ways. *Bay Area Book Reviewers Association Award, 1991.*

Matthiessen, Peter. *Killing Mister Watson.* New York: Random, 1990. 0-394-55400-0, 372p. Paper, New York: Vintage, 1991. 0-679-73405-8. R=7; I=10+.

E. J. Watson creates a reputation that stretches from that of murderer to loving father in the Everglades of Florida in the 1890's. By 1910, after the Great Hurricane, his neighbors await his return, some ready to take justice into their own hands. People show hostility towards others for a variety of reasons including disapproval of misdeeds or jealousy toward accomplishments.

Mayerson, Evelyn Wilde. *The Cat Who Escaped from Steerage.* New York: Scribner's, 1990. 0-684-19209-8, 64p. R=7; I=4.

On the journey from Poland to New York via France in 1910, Chanah, nine, loses her cat which escapes from steerage onto the other boat decks. Chanah frantically searches but is turned back each time by guards; however, the cat adopts a Polish woman who delivers it to Chanah on Ellis Island. People trying to get their freedom sometimes endure subhuman conditions.

Mazzio, Joann. *Leaving Eldorado.* Boston: Houghton Mifflin, 1993. 0-395-64381-3, 170p. R=4; I=8.

When Maude is fourteen, her mother dies, and her father leaves her in Eldorado, New Mexico, while he goes to the Yukon to search for gold in 1896. Through her diary entries, addressed to her mother, she tells of her experiences working for very little money, meeting--and surprised at herself for liking--a "fallen" woman, and getting a marriage proposal. After receiving money for saving another woman from a fire, she leaves El Dorado to take art lessons, her real desire. To refuse the security of marriage, a female needs to have external sources of money and the courage to take risks.

Naylor, Phyllis Reynolds, and Lura Schield Reynolds. *Maudie in the Middle.* Illus. Judith Gwyn Brown. New York: Atheneum, 1988. 0-689-31395-0, 161p. R=5; I=5.

As the middle of seven children in 1908, Maudie, eight, often feels neglected and either too old or too young to do things. When her parents have to leave for five weeks to help her aunt whose husband is ill, she has to comfort the baby who has a fever. She finds that being needed is a wonderful feeling. When people have to take responsibilities, they often change and begin to respect themselves.

Nelson, Theresa. *Devil Storm*. New York: Orchard/Watts, 1987. 0-531-08311-X, 214p. Paper, New York: Dell, 1991. 0-440-40409-6. R=3; I=5.

Walter's mother still mourns his brother's death a year afterward in 1900, but the family continues to try to live normally, growing watermelons on Galveston Bay. During the year, Walter, thirteen, and his sister befriend Old Tom, a tramp who has wandered into the area, and when Walter's father is out of town, Tom saves the family from a terrible storm which destroys their home. Only by trying to get to know a person can one separate the hearsay from the truth.

Pellowski, Anne. *First Farm in the Valley: Anna's Story*. Illus. Wendy Watson. New York: Philomel, 1982. 0-399-20887-9, 192p. R=5; I=4.**

Young Anna has several brothers and sisters but is happy to have another Polish friend her age on her family's Wisconsin farm in 1876. She becomes old enough to help her mother do chores, and she especially likes the Fourth of July with its fireworks. When she hears her parents discuss Poland's government leaders, the Kaiser and Bismarck who speak German, she does not understand what happened to the kings and queens who spoke Polish. Learning the reasons behind one's parents' decision to come to America remain baffling until one begins to understand the importance of individual rights.

Pendergraft, Patricia. *Hear the Wind Blow*. New York: Philomel, 1988. 0-399-21528-X, 208p. R=5; I=6.

In the early twentieth century, Isadora, twelve, goes to school in a small town where she has both enemies and friends. During the year, the male schoolteacher marries someone already pregnant, Isadora's best friend dies because her family allows only herbal instead of medicinal treatment, and she gets to take dancing lessons, one of her dreams. In a seemingly ordinary life, surprises always change the people involved.

Precek, Katharine Wilson. *Penny in the Road*. Illus. Patricia Cullen-Clark. New York: Macmillan, 1989. 0-02-774970-3, 32p. R=6; I=3.

A grandfather remembers the day in 1913, when on his way to school, he finds a penny dated 1793. He tries to imagine what the life of the person who lost it might have been like, and he never trades or sells the penny. Sometimes objects have symbolic meanings that outweigh their market value.

Rappaport, Doreen. *Trouble at the Mines.* Illus. Joan Sandin. New York: HarperCollins, 1987. 0-690-04446-1, 96p. R=4; I=3.**

In 1898, after deaths in the mines and no pay raises, the coal miners in Arnot, Pennsylvania, begin striking. Mother Jones, their wives, and daughters like Rosie, keep many of the men, except Rosie's Uncle Jack, from succumbing to the demands of the greedy mine owners. When the strike ends successfully, Rosie happily renews friendship with Jack's daughter Mary, her cousin.

Riskind, Mary. *Apple Is My Sign.* Boston: Houghton Mifflin, 1981. 0-395-30852-6, 146p. Paper, 1993. 0-395-65747-4. R=4; I=4.

In 1899, Harry, ten, travels to Philadelphia to enter the school for the deaf. His fear soon dissipates as he begins to play football and make friends with the people who like his clever drawings. Harry's honesty and difficulty communicating with people who refuse to acknowledge him reveal the special problems that the deaf have beyond those adjustments that everyone must make. *American Library Association Notable Book for Children,* 1981.

Rodowsky, Colby F. *Fitchett's Folly.* New York: Farrar, Straus & Giroux, 1987. 0-374-32342-9, 165p. R=4; I=5.

Around 1890, Sarey's father drowns off the eastern coast of the United States while saving a child from a shipwreck in which the rest of her family dies. Sarey reacts with hostility when the girl, Faith, stays with them, and she accuses Faith of causing her father's death. After Faith understands Sarey's hostility and leaves, Sarey realizes that Faith needs a family and that she must find her and bring her back.

Sebestyen, Ouida. *Words by Heart.* New York: Bantam, 1983 (1979). Paper, 0-553-27179-2, 144p. R=4; I=5.

Lena Sills, a black girl of twelve, in 1910, unexpectedly beats a white boy in a spelling bee but refuses the prize, a bow tie. Her family supports her desire to learn while everyone else works hard in the fields. A white sharecropper family with a worthless reputation tries to spoil the Sills' successes, but after a tragedy, all learn that they must work together to survive. *International Children's Book Awards*, 1980; *American Book Award*, 1981.

Sherman, Eileen B. *Independence Avenue.* Philadelphia, PA: Jewish Publication Society, 1990. 0-8276-0367-3, 145p. R=6; I=6.

Pretending to be seventeen, Elias at fourteen travels from Russia to Kansas City via Galveston, Texas, in 1907. He finds work as a tailor, begins to learn English, falls in love, and suffers the news that his parents have died in one of the czar's pogroms against the Jews. His pain, however, is relieved when his six-year-old brother arrives, saved by a family friend. For freedom, people must endure separation from family and other difficulties, but honesty and perseverance help lessen the pain.

Shiefman, Vicki. *Good-bye to the Trees.* New York: Atheneum, 1993. 0-689-31806-5, 150p. R=4; I=5.

In 1907, after her father dies and the family works to survive, Fagel leaves Russia for America. She earns boat passage money for the rest of her family, but she realizes that whatever she does, she cannot work for someone who considers her no better than a slave. People are often victims of circumstances; others, who would maltreat them, should realize that they too could have their own situations suddenly change.

Skurzynski, Gloria. *The Tempering.* New York: Clarion, 1983. 0-899-19152-5, 178p. R=7; I=8.**

Karl, at fifteen, pleased with his new job in the Pennsylvania steel mills during 1912, is quickly fired when his friend plays a foolish trick on another worker. Karl reluctantly reappears in school, falls in love with the new teacher, and thinks she is having an affair when she is secretly (and illegally) married. Although happy to have her recognize his musical ability, he decides to return to the mills at sixteen to help organize unions. When people identify injustice and want to make it right, they have to risk their safety. *Golden Kite Award*, 1984; *School Library Journal "Best Book,"* 1983; *Choice List of Internationale Jugenbibliothek of UNESCO.*

Snyder, Zilpha Keatley. *And Condors Danced.* New York: Delacorte, 1987. 0-385-29575-8, 216p. Paper, New York: Dell (Yearling), 1989. 0-440-40153-4, 224p. R=6; I=6.

In 1907, Carly, eleven, exuberant with life on a California ranch, loses her mother and her dog. But her aunt and her aunt's Chinese butler keep her while her two sisters remain at home. The aunt and the butler help her gain perspective about her situation. Trying to understand why one reacts differently than one expects can be a positive process.

Stevens, Carla. *Anna, Grandpa, and the Big Storm.* Illus. Margot Tomes. New York: Clarion, 1982. 0-89919-066-9, 60p. Paper, New York: Puffin, 1986. 0-14-031705-8, 64p. R=3; I=2.

Anna, seven, and her grandfather get caught on an elevated train in New York City during a blizzard in 1888. Her grandfather's kindness to strangers helps all those on the train return safely home. Having a chance to help others often takes one's mind off of one's own problems.

Terris, Susan. *Nell's Quilt.* New York: Scholastic, 1988 (1987). 0-590-41914-5, 162p. R=4; I=10.

In 1899, Nell, eighteen, learns that her parents want her to marry a widower ten years older with a young child when what she wants is to go to Smith College in Boston. Nell's health slowly dwindles while she sews on a quilt, and she expects to die as soon as it is finished, but during her first few hours under the completed quilt, she realizes that others, including the kittens, need her. People can do almost anything with their lives--abuse it, ignore it, waste it, or nurture it.

Tripp, Valerie. *Changes for Samantha: A Winter Story.* Illus. Nancy Niles. Madison, WI: Pleasant Company, 1990 (1988). 0-937295-46-9, 72p. Paper, 1988. 0-937295-47-7. R=7; I=4.

Samantha moves to New York City in 1904 to live with her aunt and uncle where she waits impatiently to hear from her friend Nellie. Nellie and her sisters plan to come to New York to live with Nellie's uncle since their parents have recently died from influenza. After not hearing from Nellie, Samantha traces her and finds them in an orphanage, her uncle having abandoned the girls. Samantha coerces them to run away because Nellie is scheduled to take the Orphan Train to the west. Samantha's aunt and uncle decide to keep all of the girls. Having someone care can ease the pain of loss. "The American Girls Collection."

Vogt, Esther Loewen. *A Race for Land.* Scottdale, PA: Herald Press, 1992. Paper, 0-8361-3575-X, 112p. R=6; I=4.

Ben and his family find that they must move from their rented farm in Kansas during 1893. Having immigrated from Russia, they decide to join the Oklahoma land race. They stake a claim and happily find that other Mennonites are nearby. Their faith in God helps them accept their trials and their triumphs equally.

Wallace, Bill. *Buffalo Gal.* New York: Holiday House, 1992. 0-8234-0943-0, 185p. Paper, New York: Pocket Books (Minstrel), 1993. 0-671-79899-5. R=5; I=6.

Before Amanda's sixteenth birthday in 1904, she and her mother travel from sedate San Francisco to wild Fort Sill, Oklahoma, to save buffalo from extinction. Although she dreads the trip, Amanda and her well-traveled mother have exciting experiences with kind, interesting people including the half-Indian boy who has just been accepted to Harvard and with whom she falls in love. Categorizing people according to where they live or their culture sometimes backfires because one may find that they are very different from what one may expect.

Weitzman, David, writer/illus. *Thrashin' Time: Harvest Days in the Dakotas.* Boston: Godine, 1991. 0-87923-910-7, 80p. R=7; I=6.

Peter, twelve, and his father are very interested in the new steam engine thrasher being used in North Dakota during 1912.

They use it on their farm and finish the job in much less time than their horses could do it and enjoy learning about the machine as well. In order to be effective, new machines have to win the approval of the those who might use them.

Williams, David. *Grandma Essie's Covered Wagon.* Illus. Wiktor Sadowski. New York: Knopf, 1993. 0-679-90253-8, 41p. R=5; I=2.

The narrator, a grandmother, recalls her covered wagon trip to Kansas from Missouri when she was a young girl. A drought defeats her father's farming endeavors so the family goes to Oklahoma with its oil boom. They return to Kansas after one of the children dies and the endless work tires them. People who travel to find a better life have to have courage and willingness to work hard, but even those may not be enough for success.

Wyman, Andrea. *Red Sky at Morning.* New York: Holiday House, 1991. 0-8234-0903-1, 230p. R=6; I=5.

While Callie's father has gone to Oregon, her mother dies in childbirth in Indiana during 1909. Callie and her sister continue living with their loving German grandfather until their father returns to take them away. Sickness and death lurk over the horizon, but family love and humor keep their pain from being unbearable.

Yarbro, Chelsea Quinn. *Floating Illusions.* New York: Harper, 1986. 0-06-026643-0, 215p. R=7; I=7.*

On board an ocean liner in 1910, Millicent, fourteen, is returning to school in Switzerland. She becomes friendly with a famous magician on board, and when some people are killed and his own life is threatened, she helps to identify the murderer. People who are honest allies will often risk themselves for the well-being of their friends.

Yep, Laurence. *Dragonwings.* New York: Harper, 1975. 0-06-026738-0, 256p. Paper (Trophy), 1977. 0-06-440085-9. R=5; I=6.

In 1903, Moon Shadow comes from China to join his father Windrider in San Francisco. After Windrider repairs a horseless carriage, and the owner gets him a job, he begins to correspond with the Wright brothers about their flying machine. Since Windrider must save his money to bring his wife and mother to

America rather than spend it on his own flying machine, the Wright brothers get credit for the first airplane flight instead of him. When a person's loyalty is to family instead of self, he or she may have to forego fame and fortune. *Newbery Honor*, 1976; *Friends of Children and Literature Award* (FOCAL), 1984; *Carter G. Woodson Book Award*, 1976; *International Reading Association Children's Book Award*, 1976.

1914-1929

Beatty, Patricia. *Eight Mules from Monterey*. New York: Morrow, 1982. 0-688-01047-4, 224p. Paper, 1993. 0-688-12279-5, 272p. R=5; I=7.

In 1916, Fayette's widowed mother graduates from library school and gets a job to take books to a group of people, who have requested a lending library, in the mountains of Monterey, California. Several adventures face Fayette and her mother and brother and their mule drivers. Although the journey discourages them at times, its success assures them that they can survive without the mother having to enter into a bad marriage with her deceased husband's partner.

Boyne, Walter J. *Trophy for Eagles*. New York: Crown, 1989. 0-517-57276-1, 455p. R=10; I=10+.**

While Frank Bandfield prepares to participate in the 1927 air race to Paris, an arsonist destroys his airplane, and Charles Lindbergh wins the race. Frank knows that the German pilot Hafner is responsible for the fire, and a rivalry begins between them that lasts until Bandfield shoots down Hafner's plane ten years later over Guernica in the Spanish civil war battle that destroys the city. Unscrupulous people with ambition will sacrifice others to support their own interests.

Bragg, Michael. *Betty's Wedding*. New York: Macmillan, 1988. 0-02-711880-0, 32p. R=4; I=3.**

In the 1920's, Betty gets married, and her little sister shares the event from the engagement announcement to her loneliness after the wedding when she realizes that she will no longer see Betty everyday. The warm humor underlying the family's togetherness appears in the items chosen for the scrap book, especially the sister's and brother's hair alongside that of the dog. Families often have poignant memories of major events in their lives.

Bylinsky, Tatyana, writer/illus. *Before the Wildflowers Bloom.* New York: Crown, 1989. 0-517-57052-1, 70p. R=3; I=3.**

Near Carmela's ninth birthday in 1916, her life changes when a coal mine explosion kills her father in Hastings, Colorado. The family goes to live with her grandfather on a farm. Sudden and unexpected events disrupt people's lives.

Clifford, Eth. *The Man Who Sang in the Dark.* Boston: Houghton Mifflin, 1987. 0-395-43664-8, 96p. R=4; I=4.

Leah, ten, her widowed mother, and little brother live in a tiny apartment where her mother sews to support them in 1929. After her desperate mother gives her brother to a wealthy family for adoption, Leah enlists help from the blind musician living in the apartment below, and he goes with her to retrieve Daniel. Leah's mother marries the musician and the landlord couple become surrogate grandparents. What one fears often turns out to be only one's imagination rather than reality.

Clifford, Eth. *Will Somebody Please Marry My Sister?* Illus. Ellen Eagle. Boston: Houghton Mifflin, 1992. 0-395-58037-4, 122p. R=5; I=5.

Since his grandmother says that the oldest girl must marry first in 1925, Abel, twelve, has to get his oldest sister, twenty-six, married before he can have a room of his own. She refuses the eligible bachelors he brings home because they seem uncertain about marrying a woman physician. But his problem is unexpectedly solved when his older sister takes a hospital job and his middle sister decides to marry regardless of his grandmother's "rules." Sometimes things for which one wishes happen, although not as one expects.

Corbin, William. *Me & the End of the World.* New York: Simon & Schuster, 1991. 0-671-74223-X, 222p. Paper, Englewood Cliffs, NJ: Silver Burdett. 0-663-56251-1. R=7; I=6.

Wondering if the world will really end on May 1, 1928, Tim spends his thirteenth year doing the things that he wants to complete if it does. He gains a feeling of accomplishment when he reaches his goals, and he decides to no longer childishly risk danger if the world does not end. Achievement, regardless of the motivation to act, helps people feel more confident about themselves in relationships with others.

Crews, Donald, writer/illus. *Bigmama's*. New York: Greenwillow, 1991. 0-688-09951-3, 32p. Paper, One World Friends and Neighbors Series. 0-685-64817-6. R=2; I=K.

When he was little, the narrator spent summers at his grandmother Bigmama's, riding a train south for days and nights to get there. The outhouse, the well, and the kerosene lamps reveal inconveniences that he endured. But for him as a child, they were merely characteristics of Bigmama's because he was more interested in the fun of the farm and family togetherness. A family enjoying simple things brings back many memories. *American Library Association Notable Book for Children*, 1992.

Grosser, Morton. *The Fabulous Fifty*. New York: Atheneum, 1990. 0-689-31656-9, 233p. R=2; I=6.

In 1921, the Philadelphia newspaper announces a coupon-collecting contest with fifty prizes of a trip to the World Series in New York. Solon, fifteen, and his group of friends decide to start collecting the coupons. Their group wins, but only one can join the other forty-nine winners. Solon does not win the ticket from his group, but he decides to go anyway, pretending that he belongs. Although discovered after he arrives in New York, he has a wonderful experience. To gain anything worthwhile takes a lot of effort.

Hogan, Linda. *Mean Spirit*. New York: Macmillan, 1990. 0-689-12101-6, 374p. Paper, New York: Ballantine (Ivy), 1992. 0-8041-0863-3. R=5; I=10+.

In 1922, the Dawes Act offers the Hill Indians tracts of land not claimed by the whites, and Grace Blanket chooses a piece of barren land which soon proves to have oil. This discovery jeopardizes her family, the Grayclouds, and those who try to protect them against the white government officials and businessmen wanting her land. When one unearths something of value, others will often try to take it--illegally if necessary.

Houston, Gloria. *The Year of the Perfect Christmas Tree: An Appalachian Story.* Illus. Barbara Cooney. New York: Dial, 1988. 0-8037-0300-7, 32p. R=4; I=2.

Ruthie and her father pick the Christmas tree for their small town in the spring before her father leaves Appalachia for World War I in 1918. When he has not returned home by Christmas Eve, Ruthie and her mother cut the tree and take it to the church. Her father arrives just in time to see Ruthie acting as the Christmas angel. Family members sometimes have to take each other's responsibilities in time of need.

Jones, Douglas C. *Weedy Rough.* New York: Tor, 1989 (1981). Paper, 0-8125-8463-5, 345p. R=8; I=10+.

When Barton Pay comes to Weedy Rough, he begins to spend money for different things to improve the town, but he has the stigma of being part Cherokee in an Arkansas community that hates Cherokees. When someone robs the bank in 1925, a witness accuses Pay's son, but the expert defense by the boy's grandfather Eben Pay helps him go free. Some people who hold grudges against others will accuse them of committing crimes even if they are not certain of the criminal's identity.

Ketteman, Helen. *The Year of No More Corn.* Illus. Robert Andrew Parker. New York: Orchard/Watts, 1993. 0-531-08550-3, 32p. R=3; I=2.

When young Beanie is distressed because his father will not let him help with corn planting, his grandfather, too old to help, tells him about 1928. Beginning then, he planted corn four different years, but rain, wind, heat, and lastly, crows, destroyed each crop. Some people can survive several setbacks when only one would seem enough to destroy them.

Kinsey-Warnock, Natalie. *The Night the Bells Rang.* Illus. Leslie W. Bowman. New York: Cobblehill, 1991. 0-525-65074-1, 76p. R=4; I=4.

Young Mason tries to avoid the big boy Aden who fills his hat with snow and knocks him down in 1918. But before Aden enlists to fight in World War I, he helps Mason retrieve a drawing for his father that the wind had blown out of his hand. Mason feels very sad at later hearing of Aden's death. When one disapproves of another's actions, knowing what motivates those actions may help one understand.

Kudlinski, Kathleen V. *Hero Over Here*. Illus. Bert Dodson. New York: Viking, 1990. 0-670-83050-X, 64p. Paper, New York: Puffin, 1992. 0-14-034286-9. R=4; I=5.

During the influenza epidemic of 1918 which took twenty-two million lives (more than were killed in World War I), Theodore, ten, has to care for his sick mother and sister since his father and brother are fighting in the War. He helps them first and then saves the life of another man whom he finds and drags to the hospital. In times of need, people are often stronger and able to do more than they expect. "Once Upon America Series."

Lehrman, Robert. *The Store that Mama Built*. New York: Macmillan, 1992. 0-02-754632-2, 126p. R=4; I=6.

In 1917, Birdie's Russian Jewish immigrant father dies of influenza just before opening his grocery store outside Harrisburg, Pennsylvania. Birdie's mother decides to open and to manage the store. When the family elects to give credit to black families, the store begins to make enough money for the family to keep it, even with closing on Friday nights and Saturdays for Jewish sabbath. People must adhere to their beliefs in order to keep respect for themselves.

McDonald, Megan. *The Potato Man*. Illus. Ted Lewin. New York: Orchard/Watts, 1991. 0-531-08514-7, 32p. R=6; I=2.

A grandfather tells his grandchildren about the man, blinded in one eye when fighting in the Great War in 1918, who sold vegetables on his New York street. The man catches the grandfather taking potatoes fallen from his wagon, squeezing orange juice on his sister's hair, and breaking a window, but when an apple falls off his cart and the grandfather returns it, the man gives it to him. Adults reporting actions to parents seem meddlesome when often they are trying to prevent worse behavior in the future. *School Library Journal "Best Book,"* 1991.

Mitchell, Margaree King. *Uncle Jed's Barbershop.* Illus. James Ransome. New York: Simon & Schuster, 1993. 0-671-67969-3, 34p. R=6; I=2.

Uncle Jed saves his young niece from dying by giving her parents the money for her operation. He was saving the money to open a barbershop in the 1920's. He saves more money, but his bank fails at the beginning of the Depression, and he loses it. When he is seventy-nine, he finally opens his shop exactly like he wants it. If one has a dream but also helps others in need, the dream may take longer to become reality. *Coretta Scott King Illustrator Honor Award*, 1994.

Oneal, Zibby. *A Long Way to Go: A Story of Women's Right to Vote.* Illus. Michael Dooling. New York: Viking, 1990. 0-670-82532-8, 64p. Paper, New York: Puffin, 1992. 0-14-032950-1. R=2; I=3.

In 1917, when ten-year-old Lila's grandmother goes to jail after picketing for women's suffrage in Washington, Lila begins to notice how many things men prohibit women from doing. She decides that she is as smart and as capable as any boy her age, and she tells her father. After her comments, he reconsiders the women's right to vote. Finding one's beliefs on unpopular topics takes time, but once one has decided, one needs to express them appropriately. "Once Upon America Series."

Reeder, Carolyn. *Moonshiner's Son.* New York: Macmillan, 1993. 0-02-775805-2, 208p. R=3; I=5.

At twelve in Virginia's Blue Ridge mountains, Tom helps his father protect the still where he makes moonshine (illegal whiskey) during 1919 while the Prohibition law is in effect. Soon revenuers (police) arrest Tom's father. Tom also sees other results of whiskey--wife beating and fighting. He decides that carving figures from wood which sell as crafts to townsfolk fulfills his creative spirit. When he refuses to help his father with the still, his father beats him. But soon, shocked at his overreaction, Tom's father stops running the still himself. If one no longer wants to be associated with illegality, one may face hostility, but one must do as one believes.

Ross, Rhea Beth. *The Bet's On, Lizzie Bingman!* Boston: Houghton Mifflin, 1988. 0-395-444721, 186p. Paper, 1992. 0-395-64375-9. R=6; I=6.

When Elizabeth is fourteen in 1914, she bets her brother that if she can remain self-sufficient all summer, he will have to change his speech for the statewide oratory contest to one that promotes women's rights rather than condemns them. A lot happens to her during the summer including witnessing a murder and having to testify in court, but she wins the bet. For women to overcome the male attitudes that they are things that must be protected has been and is a lengthy process.

Rostkowski, Margaret. *After the Dancing Days.* New York: HarperCollins, 1986. 0-06-025078-X. Paper (Trophy), 1988. 0-06-440248-7, 217p. R=4; I=5.

When Annie's physician father returns from World War I in 1919, he decides to work at the hospital for those wounded in the war. Annie's mother, an accomplished musician who is denying the death of her own brother in France, refuses to see any of the disfigured men and forbids Annie to visit the hospital with her grandfather. In her early teens, Annie disobeys and befriends a young man who lost much of his face when gassed while not wearing his gas mask. The maturation process can become even more painful when one must defy a parent's inappropriate decision. *Golden Kite Award*, 1987; *Jefferson Cup Award*, 1987; *International Reading Association Book Award*, 1987; *American Library Association Notable Book for Children*, 1986.

Sebestyen, Ouida. *Far from Home.* Boston: Little, Brown, 1980. 0-316-77932-0, 191p. Paper, New York: Dell (Laurel Leaf), 1983. 0-440-92640-8, 208p. R=3 I=8

During the Depression of 1929, the orphaned Salty, thirteen, asks for a job at a boarding home where his late mother, a mute, had last worked. He observes the adults living there and realizes that he understands little about their conflicts. He also learns who his father is at the same time that he sees the importance of accepting responsibility and helping others in need. *School Library Journal "Best Book,"* 1980.

Skurzynski, Gloria. *Good-bye, Billy Radish.* New York: Bradbury, 1992. 0-02-782921-9, 137p. R=5; I=7.

Hank's friend, Billy Radish (Bazyli Radichevych), is two years older and Ukrainian, living in Canaan, Pennsylvania, where their fathers work in the tough steel mills during World War I in 1917. As best friends, they go to school together, learning about each other's cultures. They share experiences such as admiring the Greek sculptures in Pittsburgh's museum and each other's triumphs--Hank's delivery of his sister-in-law's baby and Billy's naturalization as a citizen--before Billy's fatal bout with influenza. The beginnings and endings of life emphasize its pain and its preciousness.

Van Raven, Pieter. *Harpoon Island.* New York: Scribner's, 1989. 0-684-19092-3, 150p. R=4; I=9.

Mr. Barnes decides to take a job as school master on Harpoon Island off the New England coast, but he does not say that his son Brady, ten, is slow to respond to people. On the island, Brady thrives and makes friends until World War I is declared, and people accuse Brady of being German because his grandfather was a German immigrant to America. One must make decisions about one's life based not on what others decree but upon what will make one's own life most productive.

Voight, Cynthia. *Tree by Leaf.* New York: Atheneum, 1988. 0-689-31403-5, 192p. Paper, New York: Fawcett (Juniper), 1989. 0-449-70334-7. R=5; I=7.

In 1920, when Clothilde's father returns to Maine after World War I, he stays in the boathouse, unable to bear the family's horrified response to his disfigured face. When events make him reconsider and finally return home, the family begins to look to the future. War always changes things, sometimes in ways never imagined before the reality occurs.

Weaver, Lydia. *Child Star: When Talkies Came to Hollywood.* Illus. Michele Laporte. New York: Viking, 1992. 0-670-84039-4, 52p. R=4; I=4.

Joey, ten, goes with his mother to a movie studio in Hollywood where she gets day jobs playing the piano for silent movies in 1927. Someone decides to "create" him as a new child star. He makes a lot of money and survives the shift to "talkies" but finds that the drudgery of movie making has no relationship to the glamour it projects on the screen. Finding how something that seems magic actually happens may be disappointing. "Once Upon America" series.

Yep, Laurence. *The Star Fisher.* New York: Morrow, 1991. 0-688-09365-5, 150p. Paper, New York: Puffin, 1992. 0-14-036003-4. R=3; I=6.

In 1927, Jean Lee's family moves from Ohio to West Virginia to open a laundry. Jean, fifteen, has trouble making friends, but other children do not seem to mind that her younger brother and sister are Chinese. Their landlady's kindness helps them become established through a series of unusual incidences. Those who lack confidence in themselves are most likely to have prejudices against others who are different in some way. *Christopher Award*, 1992.

1930-1940

Aaron, Chester. *Lackawanna.* New York: Lippincott, 1986. 0-397-32058-2, 210p. R=4; I=8.*

By 1931, Willy, fifteen, has lost his entire family as a result of the Depression. He joins the Lackawanna, a group of children who illegally hop trains and ride with hobos in search of money and food. Severe economic hardships can damage families beyond repair, but resilient individuals can survive by bonding with others in similar situations.

Ames, Mildred. *Grandpa Jake and the Grand Christmas.* Scribner's, 1990. 0-684-19241-1, 98p. R=3; I=4.

When Lizzie's grandfather, of whom she has never heard, arrives near Christmas during the Depression, life without her deceased mother seems less dismal. His visit changes her family for the better since Lizzie, twelve, finally has the courage to tell her father that she and her sister want to celebrate Christmas at home, not with his sister's annoying family. Additionally, Lizzie offers to help her dancing teacher in return for free lessons since her father has no money to pay. If one has a goal, one often has to take risks to reach it. *School Library Journal "Best Book,"* 1991.

Amoss, Berthe. *The Mockingbird Song.* New York: HarperCollins, 1988. 0-06-020062-6, 123p. R=5; I=5.

In the 1930's, Lindy, eleven, moves out of her home where her father lives with his new wife to next door with wheel-chair confined old Miss Ellie. When the parents' baby is born prematurely and her step-mother stays weak, Lindy begins to help her after school. From finding out why Miss Ellie never married and why her own mother left, Lindy begins to understand that people have to do the best for themselves that they can--to keep strong against adverse forces.

Antle, Nancy. *Hard Times: A Story of the Great Depression.* New York: Viking, 1993. 0-670-84665-1, 64p. R=4; I=4.

In 1933, Charlie's family faces the brunt of the Depression when his father loses his job and cannot pay the mortgage. The family moves, and finally, his father gets a temporary job. People in a family can help each other cope with difficulties. "Once Upon America Series."

Armstrong, William O. *Sounder.* New York: HarperCollins, 1969. 0-06-020144-4, 128p. Paper, 1972. 0-06-440020-4. R=5; I=5.

A father departs for prison after stealing food for his starving family during the Depression, and when he returns years later, Sounder, like Ulysses' faithful dog Argus, patiently waits. The family survives the years while the father is gone through the mother's faith that God helps the weak who are morally correct. The boy sacrifices schooling to work in the fields but learns to read his beloved Bible when he meets a teacher on his searches to find his father (like Telemachus). Only Sounder has a name; the humans become Everyone who has faced irrational prejudice and endured the pain. *Newbery Award*, 1970; *Lewis Carroll Shelf Award*; *Nene Award*.

Avi. *Shadrach's Crossing.* New York: Pantheon, 1983. 0-394-95816-6, 192p. R=3; I=5.

In 1932, Shadrach becomes a product of Prohibition and the Depression when he observes smuggling and sees the wealthy boss attempt to blackmail his accomplices. Shad disobeys his parents by attempting to report the illegalities to the government. Choosing right over wrong when it threatens a family's livelihood can be a very difficult decision.

Buechner, Frederick. *The Wizard's Tide: A Story.* New York: Harper, 1990. 0-06-061160-X, 104p. Paper, 0-06-061148-0, 128p. R=7; I=10+.

When Teddy is eleven in 1936, his comfortable home is uprooted because a subway train "mysteriously" kills his father. He, his sister, and his mother go to Pittsburgh to live with his mother's family instead of spending Christmas with his wealthy New York grandparents who are seemingly untouched by the Depression. A child's understanding of serious adult problems can only be superficial because of his or her inability to know or interpret the underlying events.

Clifford, Eth. *The Remembering Box.* Illus. Donna Diamond. Boston: Houghton Mifflin, 1985. 0-395-38476-1. 70p. Paper, New York: Morrow (Beech Tree). 0-688-11777-5, 96p. R=4; I=4.

On Fridays from 1938 until he is nine in 1942, Joshua goes to see his grandmother for the Sabbath meal. She tells him stories about her past based on items she keeps in a box. One afternoon before she dies, she gives him his own box with some of her things inside it. Moments with grandparents and family can later become treasured memories.

Corcoran, Barbara. *The Sky is Falling.* New York: Atheneum, 1988. 0-689-31388-8, 185p. Paper, New York: Avon (Camelot), 1990. 0-380-70837-X. R=2; I=5.

In 1931, Annah, fourteen, has to leave her comfortable home to live with her aunt in New Hampshire while her father goes to Chicago, her mother to Florida, and her brother to finish the college semester because her father's bank fails in the Depression. She continues her correspondence with her friends but also befriends an intelligent, quiet girl at her new school who has an alcoholic mother and a stepfather who beats her. Annah also learns about her aunt, still silently mourning the death of her husband, but quick to help others in need. Giving of self and sacrificing for others can offer greater rewards than one could ever imagine.

Doctorow, E. L. *World's Fair.* New York: Random, 1985. Paper, 1992. 0-679-73628-X, 384p. R=9; I=10+.

Edgar, nine, wins "honorable mention" for an essay sponsored by the World's Fair. He and his family receive free tickets to the 1939 fair for a day of family harmony. Edgar, the adult, remembers his childhood and his family life when he enjoyed radio programs, visiting stores, film serials, excursions, and the circus where the clown plays on the high wire after the "experts" have finished. Edgar buries a capsule with mementoes from his time just as World's Fair organizers have done, but at the last minute, he keeps his ventriloquism book so he can continue to practice. Memories can fuse time so that the past merges with the present as it becomes part of the future.

Fowler, Zinita. *The Last Innocent Summer*. Forth Worth, TX: Texas Christian U, 1990. Paper, 0-87565-045-7, 145p. R=5; I=5.

In the summer of 1931, when Skeeter is ten, her whole life changes. She finds out that parents do not always love their children or vice versa and that things happen, out of anyone's control, which change lives. Members of a strong loving family with integrity will help others, and in turn, themselves, in times of need.

Greene, Constance C. *Dotty's Suitcase*. New York: Puffin, 1991 (1980). Paper, 0-14-034882-4, 160p. Paper, New York: Dell, 1982. 0-440-42108-X, 144p. R=5; I=5.

In 1934, toward the end of the Depression, when Dottie is twelve, men rob the local bank, and she and her friend find the suitcase filled with money which they have tossed out of the car when being chased. Dotty eventually leaves the money with a friend whose mother and brother have had to sell everything to survive when the friend's father died, and Dottie never tells her own father that they found the suitcase. What one expects has happened can often be very different from the reality.

Hooks, William H. *Circle of Fire*. New York: McElderry, 1982. 0-689-50241-9, 147p. R=3; I=5.

On his eleventh Christmas in 1936, Harrison experiences two sides of so-called "goodness" while he watches the gypsies' candlelight mummer's play and the Klansmen drive up in the North Carolina darkness to burn a cross and punish the man married to a South Carolina woman "outside" the tinkers' band. Since his two best friends are black, Harrison cannot understand the hostility of these men toward them, toward Catholics, and toward Jews. That some humans want to hurt others without care or provocation remains despicable.

Hunt, Irene. *No Promises in the Wind.* New York: Berkley, 1987 (1970). Paper, 0-425-09969-5, 224p. R=4; I=8.

During the Depression, in 1932, Josh and his brother leave home, angry at their father, to find work. Josh eventually gets a job playing a piano for a carnival, but the business burns, and he continues looking. After several mishaps, the two return to Chicago where their father welcomes them with relief and the hope of a new era with the election of Franklin Delano Roosevelt. In times of severe stress, individual pride can separate families.

Koller, Jackie French. *Nothing to Fear.* San Diego: Gulliver, 1991. 0-15-200544-7, 279p. Paper (Harcourt Brace), 1993. 0-15-257582-0. R=5; I=7.

During the Depression in 1932, Daniel's father leaves New York to find work, and his weakened mother has a third child while he is gone. After she collapses and goes to the hospital in a coma, Danny finds a letter to his mother telling her that his father has died four months earlier while riding the rails. Although distressed, Danny and his mother find solace in the help of another man, also victim of the Depression, whom they had nursed back to health. Times of great stress separate families and unite strangers in unexpected ways.

Levinson, Riki. *DinnieAbbieSister-r-rl.* Illus. Helen Cogancherry. New York: Bradbury, 1987. 0-02-757380-X, 90p. R=1; I=1.**

In the 1930's, Jennie, five, enjoys being with her brothers, but Abbie becomes so ill that his legs need to regain strength through therapy. One of Jennie's happiest times is riding on the train to see her brothers at *yeshiva* (Hebrew school). Families that enjoy being together usually learn to cope with difficulty.

Lord, Athena. *The Luck of Z.A.P. and Zoe.* Illus. Jean Jenkins. New York: Macmillan, 1987. 0-02-759560-9, 154p. R=6; I=5.

Zach, twelve in 1940, and his family move from a small New York town to Albany where many Greek Americans live. Zach has adventures with his little sister Zoe. After he meets a Jewish boy who had to leave Austria and spend a year in Cuba before entering America, his mother hears that Axis forces have bombed her family's Greek town. Residents of a community should try to lessen the difficulty of adjusting for people who move to their cities.

Lord, Athena. *Today's Special: Z.A.P. and Zoe.* Illus. Jean Jenkins. New York: Macmillan, 1984. 0-02-761440-9, 150p. R=6; I=4.

Zach, a Greek-American who is eleven, has to look after his sister in 1939, because both of his parents work in the family restaurant. They meet other Greek Americans who give them special favors. After he teaches Zoe her letters and numbers, she is able to enter kindergarten early, and she can take some responsibility for looking after herself. Sometimes being one of the few members of a minority, ethnic, or religious group in another country can be beneficial.

Lyon, George Ella. *Borrowed Children.* New York: Bantam, 1990 (1988). 0-553-28380-4, 154p. R=2; I=5.

In the Depression, Amanda, twelve, has to stop school to help her mother who is recovering from a difficult childbirth. Her grandmother invites her to Memphis for a mini-vacation, and she learns enough about her extended family to realize that much of what happens has a past. If one questions and searches for answers, one may learn about oneself as well as others. *Golden Kite Award,* 1989; *School Library Journal* "Best Book," 1988.

Mazer, Harry. *Cave Under the City.* New York: Crowell, 1986. 0-690-04559-X, 152p. R=2; I=5.

During the Depression, around 1930, Tolley's father has to leave New York to find work, and after he leaves, Tolley's mother collapses and has to stay in the hospital. His grandmother is also sick, so when a man comes searching for him and his little brother in the family apartment, they leave though the window and live in a cellar until Tolley himself becomes ill. Then they return home and find their father waiting. Children sometimes have unusual responsibilities when parents have financial or health problems.

Mills, Claudia. *What About Annie?* New York: Walker, 1985. 0-8027-6573-4, 68p. R=6; I=6.

On her thirteenth birthday in 1931, Annie's father loses his job, and her large family and her friends' families find new ways to support themselves during the Depression. Annie, as she grows toward eighteen, develops an interest in flying, regrets the Lindbergh baby's death, and delights over Amelia

Earhart's solo flight. People learn to cope with bad situations even though they may not be pleased with the process.

Myers, Anna. *Red-Dirt Jessie*. New York: Walker, 1992. 0-8027-8172-1, 107p. R=4; I=5.

When Jessie's baby sister dies, her father retreats into himself, defeated by death and the onset of the Depression around 1930. When Jessie's aunt and uncle leave for California, she tries to lure their dog to her house and only does so when the dog is wounded and cannot walk. The dog helps her father return to reality when it protects her from a wild dog. Some people have difficulty coping with life, but love and caring help them best.

Olsen, Violet. *The View from the Pighouse Roof.* New York: Atheneum, 1987. 0-689-31324-1, 176p. R=4; I=7.**

Marie at twelve in 1933 especially misses her sister Rosie who left their Iowa farm home to find work during the Depression, got married, and had a baby. When Rosie dies, Marie's grief leads her to decide not to enter high school, but to help her older brother and her mother recover. She finally understands that she must continue school and that their life will be happier raising Rosie's two-year-old son. Enduring the realities of life such as death and poverty make keeping one's hope difficult until one realizes that looking forward is the only way to positively face living. *Society of Midland Authors Book Awards*, 1988.

Paulsen, Gary. *The Winter Room*. Orchard/Watts, 1989. 0-531-08439-6, 103p. Paper, New York: Dell (Yearling), 1991. 0-440-40454-1. R=6; I=7.

Eldon enjoys the cycle of seasons on his northern farm, except for Fall. He especially likes the winter because his Uncle David tells stories. His brother becomes angry the winter that Eldon is eleven and says old Uncle David is a liar when he tells about his prowess as a master woodcutter. But Eldon and his brother, from their hiding place, see Uncle David prove that he can cut pieces of wood like he has described. Young people often do not believe the exploits recounted by old people and want proof of their validity. *Newbery Honor*, 1990; *American Library Association Notable Book for Children*, 1989; *Judy Lopez Memorial Award*, 1990.

Pendergraft, Patricia. *As Far As Mill Springs.* New York: Philomel, 1991. 0-399-22102-6, 153p. R=3; I=6.

In 1932, Robert has lived all his life in foster homes, and he decides he can stand it no longer when he hears through a closed door that his mother lives in a nearby town. Robert and one of the abused girls ride boxcars with other hobos, become separated, and then reunited in the town on Christmas, the day after Robert's thirteenth birthday. An old woman tells Robert that his mother has already left town, but she can hire him for a few days to do odd jobs. Since she needs him, he stays. Some people can be inhumane to others, especially children, without provocation.

Reeder, Carolyn. *Grandpa's Mountain.* New York: Macmillan, 1991. 0-02-775811-7, 171p. Paper, New York: Avon (Camelot), 1993. 0-380-71914-2. R=6; I=6.

Carrie loves visiting her grandparents each summer in Virginia's Shenandoah mountains, but her eleventh summer during the Depression is different. Her grandfather spends the summer trying to keep his land from becoming part of the new national park. He fails, but Carrie realizes that he did as much as he could. One must do the best one can, and even if one loses, one may still be satisfied with trying.

Riddell, Ruth. *Haunted Journey.* New York: Atheneum, 1988. 0-689-31429-9, 224p. R=4; I=8.**

Obie takes a journey from Michigan to Tennessee to find pearls which were supposedly lost by DeSoto and his men when they stole them from the Nun Yuna Wi Indians in Cherokee sacred lands. He is successful. But back home, he finds that his new wealth does not solve all of his problems. Education seems more productive. One must look within one's own self for strength rather than to depend on money or other people.

Ringgold, Faith, writer/illus. *Tar Beach.* New York: Crown, 1991. 0-517-58031-4, 32p. R=6; I=3.

When Cassie is eight in 1939, she realizes that she can own anything or go anywhere in her imagination. She envisions also that she helps others with their troubles as she makes her fantasy "fly overs" above Brooklyn and Tar Beach. One of the ways to combat the harshness of reality is to dream of what could be. *Caldecott Honor, 1992; California Children's Book,*

Video, and Software Award, 1991; *Coretta Scott King Award,*
1992; *New York Times Best Illustrated Children's Books of the
Year,* 1991; *Parents' Choice,* 1991; *American Library Association
Notable Book for Children,* 1992; *School Library Journal "Best
Book,"* 1991.

Ross, Rhea Beth. *Hillbilly Choir.* Boston: Houghton Mifflin,
1991. 0-395-53356-2, 166p. R=3; I=7.*

Moving back to Arkansas from New York in 1932 excites
Laurie, fifteen, who is tired of staying in her room while her
mother performs in nightclubs. But Arkansas does not satisfy
her because she is ready for something new in her life, like her
own singing career. Additionally, the town's citizens have to
unite to improve situations. If everyone sacrifices a little for the
common good, a community can have a future.

Rossiter, Phyllis. *Moxie.* New York: Four Winds, 1990.
0-02-777831-2, 192p. R=4; I=6.

Drew, thirteen, finds himself both playful and serious as he
raises his sheep during 1934, the Dust Bowl period in Kansas.
His family is constantly threatened with losing their land
without rain to grow crops, but he helps the family keep the
farm with the aid of his mule Moxie. In times of great need,
people sometimes find an inner resourcefulness of which they
were unaware.

Stolz, Mary Slattery. *Ivy Larkin.* San Diego: Harcourt Brace,
1986. 0-15-239366-8, 226p. Paper, New York: Dell (Yearling),
1989. 0-440-40175-5. R=4; I=7.

Ivy at fourteen during the Depression has two refuges--the
library and the church. She hates attending the private school
on a scholarship with her siblings and feels disturbed about her
father being out of a job. Her family is very close, and the love
and care of each member makes the days of being poor seem
less difficult.

Taylor, Mildred. *The Friendship.* Illus. Max Ginsburg. New
York: Dial, 1987. 0-8037-0418-6, 56p. R=5; I=5.

Old Tom Bee and John Wallace were once friends. In 1933,
Cassie, nine, finds out that Old Tom Bee saved John's life
twice. She also finds that John has reneged on his word that
Old Tom may always call him John rather than Mister John.

But whites have begun to complain that Old Tom is disrespectful, and to regain his white customers' respect, John shoots Old Tom in the leg. The inhumane treatment of some people by those who think themselves better is always despicable. *Boston Globe--Horn Book Award, 1988; Coretta Scott King Award, 1988; American Library Association Notable Book for Children, 1987.*

Taylor, Mildred. *Let the Circle Be Unbroken.* New York: Dial, 1982. 0-8037-4748-9, 432p. Paper, New York: Puffin, 1991. 0-14-034892-1. Paper, New York: Bantam, 1983. 0-553-23436-6. R=5; I=8.

In 1934, Cassie, the ten-year-old narrator reports several racial incidents that occur without quite understanding their significance. She sees a black boy convicted of a murder committed by two white boys; her uncle belittled by whites for sleeping with a white woman, his wife; a woman lose her sharecropper home after trying to register to vote; and Cassie herself is refused drinking privileges at a "whites only" water fountain in the court house. Adults create and perpetrate prejudice; children do not. *Coretta Scott King Award, 1982; George C. Stone Center for Children's Books Recognition of Merit Award, 1991; American Library Association Notable Book for Children, 1981*

Taylor, Mildred. *Mississippi Bridge.* New York: Dial, 1990. 0-8037-0427-5, 64p. Paper, New York: Bantam (Skylark), 1992. 0-553-15992-5. R=3; I=3.

When Jeremy is ten, in 1931, he tries to make friends with the Logan children even though they are black, and his father scorns blacks. Others are like his father including a white bus driver who makes all the blacks get off the bus in the rain because more whites want to travel. The Logans' grandmother is going to help a sick sister, and another man plans to get a job if he arrives in time, but they have to leave the bus. The rain washes out the bridge, and the bus goes into the water, drowning some of those on board. A demeaning situation saves those removed from the bus. *Christopher Award, 1991.*

Taylor, Mildred. *Roll of Thunder, Hear My Cry.* Illus. Jerry Pinkney. New York: Dial, 1976. 0-8037-7473-7. Paper, New York: Puffin, 1991. 0-14-034893-X, 276p. Paper, Bantam: New York, 1984. 0-553-25450-2, 210p. R=6; I=7.

The Logan family has to cope with the injustice of being black in Mississippi during 1933, and Cassie, nine, reports the events in their lives. Fortunately, the family owns land, but Mr. Logan has to leave home to find a job to continue to pay the mortgage while the rest of the family stays home and works hard. Although humans have no choice of their skin color, they can choose how they act toward others. *Newbery Medal*, 1977; *George C. Stone Center for Children's Books Recognition of Merit Award*, 1991.

Taylor, Mildred. *Song of the Trees.* New York: Dial, 1975. 0-8037-5453-1, 56p. Paper, New York: Bantam, 1989. 0-553-15132-0. R=3; I=4.

When Cassie is eight in 1932, while her father works in Louisiana, a white man, who wants trees from her family's land, cuts down the trees even though Cassie's grandmother refuses to sell them to him. Mr. Logan returns and threatens the man, saving the rest of the trees, but unable to restore those already demolished. People who think themselves superior to others sometimes break the law in order to take what they want.

Thesman, Jean. *Rachel Chance.* Boston: Houghton Mifflin, 1990. 0-395-50934-3, 175p. Paper, New York: Avon (Flare), 1992. 0-380-71378-0. R=7; I=7.

In 1940, when Rachel is fifteen, the campground revivalists kidnap her illegitimate brother, four. She finally locates them and goes to get him so that her mother, grandfather, and other brother can be happy again. People often take members of their family for granted until one leaves, either by moving or by death.

Uchida, Yoshiko. *The Best Bad Thing*. New York: McElderry, 1983. Paper (Aladdin), 1993. 0-689-71745-8, 136p. R=6; I=5.

In the second book of a trilogy starting with *A Jar of Dreams* and ending with *The Happiest Ending*, Rinko's mother asks her to work for the summer with Mrs. Hata, a woman Rinko thinks is slightly crazy. When Mrs. Hata calls Rinko outside to look at lovely spider webs floating in the air and an old man living nearby gives her a kite, an extension of the sky, the summer becomes the "best bad thing" ever to have happened to Rinko. Sometimes situations that seem uninteresting offer the most intriguing insights into life. *American Library Association Notable Book for Children,* 1983; *School Library Journal "Best Book,"* 1983.

Uchida, Yoshiko. *The Happiest Ending*. New York: Macmillan, 1985. 0-689-50326-1, 120p. R=4; I=5.

At twelve, Rinko, in the final book of the trilogy beginning with *A Jar of Dreams* and *The Best Bad Thing*, is more interested in being American than understanding her Japanese heritage. Adjusting to an arranged marriage between a young Japanese girl and an older man is difficult for her until she sees the man's kindness and the girl's appreciation for this quality. Creating a balance between the culture in which one has lived and the culture of one's heritage often takes much thought and care. *Bay Area Book Reviewers Association Award,* 1986.

Uchida, Yoshiko. *A Jar of Dreams*. New York: McElderry, 1981. 0-689-50210-9, 144p. Paper (Aladdin), 1993. 0-689-71672-9. R=6; I=5.

Rinko, eleven, and her family all have dreams for their future as Japanese-Americans in 1935, in the first of a trilogy with *The Best Bad Thing* and *The Happiest Ending*. An aunt comes to visit and influences each person to start working toward a goal--her mother opens a laundry, her father starts his garage, and her brother decides to finish college. Every individual develops his or her personal dreams which can only come true with hard work. *Commonwealth Club of California Book Award,* 1981; *Friends of Children and Literature Award* (FOCAL), 1986.

Van Raven, Pieter. *A Time of Troubles*. New York: Scribner's, 1990. 0-684-19212-8, 192p. R=4; I=7.

In the 1930's, Roy visits his father, who is serving a term in prison for arson, each Sunday until he is released. They go to California to look for work. Disappointed by his Dad's continued dishonesty, Roy joins the fruit pickers and strikes with them against the growers, realizing that he can no longer accept his father's lack of character. Children sometimes have to assume the adult responsibilities that their parents shirk. *Scott O'Dell Award for Historical Fiction*, 1991.

Whittaker, Dorothy. *Angels of the Swamp*. New York: Walker, 1992. 0-8027-8129-2, 209p. R=5; I=7.

Each trying to escape what seems like an unsurmountable problem in 1932, Taffy, fifteen; Jody, twelve; and Jeff, eighteen, meet in a swamp and start a new life helping each other. Taffy as an orphan does not have to go to a foster home; Jody escapes his alcoholic uncle while his leg heals; and Jeff, without a job, learns the techniques of fishing from both of them. Children must sometimes break away from adults and form different alliances for survival.

Wunderli, Stephen. *The Blue Between the Clouds*. New York: Holt, 1992. 0-8050-1772-0, 114p. R=2; I=3.

A Navaho boy comes to live with Matt, eleven, and his family in Utah during 1940. They enjoy adventures and try to help a former World War I pilot rebuild an old plane. Through their encounters with adults, both realize that seemingly strange behaviors become understandable when they know their origins.

Yolen, Jane. *LettingSwiftRiverGo*. Illus. Barbara Cooney. Boston: Little, Brown, 1992. 0-316-96899-4, 32p. R=6; I=4.

Sally Jane sees her town uprooted during the 1930's so that the Swift River Valley can be dammed and become the Quabbin Reservoir, collecting water for Boston. Villagers remove graves from the cemetery and move houses to other places. Friends leave to live in different towns. As she later sits in a boat on top of the reservoir, she decides to remember the past rather than regret its passing.

1941-1945

Aaron, Chester. *Alex Who Won his War.* New York: Walker, 1991. 0-8027-8098-9, 144p. R=4; I=6.

While delivering newspapers on a snowy day in Pequod, Connecticut, during 1944, Alex discovers a dead man and sees a man in a window of the home of an old woman and her daughter. He finds himself involved with two German spies who have taken over the house by threatening the women. War may seem like a game until the possibility of one's death becomes real.

Avi. *"Who Was that Masked Man, Anyway?"* New York: Orchard/Watts, 1992. 0-531-08607-0, 142p. R=3; I=5.

During World War II, Frankie, eleven, lives in the fantasy world of radio programs rather than doing his homework. After his brother returns wounded and his teacher's boyfriend is killed, Frankie concocts an elaborate scheme to have the two meet, and what happens is better than a radio show. Living in a "pretend" world is sometimes much less traumatic than facing reality.

Barrie, Barbara. *Lone Star.* New York: Delacorte, 1990. 0-385-30156-1, 182p. Paper, New York: Dell, 1992. 0-440-40718-4, 192p. R=2; I=5.

In 1944, Jane, ten, moves from Chicago to Corpus Christi, Texas, where she feels lonely because she has no friends and because of her parents' hostility toward each other. Her father has left Chicago to work in a new job to repay the insurance money he embezzled. After she decorates a tiny Christmas tree in her bedroom, her grandfather finds it and is furious because she has denied being Jewish just at the time when the news of Jews dying in concentration camps begins filling newspapers and radio broadcasts. Sometimes one has to experiment with other people's customs before realizing that one's own beliefs are best.

Boyne, Walter J. *Air Force Eagles.* New York: Crown, 1992.
0-517-57609-0, 455p. R=5; I=10+.**

During World War II and the Korean War, John Marshall
(*Eagles at War*) wants to be the first black American ace, but
another pilot steals his "kills." At home after the wars, another
pilot, Riley, meets and marries a German woman (*Trophy for
Eagles*) who left her husband in Berlin. The former husband
returns and kidnaps her. Then Riley and Marshall, currently
working together, rescue her and her children in Little Rock
just before the Klan and its army begin their assault on the
black community in 1957. Although reasonable people try to
keep peace, others with unscrupulous motives may destroy the
peace in order to gain power and prestige.

Boyne, Walter J. *Eagles at War.* New York: Crown, 1991.
0-517-57610-4, 392p.R=8; I=10+.

As the Americans begin to realize their imminent
involvement in World War II against the Germans, Frank
Bandfield and Hadley Roget start to create the Allied aviation
force. The air war progresses under the prodding of General
Henry Caldwell, and they have the challenge of competition
with Bruno Hafner, the German developing Hitler's jet fighter
using slave labor hidden in underground facilities. Others help
in myriad ways including one woman who becomes Goebbel's
mistress, although she despises him, in order to extract military
tactics from the enemy. People working together can accomplish
much more than people working alone.

Branscum, Robbie. *Old Blue Tilley.* New York: Macmillan, 1991.
0-02-711931-9, 96p. R=4; I=7.

Hambone, fourteen, an orphan living alone, looks forward to
traveling with Old Blue, a preacher, through the Ozarks to a
revival on the eve of war with Germany in 1941. He sees people
he has known, and for the first time, he begins to understand
their long rivalries and the strength needed to overcome them.
He too gains insight from Old Blue and realizes that he must
assume responsibility for the farm he inherited and face his
uncles. One of the ways to combat loneliness and fear is to
believe that God, whatever one's definition, will be nearby.

Chaikin, Miriam. *Friends Forever*. Illus. Richard Egielski. New York: HarperCollins, 1988. 0-06-021204-7, 120p. R=3; I=3.*

During World War II, Molly and her family in Brooklyn hear the news about the Nazis taking Jews to concentration camps, and her mother worries about her family in Poland. Molly and her friends graduate from elementary school even after she cheats in arithmetic. A boy asks her for her first date, and life seems wonderful in her neighborhood, totally removed from the rest of the world. The family love exhibited at Passover spills into the rest of the year.

Cormier, Robert. *Other Bells for Us to Ring*. New York: Delacorte, 1990. 0-385-30245-2, 137p. Paper, New York: Dell (Yearling), 1992. 0-440-40717-6. R=6; I=6.

Darcy, eleven, and her parents settle in Monument, Massachusetts, in the Frenchtown area when her father enlists in the military during World War II. There she meets an Irish Catholic girl who becomes her best friend and begins her thinking about growing up and believing in God. Darcy's searching for her religious identity and her fear when her father is reported missing lead her to a Catholic sister who helps her understand. Rules and regulations often obscure the facets of life most important for understanding one's identity and accepting such realities as death.

Ferry, Charles. *One More Time!* Boston: Houghton Mifflin, 1985. 0-395-36692-5, 171p. R=2; I=10.*

After Skeets finishes studying music at Julliard, he joins an orchestra. By the time the Japanese bomb Pearl Harbor, it has become the number two band in the nation. The grueling tour schedule plus the varied personalities of the musicians causes friction, but at the same time, they reach the peak of pleasure by becoming an almost perfect musical ensemble in their last performance before going off to fight in the war. Deciding what one wants to do can be difficult because the goals may take discipline and perseverance to reach.

Glassman, Judy. *The Morning Glory War.* New York: Dutton, 1990. 0-525-44637-0, 119p. Paper, New York: Dell, 1993. 0-440-40765-6. R=2; I=4.

Jeannie spends the second semester of fifth grade coping with a teacher everyone thought had retired and with a girl who seems to know and have everything. When the girl destroys her morning glories and lets the teacher read Jeannie's letter from her soldier pen pal in the Pacific, Jeannie decides to beat her in their Brooklyn school campaign to collect newspapers for the War Effort. Jeannie learns that humor and honesty win more friends than trying to be the best or the prettiest.

Green, Connie Jordan. *The War at Home.* New York: McElderry, 1989. 0-689-50470-5, 137p. R=4; I=5.

Annoyed with her cousin Virgil's incessant talking and his declarations that boys do things better than girls, Mattie, twelve, looks forward to the day Virgil will leave her Oak Ridge, Tennessee, apartment. When his mother dies and his deadbeat father claims him, Mattie is relieved, but she unexpectedly misses him. After Virgil's father abuses him by making him do adult work, Virgil returns. The backdrop of World War II hides the secret of Oak Ridge until the atomic bomb drops on Hiroshima, and people there learn that they have been creating parts of the bomb. As young people mature, they begin to understand and accept others for who they are rather than who they want them to be.

Greene, Bette. *Summer of My German Soldier.* New York: Dial, 1973. 0-8037-8321-1,224p. Paper, New York: Dell, 1993. 0-440-21892-6. R=6; I=6.

Bored by summer in Arkansas, Patty, twelve, protects a German prisoner of war by feeding him when he escapes in 1944. After Anton is captured and killed, the Federal Bureau of Investigation discovers Patty's involvement. With only the support of the black maid Ruth, she has to go to reform school. Contrasted to the material values of her parents, Patty's strong ethical values gained from Ruth help her to survive the ordeal. *Golden Kite Award*, 1973; *National Book Award Finalist*, 1974.

Hahn, Mary Downing. *Stepping on the Cracks.* New York: Clarion, 1991. 0-395-58507-4, 216p. Paper, New York: Avon (Camelot), 1992. 0-380-71900-2. R=4; I=4.

In College Hill, Maryland, Margaret and her friend Elizabeth spend the year of 1944 waiting for their brothers to return from World War II. They discover that a detested classmate's brother, deserted from the army, hides in the woods unable to return home to a father who abuses his family. Disgusted but concerned about the brother's cough, they are helping him recover from pneumonia when Margaret's family receives the telegram about her brother Jimmy's death. All the questions--killing or not, fighting or not, intervening in another family's private problems or not--surface, with no answers but with thoughtful discussions. *Scott O'Dell Award for Historical Fiction,* 1992; *Joan G. Sugarman Children's Book Award,* 1992; *American Library Association Notable Book for Children,* 1992; *School Library Journal "Best Book,"* 1991.

Herman, Charlotte. *A Summer on Thirteenth Street.* New York: Dutton, 1991. 0-525-44642-7, 181p. R=4; I=5.

In the summer of 1944, Shirley Cohen, eleven, plants her victory garden and meets weekly with a club of friends on her Chicago street. The war becomes more real when the druggist's son enlists (and soon dies from a vaccination reaction) and the man she thinks is a spy tells her that he left Germany because his wife, recently killed in an accident, was Jewish. Shirley learns, as her mother suggests, that before accusing people, one needs to understand their motives.

Hest, Amy. *Love You, Soldier.* New York: Four Winds, 1991. 0-02-743635-7, 48p. Paper, New York: Puffin, 1993. 0-14-036174-X. R=2; I=3.

Near the beginning of World War II, when Katie is seven, her mother dresses in her synagogue suit and they go with her father to the train when he leaves to fight. Two years later, after many exchanged letters, Katie and her mother get news of his death. Her mother's friend Louise lives with them during the war, and Katie walks with her to the hospital in a snowstorm for Louise's baby's birth. Her mother begins to correspond with her old friend, Louise's brother. When he returns from the war and goes to Texas, she decides to marry him. Katie learns that loving can cause pain but that the happiness is always worth it.

Hickman, Janet. *The Stones.* Illus. Richard Cuffair. New York: Macmillan, 1976. 0-02-743760-4, 128p. R=2; I=5.*

Garrett, eleven, waits for his father to return from fighting in World War II but receives notification that he is missing. He begins feeling sorry for an old man in town that others taunt, and one day, the man helps Garrett rescue his sister during a storm. Young people need security and love to help them gain confidence.

Holmes, Mary Z. *Dear Dad.* Illus. Geri Strigenz. Austin, TX: Raintree/ Steck-Vaughn, 1992. 0-8114-3503-2, 48p. Paper, 0-8114-6428-8. R=4; I=4.

In 1942, an extended Jewish family in Miami, Florida, does its part during World War II on both the war and home fronts. When Max and his uncle patrol the shoreline on his uncle's private boat, they unexpectedly bump into a German submarine periscope and cleverly escape. The junior high students and their families learn that war evokes emotions with which they must learn to cope as individuals and as families. "History's Children" series.

Hoobler, Dorothy and Thomas. *Aloha Means Come Back: The Story of a World War II Girl.* Illus. Cathie Bleck. Englewood Cliffs, NJ: Silver-Burdett, 1992. 55p. 0-382-24148-7. Paper, 0-382-24349-8. R=4; I=4.

Laura and her mother join her Navy father in Hawaii just before December 7, 1941. Laura meets Michiko, a Japanese-American, who teachers her to ride a surfboard and helps her wounded mother get to the hospital during the melee after the Japanese bombing of Pearl Harbor. Although Laura's parents first avoid Michiko and her family, they quickly realize that they are true friends. "Her Story" series.

Hotze, Sollace. *Summer Endings.* New York: Clarion, 1991. 0-395-56197-3, 176p. R=4; I=4.

In 1945, as Christine Kosinski cheers for the Chicago Cubs baseball team from her apartment overlooking the field, she rejoices at the end of the war. She waits to hear news of her father, a history professor detained in Poland since she, her mother, and her sister Rosie left in 1939. The diverse neighborhood members support Christine and each other in their pains and pleasures, including Rosie's wedding. When they hear that Mr. Kosinski has survived Dachau, where he was imprisoned for opposing Nazi propaganda, Christine and her mother look forward to reuniting their family--not in Poland, but in America.

Houston, Gloria. *But No Candy.* Illus. Lloyd Bloom. New York: Philomel, 1992. 0-399-22142-5, 32p. R=4; I=2.

The war starts when Lee is six, and she is disappointed by the disappearance of candy, especially her favorite Hershey bars. When her uncle returns from the European front four years later, he brings Lee a candy bar, but the pleasure of savoring each step of eating the candy, from carefully unwrapping the paper to the square of chocolate melting in her mouth, is no longer as important as his return with the war ended. As children grow up, the things that give them satisfaction may change.

Irwin, Hadley. *Kim/Kimi.* New York: McElderry, 1987. 0-689-50428-4, 200p. Paper, New York: Puffin, 1988. 0-14-032593-X. R=4; I=7.

Although not legitimate historical fiction, Kim/Kimi's story reveals the intense pain of Japanese-Americans who had to suffer the suspicions of the American government during World War II and lose nearly everything they owned through no fault of their own. As half-Japanese, Kimi goes to California to find her father's relatives even though he died before she was born. Finding one's background may provide some answers, but it often brings forth new questions.

Kudlinski, Kathleen. *Pearl Harbor is Burning!: A Story of World War II.* Illus. Ronald Himler. New York: Viking, 1991. 0-670-83475-0, 54p. Paper, New York: Puffin, 1993. 0-14-034509-4. R=2; I=4.

In 1941, Frank, ten, feels lonely in Hawaii without his Maryland friends, but he soon meets a Japanese American who loves baseball as much as he. When they play in Frank's treehouse one morning, planes bomb the harbor nearby, and Frank's friend identifies them as Japanese. When the enemy looks like one's friends, people may incorrectly assume that one's friends are the enemy. *Once Upon America* series.

Levitin, Sonia. *Annie's Promise*. New York: Atheneum, 1993. 0-689-31752-2, 192p. R=4; I=6.

In a third book about the Platt family after *Journey to America* and *Silver Days*, Annie in 1945 watches as her sister and the boy she waited two years of the war to marry break up and as her other sister move to her own apartment. Annie goes to a summer camp in the mountains of San Jacinta for the underprivileged and enjoys it enough to return when she runs away from home for two days. In a sharply changing world such as that at the end of World War II, parents may have great difficulty adjusting to their children's growing independence.

Levitin, Sonia. *Silver Days*. New York: Atheneum, 1989. 0-689-31563-5, 186p. Paper (Aladdin), 1992. 0-689-71570-6. R=3; I=7.

Lisa, her mother, and two sisters finally reach America to be with her father after a year of waiting in Switzerland in the sequel to *Journey to America*. Disappointed with difficulties in New York, they move to California where their lives improve as Lisa's father starts working in the garment industry again. She has a chance to dance again as well as become interested in boys. Adjusting to a new culture and a new life takes perseverance and courage.

Levoy, Myron. *Alan and Naomi*. New York: HarperCollins, 1987 (1977). Paper (Trophy), 0-06-440209-6, 176p. R=4; I=9.

Around 1943, Alan's mother asks him to make friends with the twelve-year-old war refugee from France, Naomi, who will not communicate with anyone after watching Nazis beat her father to death. Alan, at first, wants to refuse. He then acquiesces and eventually gets her to talk to him and even go to school. But when the neighborhood bully calls them "Jew" and bloodies Alan, Naomi runs away and returns to her shell, not talking to anyone. She has to be placed in an asylum. Sometimes humans do not have to stop breathing to stop living; either type of death is a victory for the enemy.

Lisle, Janet Taylor. *Sirens and Spies*. New York: Bradbury, 1985. 0-02-759150-6, 169p. Paper (Collier), 1990. 0-02-044341-2. R=4; I=7.

Elsie, fourteen, becomes suspicious of her violin teacher, expatriated from France after World War II. She begins researching the war in the library, and stumbles across a photograph of the woman with a child. Elsie sells her violin and starts snooping, but her sister convinces her to confront the teacher after an intruder accidently wounds the teacher. The teacher's story of her experiences as a teenager in World War II reveal that feelings of isolation and loneliness know neither time nor national boundaries.

Lord, Athena. *Z.A.P., Zoe, & the Musketeers.* New York: Macmillan, 1992. 0-02-759561-7, 157p. R=6; I=6.

Zach, thirteen, and his sister Zoe enjoy the summer of 1941 with their friends in Albany, New York. But Zach begins to worry about himself and the changes in his emotions and his Greek American body that have nothing to do with his tonsillectomy. The instability of adolescence can be surprising to the unsuspecting teenager.

Marko, Katherine. *Hang Out the Flag.* New York: Macmillan, 1992. 0-02-762320-3, 160p. R=2; I=5.

In 1943, when Leslie is eleven, her father joins the Seabees. He comes home before going overseas, and to please him, she gets her friends to paint a huge flag on the local water tower. She also helps discover a local German man who is attempting the sabotage of the steel mill where her mother works. When one decides to condemn·another of wrongdoing, one risks an indictment for false accusation.

Paterson, Katherine. *Jacob Have I Loved.* New York: Crowell, 1980. 0-690-04079-2, 228p. Paper, New York: HarperCollins (Trophy), 1990. 0-06-440368-8, 256p. R=7; I=10.

On Maryland's Chesapeake Bay during World War II, fifteen-year-old Sara Louise accuses her twin sister of being their parents' favorite child. The underlying Jacob and Esau motif along with Sara Louise's need to accept herself helps her to eventually understand her family after she becomes an adult. All children need the unequivocal love of a parent whether they seem to be strong or weak in their response to life. *Newbery Medal*, 1981; *American Library Association Notable Book for Children*, 1980; *School Library Journal "Best Book,"* 1980.

Paulsen, Gary. *The Cookcamp.* New York: Orchard/Watts, 1991.
0-531-08527-9, 116p. Paper, New York: Dell (Yearling), 1992.
0-440-40704-4. R=4; I=5.

In 1944, a five-year-old boy's mother sends him to his
grandmother in Minnesota where she cooks for a group of men
who are building a road into Canada. At first awed by the huge
men, he comes to enjoy them when they take him on their
caterpillars and trucks. The separation of families is always
painful. *School Library Journal "Best Book,"* 1991.

Poynter, Margaret. *A Time Too Swift.* New York: Atheneum,
1990. 0-689-31146-X, 216p. R=7; I=8.

Marjorie, fifteen, meets a serviceman at the skating rink in
San Diego during 1941 just before the Japanese bomb Pearl
Harbor. He leaves to fight in the war and so does her brother,
Dave, who is eventually reported missing in action. The next
year is one of waiting and worrying until Dave returns home
injured but safe, and she begins to fall in love with an old
friend. During the process of becoming aware of adult emotions,
one has to learn both patience and hope.

Ray, Deborah Kogan, writer/illus. *My Daddy Was a Soldier: A
World War II Story.* New York: Holiday House, 1990.
0-8234-0795-0, 40p. R=5; I=3.

In 1943, eight-year-old Jeannie's father goes to fight the
Japanese in World War II. Her mother starts working, and they
have to survive on items bought with ration coupons. Not until
December of 1945, do they reunite as a safe and happy family.

Ross, Ramon Royal. *Harper & Moon.* New York: Atheneum,
1993. 0-689-31803-0, 181p. R=3; I=7.

When Harper is twelve during World War II in Washington
state, one of his and his father's old friends, a World War I
hero, dies, and Harper's friend Moon joins the army. Harper
remembers Moon's alcoholic parents who abused Moon, but he
knows that Moon has artistic talent which his inability to talk
clearly belies. Moon becomes the World War II hero, saving his
platoon from an unmanned moving truck. People will often try
to protect others when they know are good and kind.

Rylant, Cynthia. *I Had Seen Castles*. San Diego: Harcourt Brace, 1993. 0-15-238003-5, 97p. R=7; I=8.

As he reflects about his past, John remembers the dividing point of his life in 1939 when his father came home, distressed at the news of Germans thinking they had a method of splitting the uranium atom. The subsequent bombs at Pearl Harbor make John anticipate saving his country by enlisting, which he does in 1942 against the wishes of his girlfriend Ginny who loves him but hates war. By 1945, however, having seen the European castles he has wanted to see since seeing pictures of them at nine, he can no longer live in an America which seems unreal, without either castles or visible suffering. People who have survived real terror may not have the words with which to speak of it.

Savin, Marcia. *The Moon Bridge*. New York: Scholastic, 1992. 0-590-45873-6, 232p. R=2; I=5.

In 1942, after the Japanese bomb Pearl Harbor, Ruthie's fifth grade friends start making unkind remarks to Mitzi, a new girl at school who is Japanese. Ruthie hates their attitude, and Mitzi becomes her best friend until the government sends her and her family to an internment camp. Ruthie tells Mitzi what happens to her in unmailed letters written during the war. After the war, the two meet again and realize that the war stole several prime years of their time together. One often does not know how brave or honest another person is until that person faces a stressful situation.

Taylor, Mildred. *The Road to Memphis*. New York: Dial, 1990. 0-8037-0340-6, 288p. Paper, New York: Puffin, 1992. 0-14-036077-8, 304p. R=3; I=9.

As Cassie travels to Memphis in 1941 to save her friend from trouble with the whites in their Mississippi county, one of the riders becomes ill, and they have to find somewhere for him to stay until they return. In Memphis, car trouble stops them, but Cassie's uncle in Chicago wires money to a lawyer friend trained at Harvard, who helps them accomplish most of their goals. The disregard of some people for the humanity of fellow humans is bordering on criminal. *Coretta Scott King Award*, 1991; *George C. Stone Center for Children's Books Recognition of Merit Award*, 1991.

Thesman, Jean. *Molly Donnelly.* Boston: Houghton Mifflin, 1993. 0-395-64348-1, 186p. R=4; I=8.

Only twelve when the Japanese bomb Pearl Harbor in 1941, Molly becomes frustrated with all the changes in Seattle, especially the quick departure of her next door neighbor and best friend Emily Tanaka, interred in a Japanese camp. After having two cousins killed, going on her first date, and being interested in a young soldier, Molly realizes that a college education is the only thing that will keep her safe from the fate of most women. When one's world falls apart, one has to build a new one.

Tripp, Valerie. *Changes for Molly.* Illus. Nick Backes and Keith Skeen. Madison, WI: Pleasant, 1990 (1988). 0-937295-48-5, 67p. Paper, 1988. 0-937295-49-3. R=3; I=4.

Molly, ten in 1944, wants to be Miss Victory in her dance recital. She worries about her hair being the wrong length, but she is also excited about her father's return from the war. On the day of the recital, she becomes ill, and in her depression at home during the show, her father's unexpected arrival makes her forget the earlier frustration in the day. People worry about many little things, but being loved makes the concerns seem trivial. "American Girls Collection Series"

Uchida, Yoshiko. *The Bracelet.* Illus. Joanna Yardley. New York: Philomel, 1993. 0-399-22503-X, 32p. R=5; I=2.

In 1942, after the Japanese bomb Pearl Harbor, Emi, seven, and her family have to leave their home in Berkeley, California, and her best friend Laurie to go to an internment camp for Japanese-Americans. Laurie gives Emi a gold bracelet with a heart charm before she leaves which Emi loses on the way to the camp. But she realizes that Laurie and her father, separately interred in Montana, are always with her in her memory. She does not need a material thing to remind her of her love for them. Stereotyping people as all bad because others of their culture have done something unacceptable is refusing to acknowledge them as individual human beings.

Uchida, Yoshiko. *Journey to Topaz.* Illus. Donald Carrick. Berkeley, CA: Creative Arts Book, 1985 (1971). Paper, 0-916870-85-5, 160p. R=5; I=5.

The United States government transports Uki Sakane, an eleven-year-old Japanese girl born in America (Nisei), her brother, and her mother to Topaz, Utah, in 1942, after the bombing of Pearl Harbor along with 110,000 other Japanese American citizens. Her father had already been taken to a camp in Montana. Eventually, the family reunites in Topaz but every member works at menial tasks far below their ability until allowed to return to their California home. Sometimes no rational explanation exists as to why something happens.

Volk, Toni. *Montana Women.* New York: Soho, 1992. 0-939149-60-5, 305p. Paper, 1993. 0-939149-89-3. R=6; I=10+.

The sisters Etta and Pearl, in their mid-twenties in 1944, suffer the loss of their fiancées in the war. Pearl meets someone, gets pregnant, and marries, only to have the marriage go bad. She and her daughter return to Etta's in Montana to live. One must live one's life as fully as possible.

Willis, Patricia. *A Place to Claim as Home.* New York: Clarion, 1991. 0-395-55395-4, 166p. R=6; I=6.

When Henry's adoptive father dies, he pretends to be fifteen instead of thirteen and goes to work in the summer for Sarah, a woman needing help on her Ohio farm. Henry rapidly adjusts and tries to help Sarah mend her spirit as well as her home. Against the backdrop of World War II, families, either in despair from the news of death or ecstatic after the latest letter, try to harvest their crops with the few able-bodied men remaining, including Henry, who soon wants to call this place "home." *Friends of American Writers Juvenile Book Merit Award*, 1992.

Yolen, Jane. *Briar Rose*. New York: Tor, 1992. 0-312-85135-9, 190p. Paper, 1993. 0-8125-5862-6. R=7; I=8.

Before Becca's grandmother dies, Becca promises to find the prince and the castle of her grandmother's Briar Rose story since her grandmother has adamantly declared that she is the princess. In the box left in the nursing home room after her grandmother dies are photographs, newspaper clippings, a ring, and a passport. They lead Becca to Fort Oswego, New York, a former World War II refugee camp, and to Chelmno, Poland, site of Nazi exterminations. Becca discovers her grandmother's secret, being found barely alive in a mass grave, receiving life from the partisan fighter who revived her, her subsequent marriage and pregnancy, and her trip to America after Nazis murdered her husband. Some truths are too painful for a person to share, even with family.

1946-1960

Bauer, Marian. *Rain of Fire.* New York: Clarion, 1983. 0-89919-190-8, 160p. R=4; I=5.

When the new boy Celestino accuses Steve's brother Matthew, who has recently returned from World War II, of being a coward, Steve tries to retaliate. Their mental war escalates until both are physically hurt. At twelve, Steve begins to understand the psychological wounds of war and why Matthew remains so sad about the bombings in Japan where he fought. *Jane Addams Book Award, 1984*

Boutis, Victoria. *Looking Out.* New York: Four Winds, 1988. 0-02-711830-4, 139p. R=5; I=7.**

Not until Julius and Ethel Rosenberg are actually executed in 1953 for giving atom bomb secrets to the Russians does Ellen, twelve, understand what it means for her parents to be communists. She also realizes that she can never be an average American girl, accepting air raid drills and not thinking about their meaning. Standing up for what one believes becomes much easier when one recognizes the risks and accepts them. *Jane Addams Book Award, 1989.*

Brooks, Jerome. *Naked in Winter.* New York: Orchard/Watts, 1990. 0-531-08466-3, 182p. R=7; I=9.

An intelligent introvert at fifteen during the 1950's in Chicago, Jake has heard his mother accuse his father endlessly for an affair he had before she arrived from Poland after World War II. Then Jake becomes an unwitting accomplice for his own brother's infidelity. He knows that succumbing to such temptations would make him hate himself. Jake matures slowly in a confusing world which crystallizes so that he knows what is important when his father almost dies.

Brooks, Martha. *Two Moons in August.* Boston: Little Brown, 1992. 0-316-10979-7, 199p. Paper, New York: Scholastic, 1993. 0-590-45923-6,208p. R=3; I=10.

After her mother's death in 1959, Sidonie at sixteen, faces a lonely summer with her sister who has returned from university and her physician father who works constantly. Her loneliness eventually finds respite in the arrival in town of two other young people, another physician's son and her sister's friend. Overcoming the painful loss of parents or friends can be exceedingly difficult and takes much time.

Cleaver, Vera and Bill. *Dust of the Earth.* New York: Lippincott-Harper, 1975. 0-397-31650-X, 160p. R=6; I=6.*

Fern's mother inherits a house upon her father's death in South Dakota, and the family moves there in the mid-twentieth century. What they find is a house and a herd of sheep which they have to learn to raise as they cope with a new environment. Although each member of a family is an individual, the unity of the group helps each one to cope with times of difficulty.

Cole, Norma. *The Final Tide.* New York: McElderry, 1990. 0-689-50510-8, 153p. R=3; I=6.

In 1948, the government decides to make a lake on top of Geneva's rural Kentucky home, and she has to coerce her grandmother into leaving. At fourteen, Geneva moves in with her grandmother, who has decided to die rather than leave. She helps her see that she should do something she has not considered--move into town. Having to relocate from a place one has always lived can be a change almost too difficult to make.

Cormier, Robert. *Tunes for Bears to Dance To.* New York: Delacorte, 1992. 0-385-30818-3, 101p. R=6; I=7.

After World War II, Henry and his mother and father move so that they can forget his brother who was killed by a car less than a year previously. Henry, only eleven, works for a grocer whose evil intent causes him to damage a Holocaust survivor's wood carving. Henry realizes his error before he accepts the cherished reward that his employer had offered him to damage the carving. One has to understand the motives of the giver as well as one's own before taking a gift.

De Hartog, Jan. *The Lamb's War.* New York: Harper, 1979. 461p. R=6; I=10+.**

At fifteen, the Dutch girl Laura goes to Schwalbenbach, a concentration camp where her father is imprisoned for trying to save Jewish babies. One of the officers there, angry at her father, ties him up and rapes Laura in front of him. Her father's rage and subsequent death haunt Laura as she survives the camp, meets and marries an American in order to enter the United States, goes to medical school, attempts to save babies in the southwest, and gets increasingly fat. When one feels guilty for something, even if one is not, the feeling influences many decisions that one makes.

Dixon, Jeanne. *The Tempered Wind.* New York: Atheneum, 1987. 0-689-31339-X, 207p. R=6; I=10.*

After becoming an orphan at thirteen and living with aunts until seventeen, Gabriella, a dwarf, goes to Montana to work in 1948. She falls in love with a minister which strengthens her will and her health. But he tries to use her and her crutches as an inducement for others to become healed at his revival meeting. Sometimes people misinterpret superficial acts of sympathy as being genuine caring love.

Filene, Peter. *Home and Away.* Cambridge, MA: Zoland Books, 1992. 0-944072-22-4, 332p. R=3; I=10+.

Murray, an intelligent Jewish boy of sixteen living in New York in 1951, decides to write a school paper about his parents after his father refuses to sign a non-Communist loyalty oath at work. Murray realizes that his father's extended trip to California to work on a new project for his company relates to problems between his parents. His research leads him to understand that his mother's accusations of his father's infidelity are unfounded. Murray himself also experiences the difficulties of dating, unsure of who he likes and why, against a background of Brooklyn Dodgers' games. Many times, people involved in a situation do not understand why they think or feel in a certain way, and therefore, an outsider may have difficulty trying to discern why things have happened.

Hall, Lynn. *Halsey's Pride.* New York: Scribner's, 1990.
0-684-19155-5, 119p. R=3; I=7.

March tells the story about going to live with her father
when thirteen in 1955 and helping him with his prize collie
Pride. Always fearful of epileptic attacks, she keeps the kennel
running after her father's disappointment that Pride's offspring
have died of torsion, and eventually she begins to breed her
own dogs. People face their disappointments in different ways;
some are better able to cope than others.

Herman, Charlotte. *Millie Cooper, Take a Chance.* Illus. Helen
Cogancherry. New York: Dutton, 1989. 0-525-44442-4, 101p.
Paper, New York: Puffin, 1990. 0-14-034119-6. R=4; I=3.

Millie fears that she will only get a few valentines from her
third grade Chicago classmates in 1947 so she tells them not to
give her any. She only gets one and is very disappointed. She
begins to understand, with her mother's help, that one has to
take the risk of being hurt in order to have the possible
pleasure of success. She begins by trying to win a bicycle in a
contest and by reciting her favorite poem for the class. Her
parents reward her for her attempts with her own two-wheeler.

Herman, Charlotte. *Millie Cooper, 3B.* Illus. Helen Cogancherry.
New York: Dutton, 1985. 0-525-44157-3, 74p. Paper, New York:
Puffin, 1986. 0-14-032072-5, 80p. R=4; I=3.

In her Chicago third grade during 1946, Millie wonders why
she almost cries each time her teacher chastises her. Her
mother says she is too sensitive. Her father finally gives her
one of the new ball point pens, but it smudges and refuses to
write. She wants to be special, and her teacher tells her that
she is artistic. The compliment and the first winter snow make
her very happy.

Higginsen, Vy, with Tonya Bolder. *Mama, I Want to Sing.*
New York: Scholastic, 1992. 0-590-44201-5, 183p. R=5; I=6.

In 1946, when Doris is only eleven, her father dies after he
tells her to follow her dream. In her teenage years, she finds
that her dream is to be a singer although her mother tries to
dissuade her. When a person chooses a career that can easily
deliver heartache instead of happiness, parents often become
fearful and plead for a more stable choice.

Howard, Ellen. *The Tower Room.* New York: Atheneum, 1993. 0-689-31856-1, 137p. R=5; I=5.

In 1953, when Mary Brooke goes to live with her aunt in Michigan after her mother dies, she expects to stay only until her father comes. What she finds instead is that her mother had never married and that complications from an illegal abortion caused her mother's recent death. Facing the truth when it is not what one wants it to be is always difficult.

Johnston, Julie. *Hero of Lesser Causes.* Boston: Joy Street, 1993. 0-316-46988-2, 192p. R=3; I=6.

Keely's older brother becomes paralyzed from polio in the summer of 1946 when Keely is twelve. He loses all interest in living, and Keely spends the next year trying to entice him back to activity. Not until he almost dies does he decide that letting his family and friends live without him would be giving up too much. When people become despondent from being in difficult situations, they sometimes need a serious jolt to remind them of the value of life, of feeling things like the sun and the rain.

Kadohata, Cynthia. *The Floating World.* New York: Ballantine, 1991 (1989). Paper, 0-345-36756-1, 176p. R=3; I=10+.

In the 1950's, a Japanese-American Olivia, her grandmother, her stepfather, her mother, and her brothers all travel along the coast of California as her stepfather works intermittently at transient jobs, and her grandmother talks incessantly. After her grandmother dies, the family settles in Arkansas. Then Olivia moves alone to California, where she remembers her grandmother's stories as guidance for her life. Sometimes people in families that seem to be the most annoying may be the ones who have the greatest influence in the future.

Learmon, Warren. *Unheard Melodies.* Marietta, GA: Longstreet, 1990. 0-929264=26-6, 214p. R=4; I=10+.

The narrator begins his story in Atlanta, Georgia, in 1948 remembering both his mother and uncle lamenting another uncle who has returned from war psychologically disturbed. As he observes his family and as he passes through the rituals of his high school basketball team and then getting into college, he realizes that the things he thought he knew about his family and his friends are illusions. One can never really know why another person makes certain decisions.

Lee, Gus. *China Boy.* New York: NAL-Dutton, 1991. 0-525-24994-X, 322p. Paper (Signet). 1992. 0-451-17434-8. R=7; I=10+.

In the 1950's, Kai Ting, seven, begins boxing lessons in his San Francisco black neighborhood YMCA. He learns to defend himself in street fights, but he has a difficult time balancing his Chinese culture with the mixture of traditions surrounding him, including his Philadelphia society step-mother who tries to squeeze the Chinese culture out of him. Realistic communication among peoples of different cultures can be very difficult.

Lelchuk, Alan. *On Home Ground.* Illus. Merle Nacht. San Diego: Gulliver, 1987. 0-15-200560-9, 72p. R=7; I=5.

Aaron, nine, has an uneasy relationship with his Russian immigrant father in 1947, preferring the company of his older friend who returned wounded from the war. His father dislikes their trips to the Brooklyn Dodgers' games during Jackie Robinson's first season. Not until Aaron's father takes him horseback riding does Aaron begin to see another side to his father's seeming intractability. One needs to accept other people's diversities rather than belittle them.

Levinson, Nancy Smiler. *Your Friend, Natalie Popper.* New York: Lodestar, 1991. 0-525-67307-5, 113p. R=4; I=5.

At twelve in 1946, Natalie goes to camp with her best friend, expecting to spend time with her. They are placed in different cabins, and Natalie meets one girl who stutters, another without a mother, and a third who makes hostile remarks about Jews. That girl gets polio while at camp, causing the camp to shut down. The first experience of a long stay away from home and family exposes a person to the very different ideas and expectations of other people.

Marino, Jan. *Eighty-eight Steps to September.* Boston: Little Brown, 1989. 0-316-54620-8, 158p. Paper, New York: Avon (Camelot), 1991. 0-380-71001-3. R=3; I=4.

When Amy is eleven, in 1948, she spends the summer at home with sitters while her parents stay in nearby Boston with her brother Robbie, who at the beginning of the summer, is diagnosed with leukemia. She waits for his return and works on the doghouse for their new puppy. She refuses to believe people who say that Robbie will not be coming home. After Robbie dies, Amy responds honestly. While hostile toward the adults and surprised at her parents' intense grief, she initially refuses to cry.

Martin, Katherine. *Night Riding.* New York: Knopf, 1989. 0-679-90064-0, 197p. R=3; I=8.*

In 1958, new neighbors move next to Princess and her family's home just as her father enters the hospital for tuberculosis treatment. Princess does not understand why she is not to play with the new girl who is fifteen, but her sister explains that she is pregnant without a husband. When the girl's father approaches Princess while she is riding her horse one night, she begins to understand what has happened to the girl. Some parents subject their children to all kinds of abuse inside the privacy of their homes.

Mickle, Shelly Fraser. *The Queen of October.* Chapel Hill, NC: Algonquin, 1989. 0-945575-21-1, 301p. Paper (Front Porch), 1992. 1-56512-003-5. R=3; I=10+.

When Sally's parents divorce in 1959, she goes to Coldwater, Arkansas, where she has lived before, to spend her eighth grade year with her grandparents. She meets old friends and makes new ones, thinks one man will wait for her to grow up for marriage, has a scatological parrot, and is especially delighted to become Coldwater's October queen. Coping with a socially degrading situation such as a parents' divorce takes a sense of humor and an empathetic family.

Moore, Yvette. *Freedom Songs.* New York: Orchard/Watts, 1991. 0-531-08412-4, 168p. Paper, New York: Puffin, 1992. 0-14-036017-4. R=6; I=8.

Traveling from Brooklyn every year to Wingate, North Carolina, to visit her mother's family, is a trip that Sheryl, fourteen, enjoys until 1963, when she finds that her young uncle has joined a band of freedom riders. Back home, she reads about the group's efforts to gain equal rights for blacks. To help the cause, her school gives a benefit concert, scheduled just after her uncle sacrifices his life. Significant experiences during adolescence not only erase innocence, but they also make young adults aware of problems never before noticed.

Nelson, Vaunda M. *Mayfield Crossing.* Illus. Leonard Jenkins. New York: Putnam, 1993. 0-399-22331-2, 96p. R=3; I=4.

Meg enters fourth grade at a different school when her town is redistricted in 1960. She is the only black in her class. All the new students in the school are ostracized until Meg and her friends challenge the others in a baseball game, and one of the opposing team members decides to join their team instead. New students of any race often have to prove their abilities more than those who are part of an established group.

Pendergraft, Patricia. *Brushy Mountain.* New York: Philomel, 1989. 0-399-21610-3, 207p. R=4; I=5.

Arney's father never returns from World War II, and he, his mother, and sister continue to help those in need in their tiny mountain town. Arney hates one old man in town and decides to kill him but saves his life three times instead. The old man names his new grandson after Arnie. Sometimes people do things from an instinct that they never knew that they had.

Rosenblum, Richard, writer/illus. *Brooklyn Dodger Days.* New York: Atheneum, 1991. 0-689-31512-0, 32p. R=6; I=4.

Buddy and his classmates enjoy the Dodgers-Giants game in 1946 when they have the day off of school to go to the game for free as members of the Knot Hole Club. Ecstatic when the Dodgers win, Buddy is not even upset that his friend, a Giants' fan, catches a home run ball. Sharing similar interests is a good way for people to enjoy each other's friendship.

Rosofsky, Iris. *Miriam.* New York: HarperCollins, 1988. 0-06-024854-8, 188p. R=3; I=7.

In the 1960's, Miriam grows up in her orthodox Jewish home, accepting but not quite understanding. After her brother dies at fourteen, she beings to realize that she will have to find her own way to reconcile her feelings about her religion and the outside world. Growing up is agonizing but being different from most others in a society can amplify the pain.

Rylant, Cynthia. *When I Was Young in the Mountains.* Illus. Diane Goode. New York: Dutton, 1982. 0-525-42525-X, 32p. Paper, 0-525-44198-0. R=7; I=3.

During the mid-twentieth century, the narrator loves living in the coal miners' mountains with her grandparents. She loves the food; the ritual of school, church, her grandfather kissing her when he returns from work; and the photograph of her family with a dead black snake draped around their necks. Having modern conveniences may not make life happier or more memorable. *American Library Association Notable Book for Children,* 1982.

Salisbury, Graham. *Blue Skin of the Sea: A Novel in Stories.* New York: Delacorte, 1992. 0-385-30596-6, 215p. R=6; I=8.

As a six-year-old, Sonny fears the sea around his Hawaiian home in 1953, but not until he reaches nineteen, and his fisherman father disappears from his sampan, does Sonny remember falling into the water when he was one. After yachters rescue his father, Sonny, who prefers school to the sea, tries to get to know his father, the man who has never even discussed Sonny's mother who died when he was only a few months old. Many people live with others for years without knowing what the other person actually thinks about life and relationships.

Schotter, Roni. *Rhoda, Straight and True.* New York: Lothrop, Lee & Shepard, 1986. 0-688-06157-5, 184p. R=4; I=6.

In 1953, Rhoda, her friends, and their families in Brooklyn suspect Mr. and Mrs. Rose of being spies, and they laugh at a large family of thirteen children. Rhoda discovers that the Roses are actors and that the family is very kind, but poor. She hears that accepting preconceived ideas about people without personal investigation is wrong. One must learn not to judge using the opinions of others.

Slepian, Jan. *Risk n' Roses.* New York: Philomel, 1990. 0-399-22219-7, 175p. Paper, New York: Scholastic (Apple), 1992. 0-590-45361-0. R=7; I=7.

In 1948, when Skip is eleven, her family moves to a new neighborhood where she begins looking for friends. The friend she finds manipulates her until Skip's slightly retarded sister does what the friend requests. This, in turn, creates great pain for a kind man who keeps searching for any members of his family who might have survived the Nazi concentration camps of World War II. Skip comprehends, too late, that true friendship never makes unreasonable demands; each person wants the other to do well.

Smalls-Hector, Irene. *Irene and the Big, Fine Nickel.* Illus. Tyrone Geter. Boston: Little, Brown, 1991. 0-316-79871-1, 32p. R=5; I=2.

Irene at seven enjoys her day in Harlem with other children who have also come from South Carolina around 1957. When she finds a nickel, she and her friends purchase a special raisin bun treat. Irene graciously shares with Charlene even though she has insulted Irene's mother earlier in the day.

Smothers, Ethel Footman. *Down in the Piney Woods.* New York: Knopf, 1992. 0-679-90360-7, 151p. R=3; I=4.

In the 1950's, Annie Rye, ten, looks forward to her Georgia summer, buying things from the "rolling" store and going possum hunting with her grandfather. What she does not anticipate is having to get along with her half-sisters who come to stay, the little white girl who unexpectedly visits, or finding rattlesnakes inside the house that have to be smoked out. Surviving everyday situations can take a lot of time and effort.

Smucker, Anna Egan. *No Star Nights.* Illus. Steve Johnson. New York: Knopf, 1989. 0-394-99925-8, 48p. R=6; I=3.

As a child in a steel mill town of the 1950's, the narrator remembers the red fires brightening the night sky, quiet days while her father slept, and going with him to Pittsburgh for baseball games. The children enjoyed holiday parades, played games in the street, and wondered how the Catholic sister teachers kept their habit collars white despite all the soot from the mills. One often forgets the unpleasant memories of childhood and remembers only the delightful times. *International Reading Association Children's Book Award*, 1990; *American Library Association Notable Book for Children*, 1990.

Steiner, Barbara. *Tessa.* New York: Morrow, 1988. 0-688-07232-1, 218p. R=4; I=7.

Tessa loves to hunt for relics in the Arkansas river bottoms with her father rather than live in town with her mother in 1946. But her teacher and the university student, who works with her father during her fourteenth summer, encourage her to consider going to college to major in archeology and be paid to do something she loves. She finally decides to stay in town and finish high school. Having to make decisions about which parent to live with or what one's career might be can be stressful.

Strauch, Eileen Walsh. *Hey You, Sister Rose.* New York: Tambourine, 1993. 0-688-11829-1, 159p. R=4; I=5.

In 1951, Arlene, eleven, enters sixth grade in Baltimore, Maryland, dreading her year under the dictatorial Sister Rose. Instead of being completely awful, Sister Rose helps Arlene find out things about herself and helps her develop her writing talent. Sometimes a teacher or an adult who seems to be too demanding is actually trying to raise one to one's level of potential.

Taylor, Mildred. *The Gold Cadillac.* New York: Dial, 1987. 0-8037-0343-0, 48p. R=6; I=5.

Her father buys a new 1950 gold Cadillac, and 'lois's mother refuses to ride in it until her father decides to drive to Mississippi from Toledo, Ohio, to see his family. The white police stop him, jail him, and fine him for speeding when he was not because they do not think that a black man should have such a costly car. Having expensive cars and material items do not make a person happy, but being with a loving, harmonious family does. *Christopher Award*, 1988.

Todd, Leonard. *Squaring Off.* New York: Viking, 1990. 0-670-83377-0, 150p. R=3; I=9.

Willy's life changes again at thirteen when his widower father meets a stripper in Savannah, Georgia, in the mid-1950's. She befriends Willy, and when Willy's father embarrasses him for watching her act, she decides to quit her job. Willy runs away, and after she helps Willy's father find him, they realize that they can both be parents for Willy. Growing up requires learning adult secrets and finding out how to handle the knowledge in perspective.

Uchida, Yoshiko. *Journey Home.* Illus. Charles Robinson. New York: McElderry, 1978. 0-689-50126-9, 144p. Paper (Aladdin), 1992. 0-689-71641-9. R=6; I=6.

Yuki and her mother return to Berkley, California, at the end of World War II after being interred by the United States government in this sequel to *Journey to Topaz.* Often targets for hostile comments and actions, Yuki, her family, and their friends learn the meaning of forgiveness when a couple whose son was killed in Japan during the war help them rebuild a fire-bombed store and invite them to celebrate Thanksgiving. Rather than looking always to the future for a better life, one needs to know how to live in the present.

Voight, Cynthia. *David and Jonathan.* New York: Scholastic, 1992. 0-590-45165-0, 256p. R=2; I=10.

In 1954, Jon and Henry, although very different except for their high intelligence, are best friends on Cape Cod, Massachusetts. When Jon's cousin, the only German Jewish relative to survive the Holocaust, comes to live with them, it changes their perspectives about themselves and their lives. They meet again in 1967 in a hospital where Henry's surgical brilliance saves Jon from a severe Viet Nam war injury. Humor and understanding are two of the best ways to lighten the burden of life's realities.

Weaver, Lydia. *Close to Home: A Story of the Polio Epidemic.* Illus. Aileen Arrington. New York: Viking, 1993. 0-670-84511-6, 64p. R=5; I=5.

During Betsy's tenth summer in 1952, one of the worst polio epidemics occurs, and her friend contracts polio. Since Betsy's mother works in Dr. Jonas Salk's laboratory in Pittsburgh, Betsy and her younger brother get the new experimental vaccine which protects them. When a debilitating or fatal disease strikes humans, it frightens all who might either be exposed to it or who might lose loved ones. "Once Upon America" series.

White, Alana. *Come Next Spring.* New York: Clarion. 1990. 0-395-52593-4, 170p. R=5; I=6.

During her year in eighth grade, 1949, Salina's Tennessee world changes. While she adjusts to influences from "outlanders" (persons not born in the valley), she makes a new friend as she loses an old one. The rituals, taffy-pulls and church socials, throughout the year reveal the value of family and community to this isolated mountain town.

White, Ruth. *Sweet Creek Holler.* New York: Farrar, Straus, & Giroux, 1988. 0-374-37360-4, 215p. Paper, 1992. 0-374-47375-7. R=4; I=5.

Although her father dies when she is six after World War II, Ginny does not understand the finality and enjoys her freedom running around her Appalachian home with her friends. Several events occur as she grows to age twelve that take away her childhood so that she welcomes the family's move to Pennsylvania and a new life. Death, of course, ends physical contact, but one can always keep the memories of a loved one. *American Library Association Notable Book for Children*, 1988.

White, Ruth. *Weeping Willow.* New York: Farrar, 1992. 0-374-38255-7, 246p. R=3; I=8.

Tiny spends her high school years from 1956 to 1960 in a rural Virginia mountain town. She is popular and musically talented with her years marred by her stepfather's attempted abuse of her and his success at abusing her younger sister. But Tiny survives and decides to attend college. A person's values during the high school years are tenuous and myopic; adults must encourage them to consider all alternatives.

Wyss, Thelma Hatch. *A Stranger Here.* New York: HarperCollins, 1993. 0-06-021439-2, 132p. R=5; I=7.

In this historical fantasy, Jada is sixteen in 1960 when she spends the summer helping her aunt and uncle on their Idaho farm. In their attic, she plays an old record, and the ghost of a young man killed in World War II appears and dances with her. She sees him often, gets to know him, and through this phantom relationship, begins to understand her aunt and herself. People need to be appreciated for their strengths rather than judged on their weaknesses.

Yount, John. *Thief of Dreams.* New York: Thorndike, 1991. Large Type, 1-56054-192-X, 375p. R=7; I=10+.

When James is thirteen in 1948, his parents separate, and he moves with his mother to the home of her parents. After a fight in which his friend is badly beaten instead of James, James decides to leave home, an act which reunites his parents after his father finds him in the woods suffering from hypothermia. Trying to understand others may not be as difficult as understanding oneself.

1961 and AFTER

Antle, Nancy. *Tough Choices: A Story of the Vietnam War.* Illus. Michele LaPorte. New York: Viking, 1993. 0-670-84879-4, 64p. R=4; I=4.

When Samantha's brother Mitch comes home from Vietnam in 1968, she proudly wears her bracelet with the name and date of one of the American soldiers missing in action. Mitch faces hostile "hippies" at the airport, and his younger brother declaims with anti-war slogans. But when Mitch receives word that his best friend in Vietnam died after he left, he decides to go back and fight the enemy that is still not defeated. When one believes in something, one must express that belief regardless of what others will think. "Once Upon America" series.

Bingham, Sallie. *Matron of Honor.* Cambridge, MA: Zoland, 1994. 0-944072-38-0, 186p. R=4; I=10+.

The day before April's wedding in 1970, her sister leaves her husband and comes home. Her arrival surprises the family since she had said that she would be unable to attend the wedding. April wants her to be her matron of honor instead of her fiancée's sister. From the points of view of various family members, the maid, and April's fiancée, the instability of Corinne's actions, April's impulsiveness, and the family loyalty come forth in this southern town. Individuals sometimes refuse to adhere to customs that their societies have carefully created in attempts to avoid controversy.

Bingham, Sallie. *Small Victories.* Cambridge, MA: Zoland, 1992. 0-944072-20-8, 298p. Paper, 0-944072-25-9. R=7; I=10+.

Louise prefers to care for her disabled sister, who is prone to fits, at home rather than sending her to a home, but her married brother Tom disagrees. Louise's nephew and Tom's son, young Tom leaves college after Louise writes him in 1958 about the lives and deaths of his grandparents. In the small North Carolina town, he learns, in a very short time, about Louise, her sister, and his father who has tried to ignore the family's realities. Most of life passes with the small victories, moments of happiness, rather than enormous achievements that glow for a long time.

Brooks, Bruce. *The Moves Make the Man.* New York: HarperCollins, 1984. 0-06-020698-5, 280p. Paper (Trophy), 1987. 0-06-447022-9. R=5; I=6.

During the 1960's, Jerome and Bix become friends who practice their best basketball "moves." On a trip across North Carolina, Bix is shocked when his favorite restaurant refuses to serve Jerome because he is black. Then he sees his mother in the mental ward at Duke Hospital. His subsequent disappearance stuns Jerome because the Bix who hated "fakes" makes the ultimate "move." Jerome survives the ordeal and continues to do well as the only black student in a white high school, but he never quite understands Bix's inability to face reality. *Newbery Honor,* 1985; *Boston Globe--Horn Book Award,* 1985; *American Library Association Notable Book for Children,* 1984; *School Library Journal "Best Book,"* 1984.

Erhart, Margaret. *Augusta Cotton.* Cambridge, MA: Zoland, 1992. 0-944072-21-6, 289p. R=4; I=10+.

In 1963, sixth grader Augusta and her new friend Helen share such events as the death of Kennedy. Helen surprises Augusta with her insights about things that Augusta has accepted without question. When Helen gets lupus, Augusta's physician father tells her that it is serious. Augusta visits Helen, learns her family secrets, and thereby expands her world beyond her Jewish-Protestant French background. Becoming aware that situations have depth as well as breadth is often unsettling to adolescents whose bodies and emotions are often functioning beyond their control.

Frank, Elizabeth Bales. *Cooder Cutlas.* New York: Harper, 1987. 0-06-17655-X, 311p. R=3; I=10.

Cooder, at twenty-three in 1975, trying to recover from the death of his girlfriend and the disintegration of his band, finds himself at the Jersey shore as a peripheral member of another band while working as a garage mechanic. He falls in love again and spends the next two or three years reconciling his life while the band goes on tour and his girlfriend models in Europe. Young people often imagine who they think they should be before they begin to accept themselves for their own assets.

Hamilton, Virginia. *Drylongso.* Illus. Jerry Pinkney. New York: Harcourt Brace, 1992. 0-15-224241-4, 56p. R=3; I=3.

In 1975, west of the Mississippi, Lindy's family is enduring drought when a dust storm brings them a boy, Drylongso. He helps them find water with his dowser and gives them seeds to plant near the newly discovered spring. After the garden begins growing, he leaves Lindy's family to find his own, leaving his good work behind to help them until the next drought season, which according to the weather cycles, will occur around twenty years later in the 1990's.

Hotze, Sollace. *Acquainted with the Night*. New York: Clarion, 1992. 0-395-61576-3, 230p. R=3; I=10.

When Molly's cousin Caleb arrives on her Maine island in 1979, they find a diary and encounter the ghost of Evaline Cobb Bloodsworth who began the diary when she was twelve in 1824. Molly, an artist of seventeen, falls in love with Caleb, twenty-one, a musician who was both physically and psychologically wounded in Vietnam. Their research reveals that Evaline's boss had seduced her at thirteen while she worked in a Lowell, Massachusetts, mill, and the baby had been adopted. Many years later, Evaline was shunned by her neighbors because she fell in love with a younger visitor and married him only for his family to realize that she was his mother. Being mature enough to keep from committing mistakes which will be regretted later takes great strength.

Jones, Adrienne. *Long Time Passing*. New York: HarperCollins, 1993 (1990). Paper (Trophy) 0-06-447070-9, 245p. R=4; I=8.

Jonas reflects about the year 1969, twenty years before, when his mother died in a car accident, and his father, a marine lieutenant colonel, went to Vietnam. He leaves his friends, including his first love, to enlist in the marines after he receives notification that his father is missing in action. He hopes to find his father, but instead, he is a misfit with no understanding of the reasons for fighting. When people make choices because others have influenced them, they sometimes have difficulty feeling comfortable or happy with their lives until they take charge of themselves.

Lasky, Kathryn. *Pageant*. New York: Four Winds, 1986. 0-02-751720-9, 221p. Paper, New York: Dell (Laurel Leaf), 1988. 0-440-20161-6. R=7; I=8.

In 1963, the fourth year that Sarah has a role as shepherd in her Indianapolis girl's school Christmas pageant, she walks out of rehearsal, gets into her parents' car, and drives alone to her sister's apartment in New York. As she attempts to understand her action, seemingly precipitated by Kennedy's assassination, it becomes clearer to her when her aunt's friend compares his escape from a bad political situation to the same thing that she has done, only perhaps on a smaller scale. Sometimes adults do not see the myriad little frustrations that can overwhelm a teenager as they leave the innocence of childhood.

Marino, Jan. *The Day That Elvis Came to Town.* Boston: Little, Brown, 1991. 0-316-54618-6, 204p. Paper, New York: Avon (Camelot), 1993. 0-380-71672-0. R=2; I=6.

During the summer of 1964, the new boarder, a jazz singer, arrives and entrances Wanda, thirteen. When Wanda hears that Mercedes went to school with Elvis and that Elvis is coming to nearby Savannah, Georgia, for a concert, Wanda thinks Elvis will send them tickets and invite them backstage. Wanda discovers that Mercedes cannot fulfill her fantasies especially since Mercedes is part colored. Instead, Wanda blames Mercedes for deceiving her. What one wants to believe about a person and what is actually true may not be the same, but facts do not lessen the reality of a person's kindness and generosity. *School Library Journal "Best Book,"* 1991.

Nelson, Theresa. *And One for All.* Orchard/Watts, 1989. 0-531-08404-3, 182p. Paper, New York: Dell, 1991. 0-440-40456-8. R=5; I=7.

Geraldine is only twelve when her older brother turns eighteen in 1967, and in the middle of his senior year, joins the marines. He leaves for Vietnam only to return in a coffin and to be eulogized by his best friend whom Geraldine has always admired except that he plans to participate in an anti-war march in Washington. People can still love the person although they abhor the cause for which that person may have died. *American Library Association Notable Book for Children,* 1990; *School Library Journal "Best Book,"* 1989.

Rostkowski, Margaret I. *The Best of Friends.* New York: Harper, 1989. 0-06-025105-0, 183p. R=3; I=10.

Around 1970, during the war in Vietnam, Dan, Sarah, and Will, all eighteen and seniors in a Utah high school, have to reassess their relationship with one another. Each has to become independent, and each has to choose appropriately for himself or herself. Individuals often have to make choices that differ from those their best friends or family would make for them.

Surat, Michele Maria. *Angel Child, Dragon Child.* Illus. Vo-Dinh Mai. Austin, TX: Raintree/Steck-Vaughn, 1983. 0-940742-12-8, 32p. Paper, New York: Scholastic, 1989. 0-590-42271-5. R=2; I=2.

At seven, Ut faces ridicule when she first attends an American school wearing her Vietnamese native dress. A boy hits her with a snowball and their fight leads the principal to isolate the two until they begin understanding each other. Their friendship influences the school families to raise money to pay for Ut's mother's passage to America. Although not historical in the traditional sense, the story and its lovely illustrations reflect what Vietnamese children have been facing since they started coming to the United States as refugees during the 1960's.

Talbert, Marc. *The Purple Heart.* New York: HarperCollins, 1992. 0-06-020429-X, 135p. R=5; I=5.

When Luke's father returns home from the Vietnam War in 1967, his disinterest in Luke and his inability to show real love greatly disturb Luke. Luke continues to pretend that his father's bravery won him the Purple Heart medal, but Luke's father dismisses the award as something one only has to be wounded to receive. The time of healing requires that all try to understand each other, within family and within community, and accept both positive and negative traits.

Young, Ronder Thomas. *Learning by Heart.* Boston: Houghton Mifflin, 1993. 0-395-65369-X, 172p. R=5; I=5.

Rachel, in the early 1960's, has to adjust to moving into a new house, a baby brother, an African-American housekeeper, and the changes in her southern United States' society. The housekeeper helps Rachel begin to accept and appreciate people in her school and in her scout activities as human regardless of their race. But when the family has financial difficulties, the parents must terminate the housekeeper's employment. Even when one has strong emotional attachments to another human, if the relationship is employer to employee, one may have to sever the affiliation when the employer can no longer pay.

CANADA

BEFORE 1800

Anderson, Joan. *Pioneer Settlers in New France.* Photos by George Ancona. New York: Lodestar, 1990. 0-525-67291-5, 60p. R=7; I=7.*

Around 1763, Jean François, a young man of the French nobility orphaned and living with his uncle and aunt in Louisbourg, Nova Scotia, dislikes working in their store, preferring the freedom of the sea and his interest in navigation. When he and a peasant fisherman's son go sailing, they are chastised for their foolishness since France and Great Britain have recently declared war, and the waterways are no longer safe. Until fighting occurs on one's doorstep, accepting the reality of a declared war is often difficult.

Bond, Nancy. *Another Shore.* New York: Macmillan, 1988. 0-689-50463-2, 308p. R=6; I=7.

In this historical fantasy, Lyn accompanies her mother to Louisburg, a town in Nova Scotia which has been restored to its 1744 condition, during the 1980's. After working as an animator for the tourists for several weeks, she finds herself actually in 1744, before war begins between the French and the British. Puzzled at her acceptance as the baker's daughter by the townspeople, she searches for a way to leave, but she falls in love with a young Frenchman instead. Even the most mysterious of situations can be bearable if one is loved.

Houston, James. *Running West.* New York: Pocket Books, 1992 (1990). Paper (Zebra), 0-8217-3505-5, 320p. R=6; I=10+.

In 1714, a boy from another Scottish clan challenges William to a duel, thinking William is his gentry cousin. When William wins, the family reluctantly decides that he must leave before the enemy pursues him. He travels to Canada where he meets a woman from the Dene nation with whom he falls in love. When one loves another human, home becomes the place where the loved one happens to be.

Hudson, Jan. *Dawn Rider.* New York: Philomel, 1990. 0-399-22178-6, 175p. Paper, New York: Scholastic (Point), 1992. 0-590-44987-7. R=4; I=6.

Kit Fox, sixteen, wants to ride the horse recently acquired by her group of Blackfeet Indians. Since they have never owned horses, they fear them and do not think females should have any contact. By sneaking to the horse every morning, Kit Fox earns its confidence and eventually saves the group from invading Snakes with her ability to ride to the friendly Cress, a tribe with guns which can defeat the Snakes. Blackfeet of 1750 had clear expectations for each tribal member. Although a definite delineation between men and women exists, love and humor help each more easily face their roles in life. *Writers Guild of Alberta Awards for Excellence* (Canada), 1990.

Kinsey-Warnock, Natalie. *Wilderness Cat.* Illus. Mark Graham. New York: Cobblehill, 1992. 0-525-65068-7, 32p. R=4; I=3.

In the late 1700's, Serena's family moves from Vermont to Canada, and Serena's father makes her leave her cat Moses with a neighbor. The family's attempt to get food during the freezing winter becomes difficult, but one night they answer a cry at the door, and Moses stands there dragging a rabbit behind him. Some animals seem to show an incredible loyalty to the humans who love them.

Marko, Katherine. *Away to Fundy Bay.* New York: Walker, 1985. 0-8027-6594-7, 145p. R=4; I=5.

In his attempt to escape a man who reports him for damning the British and the press gangs in Halifax, Nova Scotia, during 1775, Doone, thirteen, goes to his mother's friends on a farm near Fundy Bay. Later, he rescues his mother and sister, servants to his dead father's brother, and brings them to Fundy

Bay. By saving the friend's son from hanging for treason, is given his own land for his family. Trying to make life better for others can make one's own life more satisfying.

Speare, Elizabeth George. *Calico Captive.* Illus. Witold T. Mars. Boston: Houghton Mifflin, 1957. 0-395-07112-7, 288p. Paper, New York: Dell (Yearling), 1973. 0-440-41156-4. R=5; I=7.

Indians capture Miriam and her pregnant sister's family in 1754, at the outset of the French and Indian war. The Indians then take them to Montreal and sell them to French settlers. Since the Indians have kept her sister's husband, Miriam supports the family with her dress designs and sewing. She matures during this ordeal which also includes an arduous prisoner exchange requiring the family to sail from Montreal to England and back to Boston. When one replaces selfishness with selflessness, life offers many more rewards.

1800-1932

Hudson, Jan. *Sweetgrass.* New York: Philomel, 1989. 0-399-21721-5, 160p. Paper, New York: Scholastic, 1991. 0-590-43486-1. R=5; I=7.

A nineteenth century Blackfoot, Sweetgrass, thinks that she is old enough at fifteen to marry Eagle-Sun, but her father disagrees. After nursing her mother and brother back to health from smallpox and feeding them the only food available, the forbidden fish, her father recognizes her as a fully mature woman. Although waiting for men and acquiescing to their decisions seems to be the only choice for women, some women escaped these bounds by becoming warriors. *Canadian Children's Book of the Year Award,* 1984; *Canada Council Children's Literature Prize; Governor General's Literary Awards, Children's Literature Category,* 1984; *International Board of Books for Young People,* 1986; *American Library Association Notable Book for Children,* 1989; *School Library Journal "Best Book,"* 1989.

Lunn, Janet. *One Hundred Shining Candles.* Illus. Lindsay Grater. New York: Scribner's, 1991. 0-684-19280-2, 32p. R=7; I=3.

When Lucy hears about one hundred shining candles lighting homes at Christmas in the cities, she wants the same wonderful sight for her family's log cabin in Upper Canada during 1800. The family has money only for the white flour her mother needs for Christmas bread, but she and her brother thrill their parents by making red candles to light for Christmas morning. Sometimes the simplest gifts are the most thoughtful, and therefore, the most welcome.

Lunn, Janet. *Shadow in Hawthorn Bay.* New York: Puffin, 1988 (1987). Paper, 0-14-032436-4, 192p. R=6; I=9.

Around 1800 in Scotland, Mairi who has *an dà shelladh* (second sight) clearly hears her cousin Duncan calling out to her to come to Canada where he has emigrated. She goes, only to find that he has recently drowned. She refuses, however, to let his "shadow" consume her as she decides to marry and begin a new life. Some people have their insights about the present or the future verified by what happens, and such events can scare people who approach life very factually. *Canada Council Children's Literature Prizes*, 1987; *Canada Children's Book of the Year Award*, 1987; *International Board on Books for Young People*, 1988.

Major, Kevin. *Blood Red Ochre.* New York: Delacorte, 1989. 0-385-29794-7, 148p. Paper, New York: Dell (Laurel Leaf), 1990. 0-440-20730-4. R=3; I=7.

In half of the chapters of this historical fantasy, David, fifteen, becomes attracted to Nancy, an unusual new girl in his class who is also doing her heritage report on the extinct Beothuk tribe of Newfoundland. In the alternating chapters, Dauoodaset worries about helping his people, the Beothuks, known for painting their bodies with red ochre, before a white man's bullet kills him in 1829. When David takes Nancy to a nearby island where his grandfather has discovered a Beothuk skeleton and from where he found the carved bone medallion he wears, he watches Dauoodaset die and sees Nancy, who has become Dauoodaset's love, Shanawdithit, disappear as the last of the Beothuks. Sometimes unusual forces seem to control lives.

Michener, James. *Journey.* New York: Random, 1989. 0-394-57826-0, 245p. R=7; I=10+.

When news reaches London in 1897 that a ton of gold has been extracted from the Klondike in Canada, Lord Luton decides to travel with his nephew on a patriotic route through Canada to Dawson. Not prepared for the enormous distance and exposure to cold, the other men in Luton's group die, and he only stays in Klondike a few hours before he begins his return to England. People who have inflated opinions of their abilities may be temporarily blinded to the true difficulty of a project.

1933 and AFTER

Ellis, Sarah. *Next-Door Neighbors.* New York: McElderry, 1990. 0-689-50495-0, 154p. Paper, New York: Dell, 1992. 0-440-40620-X. R=6; I=5.

Peggy, twelve, dreads having to meet new people when her family moves in 1957 to a Canadian city where her father has taken a job as minister of a large church. She finds, however, that one must devise a way to make meeting people less traumatic. Her ruse, after she and a new friend put on an award-winning puppet show, is to pretend she is a puppet for a few minutes. Overcoming shyness is difficult, but learning interesting things about new people has rewards. *School Library Journal "Best Book,"* 1990.

Garrigue, Shelia. *The Eternal Spring of Mr. Ito.* New York: Bradbury, 1985. 0-02-7373002-2, 163p. R=4; I=8.

Evacuated from England in 1940 to Canadian relatives, Sara becomes friends with her uncle's World War I companion, the gardener, Mr. Ito, who helps her start a bonsai tree. After the Japanese bomb Pearl Harbor in 1941, Mr. Ito's family is interned. He hides in a cave, but Sara finds him and saves his bonsai tree, passed down from many generations and needing to go to the next. The most valuable aspects of life are not those of the physical or material but those of the spirit.

Kinsey-Warnock, Natalie. *The Canada Geese Quilt.* Illus. Leslie W. Bowman. New York: Cobblehill, 1989. 0-525-65004-0, 64p. Paper, New York: Dell (Yearling), 1992. 0-440-40719-2. R=5; I=4.

Ariel, ten, becomes distressed in 1946 when her lively grandmother has a stroke and refuses to talk with her for several weeks. When she overcomes her shyness, she helps her finish a quilt that Ariel designed with Canada geese for the new baby expected very soon, but Ariel's grandmother surprises her with another quilt made especially for her. Realizing that loved ones will die can be shocking, but one must learn to accept the natural cycles of life. *American Library Association Notable Book for Children*, 1990.

Kogawa, Joy. *Naomi's Road.* Illus. Matt Gould. Paper, New York: Oxford, 1988. 0-19-540547-1, 82p. R=3; I=3.

Separated from her parents during World War II, six-year-old Naomi goes to a Japanese internment camp in Canada with her aunt and brother. Since Naomi loves to play with her dolls and enjoys the music her brother plays on his flute, her life is not totally changed. Yet for three years, she must cope with this different life, never quite understanding why it is happening.

Lindgard, Joan. *Between Two Worlds.* New York: Lodestar, 1991. 0-525-67360-1, 186p. Paper, New York: Puffin, 1993. 0-14-036505-2. R=3; I=9.

In this sequel to *Tug of War*, the Peterson family makes a new life for itself in Toronto, having to face all of the difficulties of immigrants trying to survive in a different country. When their father has a heart attack upon their arrival in the Toronto train station, Astra and Hugo, at eighteen, have to settle the family and begin to work. They also take courses at night to learn English, and their perseverance helps them earn enough money to buy land for a home. The difficulties of living in a new country are magnified by the longing memories of the past.

Lindgard, Joan. *Tug of War.* New York: Lodestar, 1990. 0-525-673060-7, 194p. Paper, New York: Puffin. 0-14-036072-7. R=4; I=7.

When the family leaves its home in Latvia in 1944 with the Russian guns booming in the distance, Hugo becomes separated from his twin Astra, fourteen. Someone accidentally knocks off his glasses, and he cannot see people in the distance without them. The other family members reach Germany, but they cannot remain in Leipzig as they had planned because no work is available. Astra's father only gets a teaching job abroad, in 1948, after writing over two thousand letters. They coincidentally meet Hugo in Hamburg where they have gone to take the ship to Canada. The ravages of war affect everyone in many different ways.

Little, Jean. *From Anna.* Illus. Joan Sandin. New York: HarperCollins, 1972. 0-06-023912-3, 208p. Paper (Trophy), 1973. 0-06-440044-1. R=3; I=3.

In 1933, when Anna is nine, her family, fearful of the new atmosphere of hostility in Germany, leaves for Canada. A Canadian doctor discovers her poor sight and prescribes glasses for her which changes her life. No longer threatened by school because she cannot see the blackboard, Anna blossoms under the loving tutelage of her teacher and classmates.

Pearson, Kit. *Looking at the Moon.* New York: Viking, 1992. 0-670-84097-1, 212p. R=4; I=7.

In her third summer as an evacuee in Canada, in this sequel to *The Sky is Falling* set in 1944, Norah and her "family" spend the summer at their lake cottage. She has difficulty understanding her changing body and her moodiness, and she wonders how she will adjust to her real family when she returns to England, if the war ever ends. Most adolescents rush toward adulthood but stop with surprise when the decisions to be made become difficult and uncertain.

Pearson, Kit. *The Sky Is Falling.* New York: Viking, 1990. 0-670-82849-1, 248p. R=6; I=5.

Being evacuated to Canada in 1940 makes Norah, ten, very unhappy, but her parents do not give her and her younger brother a choice. Learning to live with a wealthy dowager and her timid daughter in Toronto is very difficult until, after a frightening experience, they decide to compromise. People must allow others to be themselves and to accept their backgrounds because they cannot and often do not want to forget the past. *Geoffrey Bilson Award for Historical Fiction for Young People* (Canada), 1990; *Mr. Christie's Book Awards* (Canada), 1990; *Canadian Children's Book of the Year Award*, 1990.

Roe, Elaine Corbeil. *Circle of Light.* New York: HarperCollins, 1989. 0-06-025079-8, 248p. R=7; I=7.*

Lucy, thirteen, living in Quebec, prepares for a scholarship competition when she prefers to be gossiping with her friends. Although she does not win the award, she learns a lot about her goals, and she enjoys a relationship which develops with a boy who admires her abilities. Coping with life's losses can make preparing for the future a struggle.

Turner, Bonnie. *The Haunted Igloo.* Boston: Houghton Mifflin, 1991. Sandpiper, 0-395-57037-9, 152p. R=3; I=4.

Fearful of the Inuit boys who tease him, Jean-Paul, ten and slightly crippled, hates living in Aklavik where his geologist father searches through pitchblende for radium in the 1930's. Not until Jean-Paul has to run to the home of one of the boys and get help for his mother, in childbirth in an igloo, does he feel good about himself and proud of his dog who kept the newborn warm. Being little and shy can make positive interaction with other people especially difficult.

SOUTH AND CENTRAL AMERICA
AND THE CARIBBEAN

BEFORE 1600

Conrad, Pam. *Pedro's Journal: A Voyage with Christopher Columbus.* Illus. Peter Koeppen. Honesdale, PA: Boyds Mills, 1991. 1-878093-17-7, 81p. Paper, New York: Scholastic (Apple), 1992. 0-590-46206-7. R=6; I=6.

Chosen to be cabin boy because he reads and writes, Pedro accompanies Christopher Columbus on the *Santa Maria* in 1492, expecting to reach the Indies. Pedro records the frustrations of the crew, the captain's responses to situations, the events that occur after they land, and his fear of the treacherous storms that they encounter while returning to Spain. People who explore the unknown have to be brave, hopeful, and daring.

Dorris, Michael. *Morning Girl.* New York: Hyperion, 1992. 1-56282-285-3, 74p. R=6; I=4.

Morning Girl and Star Boy live with their parents on a Bahamian island in 1492 before Columbus finds them. In their closed world, they discover things about themselves and develop various ways to do things uncomplicated by supposedly civilized people. Because a culture seems simple does not mean that its relationship to its world lacks understanding.

Foreman, Michael, and Richard Seaver. *The Boy Who Sailed with Columbus.* New York: Arcade, 1992. 1-55970-178-1, 71p. R=4; I=4.

Leif, twelve, sails with Columbus in 1492 and stays in the New World instead of returning to Spain. Captured and nurtured by a tribe because he has the blond hair of his dead Viking father, he learns the tribe's ways, and by seventeen, becomes its medicine man, traveling throughout the land telling stories and helping. Having compassion for others makes one look for more than gold from life.

Litowinsky, Olga. *The High Voyage: The Final Crossing of Christopher Columbus.* New York: Dell, 1992 (1977). Paper (Yearling), 0-440-40703-6, 147p. R=6; I=6.

Fernando, thirteen, is delighted to join his father Christopher Columbus in 1502 on another attempt to find an ocean route to India. When they beach in Jamaica, some of the crew members mutiny against Columbus, but after a brief battle, Columbus's supporters capture the leader of the revolt. Eventually Columbus gets a ship to sail back to Spain where Fernando decides he wants to stay. Learning to accept situations different from those at home can be difficult.

O'Dell, Scott. *The Amethyst Ring.* Boston: Houghton Mifflin, 1983. 0-395-33886-7, 224p. R=7; I=10.

In the third book of the trilogy beginning with *The Captive*, followed by *The Feathered Serpent*, the king of Spain, Carlos (Charles I), accuses Julian around 1530 of keeping the king's fifth of gold. Julian tries to rule as a priest, but Cortés overcomes him after Julian's friends have become indolent by constantly chewing coca plants. Julian escapes, joins Pizarro until he massacres the followers of the Incan king Atahualpa, and then trails a woman to Machu Picchu who spurns him. When people have power and wealth within their grasp, they will use many guises, including religion, to obtain them.

O'Dell, Scott. *The Captive.* Boston: Houghton Mifflin, 1979. 0-395-27811-2, 244p. R=6; I=9.

The first of a trilogy including *The Feathered Serpent* and *The Amethyst Ring*, Julian, a seminarian, sails from Seville, Spain, in 1506 for the New World. When he realizes that the ship's captain is only searching for gold, Julian refuses to keep his share, but when circumstances lead Julian to pose as the risen Kukulcán, dead for four hundred years, for the Mayan priests, the power of his position begins to seduce him. When humans become more interested in the material than the spiritual, they become captives of something else.

O'Dell, Scott. *The Feathered Serpent.* Boston, Houghton Mifflin, 1981. 0-395-30851-8, 224p. R=7; I=9.

In the second book of the trilogy including *The Captive* and *The Amethyst Ring*, Julian begins to revive the Mayan City of the Seven Serpents, but needs the advice of Montezuma (Montequma) of Tenochtitlán in Azecta. Cortés arrives, and Julian realizes that he plans to invade the city. In order to keep something desirable, one may compromise one's values.

Schlein, Miriam. *I Sailed with Columbus.* Illus. Tom Newsom. New York: HarperCollins, 1991. 0-06-022514-9, 136p. Paper (Trophy), 1992. 0-06-440423-4. R=3; I=4.

When Julio sails with Christopher Columbus (Cristobal Colon) in 1492 on the Santa Maria, he keeps a diary in which he records events and facts about the voyage. At twelve, he is chosen to participate in the expedition is because he can sing. The voyage is an experience he will never forget, but after he returns to Spain, he chooses to stay and become a farmer with the money he earned rather than returning to the New World.

1600-1799

Howard, Ellen. *When Daylight Comes.* New York: Atheneum, 1985. 0-689-31133-8, 192p. R=6; I=6.

In 1733, Helena, daughter of a wealthy plantation owner and granddaughter of the governor, witnesses the revolt of slaves on her island of St. Jan (John) in the Caribbean. After being captured, made to work in the fields, and serve a former slave (actually an African queen before being sold into slavery), she learns a lot about responsibility and love. Having to be something one never imagined may help one to understand the trials and frustrations in the lives of others.

O'Dell, Scott. *My Name Is Not Angelica.* Boston: Houghton Mifflin, 1989. 0-395-51061-9, 130p. Paper, New York: Dell (Yearling), 1990. 0-440-40379-0. R=3; I=9.

Captured deceptively, Raisha, her betrothed, and others from her tribe are taken by slave ship from Africa to St. John's in the Caribbean where they are sold into slavery. Unhappy with her new condition and name, Angelica, Raisha and the others join in the 1733 slave revolt against the plantation owners. But she cannot kill herself by jumping off the cliff as many of the other cornered slaves do including her husband because she does not want to kill her unborn child. Many times people make decisions based on their concern for the welfare of others.

1800-1899

Berry, James. *Ajeemah and His Son*. New York: HarperCollins, 1992. 0-06-021044-3, 84p. R=3; I=8.

In 1807, while walking to see his bride-to-be with his father Ajeemah, Atu, eighteen, and his father are captured, sold into slavery, and transported from Africa to Jamaica. Separated forever, each sets goals to regain his freedom, but only Ajeemah survives until August 1, 1838, when the Jamaican slaves are freed. Such separation and treatment that Africans endured can be compared to the bullish treatment of minority groups by dictators throughout history.

de Treviño, Elizabeth B. *El Güero: A True Adventure Story*. Illus. Leslie W. Bowman. New York: Farrar, 1989. 0-374-31995-2, 99p. Paper, 1991. 0-374-42028-9. R=6; I=6.

Géneral Diaz exiles El Güero (the blond one) and his family from Mexico City in 1876 to a small town near California. El Güero's father, a judge, tries to keep law in the town, but he is unsuccessful. The people claim land in the area without proper papers, and illegally imprison his father until El Güero walks to La Paz, at the foot of Baja, California, to get help. When a situation seems desperate, one may have more courage than normally expected.

O'Dell, Scott. *Carlota*. Boston: Houghton Mifflin, 1977. 0-395-25487-6, 176p. Paper, New York: Dell (Laurel Leaf), 1989. 0-440-90928-7, 144p. R=7; I=8.

At sixteen, Carlota, in 1846, becomes mistress of her family's huge Mexican ranch at the death of her father who hated "gringos." She refuses to continue her family's practice of slavery by returning a boy to his tribe, and she refuses to despise the whites. To be free, one has to make decisions based on one's own beliefs.

O'Dell, Scott. *The 290*. Boston: Houghton Mifflin, 1976.
0-395-24737-3. R=5; I=7.

Jim, sixteen, in 1862, helps design the *290*, a ship, in
Liverpool, England, not knowing that it will become a
Confederate raider of Federal ships. He also hears from his
older brother that their father's money comes from owning
slaves. Jim decides to sail with the *290* and is elated when able
to board one of his father's ships and free the captured slaves at
Port-au-Prince. To do what one believes is right often takes
enormous courage.

1900 and AFTER

Blair, David Nelson. *Fear the Condor*. New York: Lodestar,
1992. 0-525-67381-4, 138p. R=4; I=6.

Bartolina, ten, has to help her grandparents farm as well as
clean the patrón's administrator's house in their 1932 Bolivian
town while her father fights in the Chaco War. Although she
speaks only Aymara, by the time Bartolina is sixteen, she
learns ink weaving (writing) and reads for her father so that he
can attend the meetings of men who are planning to unionize in
order to have fair rights to the lands. Education is one sure
way to escape the bonds that others use to enslave the
ignorant.

De Jenkins, Lyll. *The Honorable Prison*. New York:
Lodestar/Dutton, 1988. 0-525-67238-9, 201p. Paper, New York:
Puffin, 1989. 0-14-032952-8. E=6; I=8.

Marta, seventeen, and her family, try to escape from their
South American home in 1955, but police arrest them and take
them to a house far from the city where they live for the rest of
the war, which her journalist father has denounced in print.
Marta becomes attracted to a young man at the pueblo but
realizes that staying with her family outweighs following
someone she hardly knows. People who try to tell truth
sometimes sacrifice their safety when those in power prefer the
truth to remain unspoken. *Scott O'Dell Award for Historical
Fiction, 1989.*

Foster, Cecil. *No Man in the House.* New York: Ballantine, 1992. 0-345-38067-3, 280p. R=9; I=10+.

In 1964, Howard and his two brothers live with their grandmother in their Barbados shack with no money while their parents search for a better life in England. A new headmaster arrives, and by changing the discipline and teaching methods, he helps Howard overcome the taunts of other boys for living in a fatherless home. He instills in Howard the value of having an education as a way of rising above the present into a bright future. Everyone needs someone who believes in their ability to do well.

Taylor, Theodore. *The Cay.* New York: Doubleday, 1987 (1969). 0-385-07906-0, 138p. Paper, New York: Avon (Camelot), 1977. 0-380-00142-X. R=4; I=5.

When Phillip is eleven in 1942, he and his mother sail from Curacao for Norfolk just after the German submarines begin torpedoing ships in the harbor. Germans sink their ship, and an old black man, Timothy, saves Phillip and a cat on a raft. Because Phillip becomes blind from a head injury during the ship's explosion, Timothy helps him learn independence on the isolated cay where the raft washes up so that Phillip can survive if Timothy dies. Ignoring color allows one to appreciate the inner human being, the real self, without the superficial bias of skin color. *Jane Addams Book Award, 1970; Commonwealth Club of California Book Awards, 1969; Southern California Council on Literature for Children and Young People Awards, 1970.*

Raspail, J. *Who Will Remember the People.* Trans. Jeremy Leggatt. San Francisco: Mercury House, 1988. 0-916515-42-7, 213p. R=8; I=10+.**

Lafko is the last survivor, in the twentieth century, of the Kaweskar, people who were probably the first to cross the Bering land bridge on foot and who survived in Tierra del Fuego at the southern tip of South America. Their lives seem especially primitive. They fear the land beyond the shore, mountains, and the missionaries who come to convert but ruin them instead. Before people decide that others must forsake their past and their gods for new rituals, people must be certain that they are trying to do more than satisfy their own needs for changing others.

AUSTRALIA, NEW ZEALAND, AND THE PACIFIC

BEFORE 1900

Attanasio, A. A. *Wyvern*. New York: Ticknor & Fields, 1988. 0-89919-409-5, 422p. R=7; I=10+.**

Jaki's fair skin and blond hair disturb his Borneo tribe, and all shun him except the tribal mystic. When pirates capture him, he travels to all parts of the world, finding peace only when he reaches North America where he settles in his first real home. People who have not had the warmth of community, but who have been nurtured to appreciate learning by a caring person, are still fortunate.

Lisson, Deborah. *The Devil's Own*. New York: Holiday House, 1991. 0-8234-0871-X, 169p. R=6; I=6.*

In the Abrolhos Islands off the east coast of Australia with her family, Julie, at fifteen, disdains everything that happens on board her father's new boat. In this historical fantasy, after hearing a story about the *Batavia*, shipwrecked in 1629, she ends up on shore in what seems a dream where men mistake her for Annetje, a girl traveling on the *Batavia*. Falling in love in the seventeenth century helps her see her twentieth century brattiness. Although she thinks the experience a dream, she finds tangible items that make her wonder otherwise. Sometimes one can gain perspective about one's behavior when set in other worlds and situations, even in one's dreams.

Mayne, William. *Low Tide*. Delacorte, 1993. 0-385-30904-X, 198p. R=5; I=5.

Charlie, his sister, and his Maori friend go fishing one morning when the tide is especially low circa 1890 in New Zealand and find a ship wrecked on top of a rock. While they investigate, a tidal wave resulting from a far off earthquake sweeps them into the mountains where a man rescues them and helps them return home to unexpected revelations about the man and the ship. One must not jump to a conclusion without knowing all the facts because one can make irreparable mistakes.

Pople, Maureen. *A Nugget of Gold*. New York: Knopf, 1990 (1989). Paper (Borzoi), 0-679-80284-3, 183p. R=6; I=8.

Sally discovers a brooch down a mineshaft in Australia and wonders about the inscription on the back of it. In alternate chapters, Ann Bird around 1870, meets and falls in love with Jem, who gives her a gold nugget pin with their names engraved on it. Sally hears the story of Ann Bird from the people with whom she is staying and finds that Ann is one of her ancestors. Sometimes the easiest way to face unpleasant situations is to pretend they do not exist.

Sperry, Armstrong. *Call It Courage*. New York: Macmillan, 1968 (1940). 0-02-786030-2, 96p. Paper (Aladdin), 1990. 0-689-71391-6. R=7; I=5.

Called "Boy Who Was Afraid" by his Polynesian island peers, Mafatu and his dog leave home in a canoe. Led by his albatross friend through a storm to land, he bravely protects himself and his dog by killing a tiger shark, an octopus, and a wild boar. He escapes savages in his newly built canoe only to die when reaching home, but simultaneously proves his given name, "Stout Heart," in this "timeless" novel. *Newbery Medal*, 1941.

1900 and AFTER

Collins, Alan. *Jacob's Ladder.* New York: Dutton, 1989. 0-525-67272-9, 151p. R=7; I=8.**

Jacob's family disintegrates during the Australian Depression, circa 1930, after his father commits suicide and his stepmother leaves. He and his brother survive first in a Jewish home inhabited mainly by refuge children from Europe and later in different places until a conviction for stealing takes his brother away. A life enduring prejudice and misfortune can lead one to live a solitary existence unless one makes an extra effort to establish caring relationships with others.

Duder, Tessa. *Alex in Rome.* Boston: Houghton Mifflin, 1992. 0-395-62879-2, 166p. R=7; I=8.

In the 1960 Olympics in Rome, Alex swims to a bronze medal victory for New Zealand. But on her way, she meets a young Italian man who reveals himself as a New Zealander living in Italy and studying opera. Being exposed to the international scene before reaching sixteen can be a bewildering and unsettling experience, not old enough to make major decisions and not too young to become involved in emotional relationships. *New Zealand's AIM Children's Book Award*, 1990; *Esther Glen Award* (New Zealand Library Association), 1990.

Duder, Tessa. *In Lane Three, Alex Archer.* New York: Bantam, 1991 (1989). 0-553-29020-7, 176p. R=5; I=7.

In 1959, fifteen-year-old Alex prepares for New Zealand's swimming competition as the Olympic representative to Rome. During that year of training, she participates fully in the dance and theater performances at her school and the hockey team, has a full-time boyfriend, and thinks about a competitor who wins more races than she does. People who want to win learn that they must commit themselves fully to the performance be it a race to be run or a song to be sung. *New Zealand's Children's Book of the Year AIM Award*, 1988; *Esther Glen Medal* (New Zealand Library Association); 1988.

Dunlop, Betty. *The Poetry Girl.* Boston: Houghton Mifflin, 1989. 0-395-49679-9, 209p. R=3; I=8.**

When Natalia is twelve in 1946, her family moves to another New Zealand town, but she continues to get poor grades in all her subjects except English and nature. To block out the ridicule of her teachers and the other students, she silently quotes poetry, and not until she is fifteen when her brother acknowledges her as growing up does she realize that she can be herself, even with parents who ignore her needs. Loneliness and feeling misunderstood are part of adolescence, but having a family that does not listen to problems can make the time seem worse.

Gee, Maurice. *The Champion.* New York: Simon & Schuster, 1993. 0-671-86561-7, 212p. R=3; I=7.

In 1943, Rex's Australian family decides to house an American soldier needing rest from fighting in the Pacific theater of World War II. When Jack arrives, the family is surprised that he is black. Hostile at first, Rex, twelve, learns from Jack that being supportive of others is more important than arguing, and that people who pose as something other than what they are should be avoided. Many times people against whom one has been taught to be prejudiced can offer important insights about living.

Gee, Maurice. *The Fire-Raiser.* Boston: Houghton Mifflin, 1992. 0-395-62428-2, 172p. R=2; I=6.

Someone in the New Zealand town where Kitty lives in 1915 sets fires, but no one knows who it is. Several children suspect one man, discover his benzine cans and rags, and wait for him to set another fire. When adults sometimes refuse to believe children, they may incur an unnecessary danger for all.

Klein, Robin. *All in the Blue Unclouded Weather.* New York: Viking, 1992. 0-670-83909-4, 162p. R=7; I=6.

Vivienne, the youngest of the four Melling girls, feels dejected with her hand-me-down clothes after World War II in her Australian home. She longs for new belongings until she finds that some things she gets do not fulfill her dreams of them. But her decision to spend all her money in a second-hand shop on a china plate like her mother's wedding plate as her mother's Christmas gift results in the perfect choice. Giving of oneself in little ways for people often gains one unexpected rewards.

Klein, Robin. *Dresses of Red and Gold.* New York: Viking, 1993. 0-670-84733-X, 177p. R=8; I=9.

After World War II in Australia, the Melling girls, in this sequel to *All in the Blue Unclouded Weather*, have their individual situations. Heather loves romance, but Cathy regrets that she must be a friend's bridesmaid. Vivienne spends a long time in the hospital after a tonsillectomy and wants to come home while Grace looks forward to leaving home and returning to the city after her brief holiday ends. Although families have bonds, each person has individual needs and goals to pursue.

Noonan, Michael. *McKenzie's Boots.* New York: Orchard/Watts, 1988. 0-531-08348-9, 249p. R=7; I=8.

At fourteen in 1941, Rob is an Australian already over six feet tall and clumsy. Soon he joins the army, pretending to be older, and goes to Japan to fight for his country. He needs larger and larger boots every few months until on the toes of his last boots, a Japanese soldier writes that Rob was an Australian hero. War changes everything, but sometimes people who would never have met otherwise find themselves together because of it.

Pople, Maureen. *The Other Side of the Family.* New York: Holt, 1988. 0-8050-0758-X, 167p. R=4; I=6.*

Evacuated from London via Sydney to Parsons Creek, Australia, during World War II, Katharine, at fifteen, gets to know her father's mother. She finds her deaf and poor rather than glamorously wealthy as she had been told. But Kate sees the immense respect of the neighbors for her grandmother and quickly appreciates her integrity, intelligence, and love of life.

Southall, Ivan. *Blackbird*. New York: Farrar, Straus & Giroux, 1988. 0-374-30783-0, 136p. R=6; I=8.*

Will and his family move across Australia to be nearer his father, a colonel serving in World War II defending the country from the Japanese. Will pretends to save his family's home from the invisible enemy by climbing on the roof where he faces his fear of heights. Soon afterwards, he hears a speech by a young man who has lost both legs. This young man declares that life will not always turn out as one expects, and Will realizes that he has misdirected his energies. One must prepare for whatever life has in store and be ready for whatever emergencies occur.

AFRICA

BEFORE 1900

Achebe, Chinua. *Things Fall Apart.* New York: Astor-Honor, 1958. 0-8392-1113-9. Paper, 0-8392-5006-1. New York: Knopf, 1992. 0-679-41714-1. R=7; I=10.

Okonkwo is disturbed that his family has begun listening to the Christian missionaries coming to his Ibo tribal area of Nigeria in the late nineteenth century. He becomes belligerent and tries to reassert his superiority. He is exiled, and while he is gone, the Christians prevail by creating laws to ban some of the tribal customs and schools to teach their own philosophies. People who coerce others to follow their beliefs do so without regard for the customs and traditions inherent in the others' cultures.

Carter, Peter. *The Sentinels.* New York: Oxford, 1980. R=6; I=8.**

After being shipwrecked off the African coast in 1840, John, formerly of an anti-slave patrol ship, and Lyapo, a Yoruba captured to be sold into slavery, are stranded together on the coast where they attempt to learn each other's language and respect each other's abilities. When rescued by the British Royal Navy, John returns to his patrol ship and Lyapo decides to stay in Africa. Humans who sell the freedom of other humans are less worthy than the lowest animals. *Guardian Award*, 1982; *Premio di Lettaratura d'Italie*, 1982.

1900 and AFTER

Sacks, Margaret. *Beyond Safe Boundaries.* New York: Dutton, 1989. 0-525-67281-1, 160p. Paper, New York: Puffin, 1990. 0-14-034407-1. R=7; I=9.

Elizabeth, at fifteen in 1962, strives to understand the rapid changes in herself and her country, South Africa. As a Jew, she has never had full rights, and she and her family agree with equal rights for the blacks, but they suffer under a government willing to recognize only Christian whites. Tyranny of any kind causes heartache for those who silently oppose it and pain for those overtly campaign against it. *School Library Journal "Best Book,"* 1989.

Weaver-Gelzer, Charlotte. *In the Time of Trouble.* New York: Dutton, 1993. 0-525-44973-6, 275p. R=7; I=8.

Jessie, fourteen, her twin brother, and her little sister attend boarding school in Cameroon while their missionary parents live in another section of the country. In 1959, the native Maquis, fighting the French, kidnap her parents and take them into the forest. After several difficult days for them and days of fear for the children, the Maquis return the parents safely. Learning how to help others in need when one feels desolate and fearful takes extra effort and love.

CHINA

BEFORE 1800

Chin, Tsao Hsueh. *The Dream of the Red Chamber*. Trans.
Franz Kuhn. New York: Doubleday, 1958. Paper (Anchor),
0-385-09379-1. Trans. Florence and Isabel McHugh. Westport
CT: Greenwood, 1975. 0-8371-8113-5, 582p. R=9; I=10+.

Around 1729 in China during the earlier Ching Dynasty,
Pao Yu enjoys a privileged life at eleven with his female
cousins and servants who cater to his whims as he studies for
his exams. Black Jade, one of his cousins, seems to be his alter
ego, and when his family arranges his marriage with another
cousin, Precious Clasp, but tells him he will marry Black Jade,
he becomes ill after the marriage, and Black Jade dies. At
nineteen, he passes his exams, brings good fortune to his
family, and disappears. When he reappears in the company of
two monks, his father realizes that Pao Yu, since his birth with
a jade stone around his neck, has always been from the spirit
world. To be content, one has to appreciate the spiritual as
more valuable and lasting than the material.

Lattimore, Deborah Nourse, writer/illus. *The Dragon's Robe*.
New York: HarperCollins, 1990. 0-06-023723-6, 32p. Paper
(Trophy), 1993. 0-06-443321-8. R=5; I=2.

Kwan Yin, a poor young weaver in twelfth century China,
stops to help the keeper of the Royal Dragon's shrine on her
way to ask for work at the Emperor's Palace. She follows the
lord given rice and the lord given a sword and sees them
disobey the keeper's orders. After she finishes weaving a robe
for the dragon at the keeper's request, the Tartar khan tries to
take it from her but is destroyed by the dragon instead, and the

keeper reveals himself to be the Emperor. Even though one prefers to do more interesting and entertaining things, one must always fulfill one's responsibilities and promises.

Vá, Leong. *A Letter to the King*. Illus. Leong Vá. Trans. James Anderson. New York: HarperCollins, 1991. 0-06-020070-7, 32p. R=4; I=2.

Around two thousand years ago, when the Chinese king declares that Ti Ying's physician father be imprisoned because one of his patients dies, Ti Ying goes to The Forbidden City and offers to take his place so that he can continue to save patients in their village near The Great Wall. The king is so impressed that a girl would petition him face to face that he frees her father. Love and sacrifice must underlie a family's decisions.

Yolen, Jane. *The Seeing Stick*. Illus. Remy Charlip and Demetra Maraslis. New York: Crowell, 1975. 0-690-00596-2, 32p. R=4; I=2.

Hwei Ming, the only child of the Emperor in Peking around the fifteenth century, is blind. Monks, physicians, and magician-priests try to help her in order to earn her father's reward, but an old man with a stick is the only successful candidate. He tells her stories and lets her feel the carvings that he makes on the stick so that she "sees" the characters. She then begins to feel the faces of those around her, delighted to be "seeing" them for the first time, but the old man refuses to take the emperor's monetary reward. One of the best gifts for helping another person is not the material wealth but the pleasure of having made another person's life better.

1800-1899

Dickinson, Peter. *Tulku.* New York: Dell, (1993) 1979. Paper, 0-440-21489-0. R=6; I=9.

Around 1900, Theo, thirteen, escapes from China during the Boxer rebellion via Tibet with Mrs. Jones, a plant collector he meets after his father's death. In Tibet, monks think that Theo is the reincarnation of Tulku, one of their former religious leaders. Theo continues to England, changed from being moralistic to accepting that people get their happiness in different ways. *Whitbread Book of the Year*, 1979; *Carnegie Medal*, 1980; *International Board of Books for Young People*, 1982.

Paterson, Katherine. *Rebels of the Heavenly Kingdom.* New York: Lodestar, 1983. 0-525-66911-6, 230p. Paper, New York: Avon (Flare), 1984. 0-380-68304-0, 240p. R=7; I=10.

During the Taiping Rebellion, 1850-53 in China, Wang joins the rebels and is surprised by the high status in the group of Mei Lin, a girl with ugly unbound feet. Mei Lin, however, freed one of the group's leaders from the Manchu imperial soldiers. Eventually Mei Ling, in turn, has to free herself from the group's leaders when their Christian values change as they begin to enjoy power and start murdering innocent people to gain control over a larger area of the country. A person's worth cannot be measured by appearance.

Sledge, Linda Ching & Gary Allen Sledge. *Empire of Heaven.* New York: Bantam, 1990. 0-553-05755-3, 576p. Paper, 1991. 0-553-28093-5. R=4; I=10+.

When Rulan is eleven in 1847, her mother, from a Chinese aboriginal tribe, is summoned to exorcise a spirit from Hung, the man, who claiming to be Jesus's brother, begins the Taiping Rebellion. Rulan later joins the rebels, becoming servant and mistress to spy in a Manchu house before she falls in love with a fellow rebel. She and the young man take their vows of celibacy as part of the sect fighting the rebellion. But they break their vows, and he impregnates her before they finally escape from China--he as a slave for six years and she to Hawaii to join missionaries. In order to pursue an ideal, one often has to make great sacrifices in one's personal life.

Yep, Laurence. *Mountain Light*. New York: HarperCollins, 1985.
0-06-026759-3, 282p. R=4; I=8.*

At nineteen, Squeaky finds himself not only trying to escape
the Chinese Manchu soldiers in the 1850's but also trying to
survive encounters with people who fight on the same side but
who come from different clans in China. He makes alliances,
especially with the girl Cassia. After her father's death, he goes
to America to see her brother who has been sending back
money from his work in the gold fields. Everyone has a "light"
within themselves that must be identified and allowed to shine.

1900 and AFTER

Ballard, J. G. *Empire of the Sun*. New York: Penguin, 1985.
Paper, 0-671-53053-4, 384p. R=7; I=10+.

Although World War II rages in other parts of the world,
Jim sees the war in Shanghai where he lives with his parents
as a war between the Japanese and the starving Chinese
peasants and refugees. After the bombing of Pearl Harbor, Jim,
accidentally separated from his parents, tries to surrender as he
has been told to do. Guards, however, including the British,
refuse to take a child dressed in a school uniform seriously. He
barely endures the ravages of the war, and what comes clear to
him are the excesses of western materialism juxtaposed against
the paucity of eastern goods. Human concern makes life
worthwhile, not technology.

Chang, Margaret, and Raymond Chang. *In the Eye of War*.
New York: McElderry, 1990. 0-689-50503-5, 198p. R=4; I=4.

During Shao-Shao's tenth year, 1945, his family continues its
routine in Shanghai with his father working for Chiang
Kai-shek's Nationalist Underground and the man across the
courtyard helping the Japanese invaders. Little by little,
Shao-Shao understands why his father wants him to excel at
his school work and why he does not like the children to keep
pets. The concern of the various generations of the family for

each other allows them to continue their traditions, including New Year, even though not as elaborate as in past years.

Clavell, James. *Noble House.* New York: Delacorte, 1981. 0-385-28737-2, 1200p. Paper, 1984. 0-440-16484-2. R=3; I=10+.

Hong Kong business in 1963 still functions as it did in 1841 when the first tai-pan (corporate head) of Noble House, a trading establishment, vowed to do anything for the person who presented him with the other half of specific coins. Two recently arrived Americans do not understand the unwritten rules of Hong Kong trade, the Chinese know how to work to their own advantage, and the British control everything. The intense competition between two trading houses allows intrigue and entrepreneurship to permeate the city. The situations that make individuals happy can be very different.

DeJong, Meindert. *The House of Sixty Fathers.* Illus. Maurice Sendak. New York: HarperCollins, 1984 (1956). 0-06-021481-3, 189p. Paper (Trophy), 1987. 0-06-440200-2. R=6; I=4.

After the Japanese invade China during World War II, the sampan on which young Tien Pao is sleeping washes downriver from Hengyang while his parents are working at the American airfield. When he comes ashore, he and his pig begin the long walk back through Japanese territory. After he helps an American airman whose plane crashed near him, the Americans aid him in turn. All sixty airmen want to adopt him, but his perseverance encourages them to help him find his family. People who exhibit true courage are often unaware of their achievements. *Newbery Honor*, 1957. *International Board of Books for Young People*, 1958.

Morpurgo, Michael. *King of the Cloud Forests.* New York: Viking, 1988. 0-670-82069-5, 146p. Paper, New York: Puffin, 1991. 0-14-032586-7. R=6; I=7.

When the Japanese bomb China in 1937, Ashley, fourteen, leaves his missionary physician father and travels across the mountains toward India with Uncle Sung, an old family friend from Tibet. In the cold, Ashley becomes separated from Uncle Sung but lives with the Yetis, non-human beings who find him almost frozen. When he reunites with Uncle Sung, he decides not to tell of him about his unbelievable experience. In England, however, he finds the man whose photograph the Yetis gave him. The man is delighted to find someone else who has also benefitted from the kindness of the Yetis. When things happen that others will think improbable, one need not tell those people about the experiences.

Vander Els, Betty. *The Bomber's Moon.* New York: Farrar, Straus & Giroux, 1985. 374-30864-0, 168p. Paper (Sunburst), 1992. 0-374-40877-7. R=3; I=6.

Ruth and her brother have to be evacuated from their missionary parents in China for four years beginning in 1942. They stay first in China and then in India with other children. They try to interpret the censored letters they receive, hoping to see their parents again. After waiting for several months in Shanghai, they finally reunite. War often separates families at times when children most need their parents' love and care.

Vander Els, Betty. *Leaving Point.* New York: Farrar, Straus & Giroux, 1987. 0-374-34376-4, 212p. R=3; I=9.

In 1950, Ruth, fourteen, and her younger brothers return to their missionary parents from their school, a journey of four days which stretches into three weeks because of the Chinese Communist Revolutionary rule established by Mao-Tse-tung in collaboration with the Soviet Union's leader Stalin. While living with her parents, lonely Ruth makes friends with a girl who has been indoctrinated by the anticipated equality of the revolution. Ruth jeopardizes both the girl's and her family's safety until they receive permission to leave China. Much of what happens in the world is difficult to understand because of the nuances of meaning that some adults attach to each person's words and actions.

INDIA

BEFORE 1900

Holt, Victoria. *The India Fan.* New York: Doubleday, 1988.
0-385-24600-5, 404p. Paper, New York: Fawcett (Crest), 1989.
0-449-21697-7. R=4; I=10+.

As a small child, Drusilla is the plain girl from the rectory
who plays with the wealthy Lavinia and Fabian living in the
largest house of their English village. After Lavinia marries
and Fabian goes to India, Drusilla also goes to India, discovers
Lavinia murdered, looks after her children, and inadvertently
prepares the way for Fabian to ask her to marry him back in
England. Wealth only buys things, never intangibles like
happiness.

1900 and AFTER

Scott, Paul. *The Day of the Scorpion.* New York: Avon, 1992
(1968). Paper, 380-71809-X, 512p. R=7; I=10+.

In the second novel of the "Raj Quartet," while their father is
a prisoner-of-war during World War II in 1942, Susan and
Sarah Layton live in Pankot, India. Susan marries an officer,
becomes widowed, and then bears a child, but she is unable to
cope with her situation. Sarah is the observer of both Susan
and the British-Indian conflict around them. Sarah meets
Merrick, the man responsible for falsely imprisoning a British
woman's Indian lover, when he is best man at Susan's wedding
and sees him after he is severely wounded in battle. If a person

makes a decision based on misconceptions, he or she may suffer unexpected consequences.

Scott, Paul. *A Division of the Spoils.* New York: Avon, 1992 (1975). Paper, 0-380-71811-1, 640p. R=7; I=10+.

In 1945, in the last volume of the "Raj Quartet," after World War II ends, in India Sikhs and Hindus begin murdering Muslims and vice versa as the British vote to leave. Soldiers including Sarah and Susan Layton's friends and father have to consider what they will do with the rest of their careers while the women have to readjust their roles with other British subjects who have "come out" to India but who will return home to a class structure where military rank does not raise one's status as in India. The British desire for power and control, as exemplified in Susan's second husband Merrick, destroys the potential for personal success and self-esteem in many Indian lives. When one group of people rules another, members of either group rarely are able to treat members of the other as individuals.

Scott, Paul. *The Jewel in the Crown.* New York: Avon, 1992 (1966). Paper, 0-380-71808-1, 480p. R=7; I=10+.

In the first novel of the "Raj Quartet," all the liberal and conservative racial forces of British and Indian residents of Mayapore, India, clash in August, 1942, when British police accuse Indians of raping one of their young women. Through the view points of a spinster British school teacher; the Indian Lady Chatterjee; an "angel of mercy" called Sister Ludmila; a British brigadier general; the girl supposedly abused; and finally one of those accused, a British public school educated Indian named Hari Kumar (Coomer), the real story of two people who fall into a love that cannot be tolerated in a segregated community comes to light. Unless people accept each other as unique, they will be unable to fully communicate as human beings.

Scott, Paul. *The Towers of Silence.* New York: Avon, 1992 (1971). Paper, 0-380-71810-3, 400p. R=7; I=10+.

In 1939, in the third novel of the "Raj Quartet," Barbie Batchelor, the successor to Miss Crane at the protestant mission for Indian children in Rampur, India, retires and goes to live with Mabel Layton, grandmother to Susan and Sarah, in Pankot. During her tenure there, she experiences the events in the lives of the others and becomes distressed enough after Mabel's death to become ill, lose her voice, and die at the end of the war in 1945. As people age and begin to assess what they have done with their lives, they have to face the decisions they have made whether positive or negative.

Wiggins, Marianne. *John Dollar.* New York: HarperCollins, 1990 (1989). Paper, 0-06-091655-9, 214p. R=7; I=10+.

Charlotte, widowed during World War I, decides to leave England in 1918 to go to Rangoon, Burma, and become a school teacher. There she renews her interest in life, especially after meeting and getting to know John Dollar, a sailor. Their casual trip with other friends to an island ends in disaster although Charlotte survives. Living without major events to jolt lulls one into forgetting the tenuous thread by which life hangs.

ISRAEL

1900 and AFTER

Bergman, Tamar. *The Boy From Over There*. Trans. Hillel Halkin. Boston: Houghton Mifflin, 1988. 0-395-43077-1, 181p. R=4; I=5.

Rani's father brings a boy from Poland with him to the kibbutz in Palestine after he fights for the British in World War II. Rina's father does not return, and during the war between the Palestinians and Jews to establish the country of Israel in 1948, both Rina, nine, and the Polish boy, accepting that their parents are dead, look forward to life in the Jordan Valley. Sometimes a confirmation of bad news releases the hearer from the pain and fear of not knowing an answer.

Orlev, Uri. *Lydia, Queen of Palestine*. Trans. Hillel Halkin. Boston: Houghton Mifflin, 1993. 0-395-65660-5, 170p. R=3; I=5.

During World War II, Lydia's father sends a letter from Palestine to her and her mother in Bucharest, Romania, to let them know that he is safe from the Jewish pogroms. Her mother sends her to Palestine with other children and follows later. Lydia, ten, surprised to find her father married to someone else is even more shocked when her mother arrives via Turkey with her new husband. By 1944, Lydia matures enough to realize that her situation is not all bad. That adults have problems which they cannot easily share is difficult for children to understand.

Reboul, Antoine. *Thou Shalt Not Kill.* Trans. Stephanie Craig. New York: S. G. Phillips, 1969. 87599-161-0, 157p. R=6; I=6.

Lost in the Sinai Desert during the Israeli-Egyptian war in June, 1967, Slimane and Simmy, both fourteen and enemies, first try to kill each other. But Slimane decides instead to help Simmy after he wounds her in the leg. They survive on water Slimane finds at a nearby deserted battle site. When they discover a radio and make a report about their location, they require rescuing soldiers from both sides to shake hands and share a meal. *The Grand Prize of the Salon de L'Enfance.*

Semel, Nava. *Becoming Gershona.* Trans. Seymour Simckes. New York: Viking, 1990. 0-670-83105-0, 128p. Paper, New York: Puffin, 1992. 0-14-036071-9. R=5; I=6.

Gershona learns a lot in her twelfth year in 1958. Her grandfather, now blind, comes from New York to Tel Aviv after deserting her father at six months, and he remarries her grandmother. She earns the respect of children in the neighborhood who before had taunted her. Understanding why adults make certain decisions without explaining them to the children involved can be baffling and unsettling. *National Jewish Award*, 1991.

Uris, Leon. *Exodus.* New York: Doubleday, 1958. 0-385-05082-8. Paper, New York: Bantam, 1983. 0-553-25847-8, 608p. R=7; I=10+.

To create the Jewish state of Israel during and after World War II, many people from disparate backgrounds and experiences joined together under various Jewish leaders, one being Ari Ben Canaan. He, his family, and the American widow Kitty, a nurse, battle to save the orphaned children gathered in Palestine who have escaped concentration camps. Kitty soon realizes that she can never fulfill her life in America and that she must stay in Israel to help those who need her most. The sacrifice that humans make for freedom is very dear and often includes either their own lives or those of ones whom they love.

JAPAN

BEFORE 1199

Paterson, Katherine. *Of Nightingales That Weep*. Illus. Haru
Wells. New York: Crowell, 1974. 0-690-00485-0. Paper, New
York: HarperCollins (Trophy), 1989. 0-06-440282-7, 172p. R=8;
I=10.

During Japan's Gempei War begun in 1180 between the
Genji and Heike clans, Taiko, at eleven, plays and sings so
beautifully that the Heike mother empress requests her to serve
the child emperor. During Taiko's tenure, she falls in love with
an enemy Genji and refuses to come home to help her pregnant
mother and her ugly but extraordinarily talented potter
step-father. When she finally does return, her mother and
brother have died, and an accident mars her beauty. Her
choices in life shift dramatically. True beauty lies within a
person because physical attractiveness is transitory. *Newbery
Medal*, 1981.

Paterson, Katherine *The Sign of the Chrysanthemum*. Illus.
Peter Landa. New York: Crowell, 1991 (1973). 0-690-04913-7,
132p. Paper, New York: HarperCollins (Trophy), 1988.
0-06-440232-0, 128p. R=4; I=8.

After his mother dies around 1170, Muna, thirteen, journeys
to the city to find his father. He meets a man whom he likes
but who turns out to be a Japanese ronin (a disreputable
samurai). Muna eventually begins to work for a swordmaker
who refuses to arm men unworthy of his work. When Muna
stops reporting on the Genji and Heike to the ronin, the
swordmaker deigns him worthy to become an apprentice. Pride
helps to defeat many persons who succumb to its deadliness.

1200-1599

Haugaard, Erik. *The Boy and the Samurai.* Boston: Houghton Mifflin, 1991. 0-395-56398-4, 221p. R=3; I=6.

During sixteenth century feudal Japan, both of Saru's parents die before he is six. He survives through begging and living near a temple shrine. Eventually Saru meets a kind samurai, and he helps him rescue his wife, hostage in the warlord's castle. Saru realizes that he must tell the true story because a liar must forever lie, but the truth always sets a person mentally free. *Parents' Choice,* 1991.

Haugaard, Erik. *The Samurai's Tale.* Boston: Houghton Mifflin, 1984. 0-395-34559-6, 256p. Paper, 1990, 0-395-54970-1. R=6; I=9.

Around 1550 in Japan, Taro serves his master faithfully and earns the title of samurai. He also falls in love and shows his affection by writing and sending poetry to the girl via his servant. They both escape the enemy by disguising themselves. Kind and honest masters have often rewarded loyal servants, sometimes by giving them freedom. *American Library Association Notable Book for Children,* 1984.

Namioka, Lensey. *The Coming of the Bear.* New York: HarperCollins, 1992. 0-06-020289-0, 235p. R=5; I=7.

In the sixteenth century, when Zenta and Matsuzo shipwreck on the Japanese island of Ezo (Hokkaido), the Ainu people rescue them. One of the Ainu speaks Japanese, and he explains the customs and tells them about the nearby Japanese settlement farmers usurping Ainu land. Zenta and Matsuzo help to quell the ensuing war by identifying the traitors. When people feel threatened by differences, they try to protect the status quo.

Namioka, Lensey. *Island of Ogres.* New York: HarperCollins, 1989. 0-06-24373-2, 197p. R=7; I=7.

Mistaken for a famous ronin in the sixteenth century, Kajiro decides not to let the people on the Japanese island know that he does not deserve the distinction. Instead, he helps them overcome a revolt by traitors in their former daimyo's name thereby proving that he deserves the reputation if not the name of the samurai. People often fulfill the expectations of others, whether they are positive or negative.

1600-1899

Clavell, James. *Shogun.* New York: Atheneum, 1975. Paper, New York: Dell, 1976. 0-440-17800-2, 803p. R=4; I=10+.

When John Blackthorne shipwrecks in Japanese waters during 1600, the jealous Spanish and Portuguese Jesuits in the country misrepresent his intentions in their Japanese translations. But Toranaga, the man vying to become shogun of all Japan, appreciates Blackthorne's honesty and ingenuity. Toranaga frees him from prison and gets him a trustworthy Japanese language instructor with whom Blackthorne has an affair. Toranaga realizes that Blackthorne is the only man he knows who will not conspire against him. People who want to keep power over others must know all that happens within their political realm.

Coerr, Eleanor. *Mieko and the Fifth Treasure.* New York: Putnam, 1993. 0-399-22434-3, 79p. R=5; I=5.

Meiko's four treasures--a sable brush, an inkstick, an inkstone, and a roll of rice paper--are complemented by the beauty in her heart until the 1945 bombing of Nagasaki wounds her hand and impairs her ability to do calligraphy. At ten, she thinks her artistic life has ended. But at her grandparents' home, she meets a girl who teaches her about the beauty of friendship by encouraging her to practice calligraphy again. When a person wants to do something but thinks that he or she lacks the talent, that person may need to be encouraged to proceed.

Paterson, Katherine. *The Master Puppeteer.* Illus. Haru Wells. New York: Crowell, 1991 (1976). 0-690-04905-6. Paper, New York: HarperCollins (Trophy), 1989. 0-06-440281-9), 180p. R=3; I=6.

In a five-year famine during the 1780's in Japan, Jiro becomes apprenticed to Yoshida whose son teaches him the skills of puppeteering. Both boys become especially concerned about the hunger when they see family members outside the theater starving. An accident reveals a startling situation. The integrity of friendship often guides one to make the right, although sometimes unexpected, decisions in time of hardship.

1900 and AFTER

Maruki, Toshi, writer/illus. *Hiroshima, No Pika.* New York: Lothrop, Lee, Shepard, 1982. 0-688-01297-3, 48p. R=6; I=3.

When Mii is seven in 1945, the *Enola Gay* flies over Hiroshima and bombs her city. She and her parents rush from the city fires, but her father dies, and Mii never grows any larger than she is at seven. The devastation of war lasts long after the fighting stops. *Mildred L. Batchelder Award*, 1983; *Jane Addams Children's Book Award*, 1983; *American Library Association Notable Book for Children*, 1982.

Matsubara, Hisako. *Cranes at Dusk.* Trans. Leila Vennewitz. New York: Dial, 1985. 0-385-27858-6, 253p. R=7; I=10+.**

In 1945, as Kyoto, Japan, waits for a bomb to drop, the war ends with a Japanese loss just as Saya's father, the Shinto priest Guji, had predicted with his *I Ching*. But when Saya's little brother Bo dies unexpectedly, after her other brother had been very ill, Guji laments that he had not charted his son's life on the *I Ching* and tried to protect him. Saya, ten, prays for Bo's soul. Balancing the opposites of life and being aware of them helps life have depth and meaning.

Mattingley, Christobel. *The Miracle Tree.* Illus. Marianne Yamaguchi. San Diego: Gulliver, 1986. 0-15-200530-7, 28p. R=6; I=9.

A gardener who has become a soldier rushes to Nagasaki right after the bomb drops in 1945 to find his wife who was working there in a factory. Unable to find her, he plants a tree in a garden corner which an old woman who has forgotten her daughter's husband's name admires. Another woman, scarred from the bomb, overlooks the tree from her room and writes poetry about it. Paper cranes finally reunite the gardener, his wife, and her mother, after twenty years of pain. They celebrate the holiday season together, thankful for their tree and each other.

Say, Allen, writer/illus. *Grandfather's Journey.* Boston: Houghton Mifflin, 1993. 0-395-57035-2, 32p. R=5; I=2.

When the narrator's grandfather was young, in the early twentieth century, he left Japan to see America. Wearing western clothes for the first time, he traveled around the country. He returned to Japan, married, brought his bride to San Francisco, and raised a daughter. Later, the three left America to live in Japan. The grandfather wanted to visit San Francisco again, but World War II intervened, destroying his home and the city in which he lived. Even though people may live in countries other than where they were born, they often want to return to their original homes, if only for visits. *Caldecott Medal*, 1994.

KOREA

1900 and AFTER

Choi, Sook Nyul. *Echoes of the White Giraffe*. Boston: Houghton Mifflin, 1993. 0-395-64721-5, 137p. R=5; I=7.

In the sequel to *The Year of Impossible Goodbyes*, Sookan, fifteen, her younger brother, and her mother become separated from the rest of the family in 1952 during the Korean War. They seek refuge in Pusan, South Korea. Sookan loves the poet who yells "Good morning" from the top of the mountain on which refugee huts stand, and she forms a friendship with a young man, a forbidden situation in her culture. Later, she passes exams, wins a scholarship, and leaves for America. When one's material goods disappear, one must depend on the ephemeral, music and love, to survive. *American Library Association Notable Book for Children*, 1992.

Choi, Sook Nyul. *Year of Impossible Goodbyes*. Boston: Houghton Mifflin, 1991. 0-395-57419-6, 171p. Paper, New York· Dell, 1993. 0-440-40759-1. R=5; I=5.

When Sookan is ten in 1945, World War II ends, and the destructive Japanese leave her country of Korea. Very soon, Russians come and continue the pillage, capturing people trying to escape across the 38th Parallel. Sookan and her brother succeed in escaping and join their family, only to face the outbreak of another war in 1950. A repressive government using people as slaves must try to keep people *within* its borders, while a democractic country must worry about keeping people out who will cause overpopulation. *School Library Journal "Best Book,"* 1991.

Hickey, James. *Chrysanthemum in the Snow: The Novel of the Korean War.* New York: Crown, 1990. 0-517-57402-0, 333p. R=7; I=10+.**

When Robertson is seriously wounded in Korea during 1952, his survival makes him a hospital celebrity, and he even gains the love of one of the nurses with his manners. But none of this satisifies him like feeling that he is accomplishing something good by fighting the war. He decides to end his life as the war ends, in the company of a Korean friend who also does not want to face a future that would bring with it a past that he does not want to acknowledge. People reveal unusual bravery for various reasons.

THAILAND AND CAMBODIA

1900 and AFTER

Ho, Minfong. *The Clay Marble*. New York: Farrar, Straus, & Giroux, 1991. 0-374-31340-7, 163p. R=6; I=6.

In 1980, after the Communists ravage their Cambodian village and kill her father, Dara, twelve, her brother, and mother, walk to the Thai border to a camp where they can get food. They become separated but long searching reunites them. They get supplies, especially the necessary rice plants, and return to start their life anew, to reform a "clay marble." War touches everyone, and few know the reason behind the turmoil.

Ho, Minfong. *Rice without Rain*. New York: Lothrop, Lee, & Shepard, 1990. 0-688-06355-1, 236p. R=5; I=9.

Trying to survive the poor rice harvest leads Jinda's village in 1973 to welcome, after initial suspicion, the new workers, students from Bangkok who want to learn about farming. Jinda, seventeen, falls in love with one of them, and when she visits him in Bangkok at the university, she discovers that he is famous for his speeches supporting communist ideals. He uses her father, imprisoned by the government for not giving as much rice to the landlord as required, as an example of the government's suppression in an attempt to make Communism look more appealing. To give a better life to one's children, one may have to sacrifice one's own life.

VIETNAM

1900 and AFTER

Berent, Mark. *Eagle Station*. New York: Putnam, 1992. 0-399-13722-X, 396p. R=6; I=10+.*

In a sequel to *Rolling Thunder*, *Steel Tiger*, and *Phantom Leader*, the Air Force pilots continue to fight in Vietnam during 1968 and to protect Eagle Station and its radar. When a person finally makes coded contact with prisoners of war in Hanoi to let them know that the United States government is working on their release, they feel less alone. However, other Americans who see the pilots as criminals widely speak against them. Many people often dislike war, but for the men and women fighting, it is a real danger with which they must reckon.

Berent, Mark. *Phantom Leader*. New York: Putnam, 1991. 0-399-13003-7, 414p. Paper, New York: Jove, 1992. 0-515-10785-9. R=5; I=10+.

In 1967, the Viet Cong down Flak's airplane, and he becomes imprisoned in Hanoi. After the Tet Offensive occurs, and other pilots face similar fates, Flak escapes with the help of another pilot, only to be returned to the Viet Cong by the French. In war, finding that those one thought to be friends are actually enemies can cause enormous distress.

Berent, Mark. *Rolling Thunder*. New York: Jove, 1989. Paper, 0-515-10109-7, 382p. R=7; I=10+.

Three Air Force pilots in 1965 face the conflicts of Vietnam--the bombing raids and the perils of the jungle. They cope with losing friends and risking their lives before returning to the United States where they are splattered with red dye by hippies and "peaceniks" who understand nothing of their ordeal. Those who participate in war can never find the words to accurately describe the actuality of the war--its boretom, terror, and brutality.

Berent, Mark. *Steel Tiger*. New York: Putnam, 1989. 0-399-13538-3, 399p. Paper, New York: Jove, 1990. 0-515-10467-1. R=7; I=10+.

By 1967, the Air Force officers flying together in *Rolling Thunder* reunite in Vietnam for a variety of reasons. Another pilot, a Russian, helps Bannister flee from the Viet Cong but the Russian dies in the ensuing battle. People sometimes become heroes not because they want to be but because other people need to have someone to admire.

Garland, Sherry. *Song of the Buffalo Boy*. San Diego: Harcourt Brace, 1992. 0-15-277107-7, 249p. R=3; I=9.

Loi, seventeen, remembers an American in 1973 giving her a picture of Loi, her mother, and him, but never seeing him again. After a difficult life where villagers maltreat her mother and call Loi *con-lai*, or half-breed, Loi decides to go to America with the boy she loves who has been forbidden to marry her. Before Loi leaves, her mother tells her that the man she remembers was not her father and that she had had to sell her body to get money to feed her own mother during the war. In times of war, people often have others to protect, and they have to make decisions that they would never consider during a time of peace.

Huong, Duong Thu. *Paradise of the Blind.* Trans. Phan Huy Duong and Nina McPherson. New York: Morrow, 1993. 0-688-11445-8, 270p. R=6; I=10+.

As she rides the train to Moscow to see her supposedly sick uncle, Hang remembers what her mother told her about her father and the Hanoi shack in which they lived when Hang was younger. Her mother and father had been separated by Hang's zealous uncle when he returned to their village in 1953 to initiate land reform and declare her father, a school teacher, an enemy for having hired people to work in the family noodle factory. She finds when she arrives in Moscow that her uncle is again trying to manipulate the family for his own gain. Unexpected forces can control people's lives in many ways.

Myers, Walter D. *Fallen Angels.* New York: Scholastic, 1988. 0-590-40942-5, 369p. Paper, 1989. 0-590-40943-3, 309p. R=3; I=9.

After finishing high school, Ritchie departs for Vietnam in 1967 instead of going to college so he can earn money for his brother to have clothes to wear for school. Instead of the expected truce occurring, he finds himself and the other men in his squad fighting the stealthy Viet Cong. He finally has the "luck" to be wounded badly enought that he gets to fly back to the States. The sudden brutality of battle contrasts with the long tense hours of waiting to be attacked. *Coretta Scott King Award*, 1989; *School Library Journal "Best Book,"* 1988.

Pettit, Jayne. *My Name is San Ho.* New York: Scholastic, 1992. 0-590-44172-8, 149p. R=7; I=6.

In a flashback, Sam Ho recounts having to leave his mother and grandparents in their Viet Nam village to live in Saigon for three years in 1972. In 1975, he flees to America to be with his mother and her American husband. He experiences both prejudice and protection from the Americans he meets as he tries to learn English and adjust to his new life. Knowing what a person has endured often leads one to compassion rather than contempt.

APPENDIX A. READABILITY LEVEL

Readability level, established by Edward Fry and graphed in the Fry Readability Graph, is based on the assumption that a child who has reached a grade level will be able to read a book listed at that level. The reading level will also be appropriate for any child who is in a higher grade level than the one listed. Readability generally assumes that books with shorter sentences and fewer syllables are easier to read. One assesses the reading level of a book by randomly selecting 100-word passages from the beginning, middle, and end of the book. Then one counts the number of syllables and the number of sentences in each passage. The average of the number of syllables and the average of the number of sentences in the three passages can be located on Fry's graph. Where the two averages intersect is the reading level for a specific grade. For further information about readability and the graph see Edward Fry, "Fry's Readability Graph: Clarifications, Validity, and Extension" in *Journal of Reading* 21 (Dec. 1977): 249.

Since some books written solely for adult readers have very low readability levels, knowing the interest level as well will help to decide if a book is appropriate for a particular reader. Conversely, some picture books, with interest levels in the lower grades, have very high readability levels. Adults will want and will need to read these books aloud to a child. The number next to the entry is the interest level. For interest level designations, 10+ indicates books catalogued as adult books.

GRADE 1

Byars, Betsy. *The Golly Sisters Go West* I=2 p. 179
Byars, Betsy. *Hooray for the Golly Sisters* I=1 p. 177
Levinson, Riki. *DinnieAbbieSister-r-r!* I=1 p. 228
Roop and Roop. *Keep the Lights Burning, Abbie* I=1 p. 161

GRADE 2

Avi. *The Man Who Was Poe* I=5 p. 149
Barrie, Barbara. *Lone Star* I=5 p. 237
Bedard, Michael. *Emily* I=2 p. 177
Benchley, Nathaniel. *Sam the Minuteman* I=2 p. 87
Bethancourt, T. Ernesto. *The Tommorow Connection* I=8 p. 196
Brady, Philip. *Reluctant Hero* I=7 p. 142
Brenner, Barbara. *Wagon Wheels* I=2 p. 177
Bulla, Clyde Robert. *A Lion to Guard Us* I=3 p. 115
Bulla, Clyde Robert. *Squanto, Friend of the Pilgrims* I=4 p. 115
Bulla, Clyde Robert. *The Sword in the Tree* I=4 p. 52
Cech, John. *My Grandmother's Journey* I=3 p. 31
Clements, Bruce. *The Treasure of Plunderell Manor* I=5 p. 87
Coerr, Eleanor. *Chang's Paper Pony* I=2 p. 301
Coerr, Eleanor. *The Josefina Story Quilt* I=2 p. 150
Corcoran, Barbara. *The Sky is Falling* I=5 p. 226
Crews, Donald. *Bigmama's* I=K p. 217
Dillon, Eilís. *Children of Bach.* I=5 p. 32
Ferry, Charles. *One More Time!* I=10 p. 239
Fleischman, Sid. *Humbug Mountain* I=4 p. 152
Gallaz and Innocenti. *Rose Blanche* I=6 p. 33
Gee, Maurice. *The Fire-Raiser* I=6 p. 288
Geras, Adèle. *Voyage* I=6 p. 25

GRADE 3

Almedingen, E. M. *Anna* I=6 p. 21
Ames, M. *Grandpa Jake and the Grand Christmas* I=4 p. 224
Avi. *Shadrach's Crossing* I=5 p. 225
Avi. *Something's Upstairs* I=4 p. 135
Avi. *The True Confessions of Charlotte Doyle* I=6 p. 141
Avi. *"Who Was that Masked Man, Anyway?"* I=5 p. 237
Beatty, Patricia. *Behave Yourself, Bethany Brant* I=4 p. 195
Beatty, Patricia. *Charley Skedaddle* I=6 p. 164
Beatty, Patricia. *The Coach That Never Came* I=6 p. 176
Beatty, P. *Sarah and Me and the Lady from the Sea* I=5 p. 195
Bergman, Tamar. *Along the Tracks* I=7 p. 31
Berry, James. *Ajeemah and His Son* I=8 p. 282
Bishop, Claire Huchet. *Twenty and Ten* I=3 p. 31
Brennan, J. H. *Shiva* I=6 p. 7
Brennan, J. H. *Shiva Accused* I=5 p. 8
Brooks, Martha. *Two Moons in August* I=10 p. 252
Buechner, Frederick. *Godric* I=10+ p. 51
Bulla, Clyde Robert. *Pocahontas and the Strangers* I=6 p. 115
Bylinsky, Tatyana. *Before the Wildflowers Bloom* I=3 p. 216
Chaikin, Miriam. *Friends Forever* I=3 p. 239
Clapp, Patricia. *The Tamarack Tree* I=7 p. 166
Clavell, James. *Noble House* I=10+ p. 297
Cole, Norma. *The Final Tide* I=6 p. 252
Collier and Collier. *The Clock* I=8 p. 135
Dalgliesh, Alice. *The Courage of Sarah Noble* I=3 p. 122
De Angeli, Marguerite. *The Lion in the Box* I=4 p. 197
DeFelice, Cynthia. *Weasel* I=4 p. 143
Dhondy, Farrukh. *Black Swan* I=7 p. 68
Dunlop, Betty. *The Poetry Girl* I=8 p. 288
Filene, Peter. *Home and Away* I=10+ p. 253
Fleischman, Paul. *The Borning Room* I=6 p. 152
Fleischman, Sid. *The Ghost in the Noonday Sun* I=4 p. 180
Fleischman, Sid. *Jim Ugly* I=5 p. 180

Vander Els, Betty. *Leaving Point* I=9 p. 298
Vos, Ida. *Anna Is Still Here* I=7 p. 48
Welch, Catherine A. *Danger at the Breaker* I=3 p. 192
Westall, Robert. *The Machine-Gunners* I=7 p. 108
Westall, Robert. *Fathom Five* I=8 p. 107
Westall, Robert. *The Kingdom by the Sea* I=6 p. 107
Whelan, Gloria. *Hannah* I=3 p. 192
White, Ruth. *Weeping Willow* I=8 p. 264
Wibberley, Leonard. *The Last Battle* I=7 p. 139
Wilder, Laura Ingalls. *Little House on the Prairie* I=3 p. 193
Wilder, Laura Ingalls. *These Happy Golden Years* I=6 p. 194
Yep, Laurence. *The Star Fisher* I=6 p. 223
Zei, Aliki. *The Sound of Dragon's Feet* I=5 p. 29

GRADE 4

Aaron, Chester. *Lackawanna* I=8 p. 224
Aaron, Chester. *Alex Who Won his War* I=6 p. 237
Alphin, Elaine Marie. *The Ghost Cadet* I=4 p. 164
Anand, Valerie. *The Proud Villeins* I=10+ p. 50
Anand, Valerie. *Gildenford* I=10+ p. 49
Anderson, Margaret. *Searching for Shona* I=4 p. 99
Anderson, M. *The Journey of the Shadow Bairns* I=6 p. 86
Angell, Judie. *One-Way to Ansonia* I=6 p. 195
Antle, Nancy. *Hard Times* I=4 p. 224
Antle, Nancy. *Tough Choices* I=4 p. 266
Avery, Gillian. *A Likely Lad* I=6 p. 86
Avi. *Emily Upham's Revenge* I=4 p. 175
Avi. *The Fighting Ground* I=6 p. 127
Avi. *Punch with Judy* I=5 p. 175
Baker, Betty. *Walk the World's Rim* I=7 p. 111
Baklanov, Grigory. *Forever Nineteen* I=8 p. 30
Bauer, Marian. *Rain of Fire* I=5 p. 251

Erhart, Margaret. *Augusta Cotton* I=10+ p. 267
Fenton, Edward. *The Morning of the Gods* I=6 p. 46
Fleischman, Paul. *Path of the Pale Horse* I=8 p. 136
Foreman, Seaver. *The Boy Who Sailed with Columbus* I=4 p. 279
Forman, James D. *Prince Charlie's Year* I=8 p. 75
Fox, Paula. *The Slave Dancer* I=6 p. 143
Frank, Rudolf. *No Hero for the Kaiser* I=7 p. 33
Froelich, Margaret. *Reasons to Stay* I=7 p. 199
Garfield, Leon. *Devil-in-the-Fog* I=6 p. 75
Garfield, Leon. *Footsteps* I=6 p. 76
Garfield, Leon. *The Night of the Comet* I=6 p. 76
Garrigue, Shelia. *The Eternal Spring of Mr. Ito* I=8 p. 275
Gauch, Patricia L. *This Time, Tempe Wick?* I=4 p. 130
Green, Connie Jordan. *The War at Home* I=5 p. 240
Gutman, Claude. *The Empty House* I=6 p. 34
Hahn, Mary Downing. *Stepping on the Cracks* I=4 p. 241
Hamilton, Virginia. *The Bells of Christmas* I=4 p. 200
Hamilton, Virginia. *The House of Dies Drear* I=5 p. 153
Hansen, Joyce. *Out From This Place* I=5 p. 168
Hansen, Joyce. *Which Way Freedom?* I=5 p. 167
Harrison, Ray. *Patently Murder* I=10+ p. 89
Heaven, Constance. *The Raging Fire* I=10+ p. 25
Herman, Charlotte. *The House on Walenska Street* I=4 p. 26
Herman, Charlotte. *Millie Cooper, Take a Chance* I=3 p. 254
Herman, Charlotte. *Millie Cooper, 3B* I=3 p. 254
Herman, Charlotte. *A Summer on Thirteenth Street* I=5 p. 241
Hickman, Janet. *Zoar Blue* I=7 p. 168
Hoobler, D. and T. *Treasure in the Stream* I=4 p. 154
Holland, Cecelia. *Pacific Street* I=10+ p. 154
Holt, Victoria. *The India Fan* I=10+ p. 299
Holt, Victoria. *The Road to Paradise Island* I=10+ p. 90
Holt, Victoria. *The Silk Vendetta* I=10+ p. 91
Holt, Victoria. *Snare of Serpents* I=10+ p. 91
Hooks, William H. *The Ballad of Belle Dorcas* I=4 p. 145
Hooks, William H. *A Flight of Dazzle Angels* I=8 p. 201
Hooks, William H. *The Legend of the White Doe* I=4 p. 112
Hoppe, Joanne. *Dream Spinner* I=7 p. 202

McSwigan, Marie. *Snow Treasure* I=4 p. 38
Magorian, Michelle. *Back Home* I=7 p. 110
Magorian, Michelle. *Good Night, Mr. Tom* I=6 p. 102
Magorian, Michelle. *Not a Swan* I=8 p. 102
Manson, Ainslie. *A Dog Came, Too* I=2 p. 138
Marko, Katherine. *Away to Fundy Bay* I=5 p. 245
Martin, C. L. G. *Day of Darkness, Night of Light* I=3 p. 188
Mazzio, Joann. *Leaving Eldorado* I=8 p. 207
Milton, Nancy. *The Giraffe That Walked to Paris* I=2 p. 28
Murrow, Liza K. *West Against the Wind* I=7 p. 158
Myers, Anna. *Red-Dirt Jessie* I=5 p. 230
Myers, W. *The Righteous Revenge of Artemis Bonner* I=5 p. 188
Newman, Robert. *The Case of the Etruscan Treasure* I=5 p. 94
Newman, Robert. *The Case of the Indian Curse* I=5 p. 9473
Newman, Robert. *The Case of the Threatened King* I=4 p. 95
Nixon, Joan L. *Caught in the Act* I=5 p. 159
Nixon, Joan L. *A Family Apart* I=6 p. 159
O'Dell, Scott. *The King's Fifth* I=7 p. 113
O'Dell, Scott. *Sing Down the Moon* I=7 p. 171
O'Dell, Scott. *Streams to the River, River to the Sea* I=7 p. 188
O'Dell, Scott. *Zia* I=6 p. 160
Olsen, Violet. *The View from the Pighouse Roof* I=7 p. 230
Paterson, Katherine. *Lyddie* I=8 p. 147
Paterson, Katherine. *The Sign of the Chrysanthemum* I=8 p. 305
Paulsen, Gary. *The Cookcamp* I=5 p. 246
Pearson, Kit. *Looking at the Moon* I=7 p. 278
Pendergraft, Patricia. *Brushy Mountain* I=5 p. 259
Pople, Maureen. *The Other Side of the Family* I=6 p. 289
Pullman, Philip. *The Ruby in the Smoke* I=8 p. 96
Pullman, Philip. *Shadow in the North* I=8 p. 96
Pullman, Philip. *The Tiger in the Well* I=9 p. 97
Rappaport, Doreen. *Trouble at the Mines* I=3 p. 209
Richter, Conrad. *The Light in the Forest* I=4 p. 124
Richter, Hans. *Friedrich* I=4 p. 42
Riddell, Ruth. *Haunted Journey* I=8 p. 231
Rinaldi, Ann. *The Fifth of March* I=7 p. 125
Rinaldi, Ann. *Time Enough for Drums* I=9 p. 132

Riskind, Mary. *Apple Is My Sign* I=4 p. 209

Rockwood, Joyce. *Groundhog's Horse* I=4 p. 125

Rodowsky, Colby F. *Fitchett's Folly* I=5 p. 209

Roper, Robert. *In Caverns of Blue Ice* I=7 p. 47

Rosen, Billi. *Andi's War* I=5 p. 48

Rossiter, Phyllis. *Moxie* I=6 p. 232

Rostkowski, Margaret. *After the Dancing Days* I=5 p. 221

Roth-Hano, Renee. *Touch Wood* I=6 p. 42

Rundle, Ann. *Moonbranches* I=7 p. 106

Schotter, Roni. *Rhoda, Straight and True* I=6 p. 260

Sebestyen, Ouida. *Words by Heart* I=5 p. 210

Serraillier, Ian. *The Silver Sword* I=6 p. 43

Shiefman, Vicki. *Good-bye to the Trees* I=5 p. 210

Shore, Laura Jan. *The Sacred Moon Tree* I=7 p. 173

Shub, Elizabeth. *Cutlass in the Snow* I=3 p. 139

Shura, Mary Francis. *Kate's Book* I=5 p. 148

Shura, Mary Francis. *Kate's House* I=4 p. 148

Skurzynski, Gloria. *What Happened in Hamelin* I=6 p. 16

Sledge and Sledge. *Empire of Heaven* I=10+ p. 294

Smucker, Barbara. *Runaway to Freedom* I=5 p. 162

Speare, Elizabeth George. *The Bronze Bow* I=7 p. 4

Speare, Elizabeth George. *The Sign of the Beaver* I=5 p. 126

Spinka, Penina Keen. *White Hare's Horses* I=7 p. 114

Steele, William O. *The Buffalo Knife* I=4 p. 132

Steele, William O. *Wayah of the Real People* I=5 p. 126

Steiner, Barbara. *Tessa* I=7 p. 262

Stevens, Carla. *Lily and Miss Liberty* I=0 p. 190

Stolz, Mary S. *Ivy Larkin* I=7 p. 232

Stolz, Mary. *Zekmet the Stone Carver* I=3 p. 3

Strauch, Eileen Walsh. *Hey You, Sister Rose* I=5 p. 262

Sutcliff, Rosemary. *Blood Feud* I=8 p. 16

Taylor, Theodore. *The Cay* I=5 p. 264

Terris, Susan. *Nell's Quilt* I=10 p. 211

Thesman, Jean. *Molly Donnelly* I=8 p. 248

Thomas, Elizabeth Marshall. *The Animal Wife* I=10+ p. 9

Tripp, Valerie. *Meet Felicity* I=4 p. 133

Turnbull, Ann. *Speedwell* I=4 p. 106

Turner, Ann. *Third Girl from the Left* I=9   p. 163
Uchida, Yoshiko. *The Happiest Ending* I=5   p. 235
Uchida, Yoshiko. *Samurai of Gold Hill* I=6   p. 191
Vá, Leong. *A Letter to the King* I=2   p. 294
Van Raven, Pieter. *Harpoon Island* I=9   p. 222
Van Raven, Pieter. *A Time of Troubles* I=7   p. 236
Vos, Ida. *Hide and Seek* I=5   p. 44
Weaver, Lydia. *Child Star* I=4   p. 222
Welch, Ronald. *Knight Crusader* I=8   p. 17
Westall, Robert. *Blitzcat* I=4   p. 107
Westall, Robert. *Echoes of War* I=7   p. 110
White, Ruth. *Sweet Creek Holler* I=5   p. 264
Wilder, Laura Ingalls. *Farmer Boy* I=4   p. 192
Willard, Barbara. *A Cold Wind Blowing* I=10   p. 71
Willard, Barbara. *A Flight of Swans* I=10   p. 72
Winter, Jeanette. *Follow the Drinking Gourd* I=3   p. 163
Winter, Jeanette. *Klara's New World* I=4   p. 29
Wisler, G. Clifton. *Piper's Ferry* I=5   p. 148
Wisler, G. Clifton. *Red Cap* I=6   p. 174
Wulffson, Don L. *The Upside-Down Ship* I=6   p. 81
Yarbro, Chelsea Quinn. *Four Horses for Tishtry* I=7   p. 4
Yep, Laurence. *Dragon's Gate* I=6   p. 174
Yep, Laurence. *Mountain Light* I=8   p. 296
Yolen, Jane. *The Seeing Stick* I=2   p. 294
Ziefert, Harriet. *A New Coat for Anna* I=2   p. 48

GRADE 5

Fahrmann, Willi. *The Long Journey of Lukas B.* I=7 p. 179
Fleischman, Paul. *Bull Run* I=5 p. 167
Fowler, Zinita. *The Last Innocent Summer* I=5 p. 227
Gardam, Jane. *A Long Way from Verona* I=6 p. 100
Garfield, Leon. *The Empty Sleeve* I=6 p. 76
Gear, M. and K. *People of the Sea* I=10+ p. 112
Geras, Adele. *The Tower Room* I=9 p. 109
Gipson, Fred. *Old Yeller* I=5 p. 181
Greene, Constance C. *Dotty's Suitcase* I=5 p. 227
Griffin, Peni. *Switching Well* I=5 p. 200
Grimes, Roberta. *My Thomas* I=10+ p. 122
Harnett, Cynthia. *The Great House* I=6 p. 77
Harnett, Cynthia. *Stars of Fortune* I=6 p. 69
Härtling, Peter. *Crutches* I=5 p. 46
Haugaard, Erik. *A Slave's Tale* I=8 p. 16
Hautzig, Esther. *The Endless Steppe* I=5 p. 35
Heaven, Constance. *The Craven Legacy* I=10+ p. 90
Hendry, Frances. *Quest for a Kelpie* I=7 p. 78
Hendry, Frances. *Quest for a Maid* I=7 p. 52
Hess, Donna Lynn. *In Search of Honor* I=7 p. 22
Hesse, Karen. *Letters from Rifka* I=5 p. 26
Higginsen and Bolder. *Mama, I Want to Sing* I=6 p. 254
Hill, Susan. *The Glass Angels* I=5 p. 109
Ho, Minfong. *Rice without Rain* I=9 p. 313
Hodge, Jane Aiken. *Windover* I=10+ p. 78
Hogan, Linda. *Mean Spirit* I=10+ p. 217
Holland, Cecelia. *The Lords of Vaumartin* I=10+ p. 18
Howard, Ellen. *Sister* I=6 p. 183
Howard, Ellen. *The Tower Room* I=5 p. 255
Hudson, Jan. *Sweetgrass* I=7 p. 273
James, J. Alison. *Sing for a Gentle Rain* I=10 p. 112
Kinsey-Warnock, Natalie. *The Canada Geese Quilt* I=4 p. 276
Koller, Jackie French. *Nothing to Fear* I=7 p. 228
Lattimore, D. *The Dragon's Robe* R=2 p. 293
Lawlor, Laurie. *Addie Across the Prairie* I=3 p. 185
Lawlor, Laurie. *Addie's Dakota Winter* I=4 p. 186
Lawlor, Laurie. *George on His Own* I=5 p. 186

Levine, Arthur A. *All the Lights in the Night* I=4 p. 27
Llywelyn, Morgan. *Brian Boru* I=6 p. 53
McCutcheon, Elsie. *Summer of the Zeppelin* I=5 p. 102
McGraw. Eloise. *Moccasin Trail* I=7 p. 156
McGraw, Eloise. *The Striped Ships* I=6 p. 53
MacLachlan, Patricia. *Three Names* I=2 p. 187
Mayne, William. *Low Tide* I=5 p. 286
Meyer, Carolyn. *Where the Broken Heart Still Beats* I=8 p. 170
Mooney, Bel. *The Stove Haunting* I=5 p. 83
Morpurgo, Michael. *Twist of Gold* I=7 p. 157
Morpurgo, Michael. *Why the Whales Came* I=5 p. 103
Morrow, Barbara. *Edward's Portrait* I=2 p. 158
Namioka, Lensey. *The Coming of the Bear* I=7 p. 306
Naylor and Reynolds. *Maudie in the Middle* I=5 p. 207
Nelson, Theresa. *And One for All* I=7 p. 269
Newman, Robert. *The Case of the Watching Boy* I=5 p. 95
Nixon, Joan L. *In the Face of Danger* I=5 p. 160
O'Callahan, Jan. *Tulips* I=3 p. 28
O'Dell, Scott. *The Hawk That Dare Not Hunt by Day* I=9 p. 70
O'Dell, Scott. *The 290* I=7 p. 283
Paton Walsh, Jill. *A Chance Child* I=8 p. 84
Paton Walsh, Jill. *The Dolphin Crossing* I=7 p. 103
Pellowski, Anne. *First Farm in the Valley* I=4 p. 208
Pendergraft, Patricia. *Hear the Wind Blow* I=6 p. 208
Penman, Sharon Kay. *Falls the Shadow* I=10+ p. 64
Penman, Sharon Kay. *Here Be Dragons* I=10+ p. 64
Penman, Sharon Kay. *The Reckoning* I-10+ p. 65
Penman, Sharon Kay. *The Sunne in Splendor* I=10+ p. 65
Peyton, K. M. *Flambards* I=9 p. 104
Peyton, K. M. *The Maplin Bird* I=9 p. 96
Raymond, Patrick. *Daniel and Esther* I=8 p. 105
Riley, Judith Merkle. *In Pursuit of the Green Lion* I=10+ p. 66
Rinaldi, Ann. *A Break with Charity* I=8 p. 125
Rinaldi, Ann. *In My Father's House* I=8 p. 172
Robinet, Harriette Gillem. *Children of the Fire* I=5 p. 189
Sanders, Scott R. *Bad Man Ballad* I=7 p. 139
Say, Allen. *Grandfather's Journey* I=2 p. 309

Semel, Nava. *Becoming Gershona* I=6 p. 304

Sevela, Ephraim. *We Were Not Like Other People* I=8 p. 43

Shuler, Linda Lay. *She Who Remembers* I=10+ p. 113

Shuler, Linda L. *Voice of the Eagle* I=10+ p. 114

Shura, Mary Francis. *Gentle Annie* I=7 p. 173

Skurzynski, Gloria. *Good-bye, Billy Radish* I=7 p. 222

Skurzynski, Gloria. *The Minstrel in the Tower* I=3 p. 58

Smalls-Hector, Irene. *Irene and the Big, Fine Nickel.* I=2 p. 261

Smith, Claude Clayton. *The Stratford Devil* I=9 p. 119

Speare, Elizabeth George. *Calico Captive* I=7 p. 273

Steele, William O. *Flaming Arrows* I=5 p. 132

Steele, William O. *Winter Danger* I=5 p. 133

Stolz, Mary. *Bartholomew Fair* I=8 p. 71

Sutcliff, Rosemary. *The Shining Company* I=7 p. 59

Sutcliff, Rosemary. *Warrior Scarlet* I=6 p. 9

Talbert, Marc. *The Purple Heart* I=5 p. 270

Taylor, Mildred. *The Friendship* I=5 p. 232

Taylor, Mildred. *Let the Circle Be Unbroken* I=8 p. 233

Treece, Henry. *The Dream-Time* I=7 p. 10

Turner, Ann. *Nettie's Trip South* I=4 p. 163

Uchida, Yoshiko. *The Bracelet* I=2 p. 248

Uchida, Yoshiko. *Journey to Topaz* I=5 p. 249

Voight, Cynthia. *Tree by Leaf* I=7 p. 222

Wallace, Bill. *Buffalo Gal* I=6 p. 212

Weaver, Lydia. *Close to Home* I=5 p. 264

Westall, Robert. *The Wind Eye* I=7 p. 60

Whelan, Gloria. *Next Spring an Oriole* I=3 p. 148

White, Alana. *Come Next Spring* I=6 p. 264

Whittaker, Dorothy. *Angels of the Swamp* I=7 p. 236

Wibberley, Leonard. *Red Pawns* I=7 p. 140

Wild, Margaret. *Let the Celebrations Begin!* I=3 p. 44

Wilder, Laura Ingalls. *By the Shores of Silver Lake* I=3 p. 192

Wilder, Laura Ingalls. *Little Town on the Prairie* I=5 p. 194

Wilder, Laura Ingalls. *The Long Winter* I=4 p. 194

Wilder, Laura Ingalls. *On the Banks of Plum Creek* I=3 p. 194

Willard, Barbara. *Harrow and Harvest* I=9 p. 72

Willard, Barbara. *The Lark and the Laurel* I=8 p. 67

GRADE 6

Cleaver, Vera and Bill. *Dust of the Earth* I=6 p. 252
Cole, Sheila. *The Dragon in the Cliff* I=6 p. 82
Collier and Collier. *War Comes to Willy Freeman* I=6 p. 129
Collier and Collier. *Who Is Carrie?* I=6 p. 136
Conrad, Pam. *Pedro's Journal* I=6 p. 279
Cookson, Catherine. *The Rag Nymph* I=10+ p. 88
Coolidge, Olivia. *Marathon Looks on the Sea* I=8 p. 4
Coolidge, Olivia. *People in Palestine* I=9 p. 3
Cooper, Susan. *Dawn of Fear* I=6 p. 100
Cormier, Robert. *Other Bells for Us to Ring* I=6 p. 239
Cormier, Robert. *Tunes for Bears to Dance To* I=7 p. 252
De Angeli, Marguerite. *The Door in the Wall* I=6 p. 62
de Hartog, Jan. *The Lamb's War* I=10+ p. 253
De Jenkins, Lyll. *The Honorable Prison* I=8 p. 283
de Treviño, Elizabeth B. *El Güero* I=6 p. 282
Degens, T. *On the Third Ward* I=8 p. 46
DeJong, Meindert. *The House of Sixty Fathers* I=4 p. 297
Dickinson, Peter. *Tulku* I=9 p. 295
Dixon, Jeanne. *The Tempered Wind* I=10 p. 253
Doctorow, E. L. *Ragtime* I=10+ p. 198
Dorris, Michael. *Morning Girl* I=4 p. 279
Durrell, Lawrence. *White Eagles over Serbia* I=9 p. 32
Edmonds, Walter. *The Matchlock Gun* I=3 p. 122
Ellis, Sarah. *Next-Door Neighbors* I=5 p. 275
Field, Rachel. *Calico Bush* I=7 p. 122
Fleischman, Paul. *Coming-and-Going Men* I=7 p. 136
Fleischman, Paul. *Graven Images* I=8 p. 179
Fleishman, Paul. *Saturnalia* I=8 p. 117
Forman, James D. *Becca's Story* I=8 p. 167
Garfield, Leon. *Smith* I=7 p. 76
Garrett, George. *The Succession* I=10+ p. 68
Glasco, Gordon. *Slow Through Eden* I=10+ p. 34
Greene, Bette. *Summer of My German Soldier* I=6 p. 240
Gregory, Kristiana. *Earthquake at Dawn* I=6 p. 199
Gregory, Kristiana. *Jenny of the Tetons* I=9 p. 181
Gurasich, Marj. *Letters to Oma* I=7 p. 153
Harmon, Susan. *Colorado Ransom* I=10+ p. 181

Vogt, Esther Loewen. *A Race for Land* I=4 p. 212
Volk, Toni. *Montana Women* I=10+ p. 249
Wibberley, Leonard. *John Treegate's Musket* I=7 p. 133
Wibberley, Leonard. *Leopard's Prey* I=6 p. 139
Wibberley, Leonard. *Sea Captain from Salem* I=7 p. 134
Wibberley, Leonard. *Treegate's Raiders* I=7 p. 134
Willard, Barbara. *The Eldest Son* I=10 p. 71
Willard, Barbara. *The Iron Lily* I=10 p. 72
Willis, Patricia. *A Place to Claim as Home* I=6 p. 249
Wisler, G. Clifton. *This New Land* I=5 p. 120
Wisler, G. Clifton. *Thunder on the Tennessee* I=6 p. 174
Wyman, Andrea. *Red Sky at Morning* I=5 p. 213

GRADE 7

Aaron, Chester. *Gideon* I=9 p. 30
Achebe, Chinua. *Things Fall Apart* I=10 p. 291
Almedingen, E. M. *The Crimson Oak* I=7 p. 21
Anand, Valerie. *King of the Wood* I=10+ p. 50
Anderson, Joan. *Christmas on the Prairie* I=4 p. 141
Anderson, Joan. *Pioneer Settlers in New France* I=7 p. 271
Anderson, Joan. *Spanish Pioneers of the Southwest* I=4 p. 121
Anderson, Joan. *A Williamsburg Household* I=2 p. 121
Attanasio, A. A. *Wyvern* I=10+ p. 285
Ballard, J. G. *Empire of the Sun* I=10+ p. 295
Bartone, Elisa. *Peppe the Lamplighter* I=2 p. 175
Berent, Mark. *Rolling Thunder* I=10+ p. 316
Berent, Mark. *Steel Tiger* I=10+ p. 316
Bingham, Sallie. *Small Victories* I=10+ p. 266
Blos, Joan. *A Gathering of Days* I=7 p. 141
Brooks, Jerome. *Naked in Winter* I=9 p. 251
Buechner, Frederick. *The Wizard's Tide* I=10+ p. 225
Burton, Hester. *Time of Trial* I=9 p. 74

Roe, Elaine Corbeil. *Circle of Light* I=7 p. 278
Roesch, Ethel & Paul. *Ashana* I=10+ p. 138
Rylant, Cynthia. *I Had Seen Castles* I=8 p. 247
Rylant, Cynthia. *When I Was Young in the Mountains* I=3 p. 259
Sacks, Margaret. *Beyond Safe Boundaries* I=9 p. 292
Sanders, Scott R. *Aurora Means Dawn* I=4 p. 138
Scott, Paul. *The Day of the Scorpion* I=10+ p. 299
Scott, Paul. *A Division of the Spoils* I=10+ p. 300
Scott, Paul. *The Jewel in the Crown* I=10+ p. 300
Scott, Paul. *The Towers of Silence* I=10+ p. 300
Skurzynski, Gloria. *The Tempering* I=8 p. 210
Slepian, Jan. *Risk n' Roses* I=7 p. 260
Sperry, Armstrong. *Call It Courage* I=5 p. 286
Spier, Peter. *Father, May I Come?* I=3 p. 23
Stolz, Mary. *Pangur Ban* I=7 p. 59
Sutcliff, Rosemary. *Flame-Colored Taffeta* I=7 p. 98
Sutcliff, Rosemary. *The Lantern Bearers* I=10 p. 14
Sutcliff, Rosemary. *The Mark of the Horse Lord* I=8 p. 9
Sutcliff, Rosemary. *The Shield Ring* I=7 p. 59
Sutcliff, Rosemary. *Sun Horse, Moon Horse* I=7 p. 14
Synge, Ursula. *The People and the Promise* I=8 p. 3
Thesman, Jean. *Rachel Chance* I=7 p. 234
Trease, Geoffrey. *A Flight of Angels* I=6 p. 71
Treece, Henry. *The Road to Miklagard* I=7 p. 17
Tripp, Valerie. *Changes for Samantha* I=4 p. 212
Uris, Leon. *Exodus* I=10+ p. 304
Weaver-Gelzer, Charlotte. *In the Time of Trouble* I=8 p. 292
Weitzman, David. *Thrashin' Time* I=6 p. 212
Wheeler, Thomas Gerald. *A Fanfare for the Stalwart* I=9 p. 29
Wibberley, Leonard. *Peter Treegate's War* I=7 p. 134
Wiggins, Marianne. *John Dollar* I=10+ p. 301
Willard, Barbara. *The Sprig of Broom* I=10 p. 73
Wolf, Joan. *Daughter of the Red Deer* I=10+ p. 10
Yarbro, Chelsea Quinn. *Floating Illusions* I=7 p. 213
Yolen, Jane. *Briar Rose* I=8 p. 250
Yount, John. *Thief of Dreams* I=10+ p. 265

GRADE 8

Ackerman, Karen. *Araminta's Paint Box* I=3 p. 149
Boyne, Walter J. *Eagles at War* I=10+ p. 238
Bradshaw, Gillian. *The Bearkeeper's Daughter* I=10+ p. 15
Conrad, Pam. *Prairie Songs* I=5 p. 178
Cookson, Catherine. *The Parson's Daughter* I=10+ p. 88
De Hartog, Jan. *The Peculiar People* I=10+ p. 143
De Trevino, Elizabeth. *I, Juan de Pareja* I=8 p. 21
Garfield, Leon. *The December Rose* I=8 p. 88
Garfield, Leon. *The Strange Affair of Adelaide Harris* I=8 p. 77
Garrett, George. *Death of the Fox* I=10+ p. 68
Gedge, Pauline. *Child of the Morning* I=10+ p. 1
Hackl, Erich. *Farewell Sidonia* I=10+ p. 34
Highwater, Jamake. *Eyes of Darkness* I=9 p. 201
Hunter, Mollie. *A Sound of Chariots* I=8 p. 101
Jones, Douglas C. *Weedy Rough* I=10+ p. 218
Klein, Robin. *Dresses of Red and Gold* I=9 p. 289
Mitchell, Margaret. *Gone with the Wind* I=10+ p. 170
Paterson, Katherine. *Of Nightingales That Weep* I=10 p. 305
Perry, Anne. *The Face of a Stranger* I=10+ p. 95
Raspail, J. *Who Will Remember the People* I=10+ p. 284
Renault, Mary. *The King Must Die* I=10+ p. 6
Renault, Mary. *The Last of the Wine* I=10+ p. 6
Renault, Mary. *The Mask of Apollo* I=10+ p. 7
Service, Pamela F. *The Reluctant God* I=8 p. 3
Uris, Leon. *Trinity* I=10+ p. 98
Wheeler, Thomas Gerald. *All Men Tall* I=8 p. 67
Wilder, Laura Ingalls. *The First Four Years* I=6 p. 193

GRADE 9

Alexander, Lloyd. *The Philadelphia Adventure* I=9 p. 175
Blumberg, Rhoda. *Bloomers!* I=4 p. 150
Chin, Tsao Hsueh. *The Dream of the Red Chamber* I=10+ p. 293
Doctorow, E. L. *World's Fair* I=10+ p. 225
Flanagan, Thomas. *The Year of the French* I=10+ p. 82
Foster, Cecil. *No Man in the House* I=10+ p. 284
McMurty, Larry. *Lonesome Dove* I=10+ p. 187
Rowlands, Avril. *Milk and Honey* I=6 p. 110
Santmyer, Helen H. *And Ladies of the Club* I=10+ p. 190
Sutcliff, Rosemary. *Bonnie Dundee* I=9 p. 81
Sutcliff, Rosemary. *The Eagle of the Ninth* I=9 p. 13
Sutcliff, Rosemary. *The Silver Branch* I=10 p. 14

GRADE 10

Boyne, Walter J. *Trophy for Eagles* I=10+ p. 215
Jones, Douglas C. *Come Winter* I=10+ p. 203
Jones, Douglas C. *Roman* I=10+ p. 184
Parotti, Phillip. *Fires in the Sky* I=10+ p. 5

APPENDIX B. INTEREST LEVEL

The interest level indicated for a book suggests that readers below the level listed will not be as interested in the content of the book as those readers at the level or above the level. Interest levels deal solely with the content of the book. Generally, interest level should be either the same or a higher grade level than the readability level. Some books with a higher readability level than interest level are meant for reading aloud with the adult reading the book for the child. Some books are simply too hard for the reader who will be interested in the book's content. The number next to the entry is the reading level.

The interest levels are based on a combination of reading interest studies, Lawrence Kohlberg's stages of moral development, and Carol Gilligan's modifications of Kohlberg's stages in her studies about decision-making. For further information, see Lawrence Kohlberg, *Essays on Moral Development: The Philosophy of Moral Development* (New York: HarperCollins, 1981) and Carol Gilligan, *In a Different Voice: Psychological Theory and Women's Development* (Cambridge MA: Harvard Univ., 1982).

KINDERGARTEN

Crews, Donald. *Bigmama's* R=2 p. 217
Dionetti, Michelle. *Coal Mine Peaches* R=7 p. 198

GRADE 1

Byars, Betsy. *Hooray for the Golly Sisters* R=1 p. 177
Levinson, Riki. *DinnieAbbieSister-r-r!* R=1 p. 228
Rappaport, Doreen. *The Boston Coffee Party* R=1 p. 124
Roop, P. and C. *Keep the Lights Burning, Abbie* R=1 p. 161

GRADE 2

Anderson, Joan. *A Williamsburg Household* R=7 p. 121
Bartone, Elisa. *Peppe the Lamplighter* R=7 p. 175
Bedard, Michael. *Emily* R=2 p. 177
Benchley, Nathaniel. *Sam the Minuteman* R=2 p. 87
Brenner, Barbara. *Wagon Wheels* R=2 p. 177
Byars, Betsy. *The Golly Sisters Go West* R=1 p. 179
Coerr, Eleanor. *Chang's Paper Pony* R=2 p. 301
Coerr, Eleanor. *The Josefina Story Quilt* R=2 p. 150
Cooney, Barbara. *Island Boy* R=5 p. 196
Houston, Gloria. *But No Candy* R=4 p. 243
Houston, G. *The Year of the Perfect Christmas Tree* R=4 p. 218
Howard, Elizabeth Fitzgerald. *Chita's Christmas Tree* R=3 p. 202
Howard, Ellen. *The Cellar* R=2 p. 202
Howard, Ellen. *The Chickenhouse House* R=4 p. 183
Kerry Raines. *A Birthday for Blue* R=3 p. 147
Ketteman, Helen. *The Year of No More Corn* R=3 p. 218

GRADE 3

GRADE 4

Pellowski, Anne. *First Farm in the Valley* R=5 p. 208

Prince, Alison. *How's Business* R=3 p. 105

Richter, Conrad. *The Light in the Forest* R=4 p. 124

Richter, Hans. *Friedrich* R=4 p. 42

Riskind, Mary. *Apple Is My Sign* R=4 p. 209

Rockwood, Joyce. *Groundhog's Horse* R=4 p. 125

Rosenblum, Richard. *Brooklyn Dodger Days* R=6 p. 259

Sanders, Scott R. *Aurora Means Dawn* R=7 p. 138

Schlein, Miriam. *I Sailed with Columbus* R=3 p. 281

Shaw, Janet. *Changes for Kirsten* R=3 p. 161

Shura, Mary Francis. *Kate's House* R=4 p. 148

Smothers, Ethel Footman. *Down in the Piney Woods* R=3 p. 261

Steele, William O. *The Buffalo Knife* R=4 p. 132

Taylor, Mildred. *Song of the Trees* R=3 p. 234

Tripp, Valerie. *Changes for Samantha* R=7 p. 212

Tripp, Valerie. *Changes for Molly* R=3 p. 248

Tripp, Valerie. *Meet Felicity* R=4 p. 133

Tunbo, Frances G. *Stay Put, Robbie McAmis* R=3 p. 163

Turnbull, Ann. *Speedwell* R=4 p. 106

Turner, Ann. *Grasshopper Summer* R=2 p. 191

Turner, Ann. *Nettie's Trip South* R=5 p. 163

Turner, Ann. *Time of the Bison* R=3 p. 10

Turner, Bonnie. *The Haunted Igloo* R=3 p. 278

Vogt, Esther Loewen. *A Race for Land* R=6 p. 212

Weaver, Lydia. *Child Star* R=4 p. 222

Westall, Robert. *Blitzcat* R=4 p. 107

Wilder, Laura Ingalls. *Farmer Boy* R=4 p. 192

Wilder, Laura Ingalls. *The Long Winter* R=5 p. 194

Winter, Jeanette. *Klara's New World* R=4 p. 29

GRADE 5

Aiken, Joan. *Bridle the Wind* R=5 p. 20
Amoss, Berthe. *The Mockingbird Song* R=5 p. 224
Armstrong, William O. *Sounder* R=5 p. 225
Avi. *The Man Who Was Poe* R=2 p. 149
Avi. *Punch with Judy* R=4 p. 175
Avi. *Shadrach's Crossing* R=3 p. 225
Avi. *"Who Was that Masked Man, Anyway?"* R=3 p. 239
Barrie, Barbara. *Lone Star* R=2 p. 237
Bauer, Marian. *Rain of Fire* R=4 p. 251
Bawden, Nina. *Henry* R=5 p. 99
Beatty, Patricia. *Jayhawker* R=4 p. 165
Beatty, *Sarah and Me and the Lady from the Sea* R=3 p. 195
Beatty, Patricia. *Wait for Me, Watch for Me, Eula Bee* R=4 p. 165
Bergman, Tamar. *The Boy From Over There* R=4 p. 303
Brennan, J. H. *Shiva Accused* R=3 p. 8
Brink, Carol Ryre. *Caddie Woodlawn* R=6 p. 166
Cameron, Eleanor. *The Court of the Stone Children* R=5 p. 24
Carter, Dorothy S. *His Majesty, Queen Hatshepsut* R=5 p. 1
Choi, Sook Nyul. *Year of Impossible Goodbyes* R=5 p. 311
Clements, Bruce. *The Treasure of Plunderell Manor* R=2 p. 87
Clifford, Eth. *Will Somebody Please Marry My Sister?* R=5 p. 216
Climo, Shirley. *A Month of Seven Days* R=5 p. 166
Coerr, Eleanor. *Mieko and the Fifth Treasure* R=5 p. 307
Collier and Collier. *My Brother Sam Is Dead* R=4 p. 128
Conrad, Pam. *My Daniel* R=4 p. 196
Conrad, Pam. *Prairie Songs* R=8 p. 178
Corcoran, Barbara. *The Sky is Falling* R=2 p. 226
Dexter, Catherine. *Mazemaker* R=4 p. 197
Dillon, Eilís. *Children of Bach* R=2 p. 32
Edwards, Pat. *Little John and Plutie* R=4 p. 198
Ellis, Sarah. *Next-Door Neighbors* R=6 p. 275
Fleischman, Paul. *Bull Run* R=5 p. 167

Fleischman, Sid. *Jim Ugly* R=3   p. 180

Fowler, Zinita. *The Last Innocent Summer* R=5   p. 227

Fritz, Jean. *Brady* R=3   p. 144

Gipson, Fred. *Old Yeller* R=5   p. 181

Green, Connie Jordan. *The War at Home* R=4   p. 240

Greene, Constance C. *Dotty's Suitcase* R=5   p. 227

Griffin, Peni. *Switching Well* R=5   p. 200

Hamilton, Virginia. *The House of Dies Drear* R=4   p. 153

Hansen, Joyce. *Out From This Place* R=4   p. 167

Hansen, Joyce. *Which Way Freedom?* R=4   p. 168

Härtling, Peter. *Crutches* R=5   p. 46

Hautzig, Esther. *The Endless Steppe* R=5   p. 35

Henry, Joanne L. *A Clearing in the Forest* R=7   p. 144

Hesse, Karen. *Letters from Rifka* R=5   p. 26

Herman, Charlotte. *A Summer on Thirteenth Street* R=4   p. 241

Heuck, Sigrid. *The Hideout* R=3   p. 36

Hickman, Janet. *The Stones* R=2   p. 242

Hill, Elizabeth Starr. *The Banjo Player* R=7   p. 183

Hill, Susan. *The Glass Angels* R=5   p. 109

Holland, Isabelle. *The Journey Home* R=2   p. 183

Hooks, William H. *Circle of Fire* R=3   p. 227

Howard, Ellen. *Her Own Song* R=3   p. 203

Howard, Ellen. *The Tower Room* R=5   p. 255

Jensen, Dorothea. *The Riddle of Penncroft Farm* R=3   p. 131

Kemp, Gene. *The Well* R=3   p. 102

Kordon, Klaus. *Brothers Like Friends* R=4   p. 47

Kudlinski, Kathleen. *Earthquake!* R=3   p. 204

Kudlinski, Kathleen. *Hero Over Here* R=4   p. 219

Lampman, Evelyn Sibley. *White Captives* R=4   p. 156

Lawlor, Laurie. *Addie's Long Summer* R=3   p. 186

Lawlor, Laurie. *George on His Own* R=5   p. 186

Lelchuk, Alan. *On Home Ground* R=7   p. 256

Leonard, Laura. *Finding Papa* R=6   p. 205

Levin, Betty. *Mercy's Mill* R=4   p. 118

Levinson, Nancy S. *Your Friend, Natalie Popper* R=4   p. 257

Lewis, Hilda. *The Ship That Flew* R=4   p. 2

Lord, Athena. *The Luck of Z.A. and Zoe* R=6   p. 228

Roberts, Willo Davis. *Jo and the Bandit* R=6 p. 189

Robinet, Harriette Gillem. *Children of the Fire* R=5 p. 189

Rodowsky, Colby F. *Fitchett's Folly* R=4 p. 209

Rosen, Billi. *Andi's War* R=4 p. 48

Rostkowski, Margaret. *After the Dancing Days* R=4 p. 221

Savin, Marcia. *The Moon Bridge* R=2 p. 247

Sebestyen, Ouida. *Words by Heart* R=4 p. 210

Shiefman, Vicki. *Good-bye to the Trees* R=4 p. 210

Shura, Mary Francis. *Kate's Book* R=4 p. 148

Smucker, Barbara. *Runaway to Freedom* R=4 p. 162

Speare, Elizabeth George. *The Sign of the Beaver* R=4 p. 126

Sperry, Armstrong. *Call It Courage* R=7 p. 286

Steele, William O. *Flaming Arrows* R=5 p. 132

Steele, William O. *Wayah of the Real People* R=4 p. 126

Steele, William O. *Winter Danger* R=5 p. 133

Strauch, Eileen Walsh. *Hey You, Sister Rose* R=4 p. 262

Talbert, Marc. *The Purple Heart* R=5 p. 270

Tate, Eleanora E. *The Secret of Gumbo Grove* R=3 p. 162

Taylor, Mildred. *The Friendship* R=5 p. 232

Taylor, Mildred. *The Gold Cadillac* R=6 p. 262

Taylor, Theodore. *The Cay* R=4 p. 284

Uchida, Yoshiko. *The Best Bad Thing* R=6 p. 235

Uchida, Yoshiko. *The Happiest Ending* R=4 p. 235

Uchida, Yoshiko. *A Jar of Dreams* R=6 p. 234

Uchida, Yoshiko. *Journey to Topaz* R=5 p. 249

Vos, Ida. *Hide and Seek* R=4 p. 44

Weaver, Lydia. *Close to Home* R=5 p. 264

White, Ruth. *Sweet Creek Holler* R=4 p. 264

Wilder, Laura Ingalls. *Little Town on the Prairie* R=5 p. 194

Wisler, G. Clifton. *Piper's Ferry* R=4 p. 148

Wisler, G. Clifton. *This New Land* R=6 p. 120

Wyman, Andrea. *Red Sky at Morning* R=6 p. 213

Young, Ronder Thomas. *Learning by Heart* R=5 p. 270

Zei, Aliki. *Petro's War* R=5 p. 45

Zei, Aliki. *The Sound of Dragon's Feet* R=3 p. 29

GRADE 6

Almedingen, E. M. *Anna* R=3 p. 21

Anderson, M. *The Journey of the Shadow Bairns* R=4 p. 86

Angell, Judie. *One-Way to Ansonia* R=4 p. 195

Armstrong, Jennifer. *Steal Away* R=6 p. 149

Avery, Gillian. *A Likely Lad* R=4 p. 86

Avery, Gillian. *Maria Escapes* R=6 p. 86

Avery, Gillian. *Maria's Italian Spring* R=6 p. 24

Avi. *The Fighting Ground* R=4 p. 127

Avi. *The True Confessions of Charlotte Doyle* R=3 p. 141

Bawden, Nina. *Carrie's War* R=4 p. 99

Baylis-White, Mary. *Sheltering Rebecca* R=5 p. 100

Beatty, Patricia. *Turn Homeward, Hannalee* R=6 p. 165

Beatty, P. and P. Robbins. *Eben Tyne, Powdermonkey* R=6 p. 166

Bellairs, John. *The Trolley to Yesterday* R=6 p. 18

Blair, David Nelson. *Fear the Condor* R=4 p. 283

Brennan, J. H. *Shiva* R= 3 p. 7

Brooks, Bruce. *The Moves Make the Man* R= 5 p. 267

Bulla, Clyde Robert. *Pocahontas and the Strangers* R= 3 p. 115

Cleaver, Vera and Bill. *Dust of the Earth* R= 6 p. 252

Cole, Norma. *The Final Tide* R= 3 p. 252

Cole, Sheila. *The Dragon in the Cliff* R= 6 p. 82

Collier and Collier. *Jump Ship to Freedom* R= 5 p. 135

Collier and Collier. *War Comes to Willy Freeman* R= 6 p. 129

Collier and Collier. *Who Is Carrie?* R= 6 p. 136

Conlon-McKenna, Marita. *Wildflower Girl* R= 5 p. 150

Conrad, Pam. *Pedro's Journal* R= 6 p. 279

Cooper, Susan. *Dawn of Fear* R= 6 p. 100

Corbin, William. *Me and the End of the World* R= 7 p. 216

Cormier, Robert. *Other Bells for Us to Ring* R= 6 p. 239

De Angeli, Marguerite. *The Door in the Wall* R=6 p. 62

De Treviño, Elizabeth B. *El Güero* R=6 p. 282

De Treviño, Elizabeth. *Turi's Poppa* R=7 p. 46

Edmonds, Walter. *Bert Breen's Barn* R=5 p. 198

Kittleman, Laurence R. *Canyons Beyond the Sky* R=6 p. 112
Klein, Robin. *All in the Blue Unclouded Weather* R=7 p. 288
Konigsburg, E. *A Proud Taste for Scarlet and Miniver* R=6 p. 63
Lasky, Katherine. *The Night Journey* R=6 p. 206
Lehrman, Robert. *The Store that Mama Built* R=4 p. 219
Levin, Betty. *Brother Moose* R=4 p. 186
Levitin, Sonia. *Annie's Promise* R=4 p. 244
Lisson, Deborah. *The Devil's Own* R=6 p. 285
Litowinsky, Olga. *The High Voyage* R=6 p. 280
Llywelyn, Morgan. *Brian Boru* R=5 p. 53
Lord, Athena. *Z.A., Zoe, & the Musketeers* R=6 p. 245
McCall, Edith. *Better Than a Brother* R=3 p. 206
McGraw, Eloise. *The Striped Ships* R=5 p. 53
Magorian, Michelle. *Good Night, Mr. Tom* R=4 p. 102
Malterre, Elona. *The Last Wolf of Ireland* R=6 p. 80
Marino, Jan. *The Day that Elvis Came to Town* R=2 p. 269
Marvin, Isabel R. *Bridge to Freedom* R=3 p. 38
Matas, Carol. *Daniel's Story* R=3 p. 38
Mills, Claudia. *What About Annie?* R=6 p. 229
Moeri, Louise. *Save Queen of Sheba* R=6 p. 146
Moore, Ruth Nulton. *Distant Thunder* R=6 p. 131
Newman, R. *The Case of the Baker Street Irregular* R=3 p. 93
Nixon, Joan L. *A Family Apart* R=4 p. 159
Nixon, Joan Lowery. *A Place to Belong* R=7 p. 160
O'Dell, Scott. *Island of the Blue Dolphins* R=6 p. 146
O'Dell, Scott. *Zia* R=4 p. 160
Orgel, Doris. *The Devil in Vienna* R=2 p. 40
Orlev, Uri. *The Island on Bird Street* R=3 p. 40
Paterson, Katherine. *The Master Puppeteer* R=3 p. 308
Paton Walsh, Jill. *Fireweed* R=3 p. 103
Pelgrom, Els. *The Winter When Time Was Frozen* R=6 p. 41
Pendergraft, Patricia. *As Far As Mill Springs* R=3 p. 231
Pendergraft, Patricia. *Hear the Wind Blow* R=5 p. 208
Petry, Ann. *Tituba of Salem Village* R=6 p. 119
Pettit, Jayne. *My Name is San Ho* R=7 p. 317
Phillips, Ann. *The Peace Child* R=6 p. 65
Pitt, Nancy. *Beyond the High White Wall* R=3 p. 28

Pope, Elizabeth Marie. *The Perilous Gard* R=6 p. 70
Pople, Maureen. *The Other Side of the Family* R=4 p. 289
Posell, Elsa. *Homecoming* R=6 p. 41
Reboul, Antoine. *Thou Shalt Not Kill* R=6 p. 304
Reeder, Carolyn. *Grandpa's Mountain* R=6 p. 231
Reeder, Carolyn. *Shades of Gray* R=6 p. 172
Ross, Rhea Beth. *The Bet's On, Lizzie Bingman!* R=6 p. 221
Rossiter, Phyllis. *Moxie* R=4 p. 232
Roth-Hano, Renee. *Touch Wood* R=4 p. 42
Rowlands, Avril. *Milk and Honey* R=9 p. 110
Schotter, Roni. *Rhoda, Straight and True* R=4 p. 260
Segal, Jerry. *The Place Where Nobody Stopped* R=6 p. 28
Semel, Nava. *Becoming Gershona* R=5 p. 304
Serraillier, Ian. *The Silver Sword* R=4 p. 43
Sherman, Eileen B. *Independence Avenue* R=6 p. 210
Skurzynski, Gloria. *What Happened in Hamelin* R=4 p. 16
Snyder, Zilpha Keatley. *And Condors Danced* R=6 p. 211
Sonnleitner, A. Th. *The Cave Children* R=6 p. 23
Speare, Elizabeth G. *The Witch of Blackbird Pond* R=6 p. 120
Steele, William O. *The Perilous Road* R=6 p. 173
Sutcliff, Rosemary. *Warrior Scarlet* R=5 p. 9
Trease, Geoffrey. *A Flight of Angels* R=7 p. 71
Uchida, Yoshiko. *Journey Home* R=6 p. 263
Uchida, Yoshiko. *Samurai of Gold Hill* R=4 p. 191
Vander Els, Betty. *The Bomber's Moon* R=3 p. 298
Gray, Elizabeth. *Adam of the Road* R=6 p. 62
Wallace, Bill. *Buffalo Gal* R=5 p. 212
Weitzman, David. *Thrashin' Time* R=7 p. 212
Westall, Robert. *The Kingdom by the Sea* R=3 p. 107
White, Alana. *Come Next Spring* R=5 p. 264
Wibberley, Leonard. *Leopard's Prey* R=6 p. 139
Wilder, Laura Ingalls. *The First Four Years* R=8 p. 193
Wilder, Laura Ingalls. *These Happy Golden Years* R=3 p. 194
Willis, Patricia. *A Place to Claim as Home* R=6 p. 249
Wisler, G. Clifton. *Red Cap* R=4 p. 174
Wisler, G. Clifton. *Thunder on the Tennessee* R=6 p. 174
Wulffson, Don L. *The Upside-Down Ship* R=4 p. 81

GRADE 7

Wyss, Thelma Hatch. *A Stranger Here* R=5 p. 265
Yarbro, Chelsea Quinn. *Floating Illusions* R=7 p. 213
Yarbro, Chelsea Quinn. *Four Horses for Tishtry* R=4 p. 4
Yolen, Jane. *The Devil's Arithmetic* R=5 p. 44

GRADE 8

Aaron, Chester. *Lackawanna* R=4 p. 224
Anderson, Margaret. *The Druid's Gift* R=6 p. 51
Baklanov, Grigory. *Forever Nineteen* R=4 p. 30
Benchley, Nathaniel. *Bright Candles* R=6 p. 30
Berry, James. *Ajeemah and His Son* R=3 p. 282
Bethancourt, T. Ernesto. *The Tommorow Connection* R=2 p. 196
Carter, Peter. *Borderlands* R=6 p. 178
Carter, Peter. *The Gates of Paradise* R=4 p. 75
Carter, Peter. *The Sentinels* R=6 p. 291
Collier and Collier. *The Clock* R=3 p. 135
Collins, Alan. *Jacob's Ladder* R=7 p. 287
Coolidge, Olivia. *Marathon Looks on the Sea* R=6 p. 4
Coolidge, Olivia. *Roman People* R=7 p. 11
Cross, Gillian. *The Great American Elephant Chase* R=4 p. 178
De Jenkins, Lyll. *The Honorable Prison* R=6 p. 283
De Trevino, Elizabeth. *I, Juan de Pareja* R=8 p. 21
Degens, T. *On the Third Ward* R=6 p. 46
Duder, Tessa. *Alex in Rome* R=7 p. 287
Dunlop, Betty. *The Poetry Girl* R=3 p. 288
Fleischman, Paul. *Graven Images* R=6 p. 179
Fleischman, Paul. *Path of the Pale Horse* R=4 p. 136
Fleishman, Paul. *Saturnalia* R=6 p. 117
Forman, James D. *Becca's Story* R=6 p. 167
Forman, James D. *Prince Charlie's Year* R=4 p. 75
Garfield, Leon. *The December Rose* R=8 p. 88
Garfield, Leon. *The Strange Affair of Adelaide Harris* R=8 p. 77

GRADE 9

Aaron, Chester. *Gideon* R=7 p. 30
Alexander, Lloyd. *The Philadelphia Adventure* R=9 p. 175
Blos, Joan. *Brothers of the Heart* R=4 p. 142
Brooks, Jerome. *Naked in Winter* R=7 p. 251
Burton, Hester. *Time of Trial* R=7 p. 74
Clapp, Patricia. *Witches' Children* R=6 p. 116
Coolidge, Olivia. *People in Palestine* R=6 p. 3
DeFord and Stout. *An Enemy Among Them* R=5 p. 129
Dickinson, Peter. *Tulku* R=6 p. 295
Dillon, Eilís. *The Seekers* R=4 p. 117
Durrell, Lawrence. *White Eagles over Serbia* R=6 p. 32
Garland, Sherry. *Song of the Buffalo Boy* R=3 p. 316
Geras, Adele. *The Tower Room* R=5 p. 109
Gregory, Kristiana. *Jenny of the Tetons* R=6 p. 181
Haugaard, Erik. *The Samurai's Tale* R=6 p. 306
Hendry, Diana. *Double Vision* R=7 p. 109
Highwater, Jamake. *Eyes of Darkness* R=8 p. 201
Ho, Minfong. *Rice without Rain* R=5 p. 313
Hotze, Sollace. *A Circle Unbroken* R=4 p. 145
Hunter, Mollie. *The Third Eye* R=6 p. 101
Keith, Harold. *Rifles for Watie* R=7 p. 170
Klein, Robin. *Dresses of Red and Gold* R=8 p. 289
Langenus, Ron. *Mission West* R=4 p. 80
Levoy, Myron. *Alan and Naomi* R=4 p. 244
Lindgard, Joan. *Between Two Worlds* R=3 p. 276
Luhrmann, Winifred Bruce. *Only Brave Tomorrows* R=3 p. 119
Lunn, Janet. *Shadow in Hawthorn Bay* R=6 p. 274
Mattingley, Christobel. *The Miracle Tree* R=6 p. 309
Myers, Walter D. *Fallen Angels* R=3 p. 317
Newth, Mette. *The Abduction* R=7 p. 23
O'Dell, Scott. *The Captive* R=6 p. 280
O'Dell, Scott. *The Dark Canoe* R=7 p. 160
O'Dell, Scott. *The Feathered Serpent* R=7 p. 281

O'Dell, Scott. *The Hawk That Dare Not Hunt by Day* R=5 p. 70
O'Dell, Scott. *My Name Is Not Angelica* R=3 p. 281
O'Dell, Scott. *Sarah Bishop* R=3 p. 131
Paton Walsh, Jill. *Grace* R=6 p. 84
Peyton, K. M. *Flambards* R=5 p. 104
Peyton, K. M. *Flambards in Summer* R=6 p. 104
Peyton, K. M. *The Maplin Bird* R=5 p. 96
Pullman, Phili *The Tiger in the Well* R=4 p. 97
Purtill, Richard. *Enchantment at Delphi* R=7 p. 5
Rinaldi, Ann. *Time Enough for Drums* R=4 p. 132
Sacks, Margaret. *Beyond Safe Boundaries* R=7 p. 292
Smith, Claude Clayton. *The Stratford Devil* R=5 p. 119
Sutcliff, Rosemary. *Bonnie Dundee* R=9 p. 81
Sutcliff, Rosemary. *The Eagle of the Ninth* R=9 p. 13
Taylor, Mildred. *The Road to Memphis* R=3 p. 247
Todd, Leonard. *Squaring Off* R=3 p. 263
Turner, Ann. *Third Girl from the Left* R=4 p. 163
Van Raven, Pieter. *Harpoon Island* R=4 222
Vander Els, Betty. *Leaving Point* R=3 p. 298
Wheeler, Thomas Gerald. *A Fanfare for the Stalwart* R=7 p. 29
Willard, Barbara. *Harrow and Harvest* R=5 p. 72

GRADE 10

Achebe, Chinua. *Things Fall Apart* R=7 p. 291
Bosse, Malcolm J. *Captives of Time* R=5 p. 61
Brooks, Martha. *Two Moons in August* R=3 p. 252
Carter, Peter. *Children of the Book* R=4 p. 21
Clapp, Patricia. *Constance* R=4 p. 116
Dixon, Jeanne. *The Tempered Wind* R=6 p. 253
Ferry, Charles. *One More Time!* R=2 p. 239
Frank, Elizabeth Bales. *Cooder Cutlas* R=3 p. 267
Hotze, Sollace. *Acquainted with the Night* R=3 p. 268

Hunter. Mollie. *Hold On to Love* R=7 p. 101
Hunter, Mollie. *The Stronghold* R=7 p. 12
James, J. Alison. *Sing for a Gentle Rain* R=5 p. 112
Lasky, Katherine. *Beyond the Divide* R=7 p. 156
O'Dell, Scott. *The Amethyst Ring* R=7 p. 280
O'Dell, Scott. *The Road to Damietta* R=6 p. 19
Paterson, Katherine. *Jacob Have I Loved* R=7 p. 245
Paterson, Katherine. *Of Nightingales That Weep* R=8 p. 305
Paterson, Katherine. *Rebels of the Heavenly Kingdom* R=7 p. 295
Paton Walsh, Jill. *A Parcel of Patterns* R=6 p. 80
Peyton, K. M. *The Edge of the Cloud* R=6 p. 104
Rostkowski, Margaret I. *The Best of Friends* R=3 p. 269
Shaw, Margret. *A Wider Tomorrow* R=6 p. 106
Skurzynski, Gloria. *Manwolf* R=6 p. 19
Sutcliff, Rosemary. *The Lantern Bearers* R=7 p. 14
Sutcliff, Rosemary. *The Silver Branch* R=9 p. 14
Terris, Susan. *Nell's Quilt* R=4 p. 211
Voight, Cynthia. *David and Jonathan* R=2 p. 263
Willard, Barbara. *A Cold Wind Blowing* R=4 p. 71
Willard, Barbara. *The Eldest Son* R=6 p. 71
Willard, Barbara. *A Flight of Swans* R=4 p. 72
Willard, Barbara. *The Iron Lily* R=6 p. 72
Willard, Barbara. *The Sprig of Broom* R=7 p. 73

10+

(ADULT BOOKS SUITABLE FOR YOUNG ADULTS)

Anand, Valerie. *The Disputed Crown* R=5 p. 49
Anand, Valerie. *Gildenford* R=4 p. 49
Anand, Valerie. *King of the Wood* R=7 p. 50
Anand, Valerie. *The Norman Pretender* R=6 p. 50
Anand, Valerie. *The Proud Villeins* R=4 p. 50
Attanasio, A. A. *Kingdom of the Grail* R=5 p. 51
Attanasio, A. A. *Wyvern* R=7 p. 285

Peters, Ellis. *The Raven in the Foregate* R=7 p. 57
Peters, Ellis. *The Rose Rent* R=7 p. 57
Peters, Ellis. *St. Peter's Fair* R=7 p. 57
Peters, Ellis. *The Sanctuary Sparrow* R=7 p. 58
Peters, Ellis. *The Summer of the Danes* R=7 p. 58
Peters, Ellis. *The Virgin in the Ice* R=7 p. 58
Raspail, J. *Who Will Remember the People* R=8 p. 284
Renault, Mary. *The Bull from the Sea* R=7 p. 5
Renault, Mary. *Fire from Heaven* R=7 p. 6
Renault, Mary. *The King Must Die* R=8 p. 6
Renault, Mary. *The Last of the Wine* R=8 p. 6
Renault, Mary. *The Mask of Apollo* R=8 p. 7
Renault, Mary. *The Persian Boy* R=6 p. 7
Riley, Judith Merkle. *A Vision of Light* R=6 p. 66
Riley, Judith Merkle. *In Pursuit of the Green Lion* R=5 p. 66
Roberts, Ann V. *Louisa Elliott* R=6 p. 84
Roberts, Ann V. *Morning's Gate* R=6 p. 97
Roesch, Ethel & Paul. *Ashana* R=7 p. 138
Santmyer, Helen H. *And Ladies of the Club* R=9 p. 190
Scott, Paul. *The Day of the Scorpion* R=7 p. 299
Scott, Paul. *A Division of the Spoils* R=7 p. 300
Scott, Paul. *The Jewel in the Crown* R=7 p. 300
Scott, Paul. *The Towers of Silence* R=7 p. 300
Shuler, Linda Lay. *She Who Remembers* R=5 p. 113
Shuler, Linda L. *Voice of the Eagle* R=5 p. 114
Sledge and Sledge. *Empire of Heaven* R=4 p. 294
Thomas, Elizabeth Marshall. *The Animal Wife* R=4 p. 9
Uris, Leon. *Exodus* R=7 p. 304
Uris, Leon. *Trinity* R=8 p. 98
Volk, Toni. *Montana Women* R=6 p. 249
Wiggins, Marianne. *John Dollar* R=7 p. 301
Williams, Jeanne. *The Island Harp* R=5 p. 85
Wolf, Joan. *Daughter of the Red Deer* R=7 p. 10
Yount, John. *Thief of Dreams* R=7 p. 265

APPENDIX C. HIGHLIGHTS OF HISTORY

PREHISTORY BC

40,000	Last Ice Age
28,000	Humans cross landbridge between Asia and North America
20,000	Cave painting flourishes in France and Spain
6000	First date on Egyptian Calendar
4236	Earliest date in Jewish Calendar
3372	First date in Mayan Calendar
3100	First Egyptian dynasty

3000 BC

2780	First pyramid built in Egypt
2500	Knossos founded by Minoans in Crete
	Indus Valley civilization in India
2350	Sumerian empire founded
2000	Bronze Age in northern Europe

2000 BC

1730	Hyksos rule Egypt
1728	Accession of Hammurabi the Great

1400	Knossos destroyed
1379	Accession of Amenhotep IV in Egypt
1361	Accession of Tutankhamun
1304	Accession of Rameses the Great
1122	Chou Dynasty in China
1050	Dorians invade Peloponnesus

1000 BC

994	Teutons move westward to Rhine
814	Carthage founded by Phoenicians
800	Composition of *Iliad* and *Odyssey* by Homer (traditional)
776	First Olympic Games in Greece
753	Romulus and Remus found Rome (traditional)
660	Byzantium founded
559	Cyrus the great founds Persian Empire
551	Birth of Confucius (K'ung Fu-Tzu)
521	Darius I rules Persia
509	Roman Republic founded (traditional)
500	Bantu-speaking peoples spread in East Africa

500 BC

490	Greeks defeat Persians at Marathon
480	Battles of Thermopylae and Salamis
477	Athens starts rise to power
460	Age of Pericles and First Peloponnesian War (to 451)
424	Darius II rules Persia (to 404)
431	Second Peloponnesian War (to 421)
359	Philip II, King of Macedonia (to 336)
336	Alexander III, King of Macedonia (to 323)
c.300	Maya civilization in Yucatan and in Central America
264	First Punic War (to 241)
221	Ch'in Dynasty in China (to 207)
214	Construction of the Great Wall of China
202	Han Dynasty in China (to AD 9)
149	Third Punic War (to 146); Carthage destroyed

100 BC

55   Caesar unsuccessfully invades Britain
51   Caesar completes conquest of Gaul
45   Caesar becomes dictator of Rome
44   Caesar assassinated
37   Herod the Great, King of Judea (to 4)
30   Antony and Cleopatra commit suicide
23   Augustus resigns consulship, becomes Emperor of Rome
 5   Jesus born in Bethlehem

AD

30   Crucifixion of Jesus
37   Caligula, Emperor of Rome (to 41)
54   Nero, Emperor of Rome (to 68)
77   Roman conquest of Britain (to 84)

100 AD

101   Roman Empire increasèd to maximum extent (to 107)

230   Sujin, first known ruler of Japan
250   Emperor worship made compulsory
285   Diocletian splits Roman Empire to rule Eastern Roman Empire
306   Constantine I, Emperor in the East (to 337)
325   Nicaean Creed adopted
330   Constantinople capital of Roman Empire
370   Huns from Asia invade Europe
379   Theodosius I Emperor in East (to 395)
383   Roman legions begin to leave Britain
c.400   Incas established on parts of South American Pacific coast
407   First Mongol Empire (to 553)
410   Goths sack Rome
429   Vandal kingdom in northern Africa (to 535)
451   Attila invades Gaul, and Italy (452)

476   End of Western Roman Empire

493   Theodoric, King of Ostrogoths becomes king of all Italy

500 AD

527   Justinian, Byzantine Emperor (to 565)

552   Buddhism introduced in Japan

570   Muhammad born at Mecca

584   Kingdom of Mercia founded in England

590   Gregory I, the Great, Pope (to 604)

597   St. Augustine lands in England

618   T'ang Dynasty in China (to 907)

620   Vikings begin invading Ireland

632   Death of Muhammad

700 AD

700   Production of the Lindisfarne Gospels in England

702   Arabic made the official language of Egypt

732   Charles Martel defeats Moors at Tours

756   Papal States founded in Italy

771   Charlemagne, King of the Franks (to 814)

782   Revival of learning under Charlemagne and Alcuin of York

787   First Danish invasion of Britain

850   Acropolis of Zimbabwe built

856   Main tide of Viking assaults on England (to 875)

861   Vikings discover Iceland

871   Alfred the Great, King of Wessex (to 899)

891   Founding of the Anglo-Saxon Chronicle, History of England

907   Civil wars in China

932   Wood block printing adopted in China for mass-producing books

939   Civil wars in Japan

981   Eric the Red settles in Greenland

995   Golden Age of the arts in Japan (to 1028)

999   Bagauda, first King of Kano

1000 AD

1002   Leif Ericsson explores North American coast
1016   Danes rule England (10 1042)
1019   Canute (Cnut) marries Emma of Normandy
1021   Caliph al-Hakim founds Druse sect
1046   Harold Haardraada, King of Norway (to 1066)
1052   Edward the Confessor founds Westminster Abbey, near London
1053   Death of Godwin in England; his son Harold succeeds him
1054   Eastern Church independent of Rome
1066   Battle of Hastings and succession of William of Normandy to
        King of England
1077   Almoravid Dynasty in Ghana (to 1087)
1086   Domesday Book is completed in England
1096   First Crusade

1100 AD

1147   Second Crusade (to 1149)
1151   End of Toltex Empire in Mexico
1152   Frederick I, Holy Roman Emperor (to 1190)
        Eleanor of Aquitaine annulled from marriage to Louis VII and
        married to Henry of Anjou (Henry II of England)
1156   Civil wars in Japan
1161   Explosives used in battle in China
1171   Henry II annexes Ireland
1182   Philip II of France banishes the Jews
1189   Third Crusade (to 1192)
        Richard the Lion-Hearted to King of England (1199)
1199   John Lackland (son of Henry II and Eleanor), King of England
        (to 1216)

1200 AD

1202   Fourth Crusade (to 1204)
1206   Temujin proclaimed Genghis Khan
1209   Cambridge University founded in England
1210   Mongols begin invasion of China

1215   Magna Carta
1217   Fifth Crusade, against Egypt (to 1222) fails
1228   Sixth Crusade (to 1229) reconquers Jerusalem
       Teutonic Knights begin conquering Prussia
1232   Earliest known use of rockets in war between the Mongols and
       the Chinese
1235   Sundiata Keita, King of Mali (to 1255)
1236   Alexander Nevski, Prince of Novgorod (Russia, to 1263)
1240   End of Empire of Ghana
1241   Mongols withdraw from Europe
1243   Egyptians recapture Jerusalem for Christians
1248   Seventh Crusade (to 1270) led by Louis IX of France
1260   Kublai elected Khan (to 1294)
1265   De Montfort's Parliament in England and Battle of Evesham
1271   Marco Polo visits Kublai Khan (stays to 1295)
1283   Edward I annexes Wales to England by defeating and killing
       Llewellyn, Prince of Wales
1290   Succession struggle in Scotland after death of Margaret, Maid
        of Norway
       Edward I expels all Jews from England
1291   Saracens capture Acre from Christians
1295   Model Parliament of Edward I in England

1300 AD

1305   Papal See removed to Avignon (to 1378)
1306   Philip IV expels Jews from France
1306   Robert the Bruce, King of Scotland (to 1329)
1314   Battle of Bannockburn frees Scots from English
1316   Search for Prester John in Ethiopia
1325   Aztecs found Tenochtitlán where Mexico City now stands
1338   Hundred Years' War (to 1453)
1344   First known reference to Hanseatic League
1346   Edward III defeats Philip VI at Crécy in France
1348   Black Death ravages Europe (to 1351)
1349   Persecution of the Jews in Germany
1363   Tamerlane begins conquest of Asia

1368   Ming Dynasty in China (to 1644)

1377   The Great Schism (to 1417), rival popes elected

1400 AD

1400   Richard II murdered

        Henry V of England invades and defeats France at Agincourt

1431   Jeanne d'Arc burned as a witch

1438   Inca Empire established in Peru

1453   Fall of Constantinople, end of the Hundred Years' War and the Middle Ages

1454   Printing by movable type perfected

1455   Wars of the Roses in England (to 1485)

1482   Portuguese settle Gold Coast of Africa

1485   End of England's War of Roses with defeat of Richard III at Bosworth Field and succession of Lancastrian Henry VII

1486   Henry VII of England marries Elizabeth of York, uniting the houses of Lancaster and York

1488   Diaz rounds Cape of Good Hope

1492   Christopher Columbus discovers the West Indies

1497   Jews expelled from Portugal

1498   Vasco da Gama reaches India

        Columbus discovers Trinidad and South America

1500 AD

1500   Cabral claims Brazil for Portugal

1502   Columbus discovers Nicaragua

1513   Balboa discovers Pacific Ocean

1519   Charles V, Holy Roman Emperor (to 1556)

1521   Diet of Worms

        Hernán Cortés conquers Tenochtitlán

1522   Magellan's expedition circles the world

1533   Ivan IV rules Russia (to 1584)

        Francisco Pizarro conquers Peru

1535   Jacques Cartier navigates St. Lawrence River

1541   Hernando de Soto discovers Mississippi River

1545   Council of Trent
1561   Mary Queen of Scots returns to Scotland
1562   Religious wars in France (to 1598)
1567   Portuguese settle at Rio de Janeiro
1568   Netherlands begins revolt against Spain
1571   Bornu Empire in Sudan reaches greatest height (to 1603)
1577   Francis Drake sails around the world (to 1580)
1582   Introduction of the Gregorian Calendar
1588   Defeat of the Spanish Armada
1595   First Dutch settlements on Guinea Coast
1598   Edict of Nantes equates Catholics and Hugenots in France

1600 AD

1603   Death of England's Elizabeth I and succession of James I
         (to 1625)
1604   French East India Company founded
1605   Gunpowder Plot discovered in England
1606   William Jansz sights Australia
1607   English found colony of Virginia
         Henry Hudson explores in Canada
1608   Champlain founds settlement of Quebec
1618   Thirty Years' War (to 1648)
1619   First African slaves arrive in Virginia
1620   Pilgrims reach Cape Cod and found New Plymouth
1626   Dutch found New Amsterdam
1642   Montreal founded by the French
         Civil War in England
         Abel Tasman discovers Van Diemen's Land (now Tasmania)
1649   Charles I of England executed
         Serfdom established in Russia
1652   Capetown founded by the Dutch
1655   England seizes Jamaica from Spain
1660   Charles II regains England's throne
1664   England seizes New Amsterdam and changes name to New York
1665   Great Plague in London
1666   Great Fire of London

1669   Hindu religion prohibited by Emperor of India
1676   Sikh uprising in India (to 1678)
1683   Siege of Vienna by Turkish forces
1689   Peter I, Tsar of Russia (to 1725)
1692   Salem witchcraft trials in New England

1700 AD

1745   British capture Louisburg, French fortress in Canada
1755   French and Indian War (to 1763)
1765   Stamp Act in American colonies
1770   Boston Massacre
1773   Boston Tea Party
1757   British rule established in India
1759   Battle of Quebec gives Britain control of Canada
1762   Catherine II, Tsarina of Russia (to 1796)
1768   James Cook explores Australia and New Zealand
1774   First Continental Congress meets
1775   American colonies declare war against Britain (to 1883)
1776   Declaration of Independence
1778   France joins Americans in war against Britain
1781   Cornwallis surrenders at Yorktown
1783   India Act gives Britain control of India
1787   Rice riots in Edo, Japan
1788   First convicts transported from Britain to Australia
1789   French Revolution begins
1792   China invades Nepal
        Denmark the first country to prohibit slave trade
1793   First free settlers arrive in Australia
1794   Qajar Dynasty in Persia (to 1925)

1800 AD

1800   Russia annexes Georgia
1801   Act of Unio creates United Kingdom
1803   Louisiana Purchase, Ohio 17th state
1804   Lewis and Clark explore northwestern United States

1804   Napoleon Bonaparte crowns himself Emperor of France

1805   Christian literature forbidden in China

1807   Slave trade abolished in the British Empire

1811   Luddite riots in England

1812   Britain and United States at war over shipping and territory (to 1814)

1815   Napoleon defeated at the Battle of Waterloo
         France prohibits slave trade

1818   Zulu empire founded in South Africa

1819   Spain cedes Florida to the United States

1820   Missouri Compromise
         American missionaries reach Hawaii

1833   Slavery abolished in the British colonies

1836   Texas becomes independent from Mexico

1838   Boers defeat Zulus in Natal

1839   Opium War between Britain and China

1840   Upper and Lower Canada united

1842   Hong Kong ceded to Britain
         British defeat Boers

1843   First Maori War (to 1848)

1846   Irish potato famine at its worst
         United States-Mexico war (to 1848)

1848   California gold rush begins
         Year of revolutions in Europe

1850 AD

1850   T'ai P'ing Revolt against Manchu Dynasty in China (to 1864)

1851   Gold rush in Australia

1853   David Livingston crosses Africa (to 1856)

1854   Commercial treaty between Japan and the United States
         Crimean War (to 1856)

1861   Abraham Lincoln becomes President of the United States
         American Civil War begins (to 1865)
         Gold Rush in New Zealand

1862   Bismarck becomes Prussian prime minister

1863   Battle of Gettysburg in American Civil War

1867   United States purchases Alaska from Russia

1867   Dominion of Canada formed

1868   Meiji Period in Japan (to 1912)

1869   Suez Canal opened

1871   German Empire formed with William I as Emperor

1873   Second Ashanti War (to 1874)

1876   Battle of Little Big Horn

       Korea starts trading with Japan

1879   Zulu War

       Irish Land League Formed by Irish MP Charles Stewart
Parnell

1880   Boer Uprising (to 1881)

1881   Peace declared between New Zealand settlers and Maoris

1882   Triple Alliance of Germany, Austria, and Italy (to 1914)

1890   Zansibar becomes British protectorate

1893   Ivory Coast becomes French protectorate

1894   China and Japan at war

1895   Rhodesia founded by Cecil Rhodes

1897   Greece and Turkey at war

1898   Spain and United States at war

       Social Democratic Party founded in Russia

1899   Second Boer War (to 1902)

1900 AD

1900   Britain conquers norther Nigeria

       Boxer Rebellion in China

1901   Commonwealth of Australia established

1904   Outbreak of Russo-Japanese War (to 1905)

1907   Dominion of New Zealand established

1908   Belgian Congo founded

1909   Union of South Africa formed

       American Robert Peary reaches North Pole

1910   Japan annexes Korea

1911   Revolution in Mexico

1911   Norwegian Roald Amundsen reaches South Pole

1912   Balkan Wars (to 1913)
1914   World War I (to 1918)
1916   Easter Rising in Ireland
1917   United States enters World War I
        Russian Revolution
1918   Revolution in Germany
1919   League of Nations formed

1920   Jewish state of Palestine established
1922   Egypt becomes independent
1923   Italy becomes a Fascist State
1924   New government in China under Sun Yat-sen
1926   General strike in Britain
1927   Civil War in China
        Charles Lindbergh makes first solo transatlantic flight
1929   Wall Street stock market crash

1931   Japanese occupy Manchuria
1933   Soviet Communist Party purged
1934   Mao Tse-tung's Long March (to 1935)
        Adolf Hitler becomes Führer of Germany (to 1945)
1936   Abdication of Edward VIII
        Spanish Civil War (to 1939)
        Italy annexes Ethiopia
1937   Japanese capture Shanghai and Peking
1938   Germany annexes Austria
1939   World War II (to 1945)
        Nazi-Soviet Pact

1940   Japanese join Axis
        The Battle of Britain
1941   United States enters World War II after bombing of Pearl Harbor
        Germany invades Russia
1943   Revolution in Argentina led by Juan Peron
1944   Normandy Landings D-Day
1945   Atomic bombs dropped on Hiroshima and Nagasaki in Japan
1945   United Nations formed

1946   Civil war in Indochina between nationalists and French
         Nuremberg Trials
1947   Marshall Plan for economic recovery in Europe
         Partition of Palestine
1948   War between Arab League and Israel
         Mahatma Gandhi assassinated
         North Atlantic Treaty Organization (NATO) formed
         Soviet Blockade of West Berlin (to 1949)
1949   Communist regime in China
         Apartheid policy in South Africa

1950 AD

1950   Joseph McCarthy's enquiries into "un-American" activities
         Korean War (to 1953)
1951   Pacific Security Treaty signed
1952   First national election in India
         Mau Mau rebellion in Kenya
1954   French lose battle of Dien Bien Phu; Vietnam partitioned
         South East Asia Treat Organization formed
1955   Warsaw Pact formed in opposition to NATO
         Rebellion in Argentina
         Fighting in Israel
1956   Israeli troops invade Egypt
         Soviet troops crush Hungarian uprising
1957   Race riots in southern United States
         First Soviet and United States artificial satellites
1959   Uprising in Tibet
         Communist revolt in Cuba under Fidel Castro

1960 AD

1960   Seventeen African states become independent in Civil war in
         Congo
1961   Berlin Wall built
         South Africa becomes a republic
1962   Cuban missile crisis in United States

1963   United States President John F. Kennedy assassinated
        Nuclear Test Ban Treaty
        Organization of African Unity formed
1964   Civil Rights Bill in United States
1965   Fighting breaks out in Cyprus
        Rhodesia's unilateral declaration of independence
        India and Pakistan at war
        United States sends troops to Vietnam
1966   China's "Cultural Revolution" (to 1968)
1967   Military coup in Greece
        Six-day war between Arabs and Israel
        Civil War in Nigeria (to 1970)
1968   Soviet troops invade Czechoslovakia
        Martin Luther King and Robert Kennedy assassinated in United
        States
        Crisis in Northern Ireland
1969   United States astronauts land on the moon

1970 AD

1970   United States invades Cambodia
1971   East Pakistan becomes independent as Bangladesh after civil war
1973   United States withdraws from Vietnam
        October War between Arab states and Israel
        Military coup in Chile
1974   Military coup in Portugal
        Angola and Mozambique gain independence
        United States President Richard Nixon resigns after Watergate
        scandal
1975   South Vietnam surrenders to North Vietnam, end of war
        Franco of Spain dies
1979   Shah is expelled from Iran
        Russian forces move into Afghanistan
        General Amin flees from Uganda
1980   President Tito of Yugoslavia dies

APPENDIX D. WORKS WITH PROTAGONISTS OR PLOTS CONCERNING MINORITY GROUPS

African American, Asian American, Disabled, Hispanic American, Immigrants, Jewish American, Jewish Protagonists in Europe and the British Isles, and Native American

AFRICAN AMERICAN

(or African Descent)

Bethancourt, T. E. *The Tommorow Connection* (1890-1913) p. 196

Blos, Joan. *A Gathering of Days* (1815-1845) p. 141

Brooks, Bruce. *The Moves Make the Man* (1961 and After) p. 267

Clapp, Patricia. *Witches' Children* (1600-1699) p. 116

Collier, C. and J. *Jump Ship to Freedom* (1784-1814) p. 135

Collier, C. and J. *War Comes to Willy Freeman* (1775-1783) p. 129

Collier, C. and J. *Who Is Carrie?* (1784-1814) p. 136

Crews, Donald. *Bigmama's* (1914-1929) p. 217

Doctorow, E. L. *Ragtime* (1890-1913) p. 198

Edwards, Pat. *Little John and Plutie* (1890-1913) p. 198

Foster, Cecil. *No Man in the House* (1900 and After) p. 284

Fox, Paula. *The Slave Dancer* (1815-1845) p. 143

Fritz, Jean. *Brady* (1815-1845) p. 144

Gee, Maurice. *The Champion* (1900 and After) p. 288

Hamilton, Virginia. *The Bells of Christmas* (1890-1913) p. 200

Hamilton, Virginia. *Drylongso* (1961 and After) p. 267

Hamilton, Virginia. *The House of Dies Drear* (1846-1860) p. 153

Hansen, Joyce. *Out From This Place* (1861-1865) p. 167

Hansen, Joyce. *Which Way Freedom?* (1861-1865) p. 168

Higginsen, Vy, with Tonya Bolder. *Mama, I Want to Sing* (1946-1960) p. 254

Holland, Cecelia. *Pacific Street* (1846-1860) p. 154

Holmes, Mary Z. *See You in Heaven* (1815-1845) p. 144

Hoobler, D. and T. *Next Stop, Freedom* (1846-1860) p. 154

Hooks, William H. *Circle of Fire* (1930-1940) p. 227

Hooks, William H. *The Ballad of Belle Dorcas* (1815-1845) p. 145

Hopkinson, Deborah. *Sweet Clara and the Freedom Quilt* (1846-1860) p. 154

Howard, Ellen. *When Daylight Comes* (1600-1799) p. 281

Hurmence, Brenda. *A Girl Called Boy* (1846-1860) p. 155

Hurmence, Brenda. *Tancy* (1866-1889) p. 184

Irwin, Hadley. *I Be Somebody* (1890-1913) p. 203

Lyons, Mary E. *Letters from a Slave Girl* (1784-1814) p. 137

Marino, Jan. *The Day that Elvis Came to Town* (1961 and After) p. 269

Mitchell, Margaree K. *Uncle Jed's Barbershop* (1914-1929) p. 220

Monjo, F. N. *The Drinking Gourd* (1815-1845) p. 146

ASIAN AMERICAN

Coerr, Eleanor. *Chang's Paper Pony* (1846-1860) p. 150

Garrigue, S. *The Eternal Spring of Mr. Ito* (1933 and After) p. 275

Howard, Ellen. *Her Own Song* (1890-1913) p. 203

Irwin, Hadley. *Kim/Kimi* (1941-1945) p. 243

Kadohata, Cynthia. *The Floating World* (1946-1960) p. 255

Kogawa, Joy. *Naomi's Road* (1933 and After) p. 276

Kudlinski, Kathleen. *Pearl Harbor is Burning!* (1941-1945) p. 243

Lee, Gus. *China Boy* (1946-1960) p. 256

Pettit, Jayne. *My Name is San Ho* (1900 and After) p. 317

Savin, Marcia. *The Moon Bridge* (1941-1945) p. 247

Say, Allen. *Grandfather's Journey* (1900 and After) p. 309

Snyder, Zilpha Keatley. *And Condors Danced* (1890-1913) p. 211

Surat, M. M. *Angel Child, Dragon Child* (1961 and After) p. 270

Thesman, Jean. *Molly Donnelly* (1941-1945) p. 248

Uchida, Yoshiko. *The Best Bad Thing* (1930-1940) p. 235

Uchida, Yoshiko. *The Bracelet* (1941-1945) p. 248

Uchida, Yoshiko. *The Happiest Ending* (1930-1940) p. 235

Uchida, Yoshiko. *A Jar of Dreams* (1930-1940) p. 235

Uchida, Yoshiko. *Journey Home* (1946-1960) p. 263

Uchida, Yoshiko. *Journey to Topaz* (1941-1945) p. 249

Uchida, Yoshiko. *Samurai of Gold Hill* (1866-1889) p. 191

Yep, Laurence. *Dragon's Gate* (1861-1865) p. 174

Yep, Laurence. *Dragonwings* (1890-1913) p. 213

Yep, Laurence. *Mountain Light* (1800-1899) p. 296

Yep, Laurence. *The Star Fisher* (1914-1929) p. 223

DISABLED

Clifford, Eth. *The Man Who Sang in the Dark* (1914-1929) p. 216
De Angeli, Marguerite. *The Door in the Wall* (1200-1491) p. 62
Dixon, Jeanne. *The Tempered Wind* (1946-1960) p. 253
Hall, Lynn. *Halsey's Pride* (1946-1960) p. 254
Hooks, William H. *A Flight of Dazzle Angels* (1890-1913) p. 201
Howard, Ellen. *Edith Herself* (1890-1913) p. 202
Little, Jean. *From Anna* (1933 and After) p. 277
McKenzie, Ellen Kindt. *Stargone John* (1890-1913) p. 209
Riskind, Mary. *Apple Is My Sign* (1890-1913) p. 206
Sanders, Scott R. *Bad Man Ballad* (1784-1814) p. 139
Whelan, Gloria. *Hannah* (1866-1889) p. 192
Yolen, Jane. *The Seeing Stick* (Before 1800) p. 294

HISPANIC AMERICAN

Anderson, J. *Spanish Pioneers of the Southwest* (1700-1774)
    p. 121
de Treviño, Elizabeth B. *El Güero* (1800-1899) p. 282
Howard, Elizabeth F. *Chita's Christmas Tree* (1890-1913) p. 202
Martinello and Nesmith. *With Domingo Leal in San Antonio 1734*
    (1700-1774) p. 123

IMMIGRANTS

Cech, John. *My Grandmother's Journey* (1919-1945) p. 31

Conlon-McKenna, Marita. *Wildflower Girl* (1846-1860) p. 150

Dionetti, Michelle. *Coal Mine Peaches* (1890-1913) p. 198

Doctorow, E. L. *Ragtime* (1890-1913) p. 198

Geras, Adèle. *Voyage* (1790-1918) p. 25

Goldin, Barbara Diamond. *Fire!* (1890-1913) p. 199

Gurasich, Marj. *Letters to Oma* (1846-1860) p. 153

Harvey, Brett. *Immigrant Girl* (1890-1913) p. 201

Herman, C. *The House on Walenska Street* (1790-1918) p. 26

Hesse, Karen. *Letters from Rifka* (1790-1918) p. 26

Hotze, Sollace. *Summer Endings* (1941-1945) p. 242

Kroll, Steven. *Mary McLean and the St. Patrick's Day Parade* (1846-1860) p. 156

Lasky, Katherine. *The Night Journey* (1890-1913) p. 205

Leighton, Maxinne. *An Ellis Island Christmas* (1890-1913) p.205

Lelchuk, Alan. *On Home Ground* (1946-1960) p. 256

Levitin, Sonia. *Journey to America* (1919-1945) p. 37

Lindgard, Joan. *Between Two Worlds* (1933 and After) p. 276

Lindgard, Joan. *Tug of War* (1933 and After) p. 277

Lord, Athena. *The Luck of Z.A.P. and Zoe* (1930-1940) p. 228

Lord, A. *Today's Special: Z.A.P. and Zoe* (1930-1940) p. 229

Lord, Athena. *Z.A.P., Zoe, & the Musketeers* (1941-1945) p. 245

McDonald, Megan. *The Potato Man* (1914-1929) p. 219

Mayerson, Evelyn Wilde. *The Cat Who Escaped from Steerage* (1890-1913) p. 207

Morpurgo, Michael. *Twist of Gold* (1846-1860) p. 157

Pellowski, Anne. *First Farm in the Valley* (1890-1913) p. 208

Pettit, Jayne. *My Name is San Ho* (1900 and After) p. 317

Sandin, Joan. *The Long Way to a New Land* (1866-1889) p. 190

Sandin, Joan. *The Long Way Westward* (1866-1889) p. 190

Skurzynski, Gloria. *Good-bye, Billy Radish* (1914-1929) p. 222

Winter, Jeanette. *Klara's New World* (1790-1918) p. 29

Wisler, G. Clifton. *This New Land* (1700-1774) p. 120

JEWISH AMERICAN

JEWISH PROTAGONISTS IN EUROPE AND THE BRITISH ISLES

NATIVE AMERICAN

APPENDIX E. FAMOUS GROUPS AND PEOPLE IN THE WORKS

A

ADAMS, JOHN. (1735-1826). He was the second president of the United States, married to Abigail. He served in France and England and retired to Braintree (now Quincy), Massachusetts. See *The Fifth of March* and *Jefferson: A Novel*.

ALEUTS. This native of the Aleutian Islands and the western portion of the Alaska peninsula appeared as early as 2000 BC. They are similar in appearance to Siberians and are great hunters who used kayaks to gather sea otters, whales, seal lions, seals, and walrus. See *Island of the Blue Dolphins*.

ALEXANDER III (THE GREAT). (356-323 BC). Before becoming the king of Macedonia, he was tutored by Aristotle in Athens. He defeated Darius III and founded Alexandria. He married Roxana. He also attempted to integrate subject peoples, especially the Persians, into the government and army. He died of a fever in Babylon. See *Fire from Heaven*, *The Mask of Apollo*, and *The Persian Boy*.

ALEXANDER III OF SCOTLAND. (1241-1286). This king united Isle of Man and Hebrides with Scotland and he defeated the Norwegian invasion of Haakon V as well as assisted Henry III against the barons. He designated his granddaughter Margaret, the Maid of Norway, as his heir, but she died en route to England. See *Quest for a Maid.*

ALFRED OF WESSEX. (849-899). In 871, he succeeded his brother Aethelred as King of Wessex. He defeated the second invasion of the Danes led by Guthrum in Wiltshire in 878 and captured London in 886. After receiving the submission of the Angles and Saxons, he became the sovereign of all England not under Danish rule. See *The Namesake.*

ALGONKIN. This diversified group of Indian tribes, including the Arapahoe and the Blackfeet, throughout the United States has a common linguistic link. Indian leaders speaking variants of Algonquian such as King Philip, Powhatan, Tecumseh, and Pontiac, played prominent roles in American colonial history. These tribes taught white settlers how to use the birch bark canoe, how to hunt buffalo, the importance of maize, the taste of maple syrup, and much else. See *Centennial, Dawn Rider, Red Pawns,* and *Sweetgrass.*

ALLECTUS. He murdered Marcus Aurelius Carausius in 293 and succeeded him as self-proclaimed emperor of Britain for three years. See *The Silver Branch.*

AMBROSIUS. Various authors see Ambrosius differently. According to Nennius, he was a child without a father who revealed to the British legendary king Vortigern why the fortress he was building to hold back the Saxons disintegrated each night. Geoffrey of Monmouth combines Ambrosius with Merlin explaining that his father was a spirit. See *The Lantern Bearers.*

AMENOMHET I. (1991-62 BC). In the twelfth dynasty which he founded, he reunified Egypt and strengthened Amon worship. See *The Ship That Flew.*

AMISH. This conservative body of Mennonites, characterized particularly by its dress and non-conformed way of life, exists mainly in Lancaster county, Pennsylvania; Holmes county, Ohio; and Lagrange and Elkhart counties, Indiana. See *Beyond the Divide.*

ANASAZI. From the Navaho meaning "ancient ones," this prehistoric culture of prehistoric inhabited of the region where Arizona, Colorado, New Mexico, and Utah meet. The earliest remains come from Durango, Colorado, with a tree-ring date of AD 46. They lived in pueblos with semisubterranean ceremonial structures called kivas, black-on-white painted pottery, gray utility pottery, and a type of artificial head shaping which flattens the upper part of the back of the head. They were farmers who established special techniques for conserving and using scarce water resources. The dry climate has preserved cloth, basketry, wood, feather, fur, and desiccated bodies. See *The Rainmakers, She Who Remembers, Sing for a Gentle Rain,* and *Voice of the Eagles*.

ANDROS, SIR EDMUND. (1637-1714). As British colonial governor of the "Dominion of New England" including New England colonies, New York, and New Jersey, in 1686, he interfered with colonists' rights and customs. They revolted and imprisoned him. When he was tried in England, he was not charged. He returned to govern Virginia in 1692 and Maryland in 1693. See *Cromwell's Boy*.

ANGLE. This Germanic tribe, also called Anglo, came from an area, probably Schleswig on the European continent, to invade England in the 5th century. See *The Namesake*.

ANNA IVANOVA. (1693-1740). Being the daughter of Ivan V and niece of Peter the Great allowed her succession to Empress of Russia. During her repressive regime, she abolished rights and made certain that her successor would be her great nephew, IVAN VI. See *The Crimson Oak*.

APACHE. This term denotes six culturally related Indian tribes in southwestern North America. The family lives with the wife's relatives with children belonging to the clan of the mother. Tribes in this group are the Western Apache, the Chiricahua, the Mescalero, the Jicarilla, the Lipan, and the Kiowa Apache. See *Sing Down the Moon* and *White Captives*.

ARISTOTLE. (384-322 BC). As a Greek philosopher, he tutored Alexander the Great and taught in Athens. He is considered one of the great thinkers of history and a principle shaper of Western rationalism and scientific spirit. See *Fire from Heaven*.

ARNOLD, BENEDICT. (1741-1801). After repulsing the British in various battles including Mohawk Valley in 1777, he was court-martialed in 1779 but only reprimanded for financial irregularities during his Philadelphia command. He began corresponding with the British after taking command at West Point. He arranged to surrender West Point to the British, but his plot was detected. Working for the British, he led raids in Virginia and Connecticut, but went to England in 1781 where he spent the rest of his life, disgraced and poor. See *My Brother Sam Is Dead* and *Treegate's Raiders*.

ARTHUR. (c. 500). Traditionally, he was king of the Britons who instituted the Knights of the Roundtable. He is believed to have defeated the Saxons and to have died at the Battle of Camlan (537). See *The Cargo of the Madalena* and *The Sword in the Tree*.

AZTEC. A Mexican civilization, they founded their capital, Tenochtitlán, in 1325, where Mexico City now stands. They had a religion which required many sacrifices and fought wars to obtain prisoners for those sacrifices. They were excellent architects and evolved a system of picture writing. See *The Feathered Serpent* and *White Hare's Horses*.

ASSISI, ST. FRANCIS OF. (1181?-1226). Founder of the Franciscan order, he dedicated himself to poverty and religion in 1205 and began to preach in 1208. He founded Poor Clares, an order for women, in 1212. He led movements to reform the Church before he retired to a mountain retreat. Pope Gregory IX canonized him in 1228. See *The Road to Damietta*.

ATAHUALPA. (c. 1502-1533). As the last Inca king of Peru, he disputed the succession with his brother after their father's death by deposing him. Pizarro arrested him in 1532 when he refused to become a Christian. Later he was executed for the probable murder of his brother. See *The Road to Damietta*.

ATTRIBATES [ATTREBATES]. This British tribe lived near the River Thames to the west of London although their influence probably went south at least to Atrebatum, now called Silchester. See *Sun Horse, Moon Horse*.

B

BAEDECKER. The German Karl Baedecker began publishing his travel guides in 1829 with a guide to Coblenz. Other handbooks followed in German, French, and English, for many countries. They have been revised and are currently available. See *The Exeter Blitz*.

BENEDICTINE. This label applies to the main body of monks who wear the black habit and are descendants of the traditional monasticism of early medieval Italy and Gaul. They take their name from St. Benedict of Nursia (c.480-c.457) although the name was not adopted until the late fourteenth century. See *Pangur Ban* and all of the titles of Ellis Peters in "Europe and Great Britain: 476-1199".

BEOTHUK. This Indian tribe, living in Newfoundland, were hunters and canoemen. Their habit of rubbing red ochre over their bodies might be the origin of the term "red" for Native American. The last known Beothuk died in 1829. See *Blood Red Ochre*.

BLACK SHIRTS. This designates members of fascist party organizations wearing a uniform with a black shirt. See *Wildcat Under Glass*.

BLAKE, WILLIAM. (1757-1827). As an engraver, this English poet used the new process of printing from etched copper plates for his own poems and then hand-illustrated and colored them. Many of his writings explored mystical and metaphysical concepts. See *The Gates of Paradise*.

BAGOAS. (c. 350 BC). As a Persian courtier, soldier, and eunuch, he helped place Darius III on the throne. Darius may have murdered him when Bagoas failed to murder him. See *The Persian Boy*.

BONAPARTE, NAPOLEON See NAPOLEON I

BONNIE PRINCE CHARLIE. See CHARLES EDWARD.

BOYS' HOUSE. When British tribal boys reached the age of nine, they began their warrior training in the Boys' House. There they spent seven years learning all of the skills they needed to know to help their families survive including killing a wolf single-handedly. See *Warrior Scarlet* and *The Eagle of the Ninth*.

BRIGANTES. This northern British tribe inhabited the country from the Humber estuary on the east and the Mersey to the west on northward to the Antoine wall. Their chief town was Isurium (Aldborough) and later Eburacum (York). The Romans first defeated them during Claudius' reign c. 50 A.D., but they were not subdued until c. 155 when Antoninus Pius ruled. See *The Silver Branch*.

C

CADWALADER. (d. 1172). As a Welsh prince, he conquered several towns. Owain expelled him from Wales, and he returned with an army of Irish Danes but made peace before battle. Henry II restored his lands in 1157. See *Ride to Danger*.

CAESAR, JULIUS. (100-44 BC). A Roman general and statesman, he identified himself with the popular party in Rome and became a chief rival of Sulla. He made his military reputation in Gaul, subduing revolt under Vercinqteroix. He wrote works on the Gallic wars and reformed the calendar to the Julian calendar. See *The Druids* and *Fortune's Favorites*.

CANUTE (CNUT). (d. 1035). He was both king of Denmark and of England in 1017. He married Emma of Normandy, widow of King Aethelred. As an able, just, and popular ruler, he strongly supported the church. See *Gildenford*.

CAPTAIN AHAB. In Herman Melville's *Moby Dick*, this complex one-legged character spent the later part of his life trying to conquer the White Whale, Moby Dick. See *The Dark Canoe*.

CARAUSIAS, MARCUS AURELIUS. (d. 293). As a Roman general serving Emperor Maximian, he fought rebelling Gauls in 286. As commander of a fleet at Boulogne, fighting Frankish and Saxon pirates, he took much plunder. In 286, he decided to declare himself emperor in Britain, defeating Maximian's fleet in 289 but was murdered by one of his ministers, Allectus. See *The Silver Branch*.

CARSON, KIT. (1809-1868). An American trapper, scout, and Indian agent, he raised and commanded the 1st New Mexico volunteers against Indians during the Civil War. See *The Bear Flag* and *Message from the Mountains*.

CATHERINE II OF RUSSIA. (1729-1796). Called Catherine the Great, she became Empress in 1762. Married to Peter, the nephew of the Empress Elizabeth, she deposed him soon after his accession with the help of her paramour Grigory Orlov. Although serfdom and misery increased during her reign, she extended the frontiers of her empire with large conquests. She also secularized the property of the clergy. See *Anna*.

CAXTON, WILLIAM. (C. 1422-1491). After learning printing in Cologne, he returned to England and established the first English press at Westminster in 1476. He printed his own translations as well as such texts as Mallory's *Morte d'Arthur* in 1485. See *The Cargo of the Madalena* and *The Writing on the Hearth*.

CECIL, ROBERT. (1563-1612). He succeeded his father William as Elizabeth I's adviser. As her secretary of state, he secured the succession to the throne for James VI of Scotland as James I of England. He also led her secret service. See *Death of the Fox* and *The Succession*.

CHARLEMAGNE. (742-814). King of the Franks, known as The Great, he fought with, defeated, and converted the Saxons. He also founded schools and is known for his close friendship with Roland in legend. The end of his conquests is the beginning of the Holy Roman Empire. See *Two Travelers*.

CHARLES I OF ENGLAND. (1600-1649). After enraging British commoners by disbanding Parliament and fighting many expensive battles, he declared war on the Parliamentarians at Nottingham in 1642. After finally losing at Naseby in 1645, he was eventually condemned to death and beheaded at Whitehall. See *Circle of Pearls* and *Mission West*.

CHARLES I OF SPAIN. (1500-1558). Son of Philip I of Castile and grandson of Ferdinand and Isabella, he served as king from 1516 to 1556 and as Holy Roman Emperor from 1519 to 1556. In addition to accomplishments on the European continent, he extended New World possessions with conquests of Mexico by Cort and of Peru by Pizarro. Before his death, he abdicated and retired to a monastery. See *The Amethyst Ring*.

CHARLES II OF ENGLAND. (1630-1685). After trying to save the life of his father, CHARLES I, he made promises allowing his restoration as King in 1660. He was forced to drive Catholics from office and to consent to the marriage of his niece Princess Mary to William of Orange. He died with no legitimate heir. See *Cromwell's Boy.*

CHARLES X OF FRANCE. (1757-1836). He tried to restore absolutism by dissolving the Chamber of Deputies, terminating freedom of the press, and having a new method of elections. He was overthrown in the ensuing revolution in July 1830. After naming Louis-Philippe the lieutenant general, he abdicated and fled to England. See *The Giraffe that Walked to Paris.*

CHARLES EDWARD. (1720-1788). His nicknames included the Young Pretender, the Young Chevalier, and Bonnie Prince Charlie. As grandson of James II and son of James Edward, the Old Pretender, he succeeded as head of the Jacobites. He landed in Scotland from France in 1745, garnered an army from the clans, and led an uprising known as the Forty-Five which gained control of Edinburgh and claim to the name James VIII. He briefly invaded England but was thoroughly defeated at Culloden by the Duke of Cumberland on April 16, 1746. His wanderings through Europe to gain support for STUART restoration were unfulfilled. He settled in Italy. See *Hadder MacColl* and *Prince Charlie's Year.*

CHEROKEE. An important United States tribe of Iroquoian lineage, its members were originally located in Tennessee and North and South Carolina. The Cherokee towns were either red or white and those in the red towns or war towns answered to a supreme war chief while those in the white or peace towns answered to a supreme peace chief of the tribe. The white towns were places of sanctuary. See *Flaming Arrows, Groundhog's Horse, Rifles for Watie, The Righteous Revenge of Artemis Bonner, Wayah of the Real People,* and *Winter Danger.*

CHIANG KAI-SHEK. (1887-1975). Chinese general and politician who associated with Sun Yat-Sen in the Nationalist Party but broke with the Communists in 1927, transferring the seal of government to Nanking, then fought against the Japanese in World War II. He resumed his presidency on Taiwan after Communists won control of mainland China in 1949. See *The Bomber's Moon, Empire of the Sun,* and *In the Eye of War.*

CH'ING DYNASTY. See MANCHU.

CLARK, GEORGE ROGERS. (1752-1818). Brother of William Clark, he led frontiersmen in Kentucky against Indian raids in 1776-77 and helped save the region for the Colonies. From 1779-1883, he fought to hold this territory from the British and the Indians. See *Streams to the River, River to the Sea* and *Tree of Freedom.*

CLARK, WILLIAM. (1770-1838). He fought on the frontier against the Indians in 1792-96 and joined Meriwether Lewis in leading an expedition to find a route to the Pacific Ocean from 1804-1806. His brother was George Rogers Clark. See *Streams to the River, River to the Sea* and *Tree of Freedom.*

COLUMBUS, CHRISTOPHER. (1451-1506). After deciding that the world was round, he asked and got money to fit three ships, but instead of reaching Asia, he landed in 1492 at Guanahain, which he renamed San Salvador but now called Watlings Island. He continued to Cuba and Haiti. On his second voyage in 1493, he discovered Dominica, Guadeloupe, Puerto Rico, and Jamaica, returning in 1496. In 1498, he took his third voyage and discovered Trinidad but came back to Spain in disgrace in 1500. A fourth voyage in 1502 led him to Martinique and Panama, returning after difficulties in 1504. See *The Boy Who Sailed with Columbus, The High Voyage, I Sailed with Columbus, Morning Girl,* and *Pedro's Journal.*

COMANCHE. The ancestors of the Comanches, inhabitants of the Yellowstone river country, moved south, first reported in New Mexico in 1705. They owned many horses, developing the equestrian nomadism characteristic of Plains Indians in the 1800's and 1900's. They lacked integrating tribal ceremonies, government, lineage, clans, and military societies. Since they did not hunt buffalo, they went as far south as Durango, Mexico, in a search for booty and captives. Not until June 1875 did the Comanches cease their war against the United States government. See *A Circle Unbroken; Gone the Dreams and the Dancing; Haunted Journey; Rifles for Watie; The Search for Temperance Moon; Wait for Me, Watch for Me, Eula Bee; Weedy Rough;* and *Where the Broken Heart Still Beats.*

CONSTANTINE I. (d.337). Known as the Great, he was crowned caesar by his father at Eburacum, Britain in 306, as one of six claimants to the throne of the Roman Empire. After several battles, he became sole emperor in the West in 312 and probably adopted Christianity at that time. He called the Council of Nicaea in 325 where the Nicene Creed was adopted. In 330, he renamed Byzantium to Constantinople. See *The Silver Branch.*

CONSTANTINE XI. (1404-1453). As the last emperor of the Eastern Roman Empire, he fought Mehmed II and the Ottomans when they besieged Constantinople. They killed him at one of the city gates. See *The Emperor's Winding Sheet* and *The Trolley to Yesterday.*

COPPERHEAD. This term was applied during the American Civil War to those in the North who felt that conquering the Confederacy was impossible. They opposed the war policy of the president and of congress and wanted to declare peace. The term was probably first used in 1861 by the *New York Tribune.* See *Across Five Aprils.*

CORNWALLIS, CHARLES. (1738-1805). As a major general for the British in the American Revolution, he defeated Gates at Camden and Greene at Guilford Court House before he was besieged at Yorktown and forced to surrender on October 19, 1781. See *Treegate's Raiders.*

CORONADO, FRANCIS VASQUEZ DE. (c.1510-1554). He left Spain to explore Mexico in 1535. In 1540, he commanded an expedition searching for the reportedly incredibly rich Seven Cities of Cibola. After he found the Zuni pueblos, he began looking also for the supposedly wealthy Gran and Quivara. His search ended in Kansas at the Wichita Indian village. See *Walk the World's Rim.*

CORTÉS, HERNANDO. (1485-1547). He sailed to the New World with Diego Velàsquez and took an expedition to the mainland. He defeated and made an alliance with the Tlaxcalans, and in 1519, entered the Aztec capital Tenochtitlán, now Mexico City, where he held Montezuma hostage. He left on a short expedition and returned to find the Aztecs in revolt. At Montezuma's death in 1520, he led the Spaniards and allies out of the city. He captured Mexico City and later found Lower California. He died on his Seville estate. See *Walk the World's Rim, The Feathered Serpent,* and *The Amethyst Ring.*

COSSACK. The Turkic word "kazak" means "free man," or "adventurer" or "rebel." Fugitives from the central Asian Turkic states preferring a nomadic life in the steppes north of the Black Sea instead of serfdom in the Middle Ages first acquired this designation. Later the term was used in much the same way to designate peasants escaping from Poland and servitude. Eventually Cossacks began to protect borders of both Poland and Russia. They gained certain privileges by promising to give twenty years of military service in return. See *The Trumpeter of Krakow*.

CRAZY HORSE. (1842?-1877). As an American Indian chief of the Oglala tribe of the Sioux, he helped defeat General George Crook at Rosebud Creek on June 17, 1876 and was a leader in the battle of Little Big Horn when Custer was killed on June 25. He surrendered in 1877 and was killed while resisting imprisonment. See *Eyes of Darkness*.

CROMWELL, OLIVER. (1599-1658). He became known as a Puritan and enemy of the established church. He and his Ironsides regiment helped to defeat Charles I for the Parliamentarians. He eventually led the British government after overcoming Scotland and Ireland although he refused the title of king. See *Beyond the Weir Bridge* and *Cromwell's Boy*, and *Mission West*.

CROW. A Siouan-speaking Plains Indian tribe, the Crow moved westward from the upper Missouri River in the eighteenth century. By 1740, they were established middlemen in the trading of horses, bows, shirts, and featherwork to village Indians in return for guns and metal goods which they carried to the Shoshone in Idaho. Their lives revolved around buffalo and horses. The matrilineal descent allowed paternal relatives respect but conversation between son-in-law and parent-in-law was taboo. Brothers and sisters avoided speech and bodily contact. The search for a supernatural guardian who adopted the Crow's "child" was basic to religious belief and practice. Visions were induced by tormenting the body in various ways, and mementos of the experience were gathered in "medicine" bundles which were then associated with the sun dance, medicine arrows, and tobacco. Before one could be recognized as a chief, he had to take a weapon from an enemy, strike an enemy with a coupstick, take a horse tethered within an enemy camp, and lead a war party without loss of life. War exploits were announced in every religious and social occasion. See *Moccasin Trail*.

CUMBERLAND, DUKE OF. (1721-1765). As William Augustus, he was the third son of George II and Queen Caroline. He commanded British forces which quelled the Jacobite rebellion headed by Prince Charles Edward at Culloden in 1746. He suppressed the Jacobites so severely that he earned the name "the Butcher." See *A Pistol in Greenyards* and *Quest for a Kelpie*.

CUTHBERTUS. (635?-687). As a monk, he became the prior at Lindisfarne in 664 following the reform of the Celtic church to the Roman ways. After retiring to a cell on Inner Farne in 676, he had to become Bishop of Hexham and of Lindisfarne, but again retired to his cell in 687. His body was believed to work miracles and was transferred to Durham Cathedral in approximately 999. See *The Wind Eye*.

D

DAHOMEY. This African tribe became slave traders in the eighteenth century by conquering smaller states on the Slave Coast. See *The Sentinels*.

DALRIADA. Some of these people migrated in the sixth century from the Ulster kingdom of Dalriada in Antrim to Scotland thus inhabiting both sides of the North Channel. See *The Mark of the Horse Lord*.

DANTON, GEORGES-JACQUES. (1759-1794). At first he was a French revolutionary leader who advocated extreme action, including the death of the king, but gradually, he became more moderate and was seized by the people, imprisoned, condemned by trial, and guillotined. See *In Search of Honor* and *The Wind from the Sea*.

DARIUS I. (550-486 BC). The King of Persia, Darius the Great, divided the land, introduced reforms in administration and taxation, built roads, established a postal system, and standardized weights and measures. He had two expeditions against Greece. The first in 492 BC failed because his fleet got lost in a storm. The second was a defeat at Marathon. See *Marathon Looks at the Sea* and *The Persian Boy*.

DELAWARE. These Algonquian-speaking Indians occupied an area on the Atlantic coast from Cape Henlopen, Delaware to western Long Island in New York, beginning around 1000. They called themselves the *Leni Lenape* or *Lenape*, "the people." They were the most friendly with William Penn, but as whites encroached on their lands and treated them "as women," they moved further west. After mistreatment, they decided to retaliate. They defeated the English general Braddock in the French and Indian War, but after supporting the Americans in the American Revolution, they shifted to British allegiance because of the invasion of their Ohio hunting grounds. See *The Christmas Surprise, The Light in the Forest,* and *Red Pawns.*

DEVEREUX, ROBERT. (1566-1601). As the Earl of Essex, he became a favorite of ELIZABETH I of England. However, he offended her and was deprived of his offices. Others convinced him to form a plot to remove the Queen's counselors, but he failed. He was prosecuted for treason and executed. See *The Succession.*

DIAZ, PORFIRIO. 1830-1915). A Mexican general and politician, he was eventually elected president after overthrowing Lerdo de Tejada in 1876. Peace, material prosperity, and foreign investments marked his administrations, but he also had dictatorial methods which offered little improvement for the masses. He was finally forced to resign. See *El Güero.*

DRUID. As a religious leader in Druidism for the Celts of ancient Gaul and the British Isles, the druids left no written information about either their beliefs or practices. The word in Old Irish seems to mean "he who knows." See *The Druids, The Druid's Gift, The Stronghold,* and *Warrior Scarlet.*

E

EDWARD I (1239-1307). The eldest son of Henry III, he married Eleanor of Castile. Before becoming king, he supported the barons in their insistence upon reform by cooperating with Simon de Montfort in 1258 although he eventually killed Montfort at Evesham in 1265. He joined the Eighth Crusade in 1270 and became king in 1272. He enacted a parliament representing the three estates, then banished sixteen thousand Jews from England in 1290 on charges of extortionate usury. After many battles against Scotland during his reign, he died while returning to Scotland in expectation of crushing Robert Bruce. See *Adam of the Road* and *The Reckoning.*

EDWARD II. (1284-1327). Born in Caernarvon, Wales, he was the first to bear the title, Prince of Wales. He led an army to Stirling in Scotland, the only fortress not occupied by Robert Bruce, but Bruce beat him at Bannockburn in 1314. He married the French Isabella, daughter of Philip IV in 1308. She formed a criminal connection with Roger Mortimer which forced Edward to flee from England. Baronial exiles captured him and forced him to resign the throne in 1327 before they murdered him. See *One Is One, Ransom for a Knight, The Reckoning.*

EDWARD III. (1312-1377). The oldest son of Edward II, he became king when his father was deposed by his mother and Roger Mortimer. Eventually, he executed Mortimer and claimed the French throne through the right of his mother Isabella. He fought in France, first winning and then losing Aquitaine. He introduced Flemish weavers into England. See *All Men Tall, The Door in the Wall, In Pursuit of the Green Lion, The Lords of Vaumartin, Ride to Danger,* and *A Vision of Light.*

EDWARD IV. (1442-1483). Yorkist king of England who was driven from England by the Lancastrian King Henry VI at Ludlow Field in 1459. Through a series of actions and intrigues, he prepared the way for the Tudor's absolute monarchy. His brother Richard, Duke of Gloucester, deposed his son Edward V to become king as Richard III. See *The Cargo of the Madalena.*

EDWARD, THE BLACK PRINCE. (1330-1376). Although the eldest son of EDWARD III, he died of a mortal disease contracted in Spain before he could succeed to the throne of England. He was the Prince of Wales and fought at Crécy and Calais. He caused a revolt in his southern France holdings by requiring hearth taxes for five years in order to obtain needed funds. See *Ride into Danger.*

ELEANOR OF AQUITAINE. 1122-1204). She was married to Louis VII of France and to Henry II of England. By bringing Aquitaine together with England, she set up strife between France and England which lasted for 400 years. Her sons Richard (the Lion-Heart) and John Lackland became kings of England. See *Here Be Dragons* and *A Proud Taste for Scarlet and Miniver.*

ELEANOR OF CASTILE. (1246-1290). As the wife of Edward I of England, she accompanied him on a crusade from 1270-73. See *The Reckoning.*

ELIZABETH I OF ENGLAND. (1533-1603). The only child of Henry VIII and Anne Boleyn, she succeeded to the throne in 1558 after being imprisoned in both the Tower and Woodstock. She increased her persecution of Roman Catholics after discovering the Babbington Plot in 1586 and finally signed Mary, Queen of Scots' death warrant. She defeated the Spanish and as "Good Queen Bess," helped England emerge as a world power. See *Bartholomew Fair, Black Swan, Death of the Fox, A Flight of Swans, The Iron Lily, The Last Prince of Ireland, The Perilous Gard, The Spanish Letters, Stars of Fortune,* and *The Succession.*

ELIZABETH PETROVNA. (1709-1762). As the younger daughter of Peter the Great and Catherine I of Russia, she gained the throne by overthrowing the government of Ivan VI. She reinstituted the senate and freed Russia from German dominance. She established the University of Moscow in 1755 and the Academy of Fine Arts at St. Petersburg in 1758. See *The Crimson Oak.*

ESAU. The brother of Jacob in the *Bible,* he gave up his birthright as eldest son of Isaac. See *Jacob Have I Loved.*

ESSEX, EARL OF. See DEVEREUX, ROBERT.

ESTEBAN. This man, a slave, came to the New World with Cabeza de Vaca, and they were shipwrecked on Galveston Bay. They wandered for eight years and eventually reached northern Mexico. Viceroy Antonio de Mendoza sent him to serve as guide for Fray Marcos de Niza as he tried to find the seven golden cities of Cibola beginning in 1539. See *Walk the World's Rim.*

F

FAIRY FOLK. Fairies, common in British folklore, were thieves often detected robbing stalls at fairs and markets. Their most dreaded habis was stealing a human baby and substituting a child of their own so that it might benefit from human milk. They were organized in clans with their own kings, queens, and armies living in subterranean palaces reached through caves or through gates magically opening in hillsides. Various theories have been posited as to the origin of fairies. See *The Perilous Gard.*

FERGUSON, PATRICK. (1744-1780). The inventor of the first breech-loading rifle, he served in the British army in America and was killed at the battle of King's Mountain. See *Treegate's Raiders.*

FRANKLIN, BENJAMIN. (1706-1790). He is remembered as a statesman, scientist, and philosopher. He became an important American statesman during the time of independence from the British. He invented the lightning rod and bifocles among other discoveries. His philosophy remains well known from his *Poor Richard's Almanac.* See *Sea Captain from Salem.*

FRÉMONT, JOHN. (1813-1890). He first mapped the Oregon Trail and then helped free California. Afterwards, he became the military governor of California but became involved in a quarrel and was tried for insubordination. He was one of California's first two senators. See *The Bear Flag* and *Pacific Street.*

G

GEORGE III OF ENGLAND. (1738-1820). He became king in 1760, and the policies he supported helped England lose the American colonies. He also blocked attempts to emancipate the Roman Catholics. Later in his life he lost his mental capabilities and his son who later became George IV acted as his regent. See *Sarah Bishop.*

GODWIN, HAROLD. See HAROLD II OF ENGLAND.

GOEBBELS, JOSEPH. (1897-1945). He led the NAZI party in Berlin in 1926 and was the master of modern propaganda which kept the Germans supporting the war effort during World War II. Hitler named him as his successor, but he committed suicide in Hitler's bunker in Berlin. See *Eagles at War.*

GRANT, ULYSSES. (1822-1885). The eighteenth president of the United States, Grant served in the American Civil War where he broke Confederate control of Mississippi. He took command of all the Union armies and heard Lee's surrender at Appomattox Court House. See *The Tamarack Tree.*

GUILLOTIN, JOSEPH. (1738-1814). Although a physician, during the French Revolution, he defended capital punishment and suggested the use of the beheading machine which was later named after him. See *In Search of Honor.*

GUTHORM [GUTHRUM]. (d.890). He led a large Danish invasion of Anglo-Saxon England in 878, but Alfred defeated him and required that he adopt Christianity. Afterward, he reigned peacefully. See *The Namesake.*

H

HADRIAN. (76-138). He became Roman emperor in 117 at the death of his cousin TRAJAN who designated him as his successor. He established the Euphrates River as the eastern boundary of the Roman empire and traveled throughout all parts of the empire including England in 122 where he ordered the construction of Hadrian's Wall. On another tour he visited Athens and became an avid promoter of the hellenic culture. From 132-135, he suppressed a revolt of the Jews. See *The Eagle of the Ninth.*

HAMILTON, ALEXANDER. (1755-1804). Among his important positions in the newly formed American government, he was a member of the Continental Congresses and the first United States secretary of the treasury from 1789-95. He helped the public credit reach a sound basis, but his opposition to policies led to the creation of political parties. He emerged as head of the Federalist party. He also helped defeat Aaron Burr for president, and Burr eventually mortally wounded him in a duel. See *Jump Ship to Freedom.*

HANCOCK, JOHN. (1737-1793). He served Massachusetts and was a member of the Continental Congresses, serving as president from 1775-77. He became the first signer of the Declaration of Independence and the first governor of the State of Massachusetts in 1780. See *Johnny Tremain* and *John Treegate's Musket.*

HANOVER. This electoral house began in Germany and became a royal family of England when George I gained the English crown in 1714. Other rulers in this line were George II, III, IV, William IV and Victoria. See *The Lothian Run.*

HARALD [HAROLD] HARDRADA. (1015-1066). At the battle of Stiklestad in 1030, his half-brother Olaf was killed. Then in 1033, he visited the courts of Novgorod, Kiev, and Constantinople where he had many adventures in the service of the Byzantine Emperor Michael IV. He returned to Russia in 1044 and to Norway in 1045 and became co-ruler with Magnus I Olafsson and then sole king as Harold III of Norway when Magnus died. He fought the Danes from 1047-62, and when Tostig, the brother of the English king, Harold II, asked his help in conquering England, he sailed there in 1066 but met death at the battle of Stamford Bridge. See *Gildenford, The Norman Pretender, The Proud Villeins.*

HAROLD II OF ENGLAND. (1022-1066). After serving as chief minister of his brother-in-law, Edward the Confessor, he subjugated Wales and secured his own election as king at Edward's death in 1066. He defeated his brother Tostig and Harald Hardrada at Stamford Bridge (September 25), but William, duke of Normandy, killed him in the battle of Hastings (Senlac) on October 14. See *The Disputed Crown, Gildenford, The Norman Pretender,* and *The Proud Villeins.*

HATSHEPSUT. (1503-1482 BC). After the death of her father Thutmose I, she married her half-brother Thutmose II, but after his death in 1504, she became regent for his son Thutmose III and proclaimed herself pharaoh. She promoted trade and building, renovating part of Karnak and building new temples. See *Mara, Daughter of the Nile* and *Child of the Morning.*

HECUBA, QUEEN OF TROY. (c. 1400 BC). As the wife of Priam during the wars with Greece according to Greek legend, she was also mother of Hector, Troilus, Paris, and Cassandra. See *Fires in the Sky.*

HENRY I OF ENGLAND. (1068-1135). Fourth son of William the Conqueror, he conquered Normandy and imprisoned his brother Robert. He married off his daughter Matilda to Geoffrey Plantagenet, Count of Anjou. Stephen succeeded him as king. See *Godric* and *King of the Wood* .

HENRY II OF ENGLAND. (1133-1189). Matilda's son was also count of Anjou. The Anjou family badge was a sprig of broom (planta genista) and their name, Plantagenet, was derived from it. He married Eleanor of Aquitaine and their sons, Richard and John, became kings in turn.

He created a national coinage system no longer allowing the barons to issue their own coins. When Thomas á Beckett, the man Henry appointed as Archbishop of Canterbury, refused to allow Henry to try accused clergy in royal courts, four men murdered him on Canterbury's steps. He began trial by jury. See *Here Be Dragons* and *A Proud Taste for Scarlet and Miniver*.

HENRY III OF ENGLAND. (1207-1272). After favoring foreigners and living beyond his means, he provoked a rebellion from barons who compelled him to agree with a series of reforms. He refused, and the Barons' War led by Simon de Montfort took place in 1264. He was imprisoned, but his son Edward rescued him by defeating Montfort at Evesham in 1265. Edward then succeeded him. See *Falls the Shadow*.

HENRY IV OF ENGLAND. (1366-1413). Named Bolingbroke and often called Henry of Lancaster by his contemporaries, he traveled throughout Europe on his way to the crusades. For his coronation, the golden eagle flask holding sacred oil was used for the first time. He founded the Knights of Bath, those who conduct the sovereign after he/she bathes in the City of London before being crowned to Westminster Abbey. He defeated Richard II in 1399 and suppressed Richard's sympathizers, Owen Glendower and Henry Percy (Hotspur) in the battle of Shrewsbury in 1403. His son Henry V succeeded him.

HENRY V OF ENGLAND. (1387-1422). He won the battle of Agincourt in France over Charles VI of France who had gone mad. He thus won Charles' daughter Catherine in marriage and the promise that he would succeed to the French throne with the Treaty of Troyes in 1420. His son Henry VI succeeded him. See *The Sign of the Green Falcon*.

HENRY VI OF ENGLAND. (1421-1471). Since his father died when Henry was eight, and his grandfather Charles died two months later, he became king of both England and France. Joan of Arc and others, however, expelled his forces from France except for Calais by 1453. In later age, he formed Eton and King's (Henry's) College at Cambridge for poor boys (then). His mother Catherine married Owen Tudor and had two sons. He lost his reason as he aged and was challenged by the House of York which began the Wars of Roses lasting from 1455-1485. His wife, Margaret, would not reconcile with the Yorkists, but Henry recognized Edward of York as king Edward IV. He went to the Tower of London where he was murdered. See *The Writing on the Hearth*.

HENRY VII OF ENGLAND. (1457-1509). First monarch of the house of Tudor, he lived as an exile in Brittany until he entered England, defeated Richard III at Bosworth Field on August 22, 1485, and was declared king. He married Elizabeth, daughter of Edward IV, which united the houses of Lancaster and York. He decided that nobles could have servants but no armies. He named one of his sons Arthur after the character in Mallory's *Morte d'Arthur* recently printed by William Caxton. His son Henry VIII succeeded him. See *The Lark and the Laurel* and *The Merchant's Mark*.

HENRY VIII OF ENGLAND. (1491-1547). At eighteen on becoming king, he married Catherine of Aragon, the widow of his brother Arthur. He formed various European alliances based on the advice of Cardinal Wolsey. When the Pope refused his request for a divorce from Catherine, he blamed Wolsey and appointed Sir Thomas More as chancellor in 1529. Then he married Anne Boleyn who became the mother of Elizabeth I. He accused Anne of crimes and beheaded her. Jane Seymour, his next wife, bore him a son, but she soon died. He tried a political liaison with Anne of Cleves but hated her looks. Then Catherine Howard aroused his suspicions, and he beheaded her. Finally he married Catherine Parr who outlived him. He improved naval defense, unified Wales with England, and placated Ireland. His son Edward VI succeeded him. See *A Cold Wind Blowing, The Eldest Son,* and *Stars of Fortune*.

HEPHAISTON. (d. 324 BC). He was a Macedonian general and intimate friend of Alexander the Great. He helped establish Greek colonies in conquered lands. At his sudden death in Ecbatana, Alexander ordered the erection of a vast funeral pyre and construction of temples in his honor. See *Fire from Heaven*.

HESSIANS. In the American Revolution, men from the German area of Hesse fought as mercenaries for the British Army and were called Hessians. See *Distant Thunder, An Enemy Among Them, The Fighting Ground, Peter Treegate's War,* and *Red Pawns*.

HINDU. Defining what a Hindu believes remains difficult because the beliefs and practices vary widely, dependent upon where one lives or social class. Most Hindus consider Hinduism a way of life with controls far outside the dictum of typical religions. A large difference, however, exists between the orthodox Hindu and the educated Indian

Hindu who respects the ancient religion which has existed since before 1500 BC but does not follow many of the precepts. India has over 95 percent of the world's Hindus. A distinguishing feature is the transmigration of souls with its corollary that all living beings are the same in essence. Another is its monotheism but with polytheism in the lower ranks under the one God. Hinduism has a tendency to mysticism and has a stratified system of social classes, called *castes*. See *Day of the Scorpion, A Division of the Spoils, The Jewel in the Crown,* and *The Towers of Silence*.

HIPPOLYTA AND HIPPOLYTUS. (c. 1400). The lover and son of Theseus respectively from Greek legend. Hippolyta was Queen of the Amazons, female warriors supposed to have lived in Sythia, near the Black Sea, who loved Theseus but could not marry him because of his previous engagement to Phaedra. They had a son, Hippolytus, whom Phaedra propositioned. He rejected her, and in her anger, she falsely accused him of raping her. See *The Bull from the Sea*.

HITLER, ADOLF. (1899-1945). Frustrated by his inability to become an artist, he became instead a German politician and leader (Führer). He joined the National Socialist German Worker's Party (NAZI), and used its army in his regime of terror based on the superiority of the Aryan (German) race and extreme anti-Semitism during which millions of Jews were murdered. He, was defeated in 1945. See titles in "Europe and Great Britain: 1934-1945," "United States: 1941-1945" and *When Hitler Stole Pink Rabbit*.

HUNS. A savage Asiatic people who, led by Attila, invaded eastern and central Europe in the fourth and fifth centuries AD. See *The Dancing Bear*.

I

ICENI. This British tribe occupied what is now Norfolk and Suffolk. When their king Prasutagus died in 60 A.D., the Romans annexed their territory and caused his wife, Boudicca, to revolt. When the Romans conquered the tribe, they punished it severely. See *Sun Horse, Moon Horse*.

INCA. The history of this Andean civilization begins around 1200, but its expansion did not start until 1438 and lasted until the conquest by Francisco Pizarro in 1532. It extended form the present Columbia-Ecuador border to central Chile, an area of approximately 380,000 square miles. The culture was agricultural, but the welfare state government distributed land and goods according to family size. Thus people had no initiative to improve their lives or to change locales. The emperor, or "Inca," was divine, thought to have descended from the sun. Although he had absolute power, custom kept him from being a tyrant. He most often married his sister but had a large seraglio. Human sacrifice was rare, unlike the Aztec. The culture was so highly organized that Pizarro was able to being ruling without any retaliation. See *The Amethyst Ring*.

INUIT (ESKIMO). The Inuit tribe is part of the Eskimo race living in Greenland, the Artic, the Hudson Bay coasts of North America, the Labrador coast, Alaska, and the northeastern tip of Asia. See *The Abduction* and *The Haunted Igloo*

IROQUOIS. This confederacy or league of North American Indians originally included the Mohawk, Oneida, Onondaga, Cayuga, and Seneca nations. Corn planters, they were partially sedentary, living in long multi-fireside shelters with their matrilineal crests painted on gables, which gave them the so-called long house image. Kinship and locality were the basis for political life, with each community having a ruling council of adult males, as well as peace chiefs who were appointed by women. The Iroquois liked many and long meetings. See *Red Pawns*.

J

JACOB. As the brother of ESAU in the *Bible*, he took ESAU's birthright when he accepted his father Issac's blessing as the oldest son. See *Jacob Have I Loved*.

JACOBITE. This name was given to supporters of the exiled Stuart King James II and his descendants after the revolution of 1688. See *Hadder MacColl*, *The Lothian Run*, and *Prince Charlie's Year*.

JAMES I OF ENGLAND. See JAMES VI OF SCOTLAND.

JAMES VI OF SCOTLAND. (1566-1625). After ruling Scotland as the son of Mary, Queen of Scots, he became the successor to Elizabeth I of England. In Scotland, Protestant nobles seized him in the 1582 Raid of Ruthven, but he escaped. He curbed the powers of Roman Catholic nobles in Scotland by centralizing power in the monarchy. As English king, he asserted the divine right of kings, and alienated both the Scots and English by his religious proclamations. His attitude towards Catholics precipitated the Gunpowder plot in 1605, and he spent much money on court life. The King James version of the *Bible* which he had scholars prepare by 1611 bears his name. See *Bonnie Dundee, Cromwell's Boy, Death of the Fox, The Spanish Letters, The Succession,* and *The 13th Member.*

JANISSARY [JANIZARY]. Under Mehmet II, the Janissary troops began forming from the tribute of Christian children and some boy prisoners who were considered slaves of the sultan. First assigned to households, they were trained in the Turkish language and Muslim religion and then transferred to the capital where they learned military discipline and the arts of war. They were sworn to absolute obedience, abstinence, and celibacy with all energies devoted to military training. They, in return, enjoyed many privileges. See *Children of the Book.*

JEFFERSON, THOMAS. (1743-1826). The third president of the United States, he prepared the Declaration of Independence, purchased Louisiana, sent Lewis and Clark to explore it, and prohibited the importation of slaves. He also founded the University of Virginia. See *Jefferson: A Novel, My Thomas,* and *Wolf by Ears.*

JOAN OF ARC. (1412-1431). As Jeanne d'Arc at twelve, she believed that she heard voices from angels or from God, at first giving her advice to lead a holy life, and later, to give directions to the dauphin in France's troubled times. After several campaigns, the Burgundians captured her, and a church tribunal tried her at Rouen, convicted her, and burned her at the stake. Her innocence was proclaimed in 1456, and she was canonized in 1920. See *Where the Towers Pierce the Sky.*

JOHN, KING OF ENGLAND. (1167-1216). Often called "Lackland," he was the son of Henry II and Eleanor of Aquitaine, of the house of Anjou or Plantagenet. He provoked papal interdict and excommunication but made peace by offering an annual tribute to the pope. After defeat in France in 1214, he met the barons at Runnymede where they forced him to sign the *Magna Carta*, laying the foundation for the security of English political and personal liberty. He imported foreign mercenaries to defeat the barons, but died before the war was decided. See *Here Be Dragons*.

JONES, JOHN PAUL. (1747-1792). Although born in Scotland and once in the British mercantile navy, he joined the American navy at the beginning of the American Revolution. He cruised around the British Isles, and with the French, organized a naval attack on the British. He supposedly said, "I have not yet begun to fight!" before he defeated the British ship *Serapis* in 1779. See *A Boy's Will*.

JUSTINIAN I. (483-565). Known as the Great, he married Theodora in 525 and became Emperor at the death of Justin I in 527. His reign was one of the most brilliant of the Eastern Roman Empire. His able generals helped him make many conquests with actual occupation of Rome in 536. He built many important forts, public buildings, monasteries, and churches in Ravenna and Constantinople. He tried to placate the Monophysites but alienated the Roman church in the process. His law codes form the foundation of law in most of contemporary continental Europe. See *The Bearkeepers Daughter* and *The Dancing Bear*.

K

KHAFRE (CHEPHEN). (2540-2514 BC). Of the Fourth Egyptian Dynasty, the son of Cheops (Khufu), he built the second pyramid and the sphinx which probably carries his features. See *Zekmet the Stone Carver*.

KUKULCÁN. See QUETZALCOATL.

L

LAFAYETTE. (1757-1834). A Frenchman, he entered the American military service during the American Revolution in 1777. He became a friend of George Washington and helped defeat Cornwallis in 1781. When he returned to France, he commanded the force that fired on the mob at the Champ de Mars in 1791, but at the rise of Napoleon, took no part in politics because of his opposition. See *Distant Thunder, Jefferson: A Novel,* and *Sea Captain from Salem.*

LANCASTER. This English royal house was derived from the fourth son of Edward III, John of Gaunt, who was created the Duke of Lancaster after his marriage in 1359 to the daughter and heiress of Henry, the first Duke of Lancaster. This branch of the Plantagenet family fought the house of York after 1399 in the War of Roses flying the red rose emblem. The reigning Lancastrian kings were Henry IV, V, and VI. See appropriate titles under entries for individual rulers.

LEE, ROBERT E. (1807-1870). After serving in various capacities for the military, he suppressed John Brown's raid at Harpers Ferry, Virginia in 1859. In 1861, he resigned from the United States Army and accepted the command of the army of Northern Virginia. He was defeated at both Antietam (1862) and Gettysburg (1863) but repulsed the Federals at Richmond (1862), Fredericksburg (1862), and Chancellorsville (1863). He had to surrender the Confederate Forces to Grant at Appomattox Court House in 1865. See *Across Five Aprils, The Killer Angels, Gone With the Wind, In My Father's House, The Slopes of War,* and *Thunder at Gettysburg.*

LENIN, VLADIMIR ILICH. (1870-1924). As a Marxist, he assumed control of the Bolsheviks in Russia, and took control from Kerensky's provisional government in 1917 after the overthrow of the czar. He denounced World War I as imperialistic and established the dictatorship of the proletariat. He formulated the present official Communist ideology. See *Chase Me, Catch Nobody!, The Raging Fire,* and *The Wild Children.*

LINCOLN, ABRAHAM. (1809-1865). The sixteenth president of the United States, he had little formal schooling and studied law in his few leisure hours. He was elected, after senatorial defeat, president. He issued the Emancipation Proclamation on January 1, 1863, which freed the slaves in all states. Renominated and reelected in 1864, he was shot five days after the end of the war and died on April 15. See all titles listed under "United States: 1861-1865."

LINDBERGH, CHARLES. (1902-1974). He was the American aviator who made the first solo nonstop transatlantic flight in *The Spirit of St. Louis* from Roosevelt Field, New York, to Le Bourget Air Field, Paris, in May of 1927. See *Trophy for Eagles* and *What About Annie.*

LLEWELYN (d. 1282). As the Prince of Gwynedd, he divided the land with his brother Owain and then seized Owain's portion, proclaiming himself as Prince of Wales. He received homage from other Welsh princes and joined Simon de Montfort's side in the Baron's War, but he refused to do homage to Edward I. Edward invaded Wales and subjugated him. When Llewelyn rebelled in 1282, he was killed. See *The Reckoning.*

LOLLARD. In late medieval England, followers of John Wycliffe earned this name which means "mumbler" or "mutterer." It was applied to groups suspected of combining pious pretensions with heretical beliefs. See *The Sign of the Green Falcon.*

M

MANCHU DYNASTY. (1644-1912). Last dynasty of the Chinese Empire which succeeded the Ming dynasty. It increased rapidly under the first five emperors but began a decline under the last five. They engaged in a war with the British known as the Opium Wars in 1839-42. I was finally overthrown by those who founded the Chinese Republic. See *Empire of Heaven, Mountain Light,* and *Rebels of the Heavenly Kingdom,* and *The Serpent's Children.*

MARCEL, ÉTIENNE. (1316-1358). As the French borgeois leader, he induced Dauphin Charles (later King Charles V) to issue an edict of reform. When it was suppressed, Marcel began supporting Charles the Bad, King of Navarre. He led the Paris mob into the palace of the dauphin and murdered his marshals. As Marcel prepared to open the gates of Paris for Charles the Bad's troops, one of the dauphin's agents murdered him. See *The Lords of Vaumartin.*

MARGARET, THE MAID OF NORWAY. (1283-1290). She was the granddaughter of Alexander III of Scotland, affianced to Prince Edward, son of Edward I of England in 1287. She died in the Orkneys en route to England. See *Quest for a Maid.*

MARION, FRANCIS. (1732?-1795). Called "The Swamp Fox," in the American Revolution, he commanded militia in South Carolina where he harassed British forces with raids and escaped into the swamps and forests. See *Treegate's Raiders.*

MARIUS GAIUS. (157-86 BC). A Roman general and politician who had a rivalry with Sulla which led to a civil war in 88 BC. He was driven from Rome, but with the aid of Cinna, he returned, captured the city, and revenged himself by proscribing leaders of the aristocratic party. See *The First Man in Rome, Fortune's Favorites,* and *The Grass Crown.*

MARLOW, CHRISTOPHER. (1564-1593). An English dramatist who was apparently involved in espionage service for the government while at Cambridge, and perhaps afterwards, he was killed in a tavern brawl under mysterious circumstances. Some think he wrote Shakespeare's plays. See *Black Swan.*

MARY, QUEEN OF ENGLAND. (1516-1558). Often called Bloody Mary, she, as Mary Tudor, was the daughter of Henry VIII and Catherine of Aragon who succeeded to the throne at the death of her half-brother Edward VI in 1553. She married Philip II of Spain; repealed the laws establishing Protestantism in England and reestablished Roman Catholicism; martyred at least three hundred Protestants; and lost CALAIS, the last English possession on the Continent. See *The Perilous Gard, Stars of Fortune,* and *You Never Knew Her As I Did.*

MASSASOIT. (d. 1661). As the chief of the Wampanoags, an American tribe in Massachusetts, he negotiated peace with the Pilgrims in 1621 and remained friendly with them all of his life. See *Constance* and *The Thanksgiving Story.*

MATILDA (MAUD). (1102-1167). The daughter of Henry I of England and Matilda, she and her half-brother Robert captured Stephen in 1141, after he claimed the crown, and she established herself as "Lady of England and Normandy." The citizens of London drove her out after six months because of her greed. She exercised considerable influence over her son, Henry II of England. See the titles of Ellis Peters in "Europe and Great Britain: 476-1199."

MATILDA, QUEEN OF ENGLAND. (d. 1083). The wife of William I, the Conqueror, she was crowned on her arrival in England after serving as regent in Normandy during William's absences. She is also associated with the famed Bayeux Tapestry relating the story of 1066. See *The Striped Ships.*

MENDOZA, ANTONIO DE. (1490-1552). As the viceroy of New Spain, he brought the first printing press to the New World in 1535. He tried to stop exploitation of the Indians and built schools and churches. He also tried to develop agriculture. He sent Coronado on an expedition to what is now New Mexico and Colorado. See *The King's Fifth.*

MONOPHYSITES. Christians known as monophysites teach that the person of Jesus Christ exhibited only one nature instead of two natures, divine and human, as asserted at the Council of Chalcedon in 451. See *The Dancing Bear.*

MONTEZUMA [MOCTEZUMA] II. (1466-1520). Chief of the Aztecs, he tried to persuade Cortés not to come to Mexico City in 1519, but Cortés seized him in Tenochtitlán and held him hostage after the Aztecs rose against the Spanish. He died a few days later. See *The Feathered Serpent.*

De MONTFORT, SIMON. (c.1208-1265). The Earl of Leicester, he married Henry III's sister Eleanor. He led the opposition in Parliament against the king's demand for a subsidy and then led all the barons who accused Henry III of falseness of oath in the Baron's War (1263-65). He eventually captured Henry III at the Battle of Lewes in 1264. He summoned a new Parliament with more equitable distribution, the beginning of the modern parliament. Some of the Welsh leaders joined Prince Edward against him at Evesham where he was defeated and killed. He was popularly called "Simon the Righteous." See *Falls the Shadow.*

MORGAN, DANIEL. (1736-1802). As a soldier in the American Revolution, he helped Arnold assault Quebec, opposed Gurgoyne at Saratoga, and commanded troops in North Carolina were he defeated the British at Cowpens in 1781. See *Peter Treegate's War.*

MOSES. (c. 1400 BC). This Hebrew prophet and lawgiver led the Israelites from Egypt through the wilderness into Canaan, received the Covenant, and established the religious community of Israel by organizing its cult and judicial traditions. See *The People and the Promise.*

MOSLEM (MUSLIM). As a believer in Islam, a Moslem follows *The Koran.* The basic tenet is five articles of faith which are the belief in God who is absolutely unique, in angels, in the revealed books, in the prophets, and in the Day of Judgment. The Moslem has five obligatory duties: to recite the profession of faith, to pray, to pay tax, to fast, and to take a pilgrimage to Mecca. Many other rules by which to live are part of the Islamic beliefs. In India, the custom of *sati*, when widows burn themselves alive with their deceased husbands, continued for a long time. The main fight between the Moslems and the Hindus in India from 1947 to 1956 created the Moslem state of Pakistan. See *Children of the Book, Day of the Scorpion, A Division of the Spoils, The Jewel in the Crown,* and *The Towers of Silence.*

N

NAPOLEON I. (1769-1821). He rose to command after the French Revolution and won portions of Italy and Egypt before Lord Nelson destroyed his fleet in the Battle of the Nile, 1798. In 1799, he took control of the French government, and in 1803, he abandoned hopes of an overseas empire by selling Louisiana to the United States. He declared France a hereditary empire in 1804 and had himself crowned emperor. He gained control of Europe but lost at sea when Nelson defeated his navy at Trafalgar in 1805. Finally, European land forces overcame him in 1814; he abdicated and was exiled to Elba. He reentered Paris on March 20, 1815, and raised new armies. He lost at Waterloo on June 18, 1815, and abdicated again. After surrendering to the British, he spent the remainder of his life at St. Helena. See *The Court of the Stone Children, A Fanfare for the Stalwart,* and *The Year of the French.*

NAVAHO. The largest Indian tribe in the United States, the Navaho of the southwest, with sixty clans, borrowed extensively from the Pueblo Indian culture, its agriculture, weaving, sand paintings, and ceremonial traits. Their matrilineal descent dictates that newly married couples live near the bride's mother, and the mother's brothers take responsibility for the upbringing, marriage, and property of their sister's children. No Navaho may marry a spouse from the clan of either mother or father. The religious system is quite intricate with important ceremonies which many times have the purpose of curing bodily illness or psychiatric concerns. Weaving and silversmithing are important Navaho arts. See *Sing Down the Moon.*

NAZI. Members of the National Socialist German Workers' Party, founded in Germany in 1919 and brought to power by Adolf Hitler are called this name which is a German phonetic shortening of *National-sozialist*. See *The Cay, From Anna, The Lamb's War, My Grandmother's Journey* and "Europe and Great Britain: 1934-1945."

NEZ PERCE. Although this tribe of Native Americans did not practice "nose piercing," the insertion of a shell ornament, it was from the same group. The tribes lived in Idaho, Washington, and Oregon. See *Thunder Rolling in the Mountains*.

NICHOLAS II. (1868-1918). The Russian czar, Nikolay Aleksandrovich, made peace proposals and directed the construction of the Trans-Siberian railroad. Although he was forced to grant a constitution in 1905, he did not quell the discontent of the people. Dissatisfaction with his policies led to the Russian Revolution in 1917, his abdication, and his execution with his whole family. See *All the Lights in the Night, Beyond the High White Wall, Good-bye to the Trees, Homecoming, The House on Walenska Street, Independence Avenue, Letters from Rifka, The Night Journey, One-Way to Ansonia, The Place Where Nobody Stopped, The Raging Fire, The Sound of Dragon's Feet*, and *Voyage*.

NORMAN. Originally, this term denoted Northmen "Nortmanni," the barbarians who came from Denmark, Norway, and Iceland to make plundering raids on the west in the eighth century. In the form "Normans," it refers to those Vikings who settled in northern Francia, the Frankish kingdom, and to their descendants who founded the duchy of Normandy and sent new expeditions to various places including the British Isles. The Normans became British rulers with William the Conqueror in 1066. See *Gildenford, King of the Wood, The Norman Pretender, The Proud Villeins, The Shield Ring, A Slave's Tale*, and *The Striped Ships*.

O

OTIS, JAMES. (1725-1783). Although he was the British king's advocate general in the American colonies when the royal customs collectors began to search for violations of the Sugar Act of 1773, he resigned his office and opposed the searches. He based his opposition on natural law as being superior to acts of Parliament. Along with Samuel Adams and others, he also opposed other revenue acts. See *Johnny Tremain*.

P

PAINE, THOMAS. (1739-1809). After going bankrupt in England, he emigrated to America in 1774 where in 1776 he published *Common Sense*, urging a declaration of independence. Back to England in 1787, he defended revolutionary France and tried to organize a revolt of the English against their own monarchy. The English tried him for treason and banished him in 1792. In Paris, he was imprisoned as an Englishman, but an American, James Monroe, claimed him as an American citizen. He published *The Age of Reason* while still in France, but returned to America where he lived in ostracism and poverty. See *Time of Trial*.

PARLIAMENTARIANS. Members of this group supported Parliament instead of Charles I in the English Civil War. See *Beyond the Weir Bridge, Harrow and Harvest*.

PARNELL, CHARLES STEWART. (1846-1891). An Irish Nationalist, he was elected president of the Home Rule Confederation. He united the Fenians of Ireland with America and the Land League. His reputation was ruined by his adultery with Kitty, the wife of Captain William O'Shea, a former follower. See *Parnell and the Englishwoman*.

PATRICK, SAINT. (c.400 AD). As the son of a high-ranking Celto-Roman family captured at sixteen by Irish marauders, he was sold as a slave in Antrim, escaped after six years into Gaul, and returned to his parents in Britain. In heed of a call in a dream for him to preach to the Irish, he prepared in France for fourteen years. The Druids opposed him, but the local kings protected him as he founded churches. See *A Boy's Will* and *Pangur Ban*.

PHILIP IV OF SPAIN. (1605-1665). During his reign, Spain's fortunes continued to decline and foreign wars impoverished the country. Portugal gained its independence in 1640. But in spite of the losses, he was a poet and a patron of the arts with Velázquez serving as his court painter. See *I, Juan de Pareja*.

PHILIP VI OF FRANCE. (1293-1350). The first king of the House of Valois, he had a dispute with Edward III of England which led to the beginning of the Hundred Years' War (1337). Edward III defeated him at Crécy in 1346 and took Calais in 1347. See *The Lords of Vaumartin*.

PIZARRO, FRANCISCO. (c.1475-1541). After sailing to America and exploring, he returned to Spain and enlisted men to help him on another expedition. After his discovery of Peru, he executed the Inca chieftain Atahualpa in 1533 when he refused to accept the Christian faith. He marched to Cuzco, captured it, and secured an immense amount of gold. Then he founded the new capital, Lima, in 1535. See *The Amethyst Ring*.

PLANTAGENET, HOUSE OF. This house began in 1128 with Geoffrey the Fair, nicknamed "Plantagenet," because of the sprig of broom that he wore in his hat ("broom" in French is "genêt"). Soon to be Count of Anjou, he married Matilda, heiress to Henry I, king of England. Although Henry's nephew Stephen seized the throne, eventually Stephen recognized Geoffrey and Matilda's son Henry as heir, and he became Henry II. Other Plantagenet rulers were Richard I; John; Henry III; Edward I, II, and III; and Richard II. See *The Spring of Broom* and appropriate titles under entries for individual rulers.

POCAHONTAS. (c.1595-1617). This Native American princess saved the live of Captain John Smith when she kept her father Powhatan's warriors from clubbing him. In 1612, the English took her prisoner, converted her, and named her Rebecca. She married John Rolfe, went to England with him, and died there. See *Pocahontas and the Strangers*.

PURITANS. In the 1560's the term "puritan" showed contempt for all persons within the Church of England who wanted more reform in the church as well as those who broke away from the church to carry out reforms. Puritanism in England occurred in the century following the Reformation until approximately 1660. In New England, it dates from the first settlement in 1620 to the new Massachusetts charter of 1691. Jonathan Edwards tried to create a resurgence in the 1730's. See *Constance, Only Brave Tomorrows, Sarah Morton's Day, The Seekers, Squanto, The Stratford Devil, The Thanksgiving Story, This New Land,* and *The Witch of Blackbird Pond*.

PUSHKIN, ALEKSANDR. (1799-1837). Considered the greatest Russian poet, he introduced Romanticism and the Byronic hero into Russian literature. He was killed in a duel. See *Letters from Rifka*.

Q

QUAKERS. George Fox founded the Religious Society of Friends in 1650. He said that the society's members were derisively called Quakers because "we bid them tremble at the word of God." They were severely persecuted because they refused to swear allegiance to anyone or anything other than God. See *Beyond the Weir Bridge*; *Jump Ship to Freedom*; *Lyddie; Next Stop, Freedom; The Peculiar People; Sarah Bishop; Thee, Hannah!*, and *Who Comes with Cannons*.

QUETZALCOATL. Named the "Plumed Serpent," he was first worshipped by the Aztecs in central Mexico before 300 A.D. He was the god of the wind and of dawn, identified with the planet Venus, the light, and the color white. He symbolized wisdom and knowledge as well as other positive attributes. A second figure was a king called Kukulcán who was described as being fair-skinned and bearded who reigned c.925-950. He sailed eastward but prophesied his return in the year of One Reed. See *The Captive* and *The Feathered Serpent*.

R

RALEIGH (RALEGH). (1554-1618). As an English courtier, navigator, historian, and poet, Elizabeth I granted him patent to take unknown American lands in her name. He explored the east coast from Florida to North Carolina, naming the coast north of Florida as "Virginia." He sent the settlers who occupied Roanoke Island, North Carolina, and he introduced potatoes and tobacco into England. The Earl of Essex replaced him in the Queen's favor because of a secret marriage to one of her maids. James I banished him with his wife and son to The Tower, and although he was freed to go exploring again, upon his return, he was beheaded at Whitehall under the charge of the old sentence against him. See *Death of the Fox*.

REMBRANDT VAN RIJN. (1606-1669). He was the leading representative of the Dutch school of painting and master of light and shadow. He settled in Amsterdam where he was a portrait painter and teacher. See *The Golden Tulip.*

RICHARD I OF ENGLAND. (1157-1199). Third son of Henry II and Eleanor of Aquitaine, he succeeded to the throne in 1189. The same year, he started on the Third Crusade where he aided in the capture of Acre in 1191 and recaptured Jaffa from Saladin. He was captured in Austria as he returned to Europe in 1192 and ransomed and returned to England in 1194. While fighting Philip II in France, he was killed near Limoges. See *Here Be Dragons.*

RICHARD II. (1377-99). Son of Edward the Black Prince, he became a Plantagenet king when he succeeded Edward III as king. He banished Henry of Bolingbroke (later Henry IV) but Henry came back and defeated and captured him. He was deposed by Parliament and imprisoned. See *The Peace Child.*

RICHARD III OF ENGLAND. (1452-1485). The son of Richard Plantagenet, he helped restore his brother Edward IV to the throne by defeating Lancastrians at Barnet and Tewkesbury in 1471. At Edward IV's death, he became the protectorate of young Edward V until Edward V was declared illegitimate. Then Richard III took crown in 1483. Often he is accused of the murders of Edward V and edward's younger brother Richard. The first of the Tudor family, Henry VII, defeated him at the battle of Bosworth Field on August 22, 1485. See *The Lark and the Laurel* and *The Sprig of Broom.*

ROBESPIERRE. (1758-1794). He demanded the death of the king during the French Revolution in 1793 and was responsible for much of the Reign of Terror, sending some of his friends to the guillotine in 1794. He was overthrown by the Revolution of Ninth Thermidor on July 27, 1794, and was arrested and guillotined the next day by the Revolutionary Tribunal. His death ended the Reign of Terror. See *In Search of Honor* and *The Wind from the Sea.*

ROSENBERG, JULIUS (1918-1953) **AND ETHEL** (1915-1953). Both born in New York City, they were members of the Communist party and were convicted of being American spies who received nuclear weapons data from her brother, stationed in Los Alamos, New Mexico, and passing it through a courier to the Soviet vice consul in New

York. They were convicted on her brother's testimony and were the first American citizens executed for espionage. See *Looking Out*.

ROUNDHEADS. The Royalists in the English Civil War called the Parliamentarians "roundheads," the nickname used for the unruly, close-cropped London apprentices. See *The Half Child*.

ROYALISTS. Members of this group supported Charles I in the English Civil War. See *Beyond the Weir Bridge, Circle of Pearls, Harrow and Harvest*, and *The Witch of Blackbird Pond*.

S

SACAGAWEA. (c.1786-1812). Also known as "Bird Woman," she was a member of the Shoshone tribe, captured by the Hidatasas in 1800 and sold to a Canadian trapper, Toussaint Charbonneau. She married him in 1804 by Indian rites and then accompanied him as a guide on the Lewis and Clark expedition. See *Streams to the River, River to the Sea: A Novel of Sacagawea*.

ST. JOHN OF JERUSALEM, ORDER OF THE HOSPITAL OF. Known as the Hospitallers, this order was one of the first orders of knights. Its members were dubbed at the tomb of Christ, the Holy Sepulchre, from the end of the eleventh century. They were international with a religious purpose and form. The members pledged celibacy and their grand master, provincial masters ("pillars"), grand priors, and commanders resembled the hierarchy of the church. They served on Rhodes from 1309 to 1522 and then on Malta from 1530 to 1798. Since 1834, they have been known by this name and have kept the headquarters in Rome. See *Knight Crusader* and *Manwolf*.

SAXON. This Germanic people supposedly lived in Schleswig and along the Baltic coast. They pirated Roman ships and settled, although not permanently, on the French coast. They made conquests in Britain and on the continent until 700. Charlemagne fought them beginning in 772 for thirty-two years in the Saxon wars which ended with the Saxons becoming incorporated into the Frankish empire. See *The Namesake* and *The Shining Company*.

SCHUSCHNIGG, KURT. (1897-1977). When he served Austria as federal chancellor, he tried to prevent Hitler's takeover of Austria, but the Nazis imprisoned him from 1938-45. After living in the United States until 1967, he returned to Austria. See *The Devil in Vienna.*

SENUSERT III (SESOSTRIS III). (1878-1843 BC). Son of Senusert II and father of Amenemhet III, he built the pyramid at Dashur. He raised Egypt to a state of great power, embracing one thousand miles of Nile Valley. See *The Reluctant God.*

SHAKERS. As a religious sect which observed a doctrine of celibacy, common property, and community living, it used a dance as part of its religious ritual. See *Out of Step with the Dancers.*

SHAKESPEARE, WILLIAM. (1564-1616). Often considered the greatest writer to have ever lived, he wrote poetry and plays in England during the reign of Elizabeth I. He also helped establish the Globe theater. See *Black Swan.*

SHAWNEE. This Algonquian-speaking tribe lived in the central Ohio Valley until the seventeenth century when the Iroquis scattered it. They reunited after 1725 and formed the principal barrier to westward settlement. Tecumseh failed to keep them united, and they eventually settled in different parts of Oklahoma. Long influenced by their association with the Seneca and Delaware Indians, they combined eastern woodland and prairie traits. In summer they lived in bark-covered houses while in winter they moved to hunting camps. Each village had a large council house used for religious ceremonies such as the ritual purification of warriors. Other rituals included the spring Bread Dance (field planting), the Green Corn Dance (crop ripening), and the autumn Bread Dance. The clans were patrilineal. See *The Christmas Surprise, Red Pawns,* and *Trail Through Danger.*

SHAYS, DANIEL. (1747?-1825). After fighting in the American Revolution, he led an insurrection in western Massachusetts to attack a United States government arsenal in Springfield in 1787. After being repulsed, he was sentenced to death but pardoned in 1788. See *The Winter Hero.*

SHERIDAN, PHILIP. (1831-1888). After an illustrious career as a military leader during the American Civil War where he helped gain Lee's surrender, he governed the frontier area. His severity forced his transfer to another post but he succeeded Sherman as commander-in-chief of the United States army in 1883. See *The Killer Angels.*

SHOGUN. This Japanese title first appeared in 720 to signify an emperor's supreme military commander. Minamoto Yoritomo in 1148 first used the title as a basis for asserting both military and political power over the country. In 1867, the shogun resigned his title and acceded civil and military administration back to the emperor. See *The Boy and the Samurai, Of Nightingales That Weep, Samurai of Gold Hill, The Samurai's Tale, Shogun,* and *The Sign of the Chrysanthemum.*

SHOSHONE. (also spelled "Shoshoni") A Native American tribe originally scattered over Montana, Wyoming, and Oregon, it is part of a Uto-Aztecan linguistic family, which also includes Comanche, Ute, Painte, and Hopi. The Utes come from western Colorado and eastern Utah, giving its name to that state. In 1776, the members had no horses and lived in small family clusters surviving on gathered food. In the early nineteenth century, they acquired horses and began to steal livestock from settlers. Some of them are now known as Paiutes. See *Jenny of the Tetons, The Legend of Jimmy Spoon,* and *Streams to the River, River to the Sea.*

SIKH. A person who follows an Indian religion combining Islamic and Hindu beliefs founded in the late fifteenth century by the first *guru* (teacher), Nanak. The word comes from the Sanskrit, *shishya* which means "disciple." A Sikh is a disciple of the ten gurus, some of whose writings appear in the Granth Sahib, their sacred book. World wide approximately eight million people are Sikhs, with the concentration being in East Punjab where they created a powerful state under Ranjit Singh before the British took over the country. See *Day of the Scorpion, A Division of the Spoils, The Jewel in the Crown,* and *The Towers of Silence.*

SIOUX. Part of the Siouan linguistic family, this tribe is also called Dakota. The members were Plains Indians who hunted buffalo and lived in tepees. They were nomadic, non-agricultural, and proud of their war exploits. Their greatest ceremony was the Sun Dance. The United States government took their valuable land of the Black Hills when gold was discovered. See *A Circle Unbroken, Eyes of Darkness, Featherboy and the Buffalo,* and *Save Queen of Sheba.*

SITTING BULL. (c.1831-1890). As a member of the Hunkpapa Sioux
tribe, he was made chief of the entire Sioux nation c.1867. With Gall
and Crazy Horse at the battle of Little Big Horn, he helped defeat
Custer in 1876. He retreated across the Canadian border in 1877.
After returning to surrender at Fort Buford in 1881, he gained
international fame as a member of Buffalo Bill's Wild West Show in
1885. By 1890, he had again become active in Sioux affairs and was
shot by guards. See *Thunder Rolling in the Mountains.*

SNORRI STURLUSON. (1179-1241). Before being involved in political
intrigues against King Haakon IV of Norway from 1218 and later
assassinated, he was an historian who recorded the Icelandic sagas,
the *Heimskringla* and *Younger, or Prose, Edda.* See *Westward to
Vinland.*

SOCRATES. (c.470-399 BC). As a Greek philosopher, he developed the
method of inquiry and instruction where a series of questions was
designed to elicit a clear expression of something that all rational
beings should know. Accused of various offenses, he refused to change
his attitudes, and when condemned, drank hemlock in prison. He left
none of his own writings, but his disciple Plato recorded his
philosophies. See *The Last of the Wine.*

SQUANTO. (d. 1622) A Native American of the Pawtuxet tribe, he was
captured by John Smith's expedition, sold as a slave in Spain, and
eventually made his way back to America via England. He taught the
colonists how to plant and fertilize corn. See *Squanto, Friend of the
Pilgrim; The Thanksgiving Story,* and *This New Land.*

STALIN, JOSEPH. (1879-1953). A Soviet political leader from George,
he developed the idea of five-year plans, purges of the Communist
party, and of the Russian army. He annexed the Baltic states while
repressing his people and building up his weapons in a military
rivalry with the United States. See *My Grandmother's Journey, Tug of
War,* and *Year of Impossible Goodbyes.*

STANDISH, MYLES. (1584?-1656). He sailed on the *Mayflower* in 1620
with the Pilgrims to America. As a leader, he negotiated in England
for land ownership and supplies. When he returned, he and John
Alden founded Duxbury, Massachusetts, in 1631. No historical account
exists for the tale of Alden's proposal to Priscilla as chronicled in

Longfellow's *The Courtship of Myles Standish*. See *Constance* and *This New Land*.

STANTON, ELIZABETH CADY. (1815-1902). With Lucretia Mott, she organized the first women's rights convention in Seneca Falls, New York in 1848. She then helped Susan B. Anthony with the movement and became the first president of the National Woman Suffrage Association from 1869-90. See *Bloomers*.

STEPHEN. (c. 1097-1154). At Henry I's death, he claimed the throne of England, declaring that Matilda (Maud), Henry's daughter, was the daughter of a nun, and therefore, illegitimate. He was crowned at Westminster, and then he and Matilda continued fighting over the throne until he finally recognized as his heir, Henry of Anjou (Henry II), Matilda's son. See the titles of Ellis Peters in "Europe and Great Britain: 476-1199."

STRADIVARI, ANTONIO. (1644?-1737). An Italian violin maker, he lived his entire life in Cremona. He devised the modern form of violin bridge as well as the proportions of the instrument. See *Turi's Poppa* and *The Violin Man*.

STUARTS. This Scottish and English royal house began with a follower of William the Conqueror. It provided the sovereigns of Scotland from 1371 to 1688 and various sovereigns of England. After JAMES II was deposed in 1688, the Jacobites upheld the Stuart claim for many years. See *Death of the Fox*, *The Spanish Letters*, *The Succession The 13th Member*, and *You Never Knew Her As I Did*.

SULLA. (138-78 BC). Roman general and politician who opened civil war with Gaius Marius in 88 BC and eventually defeated the younger Marius in 82. See *The First Man in Rome*, *Fortune's Favorites*, and *The Grass Crown*.

SUTTER, JOHN. (1803-1880). An American pioneer who founded a colony on the present site of Sacramento, California, he received a land grant from the Mexican government, and when gold was discovered on his land, his workmen deserted, people stole his sheep and cattle, and squatters occupied it so that he became bankrupt. See *Treasure in the Stream*.

T

TARTARS [TATAR]. The ancient name Tatar has been attributed to many groups with little or no relationship to the Turkic-speaking people whose main locale is in the Soviet Union east of the Ural Mountains. The name was given to single tribes or to all the nomads of the Asian steppes and deserts including Mongols and Turks. The term also applied to peoples and states of the Mongol Empire in the thirteenth and fourteenth centuries. See *The Trumpeter of Krakow*.

THEODORA. (c. 500-548 AD). IN her early life, she was an actress known for her beauty. She married Justinian I at twenty -five and for twenty years, she exerted a great influence over him and over the political and religious events of the Eastern Roman Empire in Constantinople. See *The Bearkeeper's Daughter*.

THESEUS. (c. 1400). A principal hero of Attica in Greek legend, he was the son of Aegeus and the King of Athens. He killed the minotar on Crete. See *The Bull from the Sea* and *The King Must Die*.

THUTMOSE III. (d. 1450 BC). When he overcame the regency of his step-mother Hatshepsut, he became one of the greatest Egyptian kings. Among his conquests were Syria, Mitanni, and other parts of Asia. He enlarged the great temple of Amon at Karnak and had his stories written on its walls. He built or restored many temples in cities such as Memphis and Heliopolis. Of many obelisks erected, two known as Cleopatra's Needles stand in London and New York. See *Mara, Daughter of the Nile* and *Child of the Morning*.

TITO. (1892-1980). A mechanic by trade, he became a Yugoslav statesman from the Communist Party. He conducted a policy of non-alignment with either the Soviet Union or the West. See *White Eagles Over Serbia*.

TORY. Meaning Loyalist, the term Tory was an Irish name suggesting a Papist outlaw and was applied to those who in 1679 supported the hereditary right of James II to succeed to the throne in spite of his Roman Catholic faith. See *Early Thunder, The Fighting Ground, Katie's Trunk, Johnny Tremain, My Brother Sam Is Dead, The Sentinels, Time Enough for Drums*, and *Treegate's Raiders*.

TUDORS. Owen Tudor, born in 1400, founded this English house which occupied the throne of England from 1485-1603. The rulers were

Henry VII and VIII, Edward VI, Mary I, and Elizabeth I. See *The Cargo of the Madalena* and *The Merchant's Mark*.

TYNDALE, WILLIAM. (c.1494-1536). As the first English translator of the New Testament and Pentateuch of the *Bible*, he began printing it in Cologne in 1525 and completed it in Worms in 1526. He escaped the seizure ordered by Wolsey, but after a controversy with Sir Thomas More in 1531, he was arrested at Antwerp and condemned for heresy, strangled, and burned at the stake. See *The Hawk That Dare Not Fly by Day*.

U

UNDERGROUND RAILWAY. A group of abolitionists functioned in secret to transport slaves north to Canada and freedom during the first half of the nineteenth century. See *The Borning Room, Brady, Charley Skedaddle, Children of the Fire, The Drinking Gourd, A Family Apart, Follow the Drinking Gourd, The House of Dies Drear, Jayhawker, Next Stop, Freedom, Runaway to Freedom, Steal Away, Sweet Clara and the Freedom Quilt, Thee Hannah!,* and *The Tin Heart*.

V

VELÁZQUEZ, DIEGO. (1599-1660). As the Spanish court painter for Philip IV, he attained fame with religious works and portraits and used light in a way that anticipated the Impressionists of the nineteenth century. See *I, Juan de Pareja*.

VERCINQETORIX. (d. 46 BC). Gallic chief of the Arverni and the leader of a rebellion which initiated the Gallic war. He was eventually besieged by Caesar in Alesia and forced to surrender in 52 BC. He was taken to Rome and exhibited as Caesar's triumph and then executed. See *The Druids*.

VERMEER, JAN. (1632-1675). His entire life was spent in Delft. In his paintings, he displayed a scientific interest in light, perspective, and color. See *The Golden Tulip*.

VESPASIAN. (9-79 AD). He was the Roman Emperor from 69-79 AD. HE commanded legions in Germany and Britain and conducted war against the Jews under Nero. He also begin erecting the Colosseum. See *Shadows in Bronze, Silver Pigs,* and *Venus in Copper.*

VICTORIA OF ENGLAND. (1819-1901). Her very long and intelligent reign, even after the death of her beloved husband, signified a new idea of British monarchy and kept the empire unified. See *Belgrave Square, The Face of a Stranger, The India Fan, The Island Harp, A Likely Lad, Parnell and the Englishwoman, A Pistol in Greenyards, Secret for a Nightingale, Snare of Serpents, Young Art and Old Hector,* and all the Robert Newman titles in "Europe and Great Britain: 1849-1918."

VIKING. The term is applied today to Scandinavians who left their homes intent on raiding or conquest, and their descendants, during a period extending roughly from AD 800-1050. They raided England, the western seas and Ireland, France or the Carolingian Empire, and into Spain and the Mediterranean. See *Blood Feud, Pangur Ban,* and *Viking's Dawn.*

VORTIGERN. (c.450). As a British ruler, he is reported to have invited the Saxons to britain in order to repel the Picts and the Scots as well as to have married Rowena, the daughter of Hengist. See *The Lantern Bearers.*

W

WASHINGTON, GEORGE. (1732-1799). Before he became the first president of the United States, he was the commanding general of the Continental Armies as they fought to defeat the British in the American Revolution. See *The Cabin Faced West, The Sign Painter's Secret* and *This Time, Tempe Wick?*

WATIE, STAND. (1806-1871). Born near Rome, Georgia, he was an American Indian leader who agreed with the removal of the Cherokee tribe to Indian territory. He raised a regiment of Cherokee mounted riflemen to serve with the Confederates in 1861 and rose to brigadier general in 1864. See *Rifles for Watie.*

WESLEY, JOHN. (1703-1791). He began an English religious leader after an experience at Aldersgate where he began to accept the

principle of justification by faith. He also traveled to Georgia where
he served as a missionary among colonists and Indian tribes. See
Peter Treegate's War and *Sea Captain from Salem*

WHIG. This term of abuse introduced in 1679 during the heated
struggle to exclude James II from succession referred to people who
wanted to exclude the heir from the throne. Cattle and horse thieves
were the original whigs, but Scottish Presbyterians also gained the
name. In the eighteenth century, people who represented the interests
of dissenters and industrialists who desired electorial, parliamentary,
and philanthropic reforms were also whigs. See *George Midgett's War,
Johnny Tremain,* and *The Sentinels.*

WILLIAM THE CONQUEROR. (c. 1028-1987). As the bastard son of a
Duke of Normandy, he was accepted by nobles as his father's
successor. He probably received a promise from Edward the Confessor
of England that he should succeed him, and Harold, Earl of Wessex,
supported his claim until Edward actually died. In 1066, William
invaded England, and with Harold's brother Tostig's support, defeated
Harold at Senlac later called Battle. After his crowning at
Westminster, he began building the Tower. He also built a "new
castle" north on the River Tyne. To complete his conquest, he made a
land survey to certify that he was receiving all his dues and had the
information recorded in the Domesday Book. He established the
feudal system and refused to pay homage to the pope. He died after
falling from his horse when entering the captured town of Mantes. He
was buried in the abbey he built in Caen. See *The Disputed Crown,
Gildenford, King of the Wood, The Norman Pretender, The Proud
Villeins,* and *The Striped Ships.*

WILLIAM OF ORANGE AND OF ENGLAND. (1650-1702). Through
his marriage to Mary, daughter of James II of England, he became
King of England in the Glorious Revolution of 1688. Both whigs and
tories asked him to become king, and when he landed in Torbay,
Devonshire with a Dutch army, before blood was shed, Parliament
invited him to accept the throne. He built Kensington Palace and
founded the Greenwich Naval Hospital. See *Bonnie Dundee.*

WILLIAM II OF GERMANY. (1859-1941). As the Emperor of German
and king of Prussia, he unsuccessfully opposed Socialism, instead
siding with Austria-Hungary in 1914 during its crisis with Serbia.

He became a dominant force of the Central Powers at the beginning of
World War II, but he fled to Holland after losing the war and
abdicated in 1918. See *The Edge of the Cloud, No Hero for the Kaiser,*
and *Summer of the Zeppelin.*

WILLIAM II (RUFUS). (c. 1056-1100). He was the second surviving son
of William the Conqueror and was crowned at Westminster in 1087.
He made many unfulfilled promises and invaded Normandy and Wales
three times each. Slain by an arrow from an unknown source
(although traditionally it is attributed to Walter Tirel, a Norman)
while hunting in New Forest. The Church refused to give him rites.
See *King of the Wood.*

WREN, CHRISTOPHER. As an English architect, he proposed a plan
for rebuilding London after the GREAT FIRE OF 1666. He designed
and built fifty-three churches in London and is perhaps best known for
his design of the new St. Paul's Cathedral. See *Circle of Pearls* and
The Great House.

Y

YETI. Known as "The Abominable Snowman," this mythical monster
supposedly inhabits the Himalayas at about the level of the snow line.
No one has ever seen one alive or dead, but certain marks found in
the snow have been attributed to it. The marks have probably been
made by falling snow or stones or produced by bears. At certain gaits,
bears place their hind feet partly over the imprint of their forefeet,
making a very large imprint that looks like an enormous human
footprint traveling in the opposite direction. See *King of the Cloud
Forests.*

YORK. This English royal house, one branch of which was Plantagenet,
had as its symbol the red rose in the Wars of Roses with the
Lancasters. Its kings were Edward IV and V and Richard III. See
appropriate titles under entries for individual rulers.

YORUBA TRIBE. Members of this tribe in modern Nigeria were taken
as slaves to the Americas. They worshipped a pantheon of gods
including the trickster, and have brought this worship into North
America. See *The Sentinels.*

APPENDIX F. WORKS WITH SEQUELS, SAME CHARACTERS, OR IN SERIES

Boyne, Walter

>
> 1927   *Trophy for Eagles* (United States)   p. 215
> 1935   *Eagles at War*   p. 238
> 1942-57   *Air Force Eagles*   p. 238

Byars, Betsy

>
> c.1880   *The Golly Sisters Go West* (United States)   p. 177
> c.1880   *Hooray for the Golly Sisters*   p. 177

Carrick, Donald

>
> c.1250   *Harald and the Giant Knight* (England)   p. 61
> c.1250   *Harald and the Great Stag*   p. 61

Choi, Sook Nyul

>
> 1945   *Year of Impossible Goodbyes* (South Korea)   p. 311
> 1952   *Echoes of the White Giraffe*   p. 311

Conlon-McKenna, Marita

>
> c.1850   *Under the Hawthorn Tree* (Ireland)   p. 82
> c.1851   *Wildflower Girl*   p. 150

Davis, Lindsey

>
> 70   *Silver Pigs* (Rome)   p. 12
> 70   *Shadows in Bronze*   p. 11
> 71   *Venus in Copper*   p. 12

Douglas, Carole Nelson

>
> c.1885   *Good Morning, Irene* (Europe)   p. 24
> c.1890   *Irene at Large*   p. 25

Duder, Tessa

>
> 1959   *In Lane Three, Alex Archer* (New Zealand)   p. 287
> 1960   *Alex in Rome*   p. 287

Hansen, Joyce

>
> 1861   *Which Way Freedom?* (United States)   p. 168
> 1863   *Out From This Place*   p. 167

Harvey, Brett

> 1889   *My Prairie Christmas* (United States) p. 182
> 1889   *My Prairie Year* p. 182

Herman, Charlotte

> 1946   *Millie Cooper, 3B* (United States) p. 254
> 1947   *Millie Cooper, Take a Chance* p. 254

Howard, Ellen

> c.1880   *The Chickenhouse House* p. 183
> 1886   *Sister* p. 183

Hunter, Mollie

> 1938   *A Sound of Chariots* (Scotland) p. 101
> 1939   *Hold On to Love* p. 101

Jones, Douglas C.

> 1861   *Elkhorn Tavern* (United States) p. 169
> 1865   *Roman* p. 184
> 1899   *Come Winter* p. 203

Jones, Douglas C.

> c.1985   *Winding Stair* (United States) p. 204
> 1898   *Remember Santiago* p. 204
> 1925   *Weedy Rough* p. 218

Klein, Robin

> 1040   *All In Blue Unclouded Weather* (Australia) p. 288
> 1948   *Dresses of Red and Gold* p. 289

Lawlor, Laurie

> 1883   *Addie Across the Prairie* p. 185
> 1884   *Addie's Dakota Winter* p. 186
> 1886   *Addie's Long Summer* p. 186
> 1887   *George on his Own* p. 186

Levitin, Sonia

    c.1939   *Journey to America* (Switzerland) p. 37
    c.1943   *Silver Days* (United States) p. 244
    1945   *Annie's Promise* p. 244

Lindgard, Joan

    1944   *Tug of War* (Germany) p. 277
    1948   *Between Two Worlds* (Canada) p. 276

Lord, Athena

    1939   *Today's Special: Z.A.P. & Zoe* (United States) p. 229
    1940   *The Luck of Z.A.P. & Zoe* p. 228
    1941   *Z.A.P., Zoe, & the Musketeers* p. 245

McCullough, Colleen

    c.110 BC   *The First Man in Rome* (Italy) p. 13
    c.80 BC   *The Grass Crown* p. 13
    c.60 BC   *Fortune's Favorites* p. 13

MacLachlan, Patricia

    c. 1850   *Sarah, Plain and Tall* (United States) p. 157
    c. 1851   *Skylark* p. 157

Matas, Carol

    1940   *Lisa's War* (Denmark) p. 39
    1945   *Code Name Kris* p. 38

Moore, Ruth

    1755   *The Christmas Surprise* (American Colonies) p. 124
    1777   *Distant Thunder* p. 131

O'Dell, Scott

    1506   *The Captive* (South and Central America) p. 280
    1520   *The Feathered Serpent* p. 281
    1530   *The Amethyst Ring* p. 280

Pearson, Kit

    1940   *The Sky Is Falling* (Canada) p. 278
    1944   *Looking at the Moon* p. 277

Penman, Sharon Kay

c.1183   *Here Be Dragons* (England) p. 64
c.1231   *Falls the Shadow* p. 64
c.1250   *The Reckoning* p. 65

Peters, Ellis

1139   *The Leper of St. Giles* (England) p. 55
1139   *St. Peter's Fair* p. 57
1139   *The Virgin in the Ice* p. 58
1140   *The Devil's Novice* p. 54
1140   *Monk's Hood* p. 56
1140   *A Morbid Taste for Bones* p. 56
1140   *The Sanctuary Sparrow* p. 58
1141   *Dead Man's Ransom* p. 54
1141   *An Excellent Mystery* p. 54
1141   *The Pilgrim of Hate* p. 56
1141   *The Raven in the Foregate* p. 57
1142   *The Confession of Brother Haluin* p. 54
1142   *The Hermit of Eyton Forest* p. 55
1142   *The Rose Rent* p. 57
1143   *The Heretic's Apprentice* p. 55
1143   *The Potter's Field* p. 56
1144   *The Holy Thief* p. 55
1144   *The Summer of the Danes* p. 58

Peyton, K. M.

1908   *Flambards* (England) p. 104
1914   *The Edge of the Cloud* p. 101
1916   *Flambards in Summer* p. 104

Pullman, Philip

1872   *The Ruby in the Smoke* (England) p. 96
1880   *Shadow in the North* p. 96
1881   *The Tiger in the Well* p. 97

Reiss, Johanna

1942   *The Upstairs Room* (Holland) p. 42
1945   *The Journey Back* p. 41

Renault, Mary

c.1400 BC   *The King Must Die* (Greece) p. 6
c.1400 BC   *The Bull from the Sea* p. 5

Renault, Mary

  352 BC   *Fire from Heaven* (Macedonia, Greece) p. 6
  326 BC   *The Persian Boy* p. 7

Riley, Judith Merkle

  1355   *A Vision of Light* (England) p. 66
  1356   *In Pursuit of the Green Lion* p. 66

Sandin, Joan

  1868   *The Long Way to a New Land* (Sweden) p. 190
  1868   *The Long Way Westward* (United States) p. 190

Scott, Paul

  1942   *The Jewel in the Crown* (India) p. 300
  1942   *The Day of the Scorpion* p. 299
  1939+   *The Towers of Silence* p. 300
  1945   *A Division of the Spoils* p. 300

Shuler, Linda Lay

  c.1200   *She Who Remembers* (Native America) p. 113
  c.1200   *Voice of the Eagle* p. 114

Shura, Mary Francis

  1843   *Kate's Book* (United States) p. 148
  1843   *Kate's House* p. 148

Taylor, Mildred

  1931   *Mississippi Bridge* (United States) p. 233
  1932   *Song of the Trees* p. 234
  1933   *Roll of Thunder, Hear My Cry* p. 234
  1933   *The Friendship* p. 232
  1934   *Let the Circle Be Unbroken* p. 233
  1941   *The Road to Memphis* p. 247

Willard, Barbara

APPENDIX G. COUNTRY AND DATES OF SETTING IN EUROPE AND THE BRITISH ISLES

Works with two major settings are cross-referenced.

AUSTRIA

Carter, Peter. *Children of the Book* (1492 1789) p. 21
Hackl, Erich. *Farewell Sidonia* (1919-1945) p. 34
Härtling, Peter. *Crutches* (1919-1945) p. 46
Orgel, Doris. *The Devil in Vienna* (1919-1945) p. 40

BELGIUM

Hesse, Karen. *Letters from Rifka* (1790-1918) p. 26
O'Dell, Scott. *The Hawk That Dare Not Hunt by Day* (1492-1789) p. 70

CONSTANTINOPLE (BYZANTIUM, ISTANBUL)

Bellairs, John. *The Trolley to Yesterday* (1200-1491) p. 18
Bradshaw, Gillian. *The Bearkeeper's Daughter* (476-1199) p. 15
Dickinson, Peter. *The Dancing Bear* (476-1199) p. 15
Paton Walsh, Jill. *The Emperor's Winding Sheet* (1200-1491) p. 19
Sutcliff, Rosemary. *Blood Feud* (476-1199) p. 16
Treece, Henry. *The Road to Miklagard* (476-1199) p. 17

DENMARK

Benchley, Nathaniel. *Bright Candles* (1919-1945) p. 30
Haugaard, Erik. *Chase Me, Catch Nobody* (1919-1945) p. 35
Holm, Ann. *North to Freedom* (1919-1945) p. 47
Lowry, Lois. *Number the Stars* (1919-1945) p. 37
Matas, Carol. *Code Name Kris* (1919-1945) p. 38
Matas, Carol. *Lisa's War* (1919-1945) p. 39

ENGLAND

Anand, Valerie. *The Disputed Crown* (476-1199) p. 49
Anand, Valerie. *Gildenford* (476-1199) p. 49
Anand, Valerie. *King of the Wood* (476-1199) p. 50
Anand, Valerie. *The Norman Pretender* (476-1199) p. 50
Anand, Valerie. *The Proud Villeins* (476-1199) p. 50
Avery, Gillian. *A Likely Lad* (1849-1918) p. 86
Avery, Gillian. *Maria Escapes* (1849-1918) p. 86
Bawden, Nina. *Carrie's War* (1919-1945) p. 99
Bawden, Nina. *Henry* (1919-1945) p. 99
Bawden, Nina. *The Peppermint Pig* (1849-1918) p. 87

FRANCE

Roper, Robert. *In Caverns of Blue Ice* (1919-1945) p. 47
Roth-Hano, Renee. *Touch Wood* (1919-1945) p. 42

GERMANY

Degens, T. *On the Third Ward* (1919-1945) p. 46
Gallaz, C. and R. Innocenti. *Rose Blanche* (1919-1945) p. 33
Gehrts, Barbara. *Don't Say a Word* (1919-1945) p. 33
Glasco, G. *Slow Through Eden* (1919-1945) (United States) p. 34
Härtling, Peter. *Crutches* (1919-1945) p. 46
Haugaard, Erik. *Chase Me, Catch Nobody* (1919-1945) p. 35
Heuck, Sigrid. *The Hideout* (1919-1945) p. 36
Kordon, Klaus. *Brothers Like Friends* (1919-1945) p. 47
Marvin, Isabel R. *Bridge to Freedom* (1919-1945) p. 38
Mattingley, C. *The Angel with a Mouth Organ* (1919-1945) p. 39
Richter, Hans. *Friedrich* (1919-1945) p. 42
Richter, Hans. *I Was There* (1919-1945) p. 42
Skurzynski, Gloria. *What Happened in Hamelin* (476-1199) p. 16
Wild, Margaret. *Let the Celebrations Begin!* (1919-1945) p. 44
Ziefert, Harriet. *A New Coat for Anna* (1919-1945) p. 48

GREECE

Fenton, Edward. *The Morning of the Gods* (1919-1945) p. 46
Rosen, Billi. *Andi's War* (1919-1945) p. 48
Zei, Aliki. *Petro's War* (1919-1945) p. 45
Zei, Aliki. *Wildcat Under Glass* (1919-1945) p. 45

HOLLAND

HUNGARY

IRELAND

Conlon-McKenna, M. *Under the Hawthorn Tree* (1790-1848) p. 82
Flanagan, Thomas. *The Year of the French* (1790-1848) p. 82
Haugaard, Erik. *A Boy's Will* (1649-1789) p. 78
Llywelyn, M. *Brian Boru: Emperor of the Irish* (476-1199) p. 53
Llywelyn, M. *The Last Prince of Ireland* (1492-1789) p. 70
Langenus, Ron. *Mission West* (1649-1789) p. 80
Leonard, Hugh. *Parnell and the Englishwoman* (1849-1918) p. 92
Malterre, Elona. *The Last Wolf of Ireland* (1649-1789) p. 80
Stolz, Mary. *Pangur Ban* (476-1199) p. 59
Treece, Henry. *Viking's Dawn* (476-1199) p. 60
Uris, Leon. *Trinity* (1849-1918) p. 98
Wheeler, Thomas G. *A Fanfare for the Stalwart* (1790-1848) p. 29

ITALY

Avery, Gillian. *Maria's Italian Spring* (1790-1918) p. 24
Coolidge, Oliva. *Roman People* (to 476 AD) p. 11
Davis, Lindsey. *Shadows in Bronze* (to 476 AD) p. 11
Davis, Lindsey. *Silver Pigs* (to 476 AD) p. 12
Davis, Lindsey. *Venus in Copper* (to 476 AD) p. 12
De Trevino, Elizabeth. *Turi's Poppa* (1919-1945) p. 46
Dillon, Eilís. *Children of Bach* (1919-1945) p. 32
Haugaard, Erik. *The Little Fishes* (1919-1945) p. 35
Holm, Ann. *North to Freedom* (1919-1945) p. 47
Hooper, Maureen Brett. *The Violin Man* (1790-1918) p. 26
Laker, Rosalind. *The Venetian Mask* (1649-1789) p. 22
McCullough, Colleen. *The First Man in Rome* (to 476 AD) p. 13
McCullough, Colleen. *Fortune's Favorites* (to 476 AD) p. 13
McCullough, Colleen. *The Grass Crown* (to 476 AD) p. 13
O'Dell, Scott. *The Road to Damietta* (1200-1491) p. 19

NORWAY

McSwigan, Marie. *Snow Treasure* (1919-1945) p. 38

POLAND

Aaron, Chester. *Gideon* (1919-1945) p. 30
Bergman, Tamar. *Along the Tracks* (1919-1945) p. 31
Frank, Rudolf. *No Hero for the Kaiser* (1919-1945) p. 33
Hautzig, Esther. *The Endless Steppe* (1919-1945) p. 35
Hautzig, Esther. *Riches* (1790-1918) p. 25
Kelly, Eric. *The Trumpeter of Krakow* (1200-1491) p. 19
Laird, Christa. *Shadow of the Wall* (1919-1945) p. 37
Matas, Carol. *Daniel's Story* (1919-1945) p. 38
Orlev, Uri. *The Island on Bird Street* (1919-1945) p. 40
Orlev, Uri. *The Man from the Other Side* (1919-1945) p. 40
Sender, Ruth Minsky. *The Cage* (1919-1945) p. 43
Serraillier, Ian. *The Silver Sword* (1919-1945) p. 43
Skurzynski, Gloria. *Manwolf* (1200-1491) p. 19
Treseder, Terry Walton. *Hear O Israel* (1919-1945) p. 44
Wheeler, Thomas Gerald. *A Fanfare for the Stalwart* (1790-1848)
    p. 29
Yolen, Jane. *The Devil's Arithmetic* (1919-1945) (United States)
    p. 44

RUSSIA

Almedingen, E. M. *Anna* (1492-1789) p. 21
Almedingen, E. M. *The Crimson Oak* (1492-1789) p. 21
Baklanov, Grigory. *Forever Nineteen* (1919-1945) p. 30
Bergman, Tamar. *Along the Tracks* (1919-1945) p. 31
Cech, John. *My Grandmother's Journey* (1919-1945) p. 31
Geras, Adèle. *Voyage* (1790-1918) p. 25
Hautzig, Esther. *The Endless Steppe* (1919-1945) p. 35
Heaven, Constance. *The Raging Fire* (1790-1918) p. 25
Herman, C. *The House on Walenska Street* (1790-1918) p. 26
Hesse, Karen. *Letters from Rifka* (1790-1918) p. 26
Holman, Felice. *The Wild Children* (1919-1945) p. 36
Levine, Arthur A. *All the Lights in the Night* (1790-1918) p. 27
Levitin, Sonia. *A Sound to Remember* (1790-1848) p. 27
Matas, Carol. *Sworn Enemies* (1790-1848) p. 27
Pitt, Nancy. *Beyond the High White Wall* (1790-1918) p. 28
Posell, Elsa. *Homecoming* (1919-1945) p. 41
Segal, Jerry. *The Place Where Nobody Stopped* (1790-1918) p. 28
Sevela, E. *We Were Not Like Other People* (1919-1945) p. 43
Wheeler, Thomas G. *A Fanfare for the Stalwart* (1790-1848) p. 29
Zei, Aliki. *The Sound of Dragon's Feet* (1790-1918) p. 29

SERBIA

Durrell, Lawrence. *White Eagles over Serbia* (1919-1945) p. 32

SCANDINAVIA

SCOTLAND

SPAIN

Aiken, Joan. *Bridle the Wind* (1492-1789) p. 20
Aiken, Joan. *The Teeth of the Gale* (1492-1789) p. 20
Conrad, Pam. *Pedro's Journal* (Before 1600) (Caribbean) p. 279
De Trevino, Elizabeth. *I, Juan de Pareja* (1492-1789) p. 21
Foreman, M., and R. Seaver. *The Boy Who Sailed With Columbus* (Before 1600) (Caribbean) p. 279
Litowinsky, O. *The High Voyage* (Before 1600) (Caribbean) p. 280
Schlein, Miriam. *I Sailed With Columbus* (Before 1600) (Caribbean) p. 281

SWEDEN

Winter, Jeanette. *Klara's New World* (1790-1918) p. 29

SWITZERLAND

Kerr, Judith. *When Hitler Stole Pink Rabbit* (1919-1945) p. 36
Levitin, Sonia. *Journey to America* (1919-1945) p. 37
Serraillier, Ian. *The Silver Sword* (1919-1945) p. 43
Sonnleitner, A. Th. *The Cave Children* (1492-1789) p. 23

WALES

Attanasio, A. A. *Kingdom of the Grail* (476-1199) p. 51
Bawden, Nina. *Carrie's War* (1919-1945) p. 99
Welch, Ronald. *Knight Crusader* (476-1199) p. 17

INDEX: AUTHORS, TITLES, AND ILLUSTRATORS

About the Author

LYNDA G. ADAMSON is author of *A Reference Guide to Historical Fiction for Children and Young Adults* (Greenwood Press, 1987). A professor of English at Prince George's Community College in Maryland, she has taught children's literature for 15 of her 25 years of college teaching.